William Henry Guillemard

Hebraisms in the Greek Testament

William Henry Guillemard

Hebraisms in the Greek Testament

ISBN/EAN: 9783744692731

Printed in Europe, USA, Canada, Australia, Japan

Cover: Foto ©ninafisch / pixelio.de

More available books at **www.hansebooks.com**

HEBRAISMS

IN THE

GREEK TESTAMENT.

EXHIBITED AND ILLUSTRATED BY NOTES AND
EXTRACTS FROM THE SACRED TEXT.

'NS OF

NT ON ITS CHARACTER AND
From the Author.   N ;
PURE GREEK STYLE.

BY

WILLIAM HENRY GUILLEMARD, D.D.

SOMETIME FELLOW OF PEMBROKE COLLEGE, CAMBRIDGE.

Cambridge:
DEIGHTON, BELL AND CO.
LONDON: GEORGE BELL AND SONS.
1879

HEBRAISMS

IN THE

GREEK TESTAMENT.

EXHIBITED AND ILLUSTRATED BY NOTES AND
EXTRACTS FROM THE SACRED TEXT.

WITH SPECIMENS OF

(1) THE INFLUENCE OF THE SEPTUAGINT ON ITS CHARACTER AND
CONSTRUCTION;

(2) THE DEVIATIONS IN IT FROM PURE GREEK STYLE.

BY

WILLIAM HENRY GUILLEMARD, D.D.
SOMETIME FELLOW OF PEMBROKE COLLEGE, CAMBRIDGE.

Cambridge:
DEIGHTON, BELL AND CO.
LONDON: GEORGE BELL AND SONS.
1879

PREFACE.

I HAVE given up my first intention of publishing an Edition of the Greek Testament: and have confined myself to Extracts from the Sacred Books, and Notes bearing on the points to which I desire to direct attention.

I avoid thereby the very great and unnecessary expense of printing the whole Text merely as a vehicle for distinctive marks exhibiting the Hebraisms and Non-Classical peculiarities of style; and also the difficulty of selecting a Text, under the present uncertainty as to final recension.

But I have preserved and re-issue the Gospel of S. Matthew previously published by me, as a sample of my original design.

I am thoroughly aware of the incomplete and fragmentary character of my little work. I earnestly disavow any claim to an *exhaustive* exhibition of *all* the Hebraisms, or *all* the deviations from Classical phraseology contained in the Greek Testament; of which I have gathered together and put forward only *a few specimens*, in the hope of stimulating others to fuller and more exact research.

PREFACE.

And I repeat what I said in my former Preface (which I subjoin herewith in explanation of my object and aim throughout, and for the perusal of which I venture to ask a few minutes), that I have thought of the perplexed and embarrassed *Student*, rather than of the accomplished Scholar, in most of what I have written; for which I beg the indulgent forbearance of more learned critics.

My extracts (except on S. Matthew) are from the Textus Receptus. But I do not anticipate, generally, any discrepancy of such a character, as to prevent my book being used side by side with any of the more recent editions.

The theory about Melchisedek (Heb. 7. 1, note) was suggested to me, nearly 40 years ago, by the late lamented Archdeacon Freeman; and formed the subject of one among many very interesting Essays on some obscure passages of Holy Writ, which he had prepared for the Press, but never published in his own name. I was not aware that it had ever been put forth by him, till I discovered it, this day, in an anonymous Article on Jerusalem in the Christian Remembrancer of Oct. 1849, to which he refers in his Principles of Divine Service, Vol. 2, page 116, and in which his views are most lucidly and fully exhibited.

I trust that the kind reception given to my S. Matthew by many eminent Scholars, Classical and Hebrew, and by several of the leading Critical Journals, in England; and in Germany by the learned Professor Schürer (Theologische Literaturzeitung, Leipzig, 1 September, 1877), may be extended to the rest of the work.

W. H. GUILLEMARD.

CAMBRIDGE, *Sept.* 26, 1879.

THE

GREEK TESTAMENT.

THE GREEK TESTAMENT,

HEBRAISTIC EDITION.

EXHIBITING AND ILLUSTRATING

(1) THE HEBRAISMS IN THE SACRED TEXT,
(2) THE INFLUENCE OF THE SEPTUAGINT ON ITS CHARACTER AND CONSTRUCTION,
(3) THE DEVIATIONS IN IT FROM PURE GREEK STYLE;

BY MEANS OF

(*a*) NOTES CHIEFLY TREATING THEREON,
(*b*) A SYSTEM OF DISTINCTIVE MARKS.

BY

WILLIAM HENRY GUILLEMARD, D.D.

SOMETIME FELLOW OF PEMBROKE COLLEGE, CAMBRIDGE.

CAMBRIDGE:
DEIGHTON, BELL AND CO.
LONDON: GEORGE BELL AND SONS.
1875.

PREFACE.

"Two distinct elements were combined in that marvellous dialect, the language of the New Testament; which was destined to preserve for ever the fullest tidings of the Gospel. On the one side there was Hebrew conception, on the other Greek expression: the thoughts of the East were wedded to the words of the West. This was accomplished by the gradual translation of the Hebrew Scriptures into the Vernacular Greek. The Greek of the LXX, like the English of the A.V. or the German of Luther, naturally determined the Greek of the mass of the Jews,...had a commanding authority over the religious dialect." B. F. W.

"The language of the Septuagint is the mould in which the thoughts and expressions of the Apostles and Evangelists are cast. In it the peculiar idioms of the Hebrew are grafted on the stock of the Greek. Hence it is a treasury of illustration for the Greek Testament." W. S.

From the Articles on "New Testament" and "Septuagint" in Smith's *Dictionary of the Bible*.

IF we regard the Greek Testament *from the religious point of view*, as the medium of communication between God and the World, in its two marked divisions of Jew and Gentile, (or as S. Paul defines them "Jew and Greek",) it is impossible to estimate fully or adequately its marvellous adaptation to the end for which it was designed in the divine economy;—as a bond of union and basis of coherence between the two dispensations, past and future, the Mosaic and the Christian;—a golden chain let down from Heaven to link together those who were standing ἐπὶ τῇ συντελείᾳ τῶν αἰώνων, εἰς οὓς τὰ τέλη τῶν αἰώνων κατήντησε:—a channel for conveying to mankind at large the mysterious truths of the new Revelation. But under its *merely human aspect*—on the philological and etymological sides—as a specimen of language, a subject of word-study—it must be conceded that it contains incongruities and anomalies which perplex and sometimes baffle the investigator. It is unlike any other Greek book, with one single exception, and absolutely unique in its peculiarities. Nor are these due, *principally or most frequently*, to variations from the old pure Attic style,—to corruptions of later dialects,—or to the natural influence of the Macedonian element, traceable in contemporary writers. They startle all the instincts of the Classical Scholar, and in many instances defy his attempts to classify or account for them satisfactorily.

It will be granted, I hope, that any attempt—if a genuine and honest one—to grapple with them, is justifiable and allowable; even though it proceed by a method not ordinary or generally recognised.

My object is not so much to suggest improvements in the translation of the Sacred Text, as to enquire how the irregularities in its fabric and texture arose, and to what causes they may be assigned; to discuss, not so much its *meaning*, as *the history of its construction*. And I desire to do this in a reverent and cautious spirit; with freedom, but with the diffidence and moderation becoming such an enquiry.

My endeavour will be—

(1) To shew how in a work, professing to be Greek, such violations of the ordinary rules of the Greek language found admission, and whence they arose.

(2) To elucidate the difficulties of the Text, thus traced to their probable origin, by illustrations drawn from the same source.

Its Authors, we must remember always, first of all, were Orientals. Greek was still a foreign tongue to them and their countrymen, only lately introduced among them. And as Oriental ideas and processes of reasoning were essentially distinct from Greek; so the vocabulary and modes of expression were all strange. They thought as men of the East, while they spoke or wrote in words borrowed from the West.

But they were also *Jews*, scions of a race whose literature, so far as we know, was all connected with the Old Testament; which, with many of them, we may believe, was the only book they knew, certainly the one they knew best; and this, probably, only in the Version of the LXX.

Their acquaintance with *written* Greek was possibly confined to that; their religious phraseology, in Greek, obtained chiefly from that, as ours from our English Version.

PREFACE. vii

We should expect then, *à priori*, that the authors of N.T. would have been influenced, in the terminology and style of their writings, by the Alexandrine Version: and that we should find reproduced in them the main characteristics of a work so familiar and so sacred. And we see that this was so, by unmistakeable proofs; we find traces of it in almost every page.

And therefore we may look upon the LXX., *not merely as a store-house of illustration* for the more difficult portions of N.T., but as the basis of its distinctive and peculiar phraseology—the fountain which has coloured its stream with most of the irregularities which confront the philologer.

This is, of course, a view familiar to all thoughtful students of the Sacred Text: and recognised, in its widest and fullest extent, by the distinguished men whose words I have set at the head of this Preface. My hope is to produce reasons to justify it: to show *the LXX. thread running through all the web;* and to lead others to acknowledge it as the predominant cause of the introduction of most of what is so strange and remarkable.

I take it for granted, according to all the received traditions, that the Alexandrine Version was the work of Jews: that it was a translation from Hebrew into Greek, by men who knew the former best, and were comparatively strangers to the latter. This is transparent on the face of it. Greek was clearly a foreign language to the Translators: a material to which they were unaccustomed, and which they had scarcely learnt how to handle. We feel, as we read the book, that they were not men adequately educated or scientifically qualified for the task; that they were not masters of the new and wonderful instrument put into their hands. We have their work before us, with all its manifold and inevitable defects: its evident and irrefragable signs of the unskilful character of the process by which it was produced.

We need not, we ought not, to shut our eyes to its true character and value as a Translation. Its very blemishes in that respect—its Oriental and Hebraic characteristics—were probably the very causes, that made it so useful to those for whom it was intended, the Hellenized Jews of the dispersion: who, though they were losing their old language, had not lost their modes of thought or idiosyncrasies of expression. It suited them better, and was more easily understood by them, than a

Version into genuine Greek would have been; preserving, as it did, Hebrew idioms under a Greek dress; literal reproductions of Hebrew phrases and turns of speech; the syntax—the grammar—the very prepositions—frequently, we may almost say generally, unaltered.

Was ever any Greek book that we possess composed under similar circumstances? Nay: *are there extant any books* written by Orientals in Greek, of the age when the Greeks were fresh in the East: i. e. the period of the compilation of the Alexandrine Version? Are the productions of contemporary Greek writers at all like it in their peculiarities and variations from the Classical Standard?

Let us regard it with all befitting respect, as *The Venerable Version*, that commanded the reverence, and shaped and moulded the religious phraseology, of God's people scattered throughout the World; as the Book probably quoted by our Blessed Lord Himself: let us gratefully own and value its many uses in Sacred Criticism. I am myself pleading now for an extension and development of its use in one particular direction, in urging that it may be advantageously employed to elucidate the process of transmuting Hebrew thought and speech into Greek forms; and so to illustrate and account for many peculiarities in the language and style of the *Greek Testament*.

It is confessedly full of irregularities of construction—syntax—grammar—diction—idiom—due to an Hebrew origin alone. If we find the same in the Greek Testament, must we not assign them to the same cause, or to one or other of two causes closely connected with it? Either that the writers of the latter *thought* in Hebrew or some Hebraic dialect, and so rendered their thoughts at times, word for word, in Greek:—or else that their ancestors had unconsciously constructed a dialect on that basis, reproducing Hebrew idioms and forms of speech in Greek guise and shape; which dialect they were themselves using;—or that their language and ways of expression, especially upon religious topics, were insensibly affected and coloured by their familiar acquaintance with the diction and style of the Book which they prized and loved beyond all others; most of which, we are told, they had learnt by heart, and could repeat from memory.

And if S. Paul,—with all his wider acquaintance than the

other contributors to the Sacred Volume, with Greek men, Greek speech, Greek philosophy,—thinks, argues, reasons as a *Jew* rather than a *Greek* :—if his logic and dialectics are *Oriental ;—Hebraic* and *not Hellenic :*—should we not expect him to *speak*, to frame his utterances, under the same influence? Should we not anticipate, as in fact we find, that his familiarity with the LXX. would be shewn in His Epistles? How can we account for his writing, at one moment, passages of perfectly grammatical Greek, and then suddenly introducing violations of all ordinary Greek constructions, deviations from the customary modes of expression,—which seem to master his pen, as it were, in the strangest way,—but on the ground of his being under the influence of some book which had filled his memory with its peculiar phrases and terms, and made it natural for him to copy and repeat them, when his subject-matter was Religion?

I propose to apply this method more widely than is usually done; to trace Oriental forms and idioms in the Greek dialect of the New Testament, and to illustrate them by parallel passages in the Greek of the Septuagint, exhibiting similar peculiarities. We *know* that the *latter* were due to the efforts of men,—if not *unlearned*, yet with small scientific knowledge of the principles of language,—to clothe Hebrew ideas and words in a Greek dress: we may clearly, in all fairness and logical accuracy, refer the *former* to a corresponding effort, under different circumstances. And it appears to be a more natural process, and more consistent with true principles of criticism, to do this, than to endeavour to account for what surprises us, by bringing forward doubtful parallelisms from obscure Greek authors, or by straining occasional solecisms or violations of grammar met with in writers of better repute, into a justification of unquestionable anomalies and irregularities of construction in the text of the Sacred Volume.

It may be regarded probably as unscientific and unphilosophical; but I venture to plead that the more scientific and philosophical method can scarcely be applied successfully to a dialect formed on so unscientific a basis, with such frequent interruptions and intermissions of grammatical precision. I think it probable,—nay, almost certain,—that this attempt may be looked upon as a departure from the principles of sound scholarship,—an infringement of the recognised maxims of modern criticism,—a return to old exploded methods;—a backward movement altogether. It is, no doubt, in some sense, a return to old methods; but such as I believe to be sound and safe, if employed with due discrimination: methods followed by the great critics of the sixteenth and seventeenth centuries, to whom we owe so much of our biblical knowledge; to some of whom we Englishmen owe our Authorized Version.

I venture to think that it was their intimate familiarity, first with the Hebrew original, and next with the Alexandrine and the Vulgate, that enabled them, above all their other qualifications for the task, to produce their wonderful translation. I doubt whether they could have done their work so well had they been better Greek and worse Hebrew scholars; if they had known more about the former, and less about the latter. They were so conversant with Hebrew idioms and constructions that they intuitively detected them and caught their meaning, in many a passage, which would have perplexed and baffled more advanced Greek scholars; and transferred them easily to English, in which they found congenial and natural and ready expression. Since their day Greek criticism has advanced with strides so rapid as to leave Hebrew far behind; and we know what zeal and devotion the most accomplished Greek scholars have brought to the study of the New Testament. I do not, in the very slightest degree, gainsay or undervalue the results of their labours. But there are still, to say the least, *some enigmas* that Greek criticism has not yet solved, *some* difficulties that seem to be beyond its sphere and out of its province, due to the complex elements of the Sacred Text, its double character, as not simply Greek, but Hebræo-Greek. May I dare to say that it seems to me too fine a weapon, forged for Plato and Xenophon and Thucydides, for the great orators and dramatists, and sharpened expressly for dealing with a language the most perfect the world has ever known? It is of a temper and polish unsuited to the unvarnished simplicity and natural artless flow of the narratives and epistles of Apostles and Evangelists. The dialect at their command was but a coarse material to work with, however admirably adapted, in the providence of God, for the majestic edifice they were inspired to construct out of it; and many of them were rough workmen, though divinely fitted for the task entrusted to them, ἄνθρωποι ἀγράμματοι καὶ ἰδιῶται.

PREFACE. xi

May we not sometimes have gone too far in the effort to prove that the material is the finest marble, and the chiselling that of the most refined and skilled artists; whereas *granite*,—cut sharp and strong, in lines of simple but imperishable beauty, by men faithful and true to the idea supernaturally impressed upon their minds, but uneducated in, and strangers to, the processes of artistic composition,—would be a worthier and more accurate description of their achievement?

I have long been wishing and hoping to see the different method for which I plead applied by other and more competent hands: and it is only because I see no indications of such an intention anywhere else, that I have resolved to put forth what I have myself observed and collected. I confess, candidly and unreservedly, that I have studied very little the works of other Commentators. From various causes,—chiefly from constant engagement in other pursuits and from physical inability to read much or long,—I have been unable to enter deeply into the labours of others. I have kept to my own line of investigation and followed it by myself alone; simply because I seemed to have come upon a track not much traversed by other feet now-a-days, by pursuing which I hoped to contribute my little share to the great cause of Biblical Criticism.

I have a sincere and very real sense of the incomplete and superficial character of much that I have advanced: I trust others, with stronger heads and more time, may go deeper into the substance. I am content to be a pioneer along a path which I cannot but think may lead hereafter to a clearer understanding of Holy Scripture.

I have not touched, save occasionally, on doctrinal questions, as not falling within the scope of my plan; nor on separate points of minute and intricate criticism,—such as the use of the article,—which I recognise as out of my depth; nor on the Recension of the Text, on which I frankly avow myself too ignorant to form an opinion. I have confined myself almost exclusively to the matters on which I seem to myself to have some little knowledge; some faint hope of assisting others.

I have taken the Text of Tischendorf, 1862.

My main object being to shew that the Greek Text owes its distinguishing characteristics to three causes—(1) Orientalisms, (2) the influence of the LXX. or Alexandrine Version, (3) deterioration of style, due either to the Macedonian element in it, or to the "scrioris Græcismi innovationes,"—I have marked the most prominent examples of each as they occur, in order to arrest attention and secure careful examination: but when a particular phrase or idiom has been once thus pointed out, I have not usually noted it again, if recurring in the immediate context.

I wish to say a few words in conclusion on the elementary character of much that I have said in this Preface and in my Notes throughout. I have made it so intentionally and from design. I am unfeignedly conscious of my very slight qualifications for any wide or deep enquiry, and of the very little hope I can possibly have to win the ear of the learned. But I may perhaps do something to smooth the path of the *Student*, and shew him the true nature of the obstacles which impede his progress, and clear a few stumblingblocks out of his way, or help him over them by a straightforward process, and so save him from the humiliation and moral injury of going round-about or avoiding or ignoring them altogether. I may be able to relieve him of some of the perplexities, which embarrassed me in the days of my first introduction to the Greek Testament. Many a man, fresh from ordinary Greek books, is bewildered and confused by the dialect there set before him. I have tried to distinguish and classify the difficulties which beset his path, and to assign them each to its separate source, that he may learn to discriminate between the changes, which the Macedonian Greek incurred by coming into the East and among Jews, and the variations from the old pure style which it brought with it, or gradually evolved and developed out of itself.

Of course, without some knowledge of Hebrew, most of what I say will be unintelligible.

But I hope to encourage those who have a fair acquaintance with the Sacred Tongue, to use it in a fresh direction, with the zest and spirit that always accompanies labour in a new field: and to stimulate others, who have as yet only mastered the elements, to strive after that proficiency which will alone give them the key to this method of investigation.

It is as an aid to such Students that I have adopted the system of *marks in the Text*, as more likely to attract notice and make an impression, than notes alone, detached from the Text, or isolated explanations in a Lexicon.

PREFACE. xiii

My chief books of reference have been "Schleusneri *Lexicon in N. T.*," and "Tromm. *Concordantiæ Græcæ in LXX. Interpretes.*"

My attention was first turned to this line of enquiry by accidentally meeting with a copy of the former some thirty years ago, but his doctrinal opinions and want of critical exactness startled and repelled me, and I took no pains to procure the book or consult it again; though I pursued, at intervals, by my own personal investigation, the path he had opened to me. More recent recourse to his pages has shewn me how much I have lost by neglecting his help in this particular, and how much time I have wasted in researches which his discoveries would have saved.

I have found the greatest assistance from Trommius, though reliance cannot always be placed on his accuracy or his judgment. His plan and arrangement are admirable, but his evident deficiency in the critical faculty has lamentably marred the execution of his design, and lessened the value of his elaborate performance.

Quite lately (in Nov. 1874) I have become acquainted with the invaluable work of Grimm, "*Lexicon Græco-Latinum in Libros N. T.*" He refers to Schleusner as one of his authorities; and would, no doubt, explicitly acknowledge his manifold obligations to the acumen and research of one from whom he has evidently derived so much assistance in this portion of his work.

"Grinfield's *Editio Hellenistica*,"—a repertory of parallel passages from the V. A., corresponding to each verse of the N. T.,—I have not found so serviceable as I had hoped, from his having selected parallelisms of sense and meaning, rather than of verbal expression.

W. H. GUILLEMARD.

CAMBRIDGE,
1 *March*, 1875.

ABBREVIATIONS AND INITIALS.

M. = Matthew, Mk. = Mark, L. = Luke, J. = John.
V.A. = Versio Alexandrina or Septuagint.
N.T. = New (i.e. Greek) Testament.
Tromm. = Trommii Concordantiæ in LXX.
Schl. = Schleusneri Lexicon in N.T.
Grimm. = Grimmii Lexicon in N.T.
E.H. = Grinfield's Editio Hellenistica N.T.
Br. = Bruder's Concordance.

Asterisks ** before and after a phrase, mark a Hebraism; either original or reflected from the V.A.

Brackets enclose instances of later Greek usage, or of debased style.

Uncial type indicates some word or phrase derived, directly and specially, from the V.A.—some peculiar use, originating apparently with its Compilers.

ΤΟ ΚΑΤΑ ΜΑΤΘΑΙΟΝ ΕΥΑΓΓΕΛΙΟΝ.

CAP.
ΒΙΒΛΟΣ γενέσεως ἸΗΣΟΥ Χριστοῦ, υἱοῦ Δαβὶδ, υἱοῦ Ἀβραάμ· 1
Ἀβραὰμ ἐγέννησε τὸν Ἰσαάκ· Ἰσαὰκ δὲ ἐγέννησε τὸν Ἰακώβ. 2
Ἰακὼβ δὲ ἐγέννησε τὸν Ἰούδαν καὶ τοὺς ἀδελφοὺς αὐτοῦ. Ἰούδας 3
δὲ ἐγέννησε τὸν Φαρὲς καὶ τὸν Ζαρὰ ἐκ τῆς Θαμάρ· Φαρὲς δὲ
ἐγέννησε τὸν Ἐσρώμ. Ἐσρὼμ δὲ ἐγέννησε τὸν Ἀράμ· Ἀρὰμ δὲ 4
ἐγέννησε τὸν Ἀμιναδάβ. Ἀμιναδὰβ δὲ ἐγέννησε τὸν Ναασσών·
Ναασσὼν δὲ ἐγέννησε τὸν Σαλμών. Σαλμὼν δὲ ἐγέννησε τὸν Βοὸζ 5
ἐκ τῆς Ῥαχάβ· Βοὸζ δὲ ἐγέννησε τὸν Ὠβὴδ ἐκ τῆς Ῥούθ. Ὠβὴδ
δὲ ἐγέννησε τὸν Ἰεσσαί· Ἰεσσαὶ δὲ ἐγέννησε τὸν Δαβὶδ τὸν βασι- 6
λέα. Δαβὶδ δὲ ὁ βασιλεὺς ἐγέννησε τὸν Σολομῶντα ἐκ τῆς τοῦ
Οὐρίου. Σολομὼν δὲ ἐγέννησε τὸν Ῥοβοάμ. Ῥοβοὰμ δὲ ἐγέννησε 7
τὸν Ἀβιά· Ἀβιὰ δὲ ἐγέννησε τὸν Ἀσά. Ἀσὰ δὲ ἐγέννησε τὸν 8
Ἰωσαφάτ· Ἰωσαφὰτ δὲ ἐγέννησε τὸν Ἰωράμ. Ἰωρὰμ δὲ ἐγέννησε
τὸν Ὀζίαν· Ὀζίας δὲ ἐγέννησε τὸν Ἰωάθαμ. Ἰωάθαμ δὲ ἐγέννησε 9
τὸν Ἄχαζ· Ἄχαζ δὲ ἐγέννησε τὸν Ἐζεκίαν. Ἐζεκίας δὲ ἐγέννησε 10
τὸν Μανασσῆ· Μανασσῆς δὲ ἐγέννησε τὸν Ἀμών. Ἀμὼν δὲ ἐγέννησε τὸν Ἰωσίαν· Ἰωσίας δὲ ἐγέννησε τὸν Ἰεχονίαν καὶ τοὺς 11
ἀδελφοὺς αὐτοῦ, *ἐπὶ τῆς μετοικεσίας Βαβυλῶνος.* Μετὰ δὲ τὴν 12
μετοικεσίαν Βαβυλῶνος, Ἰεχονίας ἐγέννησε τὸν Σαλαθιήλ. Σαλα-

Cap. I. 2. The use of the article in this genealogy, always with object, never with subject, seems to be borrowed from similar genealogies in V. A.: e.g. that in Genesis v., where the same use is found throughout the list: and in 1 Chron. passim. In most of these instances the object has אֵת before it: and the article was probably introduced to express the supposed meaning of that particle. But this does not meet all the cases; e.g. Gen. v. 1 ᾗ ἡμέρᾳ ἐποίησεν ὁ Θεὸς τὸν Ἀδάμ is the translation of בְּיוֹם בְּרֹא אֱלֹהִים אָדָם.

12. μετοικεσία Βαβυλῶνος] "the Babylonish emigration:" Hebrew genitive of qualification, equivalent to an adjective. S. Matthew uses, in all probability, a mode of expression familiar to the Jews of his day, by which the national pride was soothed, when he speaks of the captivity as a migration.

13 θιὴλ δὲ ἐγέννησε τὸν Ζοροβάβελ· Ζοροβάβελ δὲ ἐγέννησε τὸν
Ἀβιούδ. Ἀβιοὺδ δὲ ἐγέννησε τὸν Ἐλιακείμ· Ἐλιακεὶμ δὲ ἐγέν-
14 νησε τὸν Ἀζώρ. Ἀζὼρ δὲ ἐγέννησε τὸν Ζαδώκ· Ζαδὼκ δὲ ἐγέν-
15 νησε τὸν Ἀχείμ. Ἀχεὶμ δὲ ἐγέννησε τὸν Ἐλιούδ· Ἐλιοὺδ δὲ
ἐγέννησε τὸν Ἐλεάζαρ. Ἐλεάζαρ δὲ ἐγέννησε τὸν Ματθάν· Ματθὰν
16 δὲ ἐγέννησε τὸν Ἰακώβ. Ἰακὼβ δὲ ἐγέννησε τὸν Ἰωσὴφ τὸν ἄνδρα
Μαρίας, ἐξ ἧς ἐγεννήθη ΙΗΣΟΥΣ ὁ λεγόμενος Χριστός.

17 Πᾶσαι οὖν αἱ γενεαὶ ἀπὸ Ἀβραὰμ ἕως Δαβὶδ γενεαὶ δεκατέσ-
σαρες· καὶ ἀπὸ Δαβὶδ ἕως *τῆς μετοικεσίας Βαβυλῶνος* γενεαὶ
δεκατέσσαρες· καὶ ἀπὸ τῆς μετοικεσίας Βαβυλῶνος ἕως τοῦ Χριστοῦ
γενεαὶ δεκατέσσαρες.

18 ΤΟΥ δὲ Χριστοῦ ἡ γέννησις οὕτως ἦν. μνηστευθείσης γὰρ
τῆς μητρὸς αὐτοῦ Μαρίας τῷ Ἰωσήφ, πρὶν ἢ συνελθεῖν αὐτοὺς,
19 εὑρέθη ἐν γαστρὶ ἔχουσα ἐκ Πνεύματος ἁγίου. Ἰωσὴφ δὲ ὁ ἀνὴρ
αὐτῆς, δίκαιος ὢν, καὶ [μὴ] θέλων αὐτὴν δειγματίσαι, ἐβουλήθη
20 λάθρα ἀπολῦσαι αὐτήν. ταῦτα δὲ αὐτοῦ ἐνθυμηθέντος, ἰδοὺ ἄγγελος
Κυρίου κατ' ὄναρ ἐφάνη αὐτῷ λέγων, Ἰωσὴφ *υἱὸς* Δαβίδ, μὴ
φοβηθῇς παραλαβεῖν Μαριὰμ τὴν γυναῖκά σου· τὸ γὰρ ἐν αὐτῇ
21 γεννηθὲν ἐκ Πνεύματός ἐστιν ἁγίου. τέξεται δὲ υἱὸν, καὶ καλέσεις
τὸ ὄνομα αὐτοῦ Ἰησοῦν· αὐτὸς γὰρ σώσει τὸν λαὸν αὐτοῦ ἀπὸ τῶν
22 ἁμαρτιῶν αὐτῶν. [Τοῦτο δὲ ὅλον γέγονεν, ἵνα πληρωθῇ] τὸ ῥηθὲν
23 ὑπὸ Κυρίου διὰ τοῦ προφήτου λέγοντος, Ἰδοὺ, ἡ παρθένος
ἐν γαστρὶ ἕξει καὶ τέξεται υἱὸν, καὶ καλέσουσι τὸ ὄνομα αὐτοῦ
24 Ἐμμανουήλ· ὅ ἐστι μεθερμηνευόμενον, μεθ' ἡμῶν ὁ Θεός. Διεγερθεὶς
δὲ ὁ Ἰωσὴφ ἀπὸ τοῦ ὕπνου, ἐποίησεν ὡς προσέταξεν αὐτῷ
25 ὁ ἄγγελος Κυρίου· καὶ παρέλαβεν τὴν γυναῖκα αὐτοῦ, καὶ οὐκ
ἐγίνωσκεν αὐτὴν, ἕως οὗ ἔτεκεν υἱὸν, καὶ ἐκάλεσεν τὸ ὄνομα
αὐτοῦ ΙΗΣΟΥΝ.

CAP. 2 ΤΟΥ δὲ Ἰησοῦ γεννηθέντος ἐν Βηθλεὲμ τῆς Ἰουδαίας, *ἐν ἡμέ-

20. υἱός] Nominative for vocative: very common, though not universal, in V.A.: Threni ii. 13, παρθένος θύγατερ Σιών. Judges v. 12, ἀνάστα Βαράκ, υἱὸς Ἀβινεέμ. Micah v. 1, καὶ σὺ, Βηθλεέμ, οἶκος Ἐφραθά. Ps. lxxii. 1, Ὁ Θεός, τὸ κρίμα σοῦ τῷ βασιλεῖ δός. Ps. lxxxvii. 3, עִיר הָאֱלֹהִים ἡ πόλις τ. Θ. is an instance of a different construction, being the literal translation of the Hebrew definite article with noun, for vocative. See xi. 26, Mk. v. 8, 41; x. 47; Lk. viii. 54.

22. This and similar violations of the natural sequence of tenses, so common in New Testament, must, I think, be set down to debased dialect. Instances are no doubt to be found in classical authors of the like: but there they are the exception, and may be allowably assigned to inaccuracy. In the New Testament they occur so frequently as to suggest a radical deterioration of style.

23. ἡ παρθένος] as in original and in V.A.

25. A Hebraism, always literally rendered in V.A. But the phrase occurs also in Greek authors of good repute.

Cap. II. 1. בַּיָּמֵי, V.A. ἐν ᾗ. or ἐν ταῖς ἡ.] passim, e.g. 2 Chr. ix. 20, and

ραις* Ἡρώδου τοῦ βασιλέως, ἰδοὺ μάγοι ἀπὸ ἀνατολῶν παρεγένοντο
εἰς Ἱεροσόλυμα λέγοντες, Ποῦ ἐστιν ὁ τεχθεὶς βασιλεὺς τῶν Ἰου- 2
δαίων; εἴδομεν γὰρ αὐτοῦ τὸν ἀστέρα ἐν τῇ ἀνατολῇ, καὶ [ἤλθομεν
προσκυνῆσαι] αὐτῷ. Ἀκούσας δὲ Ἡρώδης ὁ βασιλεὺς ἐταράχθη, 3
καὶ πᾶσα Ἱεροσόλυμα μετ' αὐτοῦ, καὶ συναγαγὼν πάντας τοὺς 4
ἀρχιερεῖς καὶ γραμματεῖς *τοῦ λαοῦ,* ἐπυνθάνετο παρ' αὐτῶν, ποῦ
ὁ Χριστὸς γεννᾶται. οἱ δὲ εἶπον αὐτῷ, Ἐν Βηθλεὲμ τῆς Ἰουδαίας. 5
οὕτως γὰρ γέγραπται διὰ τοῦ προφήτου, Καὶ σὺ Βηθλεὲμ γῆ Ἰούδα, 6
οὐδαμῶς ἐλαχίστη εἶ ἐν τοῖς ἡγεμόσιν Ἰούδα· ἐκ σοῦ γὰρ ἐξελεύσεται ἡγούμενος, ὅστις ποιμανεῖ τὸν λαόν μου τὸν Ἰσραήλ. Τότε 7
Ἡρώδης λάθρα καλέσας τοὺς μάγους, ἠκρίβωσεν παρ' αὐτῶν τὸν
χρόνον [τοῦ φαινομένου ἀστέρος], καὶ πέμψας αὐτοὺς εἰς Βηθλεὲμ 8
εἶπεν, Πορευθέντες ἐξετάσατε ἀκριβῶς περὶ τοῦ παιδίου· ἐπὰν δὲ
εὕρητε, ἀπαγγείλατέ μοι, ὅπως κἀγὼ ἐλθὼν προσκυνήσω αὐτῷ. Οἱ 9
δὲ ἀκούσαντες τοῦ βασιλέως, ἐπορεύθησαν καὶ ἰδοὺ ὁ ἀστήρ, ὃν εἶδον

xxvi. 5. Our English idiom is the same, and the phrase is natural and familiar to us; but unnatural and incongruous in Greek, and betrays a foreign source.

2. I note once for all this infringement of the ordinary rules of grammar, too frequent to be due to accident or incuria, as the result of the deterioration alluded to i. 22. See iv. 1. To explain it by supposing the omission of τοῦ before infinitive seems far-fetched and unsatisfactory.

4. הָעָם = ὁ λαός] *the* people, i.e. Israel.

6. No quotation at all, strictly speaking. The Hebrew is (Micah v. 1) וְאַתָּה בֵּית־לֶחֶם אֶפְרָתָה צָעִיר לִהְיוֹת בְּאַלְפֵי יְהוּדָה מִמְּךָ לִי יֵצֵא לִהְיוֹת מוֹשֵׁל בְּיִשְׂרָאֵל, "And thou, Bethlehem Ephratah, insignificant to be among the families of Judah, out of thee shall come forth for me one to be a Ruler in Israel." The V.A. renders it thus: καὶ σύ, Βηθλεέμ, οἶκος Ἐφραθά, ὀλιγοστὸς εἶ τοῦ εἶναι ἐν χιλιάσιν Ἰούδα· ἐκ σοῦ μοι ἐξελεύσεται τοῦ εἶναι εἰς ἄρχοντα τοῦ Ἰσραήλ. I quote this not only to show the real words of the prophecy, and the variations from it in N.T. and V.A., but also to draw attention to the translation of לִהְיוֹת by τοῦ εἶναι twice in the latter. An apt example of the practice almost universal, in that Version, of rendering ל with infinitive, after neuter or passive verbs, by τοῦ with Greek infinitive; to the loss very often of all intelligibility or sense: e.g. 2 Sam. xix. 21, אָלֹהִ֥ים בָּאתִ֖י לְקָרַ֑את τοῦ καταβῆναί με. Gen. xviii. 25, חָלִ֣ילָה לְךָ֔ מֵעֲשֹׂ֤ת כַּדָּבָ֨ר הַזֶּ֜ה לְהָמִ֧ית צַדִּ֛יק עִם־רָשָׁ֖ע μηδαμῶς σὺ ποιήσεις ὡς τὸ ῥῆμα τοῦτο τοῦ ἀποκτεῖναι δίκαιον μετὰ ἀσεβοῦς. 1 Chr. xi. 18, וְלֹ֥א אָבָ֖ה לִשְׁתּוֹתָ֑ם καὶ οὐκ ἠθέλησε τοῦ πιεῖν. The translators appear to have concluded that a Greek idiom, which was the appropriate interpretation of the Hebrew idiom under certain conditions, e.g. verse 13, was always to be employed as its equivalent: and so have introduced into their Version renderings which are otherwise inexplicable. And to this we owe, I venture to think, in great measure, the strange and startling instances of the τοῦ with infinitive, occasionally met with in the New Testament.

The above passage illustrates likewise the use of εἶναι εἰς as equivalent to הָיָ֣ה לְ in the sense of γίγνομαι, so constantly found both in V.A. and N.T., and so familiar to the writers, that in this case they have forced the phrase into the Greek, without the occurrence of the corresponding form in the Hebrew.

7. "The time of the star that appeared," not "of the star at its appearing" or "of the appearing of the star:" though we can scarcely doubt that the writer meant to convey that meaning, or that the words, according to the usage of the time and the dialect, may have expressed it.

ἐν τῇ ἀνατολῇ, προῆγεν αὐτούς, ἕως ἐλθὼν ἐστάθη ἐπάνω οὗ ἦν τὸ
10 παιδίον. ἰδόντες δὲ τὸν ἀστέρα, ἐχάρησαν χαρὰν μεγάλην σφόδρα.
11 καὶ ἐλθόντες εἰς τὴν οἰκίαν, εἶδον τὸ παιδίον μετὰ Μαρίας τῆς
μητρὸς αὐτοῦ, καὶ πεσόντες προσεκύνησαν αὐτῷ, καὶ ἀνοίξαντες
τοὺς θησαυροὺς αὐτῶν, προσήνεγκαν αὐτῷ δῶρα, χρυσὸν καὶ λίβανον
12 καὶ σμύρναν. καὶ χρηματισθέντες κατ' ὄναρ μὴ ἀνακάμψαι πρὸς
Ἡρώδην, δι' ἄλλης ὁδοῦ ἀνεχώρησαν εἰς τὴν χώραν αὐτῶν.
13 Ἀναχωρησάντων δὲ αὐτῶν, ἰδοὺ ἄγγελος Κυρίου φαίνεται κατ'
ὄναρ τῷ Ἰωσὴφ λέγων, Ἐγερθεὶς παράλαβε τὸ παιδίον καὶ τὴν
μητέρα αὐτοῦ, καὶ φεῦγε εἰς Αἴγυπτον, καὶ ἴσθι ἐκεῖ ἕως ἂν εἴπω
σοι· μέλλει γὰρ Ἡρώδης ζητεῖν τὸ παιδίον, τοῦ ἀπολέσαι αὐτό.
14 Ὁ δὲ ἐγερθεὶς παρέλαβεν τὸ παιδίον καὶ τὴν μητέρα αὐτοῦ νυκτὸς,
15 καὶ ἀνεχώρησεν εἰς Αἴγυπτον, καὶ ἦν ἐκεῖ ἕως τῆς τελευτῆς Ἡρώδου·
ἵνα πληρωθῇ τὸ ῥηθὲν ὑπὸ τοῦ Κυρίου διὰ τοῦ προφήτου λέγοντος,
16 Ἐξ Αἰγύπτου ἐκάλεσα τὸν υἱόν μου. Τότε Ἡρώδης ἰδὼν ὅτι
ἐνεπαίχθη ὑπὸ τῶν μάγων, ἐθυμώθη λίαν, καὶ ἀποστείλας ἀνεῖλεν
πάντας τοὺς παῖδας τοὺς ἐν Βηθλεὲμ καὶ ἐν πᾶσι τοῖς ὁρίοις αὐτῆς,
ἀπὸ διετοῦς καὶ κατωτέρω, κατὰ τὸν χρόνον ὃν ἠκρίβωσεν παρὰ τῶν
17 μάγων. τότε ἐπληρώθη τὸ ῥηθὲν διὰ Ἰερεμίου τοῦ προφήτου λέγον-
18 τος, Φωνὴ ἐν Ῥαμᾶ ἠκούσθη, θρῆνος καὶ κλαυθμὸς καὶ ὀδυρμὸς πολὺς,
Ῥαχὴλ κλαίουσα τὰ τέκνα αὐτῆς· καὶ οὐκ ἤθελε παρακληθῆναι,
19 ὅτι οὐκ εἰσί. Τελευτήσαντος δὲ τοῦ Ἡρώδου, ἰδοὺ ἄγγελος Κυρίου
20 κατ' ὄναρ φαίνεται τῷ Ἰωσὴφ ἐν Αἰγύπτῳ λέγων, Ἐγερθεὶς παρά-
λαβε τὸ παιδίον καὶ τὴν μητέρα αὐτοῦ, καὶ πορεύου εἰς γῆν Ἰσραήλ·
21 τεθνήκασιν γὰρ οἱ ζητοῦντες τὴν ψυχὴν τοῦ παιδίου. ὁ δὲ ἐγερθεὶς
παρέλαβεν τὸ παιδίον καὶ τὴν μητέρα αὐτοῦ, καὶ εἰσῆλθεν εἰς γῆν
22 Ἰσραήλ. ἀκούσας δὲ ὅτι Ἀρχέλαος βασιλεύει ἐπὶ τῆς Ἰουδαίας
ἀντὶ Ἡρώδου τοῦ πατρὸς αὐτοῦ, ἐφοβήθη ἐκεῖ [ἀπελθεῖν]· χρημα-
23 τισθεὶς δὲ κατ' ὄναρ, ἀνεχώρησεν εἰς τὰ μέρη τῆς Γαλιλαίας, καὶ
ἐλθὼν κατῴκησεν εἰς πόλιν λεγομένην Ναζαρέτ· ὅπως [πληρωθῇ]
τὸ ῥηθὲν διὰ τῶν προφητῶν, Ὅτι Ναζωραῖος κληθήσεται.

CAP. 3   ΕΝ δὲ ταῖς ἡμέραις ἐκείναις παραγίνεται Ἰωάννης ὁ βαπ-
2 τιστὴς, κηρύσσων ἐν τῇ ἐρήμῳ τῆς Ἰουδαίας καὶ λέγων, Μετα-
3 νοεῖτε· ἤγγικεν γὰρ *ἡ βασιλεία τῶν οὐρανῶν.* οὗτος γάρ ἐστιν
[ὁ ῥηθεὶς] διὰ Ἡσαΐου τοῦ προφήτου λέγοντος, Φωνὴ βοῶντος ἐν
τῇ ἐρήμῳ, Ἑτοιμάσατε τὴν ὁδὸν Κυρίου· εὐθείας ποιεῖτε τὰς τρίβους

Cap. III. 2. ἡ β. τ. οὐρ.] Not found in V.A., may be inferred from Dan. ii. 42 and vii. 14. Grimm cites from Targums מִן שְׁמַיָּא מַלְכוּתָא דֶאֱלָהָא, and from Rabbins

מִן שְׁמַיָּא 'מ. M. has οὐρανῶν, the other Evangelists Θεοῦ.
3. ὁ ῥηθεὶς] "*the person* spoken of," unusual in masculine.

αὐτοῦ. αὐτὸς δὲ ὁ Ἰωάννης εἶχεν τὸ ἔνδυμα αὐτοῦ [ἀπὸ τριχῶν]
καμήλου, καὶ ζώνην δερματίνην περὶ τὴν ὀσφὺν αὐτοῦ· ἡ δὲ τροφὴ 4
ἦν αὐτοῦ ἀκρίδες καὶ μέλι ἄγριον.
Τότε ἐξεπορεύετο πρὸς αὐτὸν Ἱεροσόλυμα καὶ πᾶσα ἡ Ἰουδαία 5
καὶ πᾶσα ἡ περίχωρος τοῦ Ἰορδάνου· καὶ ἐβαπτίζοντο ἐν τῷ 6
Ἰορδάνῃ ποταμῷ ὑπ' αὐτοῦ, ἐξομολογούμενοι τὰς ἁμαρτίας αὐτῶν. 7
Ἰδὼν δὲ πολλοὺς τῶν Φαρισαίων καὶ Σαδδουκαίων ἐρχομένους
ἐπὶ τὸ βάπτισμα εἶπεν αὐτοῖς, Γεννήματα ἐχιδνῶν, τίς ὑπέδειξεν
ὑμῖν φυγεῖν ἀπὸ τῆς μελλούσης ὀργῆς; *ποιήσατε οὖν καρπὸν* 8
ἄξιον τῆς μετανοίας· καὶ μὴ δόξητε λέγειν ἐν ἑαυτοῖς, Πατέρα 9
ἔχομεν τὸν Ἀβραάμ· λέγω γὰρ ὑμῖν, ὅτι δύναται ὁ Θεὸς ἐκ
τῶν λίθων τούτων ἐγεῖραι τέκνα τῷ Ἀβραάμ. ἤδη δὲ καὶ ἡ 10
ἀξίνη πρὸς τὴν ῥίζαν τῶν δένδρων κεῖται· πᾶν οὖν δένδρον μὴ
ποιοῦν καρπὸν καλὸν, ἐκκόπτεται καὶ εἰς πῦρ βάλλεται. ἐγὼ 11
μὲν βαπτίζω ὑμᾶς *ἐν ὕδατι* εἰς μετάνοιαν· ὁ δὲ ὀπίσω μου
ἐρχόμενος, ἰσχυρότερός μου ἐστίν, οὗ οὐκ εἰμὶ ἱκανὸς τὰ ὑποδήματα
βαστάσαι· αὐτὸς ὑμᾶς βαπτίσει *ἐν Πνεύματι ἁγίῳ καὶ πυρί.*
οὗ τὸ πτύον ἐν τῇ χειρὶ αὐτοῦ, καὶ διακαθαριεῖ τὴν ἅλωνα αὐτοῦ, 12
καὶ συνάξει τὸν σῖτον αὐτοῦ εἰς τὴν ἀποθήκην, τὸ δὲ ἄχυρον κατακαύσει πυρὶ ἀσβέστῳ.

8. π. κ. = עָשָׂה פְּרִי.

9. Our idiom, "think to say," suits this exactly: and so we do not see the difficulty of extracting that meaning out of δοκέω λέγειν, according to its correct and classical use. Grimm sees it, and translates "nolite putare licere vobis dicere," which, of course, is right. Naturally the phrase means "do not think you are saying." There are three uses of δοκέω, in its sense of "cogito," in N. T. E.g. (1) Mk. vi. 49, αὐτὸν ἔδοξαν φάντασμα εἶναι. (2) J. v. 39, ὑμεῖς δοκεῖτε ζωὴν αἰώνιον ἔχειν. (3) The passage before us, where apparently ἐξεῖναι, or some similar word, is understood.

11. ἐν] Literal translation of בְּ; and used for it, in all its various shades of meaning, indiscriminately in V.A., though utterly inadequate to express its real meaning. E.g.
2 Sam. xxiii. 17, τῶν πορευθέντων ἐν ταῖς ψυχαῖς αὐτῶν הַהֹלְכִים בְּנַפְשׁוֹתָם.
1 Sam. xxiv. 22, ὀμοσόν μοι ἐν Κυρίῳ הִשָּׁבְעָה לִּי בַּיהוָה. Exod. iv. 21, τὰ τέρατα ἃ δέδωκα ἐν ταῖς χερσί σου אֲשֶׁר שַׂמְתִּי בְיָדֶךָ. Ps. cvi. 20, ἠλλάξαντο τὴν δόξαν αὐτῶν ἐν ὁμοιώματι (Rom. i. 23) הֵמִירוּ כְבוֹדָם בְּתַבְנִית. Numbers xx. 20, ἐν ὄχλῳ βαρεῖ בְּעַם כָּבֵד. 1 Kings x. 2, ἐν δυνάμει ἰσχυρᾷ בְּחַיִל כָּבֵד. Ps. lv. 19, ἐν πολλοῖς ἦσαν σὺν ἐμοί בְּרַבִּים הָיוּ עִמָּדִי. Deut. xxviii. 62, καταλειφθήσεσθε ἐν ἀριθμῷ βραχεῖ בִּמְתֵי מְעָט. Is. lviii. 1, ἀναβόησον ἐν ἰσχύι בְּגָרוֹן.

The last five may be said more or less to express *the manner* (A):
Numbers xiv. 10, κατελιθοβόλησαν ἐν λίθοις בָּאֲבָנִים *the instrument* (B): and Deut. xxiv. 16, and 2 Kings xiv. 6, ἕκαστος ἐν ταῖς ἁμαρτίαις αὐτοῦ ἀποθανεῖται אִישׁ בְּחֶטְאוֹ יָמוּת *the cause* (C).

I have cited the above in full, because the writers of N.T. have gone in the same track, in their use of ἐν, more especially in (A), (B), (C), for which we have dative alone comparatively seldom in either.

There are some startling examples of this use in N.T. E.g. vii. 6, ix. 34, L. xi. 20, 1 Cor. iv. 21, ἐν ῥάβδῳ ἔλθω πρὸς ὑμᾶς;
V.A. Θεὸς ἰσχυρός Deut. x. 17 and Θεὸν ἰσχύοντα Is. xx. 21 for אֵל גִּבּוֹר. The Greek word here and Mk. i. 7, L. iii. 11, would seem too weak to express the idea, but for this use of it in V.A.

13 Τότε παραγίνεται ὁ Ἰησοῦς ἀπὸ τῆς Γαλιλαίας ἐπὶ τὸν
14 Ἰορδάνην πρὸς τὸν Ἰωάννην, τοῦ βαπτισθῆναι ὑπ' αὐτοῦ. ὁ δὲ
διεκώλυεν αὐτὸν λέγων, Ἐγὼ χρείαν ἔχω ὑπὸ σοῦ βαπτισθῆναι,
15 καὶ σὺ ἔρχῃ πρός με; ἀποκριθεὶς δὲ ὁ Ἰησοῦς εἶπεν αὐτῷ [Ἄφες
ἄρτι·] οὕτως γὰρ πρέπον ἐστὶν ἡμῖν πληρῶσαι πᾶσαν δικαιο-
16 σύνην. τότε ἀφίησιν αὐτόν. βαπτισθεὶς δὲ ὁ Ἰησοῦς εὐθὺς ἀνέβη
ἀπὸ τοῦ ὕδατος· καὶ ἰδοὺ ἀνεῴχθησαν αὐτῷ οἱ οὐρανοί, καὶ εἶδεν
τὸ Πνεῦμα τοῦ Θεοῦ καταβαῖνον ὡσεὶ περιστερὰν, ἐρχόμενον
17 ἐπ' αὐτόν. καὶ ἰδοὺ φωνὴ ἐκ τῶν οὐρανῶν λέγουσα, Οὗτός ἐστιν
ὁ υἱός μου ὁ ἀγαπητός, ἐν ᾧ εὐδόκησα.

CAP.
4 Τότε ὁ Ἰησοῦς ἀνήχθη εἰς τὴν ἔρημον ὑπὸ τοῦ Πνεύματος,
2 [πειρασθῆναι] ὑπὸ τοῦ διαβόλου. καὶ νηστεύσας ἡμέρας τεσσα-
3 ράκοντα καὶ νύκτας τεσσαράκοντα, ὕστερον ἐπείνασε. καὶ προσελθὼν αὐτῷ ὁ πειράζων εἶπεν, Εἰ υἱὸς εἶ τοῦ Θεοῦ, εἰπὲ ἵνα οἱ λίθοι
4 οὗτοι ἄρτοι γένωνται. Ὁ δὲ ἀποκριθεὶς εἶπεν, Γέγραπται, * Οὐκ
ἐπ' ἄρτῳ μόνῳ ζήσεται ἄνθρωπος, ἀλλ' ἐπὶ παντὶ ῥήματι ἐκπο-
5 ρευομένῳ διὰ στόματος Θεοῦ.* Τότε παραλαμβάνει αὐτὸν ὁ διάβολος εἰς τὴν ἁγίαν πόλιν, καὶ ἵστησιν αὐτὸν ἐπὶ τὸ πτερύγιον
6 τοῦ ἱεροῦ καὶ λέγει αὐτῷ, Εἰ υἱὸς εἶ τοῦ Θεοῦ, βάλε σεαυτὸν
κάτω· γέγραπται γὰρ, Ὅτι τοῖς ἀγγέλοις αὐτοῦ ἐντελεῖται περὶ
σοῦ, καὶ ἐπὶ χειρῶν ἀροῦσί σε, μήποτε προσκόψῃς πρὸς λίθον τὸν
7 πόδα σου. Ἔφη αὐτῷ ὁ Ἰησοῦς, Πάλιν γέγραπται, Οὐκ ἐκπειρά-
8 σεις Κύριον τὸν Θεόν σου. Πάλιν παραλαμβάνει αὐτὸν ὁ διάβολος
εἰς ὄρος ὑψηλὸν λίαν, καὶ δείκνυσιν αὐτῷ πάσας τὰς βασιλείας
9 τοῦ κόσμου καὶ τὴν δόξαν αὐτῶν, καὶ λέγει αὐτῷ, Ταῦτα πάντα
10 σοι δώσω, ἐὰν πεσὼν προσκυνήσῃς μοι. Τότε λέγει αὐτῷ ὁ Ἰησοῦς,
Ὕπαγε ὀπίσω μου Σατανᾶ· γέγραπται γὰρ, Κύριον τὸν Θεόν
11 σου προσκυνήσεις, καὶ αὐτῷ μόνῳ λατρεύσεις. Τότε ἀφίησιν αὐτὸν
ὁ διάβολος· καὶ ἰδοὺ ἄγγελοι προσῆλθον καὶ διηκόνουν αὐτῷ.

15. πᾶσαν δικαιοσύνην] every claim of religious duty and piety.

17. εὐδόκησεν ἐν = בְּ חָפֵץ and is frequently put for it, e.g. 2 Sam. xxii. 19, by V.A.: which also follows literally other varieties of the Hebrew idiom connected with חָפֵץ and its cognate רָצָה, e.g. Ps. li. 16, עוֹלָה לֹא תִרְצֶה ὁλοκαυτώματα οὐκ εὐδόκησεις. Ps. lxxxv. 1, רָצִיתָ יְהוָה אַרְצֶךָ εὐδόκησας, Κύριε, τὴν γῆν σου.

Cap. IV. 4. V.A. Deut. viii. 3: כִּי עַל כָּל־מוֹצָא פִּי יְהוָה not "every word" but "any thing—coming out from the mouth of the Lord," "any thing appointed by God." Ordinary food is not necessary for human life when God provides extraordinary. ζῆν ἐπὶ = חָיָה עַל literally: but not really.

6. V.A. for עַל כַּפַּיִם. ὅτι is an integral part of the quotation from V.A. answering to כִּי in the Hebrew. I note this, that it may not be considered an instance of the ὅτι recitativum, as Grimm styles it; classing under this head ii. 23, vii. 23, xvi. 7, &c.: on which I hope to offer some observations hereafter.

ΑΚΟΥΣΑΣ δὲ ὁ Ἰησοῦς ὅτι Ἰωάννης παρεδόθη, ἀνεχώρησεν 12 εἰς τὴν Γαλιλαίαν, καὶ καταλιπὼν τὴν Ναζαρὲτ, ἐλθὼν κατῴκησεν 13 εἰς Καφαρναοὺμ τὴν παραθαλασσίαν, ἐν ὁρίοις Ζαβουλὼν καὶ Νεφθαλείμ· [ἵνα πληρωθῇ] τὸ ῥηθὲν διὰ Ἡσαΐου τοῦ προφήτου 14 λέγοντος, Γῆ Ζαβουλὼν καὶ γῆ Νεφθαλείμ, *ὁδὸν θαλάσσης* 15 πέραν τοῦ Ἰορδάνου, Γαλιλαία τῶν ἐθνῶν, ὁ λαὸς ὁ καθήμενος ἐν 16 σκότιᾳ φῶς εἶδεν μέγα, καὶ τοῖς καθημένοις *ἐν χώρᾳ καὶ σκιᾷ θανάτου,* φῶς ἀνέτειλεν αὐτοῖς.
Ἀπὸ τότε ἤρξατο ὁ Ἰησοῦς κηρύσσειν καὶ λέγειν, Μετανοεῖτε· 17 ἤγγικεν γὰρ *ἡ βασιλεία τῶν οὐρανῶν.* Περιπατῶν δὲ ὁ Ἰησοῦς 18 παρὰ τὴν θάλασσαν τῆς Γαλιλαίας, εἶδεν δύο ἀδελφούς, Σίμωνα τὸν λεγόμενον Πέτρον, καὶ Ἀνδρέαν τὸν ἀδελφὸν αὐτοῦ, βάλλοντας ἀμφίβληστρον εἰς τὴν θάλασσαν· ἦσαν γὰρ ἁλιεῖς. καὶ λέγει 19 αὐτοῖς, Δεῦτε ὀπίσω μου, καὶ ποιήσω ὑμᾶς ἁλιεῖς ἀνθρώπων. οἱ 20 δὲ εὐθέως [ἀφέντες] τὰ δίκτυα, ἠκολούθησαν αὐτῷ. Καὶ προβὰς 21 ἐκεῖθεν, εἶδεν ἄλλους δύο ἀδελφούς, Ἰάκωβον τὸν τοῦ Ζεβεδαίου, καὶ Ἰωάννην τὸν ἀδελφὸν αὐτοῦ, ἐν τῷ πλοίῳ μετὰ Ζεβεδαίου τοῦ πατρὸς αὐτῶν, καταρτίζοντας τὰ δίκτυα αὐτῶν, καὶ ἐκάλεσεν αὐτούς· οἱ δὲ εὐθέως [ἀφέντες] τὸ πλοῖον καὶ τὸν πατέρα αὐτῶν, 22 ἠκολούθησαν αὐτῷ.
Καὶ [περιῆγεν] ἐν ὅλῃ τῇ Γαλιλαίᾳ ὁ Ἰησοῦς, διδάσκων ἐν 23 ταῖς συναγωγαῖς αὐτῶν, καὶ κηρύσσων τὸ εὐαγγέλιον τῆς βασιλείας, καὶ θεραπεύων πᾶσαν νόσον καὶ πᾶσαν מַלאכִין ἐν τῷ λαῷ. καὶ [ἀπῆλθεν] *ἡ ἀκοὴ αὐτοῦ* εἰς ὅλην τὴν Συρίαν· καὶ προσή- 24 νεγκαν αὐτῷ πάντας τοὺς κακῶς ἔχοντας, ποικίλαις νόσοις καὶ βασάνοις συνεχομένους, καὶ δαιμονιζομένους, καὶ σεληνιαζομένους, καὶ παραλυτικούς· καὶ ἐθεράπευσεν αὐτούς. καὶ ἠκολούθησαν 25 αὐτῷ ὄχλοι πολλοὶ ἀπὸ τῆς Γαλιλαίας καὶ Δεκαπόλεως, καὶ Ἱεροσολύμων καὶ Ἰουδαίας, καὶ πέραν τοῦ Ἰορδάνου.

15. The confessedly obscure passage Isaiah viii. 23 and ix. 1 is made hopelessly unintelligible in V.A. We have here a literal translation of it. ὁδὸν θαλάσσης] for דֶּרֶךְ הַיָּם, which is correctly rendered in our Auth. Vers. "by the way of the sea." χώρα καὶ σκιὰ θανάτου for בְּאֶרֶץ צַלְמָוֶת "in the land of the shadow of death :" a purely Hebrew idiom ; as in Ps. xxiii. 4, xliv. 19, cvii. 10, Jerem. ii. 6, derived, apparently, from the idea of death as a dark mountain-barrier casting its gloomy shadow up the long valley through which it must be approached.

23. ix. 35. μαλακία in V. A. = חֳלִי, e.g. Deut. vii. 15, xxviii. 61, from חלה "delinivit, demulsit," and so μαλακὸν ἐποίησε: as if μαλακὸς = "languidus."
Is. xxxix. 1, כִּי חָלָה שָׁמַע· ἤκουσεν ὅτι ἐμαλακίσθη. The word is found in this sense in Arrian de Ven. VIII. 4, and Xenophon de Ven. v. 2, as Schleusner shows.

24. ἡ ἀκοὴ αὐτοῦ = שָׁמְעוֹ] Is. lxvi. 19. שָׁמְעִי = τὸ ὄνομά μου V.A. The Hebrew idiom seems to have influenced the LXX. in their frequent use of ἀκοὴ in this sense: though it is also found in classical authors.

MATTHEW, V. 1—16.

CAP.
5 ΙΔΩΝ δὲ τοὺς ὄχλους ἀνέβη εἰς τὸ ὄρος· καὶ καθίσαντος
2 αὐτοῦ, προσῆλθον αὐτῷ οἱ μαθηταὶ αὐτοῦ· καὶ *ἀνοίξας τὸ στόμα
3 αὐτοῦ,* ἐδίδασκεν αὐτοὺς λέγων, Μακάριοι οἱ πτωχοὶ [τῷ πνεύματι]·
4 ὅτι αὐτῶν ἐστιν ἡ βασιλεία τῶν οὐρανῶν. μακάριοι οἱ πραεῖς·
5 ὅτι αὐτοὶ κληρονομήσουσι τὴν γῆν. μακάριοι οἱ πενθοῦντες· ὅτι
6 αὐτοὶ παρακληθήσονται. μακάριοι οἱ [πεινῶντες καὶ διψῶντες] τὴν
7 δικαιοσύνην· ὅτι αὐτοὶ χορτασθήσονται. μακάριοι οἱ ἐλεήμονες·
8 ὅτι αὐτοὶ ἐλεηθήσονται. μακάριοι οἱ καθαροὶ τῇ καρδίᾳ· ὅτι αὐτοὶ
9 τὸν Θεὸν ὄψονται. μακάριοι οἱ εἰρηνοποιοί· ὅτι αὐτοὶ υἱοὶ Θεοῦ
10 κληθήσονται. μακάριοι οἱ δεδιωγμένοι ἕνεκεν δικαιοσύνης· ὅτι
11 αὐτῶν ἐστιν ἡ βασιλεία τῶν οὐρανῶν. μακάριοί ἐστε, ὅταν ὀνειδίσωσιν ὑμᾶς καὶ διώξωσι, καὶ *εἴπωσιν* καθ᾽ ὑμῶν πᾶν πονη-
12 ρὸν ἕνεκεν ἐμοῦ. χαίρετε καὶ ἀγαλλιᾶσθε, ὅτι ὁ μισθὸς ὑμῶν πολὺς ἐν τοῖς οὐρανοῖς· οὕτως γὰρ ἐδίωξαν τοὺς προφήτας τοὺς πρὸ ὑμῶν.
13 Ὑμεῖς ἐστε τὸ ἅλας τῆς γῆς· ἐὰν δὲ τὸ ἅλας *μωρανθῇ, ἐν τίνι* ἁλισθήσεται; εἰς οὐδὲν ἰσχύει ἔτι, εἰ μὴ βληθὲν ἔξω, κατα-
14 πατεῖσθαι ὑπὸ τῶν ἀνθρώπων. Ὑμεῖς ἐστε τὸ φῶς τοῦ κόσμου.
15 οὐ δύναται πόλις κρυβῆναι ἐπάνω ὄρους κειμένη· οὐδὲ καίουσι λύχνον καὶ τιθέασιν αὐτὸν ὑπὸ τὸν μόδιον, ἀλλ᾽ ἐπὶ τὴν λυχνίαν,
16 καὶ λάμπει πᾶσι τοῖς ἐν τῇ οἰκίᾳ. οὕτως λαμψάτω τὸ φῶς ὑμῶν ἔμπροσθεν τῶν ἀνθρώπων, ὅπως ἴδωσιν ὑμῶν τὰ καλὰ ἔργα, καὶ δοξάσωσι τὸν πατέρα ὑμῶν τὸν ἐν τοῖς οὐρανοῖς.

Cap. V. 3. 4. πτωχὸς and ταπεινὸς are used indifferently in V. A. for עָנִי or עָנָו in sense of "humble, modest, gentle, meek" as opposed to רָם "proud:" e.g. 2 Sam. xxii. 28, Ps. xviii. 28, which are two copies of the same hymn; where עָנָו is rendered by πτωχὸς in the one and ταπεινὸς in the other. But the word is much more frequently translated by πτωχὸς, even where the meaning is "humility" and not "poverty." See Trommius. This is an instance in which the Septuagint use of a word seems to have won for it, by mere force of familiarity, a meaning not its own before, in the popular phraseology. See cap. xi. 29, where our Lord, applying to Himself the terms πραὸς and ταπεινὸς τῇ καρδίᾳ, corresponding to the adjectives in vv. 3, 4, bids His followers learn of Him and so find peace and blessing. Ps. xxxvii. 11, οἱ πραεῖς κληρονομήσουσι γῆν.

13. μωρὸς] = dull, sluggish, slow: hence metaphorically (a) of the mind, "silly, foolish;" (b) and of taste, "insipid, flat:" as fatuus in Latin, with its double meaning answering to (a) and (b): and תָּפֵל (which is primarily "calx tectoria," mortar, Ez. xiii. 10, 12) signifies in Job vi. 6, "insulsum;" and in Threni ii. 14, "ineptum quiddam," and is rendered in V.A. ἀφροσύνη.

16. ἔμπροσθεν] "in front of," for ἐνώπιον "in presence of:" both being equivalent to לִפְנֵי, which has the two meanings, are constantly confused in V. A., and not kept distinct: and so, naturally, and as might be expected, in N.T.; e.g. L. i. 17 ἐνώπιον for ἔμπροσθεν, M. xi. 27, xvii. 2. Ἐναντίον also which corresponds to נֶגֶד "against," is similarly misplaced in Mark ii. 12, instead of ἐνώπιον; whereas in Matt. xxiii. 14 we have ἔμπροσθεν instead of ἐναντίον.

This seems to be peculiar to V. A. and N. T. Neither Grimm nor Schleusner, nor Liddell and Scott, give any instance,

MATTHEW, V. 17—24.

Μὴ νομίσητε ὅτι [ἦλθον καταλῦσαι] τὸν νόμον ἢ τοὺς προ- 17
φήτας· οὐκ ἦλθον καταλῦσαι, ἀλλὰ πληρῶσαι. *ἀμὴν* γὰρ λέγω 18
ὑμῖν, ἕως ἂν παρέλθῃ ὁ οὐρανὸς καὶ ἡ γῆ, ἰῶτα ἓν ἢ μία κεραία
οὐ μὴ παρέλθῃ ἀπὸ τοῦ νόμου, ἕως ἂν πάντα γένηται. [ὃς ἐὰν 19
οὖν λύσῃ] μίαν τῶν ἐντολῶν τούτων τῶν ἐλαχίστων καὶ διδάξῃ
οὕτως τοὺς ἀνθρώπους, ἐλάχιστος *κληθήσεται* ἐν τῇ βασιλείᾳ
τῶν οὐρανῶν· ὃς δ᾽ ἂν ποιήσῃ καὶ διδάξῃ, οὗτος *μέγας κληθήσεται* ἐν τῇ βασιλείᾳ τῶν οὐρανῶν. λέγω γὰρ ὑμῖν, ὅτι ἐὰν μὴ 20
περισσεύσῃ ἡ δικαιοσύνη ὑμῶν πλεῖον τῶν γραμματέων καὶ Φαρισαίων, οὐ μὴ εἰσέλθητε εἰς τὴν βασιλείαν τῶν οὐρανῶν. Ἠκού- 21
σατε ὅτι ἐρρήθη [τοῖς ἀρχαίοις], Οὐ φονεύσεις· ὃς δ᾽ ἂν φονεύσῃ,
ἔνοχος ἔσται τῇ κρίσει. Ἐγὼ δὲ λέγω ὑμῖν, ὅτι πᾶς ὁ ὀργιζόμενος 22
τῷ ἀδελφῷ αὐτοῦ, ἔνοχος ἔσται τῇ κρίσει· ὃς δ᾽ ἂν εἴπῃ τῷ
ἀδελφῷ αὐτοῦ *ῥακὰ,* ἔνοχος ἔσται τῷ συνεδρίῳ· ὃς δ᾽ ἂν εἴπῃ
μωρὲ, ἔνοχος ἔσται *εἰς τὴν γέενναν τοῦ πυρός.* ἐὰν οὖν προσ- 23
φέρῃς τὸ δῶρόν σου ἐπὶ τὸ θυσιαστήριον, κἀκεῖ μνησθῇς ὅτι ὁ
ἀδελφός σου ἔχει τὶ κατὰ σοῦ, ἄφες ἐκεῖ τὸ δῶρόν σου ἔμπροσθεν 24
τοῦ θυσιαστηρίου, καὶ ὕπαγε, πρῶτον διαλλάγηθι τῷ ἀδελφῷ σου,

in classical authors, of ἔμπροσθεν "in sight of."

18. ἀμὴν] never used in this sense by V.A.: seldom put at all as a Greek word: generally rendered by γένοιτο.

19. ὃς ἐὰν λύσῃ] I mark once for all this use of ἐὰν, so frequent in N.T., as indicative of deviation from pure Greek style.

22. ῥακὰ] from Heb. רֵיק evacuari, or רָקַק conspuit: each of them suggesting contempt and insult.

גֵּי הִנֹּם or גֵּי בְנֵי־הִנֹּם] the ravine under Mount Zion, where was הַתֹּפֶת or בָּמוֹת הַתֹּפֶת, spoken of 2 Kings xxiii. 10 and Jerem. vii. 31; the "locus combustionis" (Gesenius), the "furnace" or "fire" sacred to Molech, the fire-shrine, where the children passed through the fire: which was desecrated by Josiah, and made the place for burning the filth of the city, carcases of criminals, and the offal of the victims sacrificed in the Temple, brought down into it by the great sewers recently discovered. The name γέ-εννα τοῦ πυρός, "The flaming Gehenna," would have been appropriate, in the days of its honour and dishonour alike. The loathsome task of burning the garbage was probably performed by convicts, employed, both in ancient and modern times, as scavengers of great cities: as in Spain and Portugal till quite recently. Hence the force of ἔνοχος εἰς τὴν γέενναν τοῦ πυρός. "Obnoxius poenæ usque ad Gehennam ardentem." Our Lord names three degrees of offence, deserving of citation before a recognized tribunal, of less or greater jurisdiction, naming in the last case, not the tribunal (as in the others) but the penalty. We must carefully note the difference of construction: ἔνοχος κρίσει (a), συνεδρίῳ (b), εἰς γέενναν (c). The latter cannot be considered as equivalent to the dative γεέννᾳ,—so ἔνοχος (in c) must be taken alone, as "poenæ obnoxius." In V.A. it stands, I believe, always alone (except in two cases: Deut. xix. 10 וְלֹא יִהְיֶה עָלֶיךָ דָּמִים, i. e. "and there shall not be upon thee the guilt of blood," οὐκ ἔσται ἐν σοὶ αἵματι ἔνοχος, "there shall not be in the midst of thee any one liable to punishment by reason of blood," i. e. "guilty of manslaughter;" and Gen. xxvi. 11, מוֹת יוּמָת, θανάτῳ ἔνοχος ἔσται, morti obnoxius erit): Schl. gives three meanings: (1) ὑποκείμενος. Heb. ii. 15, ἔνοχος δουλείας. (2) ὑπεύθυνος, as above, and Mk. iii. 29. (3) ὑπαίτιος, as 1 Cor. xi. 27, ἔνοχος τοῦ σώματος τοῦ Κυρίου, and James ii. 10, πάντων ἔνοχος. But throughout N. T. its construction is very irregular, and it appears to take genitive or dative indifferently.

25 καὶ τότε ἐλθὼν πρόσφερε τὸ δῶρόν σου. [ἴσθι εὐνοῶν] τῷ ἀντιδίκῳ σου ταχύ, ἕως ὅτου εἶ ἐν τῇ ὁδῷ μετ' αὐτοῦ· μήποτέ σε παραδῷ ὁ ἀντίδικος τῷ κριτῇ, καὶ ὁ κριτής σε παραδῷ τῷ ὑπηρέτῃ,
26 καὶ εἰς φυλακὴν βληθήσῃ. ἀμὴν λέγω σοι, οὐ μὴ ἐξέλθῃς ἐκεῖθεν
27 ἕως ἂν ἀποδῷς τὸν ἔσχατον κοδράντην. Ἠκούσατε ὅτι ἐρρήθη
28 τοῖς ἀρχαίοις, Οὐ μοιχεύσεις. Ἐγὼ δὲ λέγω ὑμῖν, ὅτι πᾶς ὁ [βλέπων γυναῖκα] πρὸς τὸ ἐπιθυμῆσαι αὐτῆς, ἤδη ἐμοίχευσεν αὐτὴν
29 ἐν τῇ καρδίᾳ αὐτοῦ. εἰ δὲ ὁ ὀφθαλμός σου ὁ δεξιὸς *σκανδαλίζει* σε, ἔξελε αὐτὸν καὶ βάλε ἀπὸ σοῦ· συμφέρει γάρ σοι [ἵνα ἀπόληται] ἓν τῶν μελῶν σου, καὶ μὴ ὅλον τὸ σῶμά σου βληθῇ *εἰς*
30 γέενναν.* καὶ εἰ ἡ δεξιά σου χεὶρ σκανδαλίζει σε, ἔκκοψον αὐτὴν καὶ βάλε ἀπὸ σοῦ· συμφέρει γάρ σοι ἵνα ἀπόληται ἓν τῶν μελῶν σου, καὶ μὴ ὅλον τὸ σῶμά σου εἰς γέενναν ἀπέλθῃ.
31 Ἐρρήθη δέ, ὃς ἂν ἀπολύσῃ τὴν γυναῖκα αὐτοῦ, δότω αὐτῇ
32 ἀποστάσιον. Ἐγὼ δὲ λέγω ὑμῖν, ὅτι ὃς ἂν ἀπολύσῃ τὴν γυναῖκα αὐτοῦ, παρεκτὸς *λόγου πορνείας,* ποιεῖ αὐτὴν μοιχευθῆναι· καὶ ὃς
33 ἐὰν ἀπολελυμένην γαμήσῃ, μοιχᾶται. Πάλιν ἠκούσατε ὅτι ἐρρήθη τοῖς ἀρχαίοις, Οὐκ ἐπιορκήσεις, ἀποδώσεις δὲ τῷ Κυρίῳ τοὺς

29. In the parallel passage, Mk. ix. 43, 44, we have the additional description, ὅπου ὁ σκώληξ αὐτῶν οὐ τελευτᾷ καὶ τὸ πῦρ οὐ σβέννυται. Compare Isai. lxvi. 24. V.A. ἥξει πᾶσα σὰρξ τοῦ προσκυνῆσαι ἐνώπιον ἐμοῦ ἐν Ἱερουσαλὴμ εἶπε Κύριος. Καὶ ἐξελεύσονται καὶ ὄψονται τὰ κῶλα τῶν ἀνθρώπων τῶν παραβεβηκότων ἐν ἐμοί, הַפֹּשְׁעִים֙. ὁ γὰρ σκώληξ αὐτῶν οὐ τελευτήσει καὶ τὸ πῦρ αὐτῶν οὐ σβεσθήσεται, καὶ ἔσονται εἰς ὅρασιν πάσῃ σαρκί, וְהָי֣וּ דֵרָא֔וֹן.

LXX. seem to have had לִרְאוֹן. Note the use of εἰμὶ εἰς for הָיָה לְ = γίγνομαι. Comp. Dan. xii. 2, where דֵּרָאוֹן is ὀνειδισμὸν in V.A., "shame and everlasting contempt," "abominatio." The carcases of offenders against God were to be seen by all who should come up to Jerusalem, devoured by worms, rotting away, or consumed by a fire kept constantly burning,—apparently in γέεννα, the ravine of Hinnom "outside" the city: verse 22.

The horrible and loathsome sight, ever before their eyes, day and night, with all its foul accompaniments of smell and sound, where the bodies of transgressors against God or man, exposed to "*shame and contempt,*" suffered the extreme penalty of their crimes, suggested naturally the idea of the place of torment in Hades, recognized as the doom of sinners by our Lord, x. 28, xxiii. 33, L. xii. 5, xvi. 23, more especially as Daniel used the same word in describing the future doom of the wicked. Whether the particular passage before us here (verses 29, 30) refers to punishment of *this* world or *the next*, may be thought doubtful, as it makes no allusion to the soul. It may possibly contain only the counsel to destroy an offending member,—remove the cause of temptation and instrument of some besetting sin,—to prevent any chance of its leading to such crime, as would entail the death of a criminal and subsequent exposure to worm and fire in the reeking pit of Gehenna. A counsel of worldly prudence, as vv. 25, 26; capable, no doubt, of a higher and spiritual application; but not, in the first instance, necessarily and essentially involving it.

32. λ. π.] = דְּבַר וְגִוּת, "*the matter of adultery,*" "*the case of...,*" as Phil. iv. 15 εἰς λόγον δόσεως = עַל דְּבַר, a common Hebrew idiom, here literally translated. Grimm gives *ratio* as the meaning of λόγος, and quotes many passages from class. authors; but in all these λόγος stands alone, with no genitive, as here: e.g. ἐκ τίνος λόγου; τίνι δικαίῳ λόγῳ;... This does not cover our phrase, which is simply Hebraic.

ὅρκους σου. Ἐγὼ δὲ λέγω ὑμῖν μὴ ὀμόσαι ὅλως, μήτε *ἐν τῷ 34
οὐρανῷ,* ὅτι θρόνος ἐστὶν τοῦ Θεοῦ· μήτε ἐν τῇ γῇ, ὅτι ὑποπόδιόν 35
ἐστιν τῶν ποδῶν αὐτοῦ· μήτε [εἰς] Ἱεροσόλυμα, ὅτι πόλις ἐστὶν τοῦ
μεγάλου βασιλέως· μήτε ἐν τῇ κεφαλῇ σου ὀμόσῃς, ὅτι οὐ δύνασαι 36
μίαν τρίχα λευκὴν ἢ μέλαιναν ποιῆσαι. ἔσται δὲ ὁ λόγος ὑμῶν, 37
ναὶ ναί, οὒ οὔ· τὸ δὲ περισσὸν τούτων ἐκ τοῦ πονηροῦ ἐστιν.
Ἠκούσατε ὅτι ἐρρήθη, Ὀφθαλμὸν ἀντὶ ὀφθαλμοῦ, καὶ ὀδόντα ἀντὶ 38
ὀδόντος. Ἐγὼ δὲ λέγω ὑμῖν μὴ ἀντιστῆναι τῷ πονηρῷ· ἀλλ' ὅστις 39
σε ῥαπίσει ἐπὶ τὴν δεξιάν σου σιαγόνα, στρέψον αὐτῷ καὶ τὴν
ἄλλην· καὶ τῷ θέλοντί σοι κριθῆναι καὶ τὸν χιτῶνά σου λαβεῖν, 40
ἄφες αὐτῷ καὶ τὸ ἱμάτιον· καὶ ὅστις σε ἀγγαρεύσει μίλιον 41
ἕν, ὕπαγε μετ' αὐτοῦ δύο. τῷ αἰτοῦντί σε δός· καὶ τὸν θέλοντα 42
ἀπὸ σοῦ δανείσασθαι μὴ ἀποστραφῇς. Ἠκούσατε ὅτι ἐρρήθη, 43
Ἀγαπήσεις τὸν πλησίον σου, καὶ μισήσεις τὸν ἐχθρόν σου. 44
Ἐγὼ δὲ λέγω ὑμῖν, ἀγαπᾶτε τοὺς ἐχθροὺς ὑμῶν, καὶ προσεύχεσθε ὑπὲρ τῶν διωκόντων ὑμᾶς· ὅπως γένησθε υἱοὶ τοῦ πατρὸς ὑμῶν τοῦ ἐν οὐρανοῖς· ὅτι τὸν ἥλιον αὐτοῦ ἀνατέλλει ἐπὶ 45
πονηροὺς καὶ ἀγαθοὺς, καὶ βρέχει ἐπὶ δικαίους καὶ ἀδίκους.
ἐὰν γὰρ ἀγαπήσητε τοὺς ἀγαπῶντας ὑμᾶς, τίνα μισθὸν ἔχετε; 46
οὐχὶ καὶ οἱ τελῶναι οὕτως ποιοῦσι; Καὶ ἐὰν ἀσπάσησθε τοὺς 47
ἀδελφοὺς ὑμῶν μόνον, [τί περισσὸν ποιεῖτε;] οὐχὶ καὶ οἱ ἐθνικοὶ
τὸ αὐτὸ ποιοῦσιν; *ἔσεσθε* οὖν ὑμεῖς τέλειοι, ὥσπερ ὁ πατὴρ ὑμῶν 48
ὁ ἐν τοῖς οὐρανοῖς τέλειός ἐστι.

CAP.
[ΠΡΟΣΕΧΕΤΕ] δὲ τὴν δικαιοσύνην ὑμῶν μὴ ποιεῖν ἔμπροσθεν 6

34. ἐν τῷ οὐρανῷ] בְּ יְשַׁבֵּעַ, "*juravit per:*" rendered literally here, as in V. A. passim: e. g. יְשַׁבַּע בְּלָא אֱלֹהִים, Jerem. v. 7, ὤμνυον ἐν τοῖς οὐκ οὖσι θεοῖς. I do not understand the force of the preposition in εἰς Ἱεροσόλυμα. Grimm explains "animo in Jerusalem directo," very unsatisfactorily.

37. ἐκ τοῦ πονηροῦ] "on the side of," "under the category of," as Gal. iii. 9, 10, 12, οἱ ἐκ πίστεως, the *faith* party, ἐξ ἔργων νόμου, "on the side of religious works," ὁ νόμος οὐκ ἔστιν ἐκ πίστεως, "the Jewish religion is not a rule or system of faith." 1 John ii. 21, πᾶν ψεῦδος ἐκ τῆς ἀληθείας οὐκ ἔστι, "there can be no lie in the ranks of the truth:" where mark Hebraism πᾶν ψ. οὐκ = לֹא ... כָּל.

48. ἔσεσθε] Future for imperative (or optative), a common Hebraism. Ps. xix.

15. V.A. has ἔσονται: our Engl. Version *optative* rightly, "Let the words of my mouth..."

Cap. VI. 1. This is the only instance of προσέχειν alone followed by μή. The general uses in the N.T. are (*a*) προσέχειν ἀπὸ, infra vii. 15, x. 7, and L. xx. 46, which is found in Apocrypha; or (*b*) προσέχειν ἑαυτοῖς ἀπὸ, L. xii. 1; or (*c*) προσέχειν ἑαυτοῖς, L. xvii. 3, Acts v. 35, which both occur constantly in V.A. for חָדַל, 2 Chr. xxv. 13, or הִשָּׁמֶר, Deut. iv. 23, iv. 9; Gen. xxiv. 6. This usage seems unknown to class. authors.

Many MSS. have ἐλεημοσύνην. V.A. for צְדָקָה, Dan. iv. 24, has ἐν ἐλεημοσύναις. Hence we gather that ἐλεημοσύνη, an essential element in Jewish δικαιοσύνη, had come to be used as equivalent to it: a part for the whole.

τῶν ἀνθρώπων, πρὸς τὸ θεαθῆναι αὐτοῖς· εἰ δὲ μήγε, μισθὸν οὐκ
2 ἔχετε παρὰ τῷ πατρὶ ὑμῶν τῷ ἐν τοῖς οὐρανοῖς. ὅταν οὖν ποιῇς
ἐλεημοσύνην, μὴ σαλπίσῃς ἔμπροσθέν σου, ὥσπερ οἱ ὑποκριταὶ
ποιοῦσιν ἐν ταῖς συναγωγαῖς καὶ ἐν ταῖς ῥύμαις, ὅπως δοξασθῶσιν
ὑπὸ τῶν ἀνθρώπων· ἀμὴν λέγω ὑμῖν, ἀπέχουσι τὸν μισθὸν αὐτῶν.
3 σοῦ δὲ ποιοῦντος ἐλεημοσύνην, μὴ γνώτω ἡ ἀριστερά σου [τί] ποιεῖ
4 ἡ δεξιά σου, ὅπως ᾖ σου ἡ ἐλεημοσύνη ἐν τῷ κρυπτῷ· καὶ ὁ
5 πατήρ σου ὁ βλέπων ἐν τῷ κρυπτῷ, ἀποδάσει σοι. Καὶ ὅταν
προσεύχησθε, οὐκ ἔσεσθε ὥσπερ οἱ ὑποκριταί, ὅτι φιλοῦσιν ἐν ταῖς
συναγωγαῖς καὶ ἐν ταῖς γωνίαις τῶν πλατειῶν ἑστῶτες προσεύχε-
σθαι, ὅπως [φανῶσιν] τοῖς ἀνθρώποις· ἀμὴν λέγω ὑμῖν, ἀπέ-
6 χουσι τὸν μισθὸν αὐτῶν. σὺ δὲ ὅταν προσεύχῃ, εἴσελθε εἰς τὸ
ΤΑΜΙΕῖΟΝ σου, καὶ κλείσας τὴν θύραν σου, πρόσευξαι τῷ πατρί σου
τῷ ἐν τῷ κρυπτῷ· καὶ ὁ πατήρ σου ὁ βλέπων ἐν τῷ κρυπτῷ,
7 ἀποδώσει σοι. Προσευχόμενοι δὲ μὴ βαττολογήσητε, ὥσπερ
[οἱ ἐθνικοί]· δοκοῦσι γὰρ ὅτι *ἐν τῇ πολυλογίᾳ* αὐτῶν
8 εἰσακουσθήσονται. μὴ οὖν ὁμοιωθῆτε αὐτοῖς· οἶδεν γὰρ ὁ πατὴρ
9 ὑμῶν ὧν χρείαν ἔχετε, πρὸ τοῦ ὑμᾶς αἰτῆσαι αὐτόν. οὕτως οὖν
προσεύχεσθε ὑμεῖς· Πάτερ ἡμῶν ὁ ἐν τοῖς οὐρανοῖς, ἁγιασθήτω τὸ
10 ὄνομά σου· ἐλθέτω ἡ βασιλεία σου· γενηθήτω τὸ θέλημά σου, ὡς
11 ἐν οὐρανῷ, *καὶ* ἐπὶ γῆς· τὸν ἄρτον ἡμῶν τὸν [ἐπιούσιον] δὸς
12 ἡμῖν σήμερον· καὶ ἄφες ἡμῖν *τὰ ὀφειλήματα* ἡμῶν, ὡς καὶ
13 ἡμεῖς ἀφίεμεν *τοῖς ὀφειλέταις* ἡμῶν· καὶ μὴ εἰσενέγκῃς ἡμᾶς
14 εἰς πειρασμὸν, ἀλλὰ ῥῦσαι ἡμᾶς ἀπὸ τοῦ πονηροῦ. Ἐὰν γὰρ
ἀφῆτε τοῖς ἀνθρώποις τὰ παραπτώματα αὐτῶν, ἀφήσει καὶ
ὑμῖν ὁ πατὴρ ὑμῶν ὁ οὐράνιος· ἐὰν δὲ μὴ ἀφῆτε τοῖς ἀνθρώποις
15 τὰ παραπτώματα αὐτῶν, οὐδὲ ὁ πατὴρ ὑμῶν ἀφήσει τὰ παραπτώματα ὑμῶν. Ὅταν δὲ νηστεύητε, μὴ γίνεσθε ὥσπερ οἱ ὑποκριταὶ
16 σκυθρωποί· [ἀφανίζουσι] γὰρ τὰ πρόσωπα αὐτῶν, ὅπως φανῶσι
τοῖς ἀνθρώποις νηστεύοντες· ἀμὴν λέγω ὑμῖν, ἀπέχουσιν τὸν
17 μισθὸν αὐτῶν. σὺ δὲ νηστεύων ἄλειψαί σου τὴν κεφαλὴν, καὶ τὸ
18 πρόσωπόν σου νίψαι· ὅπως μὴ φανῇς τοῖς ἀνθρώποις νηστεύων,

---

6. Βάδιζε λαός μου, εἴσελθε εἰς τὰ ταμεῖα σοῦ, Is. xxvi. 20. V.A. for לֵךְ עַמִּי בֹּא בַחֲדָרֶיךָ; which probably accounts for the use of the word in N.T.

7. ἐν with dative for "cause," "because of."

12. V.A. does not use ὀφείλημα as =ἁμαρτία. But the Rabbins in their Targums employed this phraseology.—

Schleusner quotes Gen. xx. 9 מָצְאָה גְדֹלָה paraphrased by חוֹבָא רַבָּא, and Ps. xxv. 18 חַסָּאתַי rendered חוֹבֵי in the Targum, חוֹב being Chaldee for *debt*. Also Gen. xviii. 20, Ex. xxxii. 32. Hence we see that the idea of *sin* as *debt* was familiar to the Jews; and our Lord recognizes it in His parables.

ἀλλὰ τῷ πατρί σου τῷ ἐν τῷ κρυφαίῳ· καὶ ὁ πατήρ σου ὁ βλέπων ἐν τῷ κρυφαίῳ, ἀποδώσει σοι.

Μὴ θησαυρίζετε ὑμῖν θησαυροὺς ἐπὶ τῆς γῆς, ὅπου σὴς καὶ 19 βρῶσις ἀφανίζει, καὶ ὅπου κλέπται διορύσσουσι καὶ κλέπτουσιν· θη- 20 σαυρίζετε δὲ ὑμῖν θησαυροὺς ἐν οὐρανῷ, ὅπου οὔτε σὴς οὔτε βρῶσις ἀφανίζει, καὶ ὅπου κλέπται οὐ διορύσσουσιν οὐδὲ κλέπτουσιν. ὅπου 21 γάρ ἐστιν ὁ θησαυρός σου, ἐκεῖ ἔσται καὶ ἡ καρδία σου. Ὁ 22 λύχνος τοῦ σώματός ἐστιν ὁ ὀφθαλμός· ἐὰν οὖν ὁ ὀφθαλμός σου ἁπλοῦς ᾖ, ὅλον τὸ σῶμά σου φωτεινὸν ἔσται· ἐὰν δὲ ὁ ὀφθαλμός 23 σου πονηρὸς ᾖ, ὅλον τὸ σῶμά σου σκοτεινὸν ἔσται. εἰ οὖν τὸ φῶς τὸ ἐν σοὶ σκότος ἐστί, τὸ σκότος πόσον; οὐδεὶς δύναται δυσὶ 24 κυρίοις δουλεύειν· ἢ γὰρ τὸν ἕνα μισήσει, καὶ τὸν ἕτερον ἀγαπήσει· ἢ ἑνὸς ἀνθέξεται, καὶ τοῦ ἑτέρου καταφρονήσει. οὐ δύνασθε Θεῷ δουλεύειν καὶ μαμμωνᾷ. διὰ τοῦτο λέγω ὑμῖν, μὴ μεριμνᾶτε 25 τῇ ψυχῇ ὑμῶν, [τί φάγητε] καὶ τί πίητε· μηδὲ τῷ σώματι ὑμῶν τί ἐνδύσησθε. οὐχὶ ἡ ψυχὴ πλεῖόν ἐστι τῆς τροφῆς, καὶ τὸ σῶμα τοῦ ἐνδύματος; ἐμβλέψατε εἰς τὰ πετεινὰ τοῦ οὐρανοῦ, ὅτι οὐ 26 σπείρουσιν, οὐδὲ θερίζουσιν, οὐδὲ συνάγουσιν εἰς ἀποθήκας, καὶ ὁ πατὴρ ὑμῶν ὁ οὐράνιος τρέφει αὐτά· οὐχ ὑμεῖς μᾶλλον διαφέρετε αὐτῶν; τίς δὲ ἐξ ὑμῶν μεριμνῶν δύναται προσθεῖναι ἐπὶ τὴν ἡλικίαν 27 αὐτοῦ πῆχυν ἕνα; καὶ περὶ ἐνδύματος τί μεριμνᾶτε; καταμάθετε τὰ 28 κρίνα τοῦ ἀγροῦ [πῶς] αὐξάνουσιν· οὐ κοπιῶσιν, οὐδὲ νήθουσιν. λέγω δὲ ὑμῖν, ὅτι οὐδὲ Σολομὼν ἐν πάσῃ τῇ δόξῃ αὐτοῦ περιε- 29 βάλετο ὡς ἓν τούτων. εἰ δὲ τὸν χόρτον τοῦ ἀγροῦ, σήμερον ὄντα, 30 καὶ αὔριον εἰς κλίβανον βαλλόμενον, ὁ Θεὸς οὕτως ἀμφιέννυσιν, οὐ πολλῷ μᾶλλον ὑμᾶς, ὀλιγόπιστοι; μὴ οὖν μεριμνήσητε λέγον- 31 τες, Τί φάγωμεν, ἢ τί πίωμεν, ἢ τί περιβαλώμεθα; πάντα γὰρ 32 ταῦτα τὰ ἔθνη ἐπιζητοῦσιν· οἶδεν γὰρ ὁ πατὴρ ὑμῶν ὁ οὐράνιος ὅτι χρῄζετε τούτων ἁπάντων. ζητεῖτε δὲ πρῶτον τὴν βασιλείαν τοῦ 33 Θεοῦ καὶ τὴν δικαιοσύνην αὐτοῦ, καὶ ταῦτα πάντα *προστεθήσεται*

22. ἁπλότης· V.A. for םת "integritas." 2 Kings xv. 11, Prov. xix. 1.

33. προστεθήσεται] here and L. xii. 31, in sense of "come in afterwards," "come next," as Acts xii. 3, προσέθετο συλλαβεῖν Πέτρον: "he seized Peter afterwards." L. xx. 11. Always used by V. A. for יסף in same sense. Here the *future* stands for imperative or permissive, a usage not uncommon in Hebrew; and vice versâ. Is. lv. 2, "Hearken unto me and eat:" i. e. "ye shall eat;" and the commandments in Ex. xx.—V.A. frequently renders Hebrew imperative by future: e.g. Is. vi. 9, a passage very loosely translated in it: see infra, cap. xiii. 14—16. My conclusion is that this verse does not contain a promise of the supply of our bodily and temporal wants, as the consequence of our devotion to God's service (as our English Version seems to imply); but a permission from the mouth of our great Teacher and Lawgiver to provide for *them* after we have first discharged our duties to God; "seek ye first the kingdom of God and His righteousness, and then all these claims of the world and the flesh may allowably and innocently be attended to:" the life of the soul to be the first care and thought, the life of the body the second.

34 ὑμῖν· μὴ οὖν μεριμνήσητε εἰς τὴν αὔριον· ἡ γὰρ αὔριον μεριμνήσει ἑαυτῆς. ἀρκετὸν τῇ ἡμέρᾳ [ἡ κακία] αὐτῆς.

CAP. 7

ΜΗ κρίνετε, ἵνα μὴ κριθῆτε. *ἐν ᾧ γὰρ κρίματι* κρίνετε, 3 κριθήσεσθε· καὶ ἐν ᾧ μέτρῳ μετρεῖτε, μετρηθήσεται ὑμῖν. Τί δὲ βλέπεις τὸ κάρφος τὸ ἐν τῷ ὀφθαλμῷ τοῦ ἀδελφοῦ σου, τὴν 4 δὲ ἐν τῷ σῷ ὀφθαλμῷ δοκὸν οὐ κατανοεῖς; ἢ πῶς ἐρεῖς τῷ ἀδελφῷ σου, Ἄφες ἐκβάλω τὸ κάρφος ἀπὸ τοῦ ὀφθαλμοῦ σου, 5 καὶ ἰδοὺ ἡ δοκὸς ἐν τῷ ὀφθαλμῷ σου; ὑποκριτά, ἔκβαλε πρῶτον τὴν δοκὸν ἐκ τοῦ ὀφθαλμοῦ σου, καὶ τότε διαβλέψεις ἐκβαλεῖν τὸ 6 κάρφος ἐκ τοῦ ὀφθαλμοῦ τοῦ ἀδελφοῦ σου. Μὴ δῶτε τὸ ἅγιον τοῖς κυσί· μηδὲ βάλητε τοὺς μαργαρίτας ὑμῶν ἔμπροσθεν τῶν χοίρων, μήποτε καταπατήσωσιν αὐτοὺς * ἐν τοῖς ποσὶν * αὐτῶν, καὶ 7 στραφέντες ῥήξωσιν ὑμᾶς. Αἰτεῖτε, καὶ δοθήσεται ὑμῖν. ζητεῖτε, καὶ 8 εὑρήσετε· κρούετε, καὶ ἀνοιγήσεται ὑμῖν· πᾶς γὰρ ὁ αἰτῶν λαμβάνει, 9 καὶ ὁ ζητῶν εὑρίσκει, καὶ τῷ κρούοντι ἀνοιγήσεται. ἢ τίς ἐξ ὑμῶν ἄνθρωπος, [ὃν αἰτήσει ὁ υἱὸς αὐτοῦ ἄρτον, μὴ λίθον ἐπιδώ-10 σει αὐτῷ; ἢ καὶ ἰχθὺν αἰτήσει, μὴ ὄφιν ἐπιδώσει αὐτῷ;] εἰ οὖν 11 ὑμεῖς, πονηροὶ ὄντες, οἴδατε δόματα ἀγαθὰ διδόναι τοῖς τέκνοις ὑμῶν, πόσῳ μᾶλλον ὁ πατὴρ ὑμῶν ὁ ἐν τοῖς οὐρανοῖς δώσει ἀγαθὰ 12 τοῖς αἰτοῦσιν αὐτόν; Πάντα οὖν ὅσα ἂν θέλητε ἵνα ποιῶσιν ὑμῖν οἱ ἄνθρωποι, οὕτως καὶ ὑμεῖς ποιεῖτε αὐτοῖς· [οὗτος] γάρ ἐστιν ὁ νόμος καὶ οἱ προφῆται.

13 Εἰσέλθατε διὰ τῆς στενῆς πύλης· ὅτι πλατεῖα ἡ πύλη, καὶ εὐρύχωρος ἡ ὁδὸς ἡ ἀπάγουσα εἰς τὴν ἀπώλειαν, καὶ πολλοί εἰσιν 14 οἱ εἰσερχόμενοι δι᾽ αὐτῆς· ὅτι στενὴ ἡ πύλη, καὶ τεθλιμμένη ἡ ὁδὸς ἡ ἀπάγουσα εἰς τὴν ζωήν, καὶ ὀλίγοι εἰσὶν οἱ εὑρίσκοντες αὐτήν. 15 Προσέχετε δὲ ἀπὸ τῶν ψευδοπροφητῶν, οἵτινες ἔρχονται πρὸς ὑμᾶς 16 *ἐν ἐνδύμασι προβάτων,* ἔσωθεν δέ εἰσιν λύκοι ἅρπαγες. * ἀπὸ τῶν καρπῶν* αὐτῶν ἐπιγνώσεσθε αὐτούς· μήτι συλλέγουσιν ἀπὸ 17 ἀκανθῶν σταφυλήν, ἢ ἀπὸ τριβόλων σῦκα; οὕτως πᾶν δένδρον ἀγαθὸν καρποὺς καλοὺς ποιεῖ· τὸ δὲ σαπρὸν δένδρον καρποὺς 18 πονηροὺς ποιεῖ. οὐ δύναται δένδρον ἀγαθὸν καρποὺς πονηροὺς 19 ποιεῖν, οὐδὲ δένδρον σαπρὸν καρποὺς καλοὺς ποιεῖν. πᾶν δένδρον

---

34. ἡ γὰρ......] "for the morrow will have to care for its own matters," "is sure to have," "will certainly have," "cares enough of its own."

κακία] V.A. for "vexatio, aerumna." 1 Kings xx. 28, Eccl. xii. 1, Am. iii. 6. Is the word ever thus used in pure Greek?

Cap. VII. 2. Instances are given by Lightfoot of an old Rabbinical proverb of the mote and beam: the words are not found in V.A.

9. Confessedly ungrammatical.

12. οὗτός ἐστιν ὁ ν. κ. ὁ. π.] A strange construction utterly at variance with ordinary forms.

16. ἀπὸ] = לְ used to express cause; in xviii. 7, instrument or manner: Hebrew rather than Greek: Gen. ix. 11, Ps. lxxvi. 7.

μὴ ποιοῦν καρπὸν καλὸν, ἐκκόπτεται καὶ εἰς πῦρ βάλλεται. ἄραγε 20
ἀπὸ τῶν καρπῶν αὐτῶν ἐπιγνώσεσθε αὐτούς.

Οὐ πᾶς ὁ λέγων μοι, Κύριε, Κύριε, εἰσελεύσεται εἰς *τὴν 21
βασιλείαν τῶν οὐρανῶν·* ἀλλ' ὁ ποιῶν τὸ θέλημα τοῦ πατρός μου
τοῦ ἐν τοῖς οὐρανοῖς. πολλοὶ ἐροῦσίν μοι ἐν ἐκείνῃ τῇ ἡμέρᾳ, Κύριε, 22
Κύριε, οὐ [τῷ σῷ ὀνόματι] προεφητεύσαμεν, καὶ τῷ σῷ ὀνόματι
δαιμόνια ἐξεβάλομεν, καὶ τῷ σῷ ὀνόματι *δυνάμεις* πολλὰς
ἐποιήσαμεν; καὶ τότε [ὁμολογήσω] αὐτοῖς, *ὅτι* οὐδέποτε ἔγνων 23
ὑμᾶς· ἀποχωρεῖτε ἀπ' ἐμοῦ οἱ ἐργαζόμενοι τὴν ἀνομίαν. Πᾶς οὖν 24
ὅστις ἀκούει μου τοὺς λόγους τούτους, καὶ ποιεῖ αὐτοὺς, ὁμοιώσω
αὐτὸν ἀνδρὶ φρονίμῳ, ὅστις ᾠκοδόμησεν τὴν οἰκίαν αὐτοῦ ἐπὶ τὴν
πέτραν· καὶ κατέβη ἡ βροχὴ καὶ ἦλθον οἱ ποταμοὶ καὶ ἔπνευσαν 25
οἱ ἄνεμοι, καὶ προσέπεσον τῇ οἰκίᾳ ἐκείνῃ, καὶ οὐκ ἔπεσεν· τεθε-
μελίωτο γὰρ ἐπὶ τὴν πέτραν. καὶ πᾶς ὁ ἀκούων μου τοὺς λόγους 26
τούτους, καὶ μὴ ποιῶν αὐτοὺς, ὁμοιωθήσεται ἀνδρὶ μωρῷ, ὅστις
ᾠκοδόμησε τὴν οἰκίαν αὐτοῦ ἐπὶ τὴν ἄμμον· καὶ κατέβη ἡ βροχὴ 27
καὶ ἦλθον οἱ ποταμοὶ καὶ ἔπνευσαν οἱ ἄνεμοι, καὶ προσέκοψαν
τῇ οἰκίᾳ ἐκείνῃ, καὶ ἔπεσεν· καὶ ἦν ἡ πτῶσις αὐτῆς μεγάλη. Καὶ 28
[ἐγένετο] ὅτε ἐτέλεσεν ὁ Ἰησοῦς τοὺς λόγους τούτους, [ἐξεπλήσ-

22. τῷ σῷ ὀνόματι] Here, where we should naturally expect ἐν, we have dative alone: not easy to account for: unless as, in some sense, conveying the idea of instrumentality, though this seems forced and unnatural. And besides, M. *very seldom* uses dative for this.

δυνάμεις] Found once only *in this sense* in V.A. for מִפְלָאוֹת Job xxxvii. 16. גְּבוּרָה, to which Schleusner considers it parallel, is rather the abstract, δύναμις, *power*, than its manifestation by a miracle; and besides there are no other instances, but that above, of the plural in V.A. In N.T. we have both (*a*) singular and (*b*) plural, in this sense: (*a*) Mk. ix. 39, (*b*) infra xi. 20, 21, 22, Acts ii. 22.

23. I select *this* instance of ὅτι, in a collocation frequent in N.T., to offer a few remarks on its probable force and meaning, because it has been allowed to remain in the text by Tischendorf, who has so unsparingly eliminated the word elsewhere. I cannot regard it as universally pleonastic or superfluous, or as merely introductory to a quotation or the statement of another person's opinion, though this, of course, is occasionally its use and meaning, what Grimm calls "ὅτι recitativum," specifying this passage and infra cap. xxvi. 72, 74, xxvii. 43 among others. I purposely confine myself to S. Matt., although I might cite the other sacred authors largely. I cannot, in any of these instances, nor in many others, e.g. cap. xix. 8, xxvi. 65, x. 7, xiv. 26, acquiesce in this annihilation of its significance. Twice, at least, in V.A., Gen. xxviii. 16, xliv. 28, it is given for אַךְ or אָבֵן, "verily," in strong asseveration, as emphatic, which would suit all the passages above. Nor may we forget how frequently it is used in V.A. as = כִּי, in all its various meanings, and that one of those is *asseveration*, as recognized by lexicographers and by our Auth. Version. Gen. xxix. 33 וַתֹּאמֶר כִּי שָׁמַע יְהוָה, καὶ εἶπεν, ὅτι ἤκουσε Κύριος. Josh. ii. 24 וַיֹּאמְרוּ כִּי נָתַן יְהוָה בְּיָדֵנוּ אֶת־כָּל־הָאָרֶץ καὶ εἶπαν, ὅτι παραδέδωκεν ὁ Κύριος πᾶσαν τὴν γῆν ἐν χειρὶ ἡμῶν. Jerem. xxii. 22 כִּי אָז תֵּבֹשִׁי, ὅτι τότε αἰσχυνθήσῃ, "surely then thou shalt be ashamed." I think therefore that we may claim this meaning for ὅτι in those passages where it manifestly suits the sense and gives force to the expression.

28. The omission of any conjunction to connect the two verbs, so frequent in

29 σοντο] οἱ ὄχλοι ἐπὶ τῇ διδαχῇ αὐτοῦ· ἦν γὰρ διδάσκων αὐτοὺς
CAP. ὡς ἐξουσίαν ἔχων, καὶ οὐχ ὡς οἱ γραμματεῖς αὐτῶν.
8   ΚΑΤΑΒΑΝΤΙ δὲ αὐτῷ ἀπὸ τοῦ ὄρους, ἠκολούθησαν αὐτῷ ὄχλοι
2 πολλοί· καὶ ἰδοὺ λεπρὸς προσελθὼν προσεκύνει αὐτῷ λέγων, Κύριε,
3 ἐὰν θέλῃς, δύνασαί με καθαρίσαι. καὶ ἐκτείνας τὴν χεῖρα, ἥψατο
αὐτοῦ ὁ Ἰησοῦς λέγων, Θέλω, καθαρίσθητι. καὶ εὐθέως ἐκαθαρίσθη
4 αὐτοῦ ἡ λέπρα. καὶ λέγει αὐτῷ ὁ Ἰησοῦς, Ὅρα μηδενὶ εἴπῃς·
ἀλλ' ὕπαγε, σεαυτὸν δεῖξον τῷ ἱερεῖ, καὶ προσένεγκε τὸ δῶρον ὃ
προσέταξεν Μωσῆς, *εἰς μαρτύριον* αὐτοῖς.
5   Εἰσελθόντι δὲ αὐτῷ εἰς Καφαρναούμ, προσῆλθεν αὐτῷ
6 ἑκατόνταρχος παρακαλῶν αὐτὸν καὶ λέγων, Κύριε, ὁ παῖς μου
7 [βέβληται] ἐν τῇ οἰκίᾳ παραλυτικὸς, δεινῶς βασανιζόμενος. καὶ
8 λέγει αὐτῷ ὁ Ἰησοῦς, Ἐγὼ ἐλθὼν θεραπεύσω αὐτόν. καὶ ἀποκριθεὶς
ὁ ἑκατόνταρχος ἔφη, Κύριε, οὐκ εἰμὶ [ἱκανὸς] ἵνα μου ὑπὸ τὴν στέγην
9 εἰσέλθῃς· ἀλλὰ μόνον εἰπὲ λόγῳ, καὶ ἰαθήσεται ὁ παῖς μου. καὶ
γὰρ ἐγὼ ἄνθρωπός εἰμι [ὑπὸ ἐξουσίαν, ἔχων ὑπ' ἐμαυτὸν] στρατι-
ώτας· καὶ λέγω τούτῳ, Πορεύθητι, καὶ πορεύεται· καὶ ἄλλῳ, Ἔρχου,
10 καὶ ἔρχεται· καὶ τῷ δούλῳ μου, Ποίησον τοῦτο, καὶ ποιεῖ. Ἀκούσας
δὲ ὁ Ἰησοῦς ἐθαύμασεν, καὶ εἶπεν τοῖς ἀκολουθοῦσιν, Ἀμὴν λέγω ὑμῖν,
11 παρ' οὐδενὶ τοσαύτην πίστιν ἐν τῷ Ἰσραὴλ εὗρον. λέγω δὲ ὑμῖν,
ὅτι πολλοὶ ἀπὸ ἀνατολῶν καὶ δυσμῶν ἥξουσι, καὶ ἀνακλιθήσονται
μετὰ Ἀβραὰμ, καὶ Ἰσαὰκ, καὶ Ἰακὼβ ἐν τῇ βασιλείᾳ τῶν οὐρανῶν·
12 *οἱ δὲ υἱοὶ τῆς βασιλείας* ἐκβληθήσονται εἰς τὸ σκότος τὸ ἐξώ-
13 τερον· ἐκεῖ ἔσται *ὁ κλαυθμὸς καὶ ὁ βρυγμὸς τῶν ὀδόντων.* καὶ
εἶπεν ὁ Ἰησοῦς τῷ ἑκατοντάρχῃ, Ὕπαγε, ὡς ἐπίστευσας γενηθήτω
σοι. καὶ ἰάθη ὁ παῖς αὐτοῦ ἐν τῇ ὥρᾳ ἐκείνῃ.
14 Καὶ ἐλθὼν ὁ Ἰησοῦς εἰς τὴν οἰκίαν Πέτρου, εἶδεν τὴν πενθερὰν

N.T., is due to depravation of style; as also cap. viii. 6, 8, 9, βέβληται for "aegrotus decumbit lecto affixus," as Grimm paraphrases it; and ἱκανός, "a sufficiently great person," "grand enough;" and ὑπὸ ἐξουσίαν in accusative.

Cap. VIII. 12. The Hebrew idioms, in which בֵּן, in its various derivative or metaphorical significations, is employed,—rendered literally in V.A. by υἱός, and in our Auth. V. by "son" or "child,"—are so familiar to us, that we very often do not stop to get a clear and definite idea of their meaning: e.g. "sons of Belial," Deut. xiii. 13, 1 Sam. ii. 12, and υἱὸς θανάτου, "death's child," doomed to die, 1 Sam. xx. 31, 2 Sam. xii. 5; and infra cap. xxiii. 15 υἱὸς γεέννης, "a child of hell," and υἱοὶ τοῦ νυμφῶνος, ix. 15, "children of the bride-chamber;" John xvii. 12, υἱὸς ἀπωλείας, "the son of perdition." No general rule can be given: each case requires its own special consideration.

τὸ σκ. τὸ ἐξ.] "the darkness outside," contrasted with the brilliancy and splendour which light up the banquet of the king, referred to in verse 11, and in the Parable of the Marriage Feast, cap. xxii. 1—14. It is a periphrasis for the place of punishment.

ὁ κλ. κ. ὁ βρ.] The article here and in L. xiii. 38 seems to imply a well-known form of expression for the misery of the scene: "*the* wailing...that all have heard of." Possibly a phrase of some sacred writer that had passed into a proverb. Ps. cxi. 10, τοὺς ὀδόντας αὐτοῦ βρύξει ὁ ἁμαρτωλός.

αὐτοῦ [βεβλημένην] καὶ πυρέσσουσαν, καὶ ἥψατο τῆς χειρὸς αὐτῆς, 15
καὶ ἀφῆκεν αὐτὴν ὁ πυρετός· καὶ ἠγέρθη, καὶ διηκόνει αὐτῷ.
Ὀψίας δὲ γενομένης προσήνεγκαν αὐτῷ δαιμονιζομένους πολλούς· 16
καὶ ἐξέβαλε τὰ πνεύματα λόγῳ, καὶ πάντας τοὺς κακῶς ἔχοντας
ἐθεράπευσεν· [ἵπως πληρωθῇ] τὸ ῥηθὲν διὰ Ἡσαΐου τοῦ προφήτου 17
λέγοντος, Αὐτὸς τὰς ἀσθενείας ἡμῶν ἔλαβεν καὶ τὰς νόσους ἐβάστασεν.

Ἰδὼν δὲ ὁ Ἰησοῦς πολλοὺς ὄχλους περὶ αὐτόν, ἐκέλευσεν 18
ἀπελθεῖν εἰς τὸ πέραν. καὶ προσελθὼν [εἷς] γραμματεὺς εἶπεν 19
αὐτῷ, Διδάσκαλε, ἀκολουθήσω σοι, [ὅπου ἐὰν ἀπέρχῃ.] καὶ λέγει 20
αὐτῷ ὁ Ἰησοῦς, Αἱ ἀλώπεκες φωλεοὺς ἔχουσι, καὶ τὰ πετεινὰ τοῦ
οὐρανοῦ κατασκηνώσεις· ὁ δὲ υἱὸς τοῦ ἀνθρώπου οὐκ ἔχει, [ποῦ]
τὴν κεφαλὴν κλίνῃ. Ἕτερος δὲ τῶν μαθητῶν εἶπεν αὐτῷ, Κύριε, 21
ἐπίτρεψόν μοι πρῶτον ἀπελθεῖν καὶ θάψαι τὸν πατέρα μου.
ὁ δὲ Ἰησοῦς λέγει αὐτῷ, Ἀκολούθει μοι, καὶ [ἄφες τοὺς νε- 22
κροὺς] θάψαι τοὺς ἑαυτῶν νεκρούς. Καὶ ἐμβάντι αὐτῷ εἰς 23
πλοῖον, ἠκολούθησαν αὐτῷ οἱ μαθηταὶ αὐτοῦ. καὶ ἰδοὺ σεισμὸς 24
μέγας ἐγένετο ἐν τῇ θαλάσσῃ, ὥστε τὸ πλοῖον καλύπτεσθαι ὑπὸ
τῶν κυμάτων· αὐτὸς δὲ ἐκάθευδεν. καὶ προσελθόντες ἤγειραν 25
αὐτὸν λέγοντες, Κύριε, σῶσον, ἀπολλύμεθα. καὶ λέγει αὐτοῖς, 26
Τί δειλοί ἐστε ὀλιγόπιστοι; τότε ἐγερθεὶς ἐπετίμησεν τοῖς ἀνέμοις
καὶ τῇ θαλάσσῃ, καὶ ἐγένετο γαλήνη μεγάλη. οἱ δὲ ἄνθρωποι 27
ἐθαύμασαν λέγοντες, Ποταπός ἐστιν οὗτος, ὅτι οἱ ἄνεμοι καὶ ἡ
θάλασσα ὑπακούουσιν αὐτῷ;

Καὶ ἐλθόντι αὐτῷ εἰς τὸ πέραν εἰς τὴν χώραν τῶν Γαδαρηνῶν, 28
ὑπήντησαν αὐτῷ δύο δαιμονιζόμενοι ἐκ τῶν μνημείων ἐξερχόμενοι
χαλεποὶ λίαν, ὥστε μὴ ἰσχύειν [τινὰ] παρελθεῖν διὰ τῆς ὁδοῦ
ἐκείνης. καὶ ἰδοὺ ἔκραξαν λέγοντες, * Τί ἡμῖν καὶ σοί,* Ἰησοῦ υἱὲ 29
τοῦ Θεοῦ; [ἦλθες ᾧδε πρὸ καιροῦ βασανίσαι] ἡμᾶς; ἦν δὲ μακρὰν 30
ἀπ' αὐτῶν ἀγέλη χοίρων πολλῶν βοσκομένη. οἱ δὲ δαίμονες 31
παρεκάλουν αὐτὸν λέγοντες, Εἰ ἐκβάλλεις ἡμᾶς, ἀπόστειλον
ἡμᾶς εἰς τὴν ἀγέλην τῶν χοίρων. καὶ εἶπεν αὐτοῖς, Ὑπάγετε. 32
οἱ δὲ ἐξελθόντες ἀπῆλθον εἰς τὴν ἀγέλην τῶν χοίρων· καὶ ἰδοὺ
ὥρμησεν πᾶσα ἡ ἀγέλη τῶν χοίρων κατὰ τοῦ κρημνοῦ εἰς τὴν
θάλασσαν, καὶ ἀπέθανον ἐν τοῖς ὕδασιν. οἱ δὲ βόσκοντες ἔφυγον, 33
καὶ ἀπελθόντες εἰς τὴν πόλιν, ἀπήγγειλαν πάντα, καὶ τὰ τῶν
δαιμονιζομένων. καὶ ἰδοὺ πᾶσα ἡ πόλις ἐξῆλθεν εἰς συνάντησιν 34

19, 20. εἰς γρ. for γρ. τίς. τοῦ for ὅπου.
28. χαλεπὸς] V.A. Is. xviii. 2, for נִבְזֶה "terribilis, formidandus," Niph. well defined to mean "hard of things, harsh of men, fierce of beasts." W. W.

MATTHEW, IX. 1—17.

τῷ Ἰησοῦ· καὶ ἰδόντες αὐτὸν, παρεκάλεσαν ὅπως [μεταβῇ] ἀπὸ τῶν ὁρίων αὐτῶν.

CAP. 9 ΚΑΙ ἐμβὰς εἰς πλοῖον διεπέρασεν καὶ ἦλθεν εἰς τὴν ἰδίαν 2 πόλιν. καὶ ἰδοὺ προσέφερον αὐτῷ παραλυτικὸν ἐπὶ κλίνης [βεβλημένον] καὶ ἰδὼν ὁ Ἰησοῦς τὴν πίστιν αὐτῶν, εἶπεν τῷ παραλυ- 3 τικῷ, Θάρσει τέκνον· [ἀφέωνταί] σου αἱ ἁμαρτίαι. καὶ ἰδού τινες 4 τῶν γραμματέων εἶπον ἐν ἑαυτοῖς, Οὗτος βλασφημεῖ. καὶ ἰδὼν ὁ Ἰησοῦς τὰς ἐνθυμήσεις αὐτῶν, εἶπεν, Ἱνατί ὑμεῖς [ἐνθυμεῖσθε πο- 5 νηρὰ] ἐν ταῖς καρδίαις ὑμῶν; [τί γάρ ἐστιν εὐκοπώτερον], εἰπεῖν, 6 Ἀφέωνταί σου αἱ ἁμαρτίαι· ἢ εἰπεῖν, Ἔγειρε καὶ περιπάτει; ἵνα δὲ εἰδῆτε, ὅτι ἐξουσίαν ἔχει ὁ υἱὸς τοῦ ἀνθρώπου ἐπὶ τῆς γῆς ἀφιέναι ἁμαρτίας· τότε λέγει τῷ παραλυτικῷ· Ἐγερθεὶς ἆρόν σου 7 τὴν κλίνην, καὶ ὕπαγε εἰς τὸν οἶκόν σου. καὶ ἐγερθεὶς ἀπῆλθεν 8 εἰς τὸν οἶκον αὐτοῦ. ἰδόντες δὲ οἱ ὄχλοι ἐφοβήθησαν, καὶ ἐδόξασαν τὸν θεὸν, τὸν δόντα ἐξουσίαν τοιαύτην τοῖς ἀνθρώποις.

9 Καὶ [παράγων] ὁ Ἰησοῦς ἐκεῖθεν, εἶδεν ἄνθρωπον καθήμενον *ἐπὶ τὸ τελώνιον,* Ματθαῖον λεγόμενον, καὶ λέγει αὐτῷ, Ἀκο- 10 λούθει μοι. καὶ ἀναστὰς ἠκολούθησεν αὐτῷ. *Καὶ ἐγένετο* αὐτοῦ ἀνακειμένου ἐν τῇ οἰκίᾳ, *καὶ ἰδοὺ* πολλοὶ τελῶναι καὶ ἁμαρτω- 11 λοὶ ἐλθόντες συνανέκειντο τῷ Ἰησοῦ καὶ τοῖς μαθηταῖς αὐτοῦ. καὶ ἰδόντες οἱ Φαρισαῖοι ἔλεγον τοῖς μαθηταῖς αὐτοῦ, Διατί μετὰ τῶν 12 τελωνῶν καὶ ἁμαρτωλῶν ἐσθίει ὁ διδάσκαλος ὑμῶν; ὁ δὲ ἀκούσας εἶπεν, Οὐ χρείαν ἔχουσιν οἱ ἰσχύοντες ἰατροῦ, ἀλλ᾽ οἱ κακῶς ἔχοντες. 13 πορευθέντες δὲ μάθετε τί ἐστιν, Ἔλεος θέλω, καὶ οὐ θυσίαν· οὐ γὰρ [ἦλθον καλέσαι] δικαίους, ἀλλὰ ἁμαρτωλούς.

14 Τότε προσέρχονται αὐτῷ οἱ μαθηταὶ Ἰωάννου λέγοντες, Διατί ἡμεῖς καὶ οἱ Φαρισαῖοι νηστεύομεν πολλὰ, οἱ δὲ μαθηταί σου 15 οὐ νηστεύουσι; καὶ εἶπεν αὐτοῖς ὁ Ἰησοῦς, Μὴ δύνανται *οἱ υἱοὶ τοῦ νυμφῶνος* πενθεῖν, ἐφ᾽ ὅσον μετ᾽ αὐτῶν ἐστιν ὁ νυμφίος; ἐλεύσονται δὲ ἡμέραι [ὅταν ἀπαρθῇ] ἀπ᾽ αὐτῶν ὁ 16 νυμφίος, καὶ τότε νηστεύσουσιν. οὐδεὶς δὲ ἐπιβάλλει ἐπίβλημα ῥάκους ἀγνάφου ἐπὶ ἱματίῳ παλαιῷ· αἴρει γὰρ [τὸ πλήρωμα 17 αὐτοῦ] ἀπὸ τοῦ ἱματίου, καὶ χεῖρον σχίσμα γίνεται. οὐδὲ [βάλλουσιν] οἶνον νέον εἰς ἀσκοὺς παλαιούς· εἰ δὲ μή γε, ῥήγνυνται οἱ

Cap. IX. 9. ἐπί] Here probably used as = אֶל, "apud," as εἰς and πρός are in V.A. or N.T. See xiii. 56. It is found in V.A. frequently for אֶל, with all its varieties of meaning, e.g. 2 Sam. xxi. 2 אֶל־שָׁאוּל, ἐπὶ τὸν Σαούλ, "It is for Saul and for his bloody house."

10. Gen. xxiv. 30 וַיְהִי ... וַיָּבֹא, καὶ ἐγένετο...καὶ ἦλθε. V.A. passim; as also in N.T.

ἀσκοὶ, καὶ ὁ οἶνος ἐκχεῖται, καὶ οἱ ἀσκοὶ ἀπολοῦνται· ἀλλὰ βάλλουσιν οἶνον νέον εἰς ἀσκοὺς καινούς, καὶ ἀμφότεροι συντηροῦνται.

Ταῦτα αὐτοῦ λαλοῦντος αὐτοῖς, ἰδοὺ ἄρχων ἐλθὼν προσεκύνει 18 αὐτῷ λέγων, Ὅτι ἡ θυγάτηρ μου ἄρτι ἐτελεύτησεν· ἀλλὰ ἐλθὼν ἐπίθες τὴν χεῖρά σου ἐπ᾽ αὐτήν, καὶ ζήσεται. καὶ ἐγερθεὶς ὁ Ἰησοῦς 19 ἠκολούθησεν αὐτῷ καὶ οἱ μαθηταὶ αὐτοῦ.

Καὶ ἰδοὺ γυνὴ αἱμορροοῦσα δώδεκα ἔτη, προσελθοῦσα ὄπισθεν, 20 ἥψατο τοῦ κρασπέδου τοῦ ἱματίου αὐτοῦ. ἔλεγεν γὰρ ἐν ἑαυτῇ, 21 Ἐὰν μόνον ἅψωμαι τοῦ ἱματίου αὐτοῦ, [σωθήσομαι.] ὁ δὲ Ἰησοῦς 22 στραφεὶς καὶ ἰδὼν αὐτήν, εἶπεν, Θάρσει θύγατερ· ἡ πίστις σου σέσωκέν σε. καὶ ἐσώθη ἡ γυνὴ ἀπὸ τῆς ὥρας ἐκείνης. Καὶ ἐλθὼν 23 ὁ Ἰησοῦς εἰς τὴν οἰκίαν τοῦ ἄρχοντος, καὶ ἰδὼν τοὺς αὐλητὰς καὶ τὸν ὄχλον θορυβούμενον, ἔλεγεν Ἀναχωρεῖτε· οὐ γὰρ ἀπ- 24 έθανεν τὸ κοράσιον, ἀλλὰ καθεύδει. καὶ κατεγέλων αὐτοῦ. ὅτε 25 δὲ ἐξεβλήθη ὁ ὄχλος, εἰσελθὼν ἐκράτησεν τῆς χειρὸς αὐτῆς, καὶ ἠγέρθη τὸ κοράσιον. καὶ ἐξῆλθεν ἡ φήμη αὕτη εἰς ὅλην τὴν γῆν 26 ἐκείνην.

Καὶ [παράγοντι] ἐκεῖθεν τῷ Ἰησοῦ, ἠκολούθησαν αὐτῷ δύο 27 τυφλοί, κράζοντες καὶ λέγοντες, Ἐλέησον ἡμᾶς υἱὸς Δαυίδ. ἐλ- 28 θόντι δὲ εἰς τὴν οἰκίαν, προσῆλθον αὐτῷ οἱ τυφλοί, καὶ λέγει αὐτοῖς ὁ Ἰησοῦς, Πιστεύετε ὅτι δύναμαι τοῦτο ποιῆσαι; λέγουσιν αὐτῷ, Ναὶ Κύριε. τότε ἥψατο τῶν ὀφθαλμῶν αὐτῶν λέγων, 29 Κατὰ τὴν πίστιν ὑμῶν γενηθήτω ὑμῖν. καὶ ἠνεῴχθησαν αὐτῶν 30 οἱ ὀφθαλμοί· καὶ [ἐνεβριμήθη] αὐτοῖς ὁ Ἰησοῦς λέγων, Ὁρᾶτε μηδεὶς γινωσκέτω. οἱ δὲ ἐξελθόντες [διεφήμισαν] αὐτὸν ἐν ὅλῃ 31 τῇ γῇ ἐκείνῃ.

Αὐτῶν δὲ ἐξερχομένων, ἰδοὺ προσήνεγκαν αὐτῷ ἄνθρωπον 32 κωφὸν [δαιμονιζόμενον]. καὶ ἐκβληθέντος τοῦ ΔΑΙΜΟΝΙΟΥ, ἐλάλησεν 33 ὁ κωφός· καὶ ἐθαύμασαν οἱ ὄχλοι λέγοντες, Οὐδέποτε [ἐφάνη] οὕτως

21. σωθήσομαι] Schleus. cites Xen. *Mem.* II. 10. 1 to show that σώζειν="to heal," and that σωτήρ=physician, and σῶστρον his fee for restoring health. But it is not a common use of the words in Greek authors. It is not found in this sense, so far as I can discover, in V.A. in which it stands for יָשַׁע, as ἰᾶσθαι for רָפָא, uniformly. But in N.T. it very often means "to heal:" as here: and Mk. v. 23, vi. 56: L. viii. 36, J. xi. 12, Acts iv. 9. And our Auth. Version curiously renders σωτηρία, "health," Ps. xlii. 11, xliii. 5; and "saving health," Ps. lxvii. 2: most probably from the double meaning of "salus," (a) health and (b) salvation; which latter they distinguish from (a), as "*saving* health:" Vulgate has in the above "salutare vultûs mei," "salutare tuum": in fact "salutare" is its usual rendering of σωτήριον and σωτηρία.

33. The notion of "*evil* spirits" attached to δαιμόνια seems to be entirely Jewish: we have the term used of an inferior race of divine beings by Plato and Xenophon: and hence, probably, its application to the gods of the heathen by V. A. for שֵׁדִים. Deut. xxxii. 17 יִזְבְּחוּ לַשֵּׁדִים לֹא אֱלֹהַּ, δαιμονίοις ἔθυσαν καὶ οὐ Θεῷ, quoted by S. Paul, 1 Cor. x. 20, apparently in same sense, and Ps. xcvi. 5

34 ἐν τῷ Ἰσραήλ. οἱ δὲ Φαρισαῖοι ἔλεγον, *Ἐν τῷ ἄρχοντι * τῶν δαιμονίων ἐκβάλλει τὰ δαιμόνια.

35 ΚΑΙ περιῆγεν ὁ Ἰησοῦς τὰς πόλεις πάσας καὶ τὰς κώμας, διδάσκων ἐν ταῖς συναγωγαῖς αὐτῶν, καὶ κηρύσσων τὸ εὐαγγέλιον τῆς βασιλείας, καὶ θεραπεύων πᾶσαν νόσον καὶ πᾶσαν 36 ΜΑΛΑΚΙΑΝ. ἰδὼν δὲ τοὺς ὄχλους, ἐσπλαγχνίσθη περὶ αὐτῶν, ὅτι ἦσαν [ἐσκυλμένοι καὶ ἐρριμμένοι] ὡσεὶ πρόβατα [μὴ] ἔχοντα 37 ποιμένα. τότε λέγει τοῖς μαθηταῖς αὐτοῦ, Ὁ μὲν θερισμὸς 38 πολύς, οἱ δὲ ἐργάται ὀλίγοι· δεήθητε οὖν τοῦ κυρίου τοῦ CAP. 10 θερισμοῦ, ὅπως [ἐκβάλῃ] ἐργάτας εἰς τὸν θερισμὸν αὐτοῦ. Καὶ προσκαλεσάμενος τοὺς δώδεκα μαθητὰς αὐτοῦ, ἔδωκεν αὐτοῖς ἐξουσίαν πνευμάτων ἀκαθάρτων, ὥστε ἐκβάλλειν αὐτά, καὶ θε- 2 ραπεύειν πᾶσαν νόσον καὶ πᾶσαν ΜΑΛΑΚΙΑΝ. Τῶν δὲ δώδεκα ἀποστόλων τὰ ὀνόματά ἐστιν ταῦτα· πρῶτος Σίμων ὁ λεγόμενος Πέτρος, καὶ Ἀνδρέας ὁ ἀδελφὸς αὐτοῦ· Ἰάκωβος ὁ τοῦ Ζεβε- 3 δαίου, καὶ Ἰωάννης ὁ ἀδελφὸς αὐτοῦ· Φίλιππος, καὶ Βαρθολομαῖος· Θωμᾶς, καὶ Ματθαῖος ὁ τελώνης· Ἰάκωβος ὁ τοῦ Ἀλφαίου, 4 καὶ Λεββαῖος, Σίμων * ὁ Καναναῖος,* καὶ Ἰούδας Ἰσκαριώτης ὁ καὶ παραδοὺς αὐτόν.

5 Τούτους τοὺς δώδεκα ἀπέστειλεν ὁ Ἰησοῦς, παραγγείλας αὐτοῖς λέγων, Εἰς ὁδὸν ἐθνῶν μὴ ἀπέλθητε, καὶ εἰς πόλιν Σαμα- 6 ρειτῶν μὴ εἰσέλθητε· πορεύεσθε δὲ μᾶλλον πρὸς τὰ πρόβατα 7 τὰ ἀπολωλότα *οἴκου Ἰσραήλ.* πορευόμενοι δὲ κηρύσσετε 8 λέγοντες, Ἤγγικεν ἡ βασιλεία τῶν οὐρανῶν. ἀσθενοῦντας θεραπεύετε, λεπροὺς καθαρίζετε, δαιμόνια ἐκβάλλετε, δωρεὰν 9 ἐλάβετε, δωρεὰν δότε. Μὴ [κτήσησθε] χρυσὸν, μηδὲ ἄργυρον, 10 μηδὲ χαλκὸν εἰς τὰς ζώνας ὑμῶν, μὴ πήραν εἰς ὁδὸν, μηδὲ δύο χιτῶνας, μηδὲ ὑποδήματα, μηδὲ ῥάβδους· ἄξιος γὰρ ὁ ἐργά- 11 της τῆς τροφῆς αὐτοῦ. Εἰς ἣν δ' ἂν πόλιν ἢ κώμην εἰσέλθητε, ἐξετάσατε τίς ἐν αὐτῇ ἄξιός ἐστιν· κἀκεῖ μείνατε, ἕως ἂν

כָּל־אֱלֹהֵי הָעַמִּים אֱלִילִים, πάντες οἱ θεοὶ τῶν ἐθνῶν δαιμόνια. And so the term easily passed to mean "Devils," "Spirits of evil," *about* men and *in* men: the fallen angels, Satan and his agents.

38. βάλλειν = "put" (a), and ἐκβάλλω = "put forth" or "send out" (b), constantly in N.T.—(a) M. xii. 35, xxv. 27, xxvi. 12, Mk. vii. 30, 33; (b) here and Mk. i. 43, Jo. x. 4.

V.A. uses ἐμβάλλειν for שׂוּם pono Gen. xxxi. 34, xliv. 1, Deut. x. 2, and ἐκβάλλειν for הָיָה 2 Chr. xxiii. 14, xxix. 5. It seems clear from this that βάλλειν could be used in a much milder sense in later Greek than it bore in earlier authors. See x. 34.

4. Κανανίτης or Καναναῖος from קָנָא, "zelotypus fuit," and so = Ζηλωτής. Ἀλφαῖος, Hebr. חַלְפִּי, seems to be from the same root as Cleophas; and probably the same name, if not the same person, as in J. xix. 25.

6. οἶκος Ἰσραήλ] = בֵּית יִשְׂרָאֵל = "the descendants of Jacob," "the family of Israel."

ἐξέλθητε. εἰσερχόμενοι δὲ εἰς τὴν οἰκίαν, ἀσπάσασθε αὐτήν. καὶ 12
ἐὰν μὲν ᾖ ἡ οἰκία ἀξία, ἐλθέτω ἡ εἰρήνη ὑμῶν ἐπ᾽ αὐτήν· ἐὰν 13
δὲ μὴ ᾖ ἀξία, ἡ εἰρήνη ὑμῶν πρὸς ὑμᾶς ἐπιστραφήτω. καὶ ὃς 14
ἐὰν μὴ δέξηται ὑμᾶς, μηδὲ ἀκούσῃ τοὺς λόγους ὑμῶν, ἐξερχόμενοι ἔξω τῆς οἰκίας ἢ τῆς πόλεως ἐκείνης, ἐκτινάξατε τὸν κονιορ-
τὸν τῶν ποδῶν ὑμῶν. ἀμὴν λέγω ὑμῖν, ἀνεκτότερον ἔσται γῇ 15
Σοδόμων καὶ Γομόρρας ἐν ἡμέρᾳ κρίσεως, ἢ τῇ πόλει ἐκείνῃ.

Ἰδοὺ ἐγὼ ἀποστέλλω ὑμᾶς ὡς πρόβατα ἐν μέσῳ λύκων· γί- 16
νεσθε οὖν φρόνιμοι ὡς οἱ ὄφεις, καὶ ἀκέραιοι ὡς αἱ περιστεραί.
[προσέχετε δὲ ἀπὸ] τῶν ἀνθρώπων· παραδώσουσιν γὰρ ὑμᾶς εἰς 17
συνέδρια, καὶ ἐν ταῖς συναγωγαῖς αὐτῶν μαστιγώσουσιν ὑμᾶς· καὶ 18
ἐπὶ ἡγεμόνας δὲ καὶ βασιλεῖς ἀχθήσεσθε ἕνεκεν ἐμοῦ, [εἰς μαρ-
τύριον] αὐτοῖς καὶ τοῖς ἔθνεσιν. ὅταν δὲ παραδῶσιν ὑμᾶς, μὴ 19
μεριμνήσητε πῶς ἢ τί λαλήσητε· δοθήσεται γὰρ ὑμῖν ἐν ἐκείνῃ
τῇ ὥρᾳ τί λαλήσετε· οὐ γὰρ ὑμεῖς ἐστε οἱ λαλοῦντες, ἀλλὰ τὸ 20
πνεῦμα τοῦ πατρὸς ὑμῶν τὸ λαλοῦν ἐν ὑμῖν. Παραδώσει δὲ 21
ἀδελφὸς ἀδελφὸν εἰς θάνατον, καὶ πατὴρ τέκνον· καὶ ἐπαναστή-
σονται τέκνα ἐπὶ γονεῖς, καὶ θανατώσουσιν αὐτούς. καὶ ἔσεσθε 22
μισούμενοι ὑπὸ πάντων διὰ τὸ ὄνομά μου· ὁ δὲ ὑπομείνας εἰς
τέλος, οὗτος σωθήσεται. ὅταν δὲ διώκωσιν ὑμᾶς ἐν τῇ πόλει 23
ταύτῃ, φεύγετε [εἰς τὴν ἄλλην.] ἀμὴν γὰρ λέγω ὑμῖν, οὐ μὴ
τελέσητε τὰς πόλεις Ἰσραὴλ, [ἕως ἔλθῃ] ὁ υἱὸς τοῦ ἀνθρώπου. Οὐκ ἔστιν μαθητὴς ὑπὲρ τὸν διδάσκαλον, οὐδὲ δοῦλος 24
ὑπὲρ τὸν κύριον αὐτοῦ. ἀρκετὸν τῷ μαθητῇ ἵνα γένηται ὡς ὁ 25
διδάσκαλος αὐτοῦ, καὶ ὁ δοῦλος ὡς ὁ κύριος αὐτοῦ. εἰ τὸν
οἰκοδεσπότην Βεελζεβοὺλ ἐκάλεσαν, πόσῳ μᾶλλον τοὺς οἰκιακοὺς
αὐτοῦ; Μὴ οὖν φοβηθῆτε αὐτούς· οὐδὲν γάρ ἐστιν κεκαλυμμένον 26
ὃ οὐκ ἀποκαλυφθήσεται· καὶ κρυπτὸν, ὃ οὐ γνωσθήσεται. ὃ 27
λέγω ὑμῖν ἐν τῇ σκοτίᾳ, εἴπατε ἐν τῷ φωτί· καὶ ὃ *εἰς τὸ οὖς*
ἀκούετε, κηρύξατε ἐπὶ τῶν δωμάτων. καὶ μὴ *φοβεῖσθε ἀπὸ* 28
τῶν ἀποκτεννόντων τὸ σῶμα, τὴν δὲ ψυχὴν μὴ δυναμένων ἀπο-
κτεῖναι· φοβήθητε δὲ μᾶλλον τὸν δυνάμενον καὶ ψυχὴν καὶ σῶμα
ἀπολέσαι *ἐν γεέννῃ.* οὐχὶ δύο στρουθία ἀσσαρίου πωλεῖται; 29
καὶ ἓν ἐξ αὐτῶν οὐ πεσεῖται ἐπὶ τὴν γῆν ἄνευ τοῦ πατρὸς ὑμῶν·
ὑμῶν δὲ καὶ αἱ τρίχες τῆς κεφαλῆς πᾶσαι ἠριθμημέναι εἰσίν. 30

23. ἕως] for πρὶν often in N.T.
27. This peculiar use of εἰς τὸ οὖς or εἰς τὰ ὦτα had probably become habitual from its frequent occurrence in V.A. for בְּאָזְנֵי. Gen. xx. 8, xxiii. 16, Ex. x. 2, Is. v. 9. ἠκούσθη εἰς τὰ ὦτα: as Acts xi. 22. It seems to have been adopted as an idiomatic equivalent.

28. φοβεῖσθαι ἀπό] in V.A. and N.T. is a literal rendering of a common Hebraism: יָרֵא מִן Deut. i. 29, v. 5, Ps. iii. 7, xxvii. 1.

31 μὴ οὖν φοβεῖσθε [πολλῶν στρουθίων διαφέρετε] ὑμεῖς. Πᾶς οὖν
32 ὅστις * ὁμολογήσει ἐν ἐμοὶ * ἔμπροсθεν τῶν ἀνθρώπων, ὁμολογήσω
κἀγὼ ἐν αὐτῷ ἔμπροсθεν τοῦ πατρός μου τοῦ ἐν τοῖς οὐρανοῖς.
33 ὅστις δὲ ἀρνήσηταί με ἔμπροσθεν τῶν ἀνθρώπων, ἀρνήσομαι αὐτὸν
34 κἀγὼ ἔμπροσθεν τοῦ πατρός μου τοῦ ἐν τοῖς οὐρανοῖς. Μὴ νομίσητε ὅτι [ἦλθον βαλεῖν] εἰρήνην ἐπὶ τὴν γῆν· οὐκ ἦλθον βαλεῖν
35 εἰρήνην, ἀλλὰ μάχαιραν. ἦλθον γὰρ [διχάσαι] ἄνθρωπον κατὰ τοῦ
πατρὸς αὐτοῦ, καὶ θυγατέρα κατὰ τῆς μητρὸς αὐτῆς, καὶ νύμφην
36 κατὰ τῆς πενθερᾶς αὐτῆς· καὶ ἐχθροὶ τοῦ ἀνθρώπου οἱ οἰκιακοὶ
37 αὐτοῦ. ὁ φιλῶν πατέρα ἢ μητέρα ὑπὲρ ἐμὲ, οὐκ ἔστίν μου ἄξιος·
38 καὶ ὁ φιλῶν υἱὸν ἢ θυγατέρα ὑπὲρ ἐμὲ, οὐκ ἔστίν μου ἄξιος· καὶ
ὃς οὐ λαμβάνει τὸν σταυρὸν αὐτοῦ καὶ ἀκολουθεῖ ὀπίσω μου,
39 οὐκ ἔστίν μου ἄξιος. ὁ εὑρὼν τὴν ψυχὴν αὐτοῦ, ἀπολέσει αὐτήν·
καὶ ὁ ἀπολέσας τὴν ψυχὴν αὐτοῦ ἕνεκεν ἐμοῦ, εὑρήσει αὐτήν.
40 Ὁ δεχόμενος ὑμᾶς, ἐμὲ δέχεται· καὶ ὁ ἐμὲ δεχόμενος, δέχεται
41 τὸν ἀποστείλαντά με. ὁ δεχόμενος προφήτην * εἰς ὄνομα * προφήτου, μισθὸν προφήτου λήμψεται· καὶ ὁ δεχόμενος δίκαιον εἰς
42 ὄνομα δικαίου, μισθὸν δικαίου λήμψεται· καὶ [ὃς ἐὰν ποτίσῃ] ἕνα
τῶν μικρῶν τούτων ποτήριον ψυχροῦ μόνον εἰς ὄνομα μαθητοῦ,
CAP. ἀμὴν λέγω ὑμῖν, οὐ μὴ ἀπολέσῃ τὸν μισθὸν αὐτοῦ.
11 Καὶ * ἐγένετο ὅτε * ἐτέλεσεν ὁ Ἰησοῦς διατάσσων τοῖς δώδεκα
μαθηταῖς αὐτοῦ, * μετέβη * ἐκεῖθεν τοῦ διδάσκειν καὶ κηρύσσειν ἐν
ταῖς πόλεσιν αὐτῶν.
2 Ὁ ΔΕ Ἰωάννης ἀκούσας ἐν τῷ δεσμωτηρίῳ τὰ ἔργα τοῦ
3 Χριστοῦ, πέμψας διὰ τῶν μαθητῶν αὐτοῦ, εἶπεν αὐτῷ, Σὺ εἶ ὁ
4 ἐρχόμενος, ἢ ἕτερον προσδοκῶμεν; καὶ ἀποκριθεὶς ὁ Ἰησοῦς εἶπεν
αὐτοῖς, Πορευθέντες ἀπαγγείλατε Ἰωάννῃ, ἃ ἀκούετε καὶ βλέπετε·
5 τυφλοὶ ἀναβλέπουσιν, καὶ χωλοὶ περιπατοῦσιν· λεπροὶ καθαρίζον-
ται, καὶ κωφοὶ ἀκούουσιν· νεκροὶ ἐγείρονται, καὶ πτωχοὶ εὐαγγε-
6 λίζονται· καὶ μακάριός ἐστιν ὃς ἐὰν μὴ * σκανδαλισθῇ ἐν ἐμοί.*
7 Τούτων δὲ πορευομένων, ἤρξατο ὁ Ἰησοῦς λέγειν τοῖς ὄχλοις περὶ
Ἰωάννου, Τί [ἐξήλθετε] εἰς τὴν ἔρημον [θεάσασθαι;] κάλαμον ὑπὸ
8 ἀνέμου σαλευόμενον; ἀλλὰ τί ἐξήλθετε ἰδεῖν; ἄνθρωπον [ἐν μα-
λακοῖς] ἠμφιεσμένον; ἰδοὺ οἱ τὰ μαλακὰ φοροῦντες ἐν τοῖς
9 οἴκοις τῶν βασιλέων εἰσίν. ἀλλὰ τί ἐξήλθετε; προφήτην

32. ὁμολογήσει ἐν ἐμοί] here and L. xii. 8, have no parallel in V.A.
41. εἰς ὄνομα π.] Grimm renders "respiciens nomen prophetae quod gerit," "out of regard to." But it may possibly be nothing more than an inaccurate use of εἰς for ἐν, of which we have so many examples in V.A. and N.T. The phrase בְּשֵׁם is rendered ἐπὶ τῷ ὀνόματι by V.A. Ex. v. 23, Jerem. xi. 21.

MATTHEW, XI. 10—19.

ἰδεῖν; ναὶ λέγω ὑμῖν, καὶ περισσότερον προφήτου. οὗτος γάρ 10
ἐστιν περὶ οὗ γέγραπται, Ἰδοὺ ἐγὼ ἀποστέλλω τὸν ἀγγελόν
μου *πρὸ προσώπου σου,* καὶ κατασκευάσει τὴν ὁδόν σου ἔμπροσθέν σου. Ἀμὴν λέγω ὑμῖν, οὐκ ἐγήγερται ἐν ΓΕΝΝΗΤΟῖϹ ΓΥΝΑΙ- 11
ΚῶΝ μείζων Ἰωάννου τοῦ βαπτιστοῦ· [ὁ δὲ μικρότερος] ἐν τῇ
βασιλείᾳ τῶν οὐρανῶν, μείζων αὐτοῦ ἐστιν. ἀπὸ δὲ τῶν ἡμερῶν 12
Ἰωάννου τοῦ βαπτιστοῦ ἕως ἄρτι *ἡ βασιλεία τῶν οὐρανῶν*
βιάζεται, καὶ βιασταὶ ἁρπάζουσιν αὐτήν. πάντες γὰρ οἱ προ- 13
φῆται καὶ ὁ νόμος ἕως Ἰωάννου ἐπροφήτευσαν· καὶ εἰ θέλετε 14
δέξασθαι, αὐτός ἐστιν Ἡλίας ὁ μέλλων ἔρχεσθαι. ὁ ἔχων ὦτα, 15
ἀκουέτω. Τίνι δὲ ὁμοιώσω τὴν γενεὰν ταύτην; ὁμοία ἐστὶν παι- 16
δαρίοις ἐν ἀγοραῖς καθημένοις, ἃ προσφωνοῦντα τοῖς ἑτέροις λέ- 17
γουσιν, Ηὐλήσαμεν ὑμῖν, καὶ οὐκ ὠρχήσασθε· ἐθρηνήσαμεν, καὶ
οὐκ ἐκόψασθε. ἦλθε γὰρ Ἰωάννης [μήτε] ἐσθίων μήτε πίνων 18
καὶ λέγουσιν, Δαιμόνιον ἔχει. ἦλθεν ὁ υἱὸς τοῦ ἀνθρώπου ἐσθίων 19
καὶ πίνων· καὶ λέγουσιν, Ἰδοὺ ἄνθρωπος φάγος καὶ οἰνοπότης,
τελωνῶν φίλος καὶ ἁμαρτωλῶν. καὶ *ἐδικαιώθη ἡ σοφία ἀπὸ*

Cap. XI. 11. Job xiv. 1, xv. 14, xxv. 4 יְלוּד אִשָּׁה, V.A. γεννητὸς γυναικὸς: evidently taking γεννητὸς as a noun. The phrase is very peculiar: apparently Hebr. and brought into familiar use, possibly, from these passages.

15. Ez. xii. 2 אָזְנַיִם לָהֶם לִשְׁמֹעַ, ὦτα ἔχουσι τοῦ ἀκούειν V.A., and Deut. xxix. 3 without τοῦ. See above ii. 6 for ל with infinitive.

19. ἡ σοφία = הַחָכְמָה, "Divine wisdom," or "wisdom-in-divine-things," "The true Religion has ever been and always is cleared of any charge of inconsistency,—acquitted of any unreality,—by her children," "declared faultless," "proclaimed to be always right and true." Compare 1 Tim. iii. 16, ἐδικαιώθη ἐν Πνεύματι "was declared to be true Christ," "authenticated" "by the Holy Spirit;" i.e. at His Baptism: Schleusner "declaratus est talis qualis vere est," which Grimm also gives.

For this sense of δίκαιος and its derivatives, as equivalent to ἀληθής, see Luke xvi. 9, x. 11. The words צֶדֶק and אֱמֶת, from their usage in the Old Test., would seem to be almost convertible terms. Ps. lii. 3 אָהַבְתָּ רָע מִטּוֹב שֶׁקֶר מִדַּבֵּר צֶדֶק in which צֶדֶק stands for אֱמֶת. Is. xlv. 19 אֲנִי יְהוָה דֹּבֵר צֶדֶק. Is. xlii. 3 לֶאֱמֶת יוֹצִיא מִשְׁפָּט; where אֱמֶת clearly means צֶדֶק; "he shall make judgment to proceed according to justice and right." Proverbs viii. 7, 8, where the two words might be used one for the other. And V.A., apparently recognizing this, constantly uses (1) ἀλήθεια for δικαιοσύνη, (2) ἀληθινὸς and ἀληθὴς for δίκαιος, (3) ἄδικος for ψευδής, (4) ἀδικία for ψεῦδος; and vice versâ. (1) Is. xlv. 19, Ps. lii. 3 above. (2) Is. xli. 26. (3) Deut. xix. 18, Jerem. v. 31, Ps. cxx. 2 (Hebr. cxix. 2), Pr. xii. 19. (4) Ps. lii. 3, Lev. vi. 3 ἀδίκως for עַל־שָׁקֶר (Hebr. Text v. 22), Micah vi. 12. And we, in our English Version, have often followed suit, translating literally, to the great obscuration of the meaning: e.g. Ps. lii. 3, "Thou hast loved lying rather than to speak righteousness." The N.T. writers carry on the same interchange of the words, to which doubtless their acquaintance with V.A. had familiarised them: e.g. Luke xvi. 9, 10, 11, where we have μαμωνᾶ τῆς ἀδικίας in 9, corresponding to τὸ ἄδικον μ. in 11, and contrasted with τὸ ἀληθινόν; i.e. ἄδικος = ψευδής; and in 10, πιστὸς contrasted with ἄδικος. Here therefore ἄδικος means "false, untrue, unreal, unreliable;" ἀληθινὸς = "true, real, substantial." Compare J. iii. 21 (ἀλήθεια for δικαιοσύνη, as opposed to φαῦλα in 20) and vii. 18 οὗτος ἀληθής ἐστι καὶ ἀδικία ἐν αὐτῷ οὐκ ἔστιν (ἀδικία for ψεῦδος); as in Romans ii. 8. 1 Cor. xv. 34, ἐκνήψατε δικαίως, i.e. "truly, in earnest:" xiii. 6 ἡ ἀγάπη οὐ χαίρει ἐπὶ

20 τῶν τέκνων αὐτῆς. Τότε ἤρξατο ὀνειδίζειν τὰς πόλεις, ἐν αἷς
21 ἐγένοντο [αἱ πλεῖσται δυνάμεις] αὐτοῦ, ὅτι οὐ μετενόησαν. Οὐαί
σοι Χοραζίν, οὐαί σοι Βηθσαϊδάν, ὅτι εἰ ἐν Τύρῳ καὶ Σιδῶνι
ἐγένοντο αἱ δυνάμεις αἱ γενόμεναι ἐν ὑμῖν, πάλαι ἂν ἐν σάκκῳ
22 καὶ σποδῷ μετενόησαν. πλὴν λέγω ὑμῖν, Τύρῳ καὶ Σιδῶνι ἀνεκ-
23 τότερον ἔσται ἐν ἡμέρᾳ κρίσεως, ἢ ὑμῖν. Καὶ σὺ Καπερναούμ,
ἡ ἕως οὐρανοῦ ὑψώθης, ἕως ᾅδου καταβήσῃ· ὅτι εἰ ἐν Σοδόμ-
οις ἐγένοντο αἱ δυνάμεις αἱ γενόμεναι ἐν σοί, ἔμειναν ἂν μέχρι
24 τῆς σήμερον. πλὴν λέγω ὑμῖν, ὅτι γῇ Σοδόμων ἀνεκτότερον
25 ἔσται ἐν ἡμέρᾳ κρίσεως, ἢ σοί. Ἐν ἐκείνῳ τῷ καιρῷ ἀποκριθεὶς ὁ Ἰησοῦς εἶπεν, Ἐξομολογοῦμαί σοι πάτερ κύριε τοῦ οὐρανοῦ καὶ τῆς γῆς, ὅτι ἀπέκρυψας ταῦτα ἀπὸ σοφῶν καὶ συν-
26 ετῶν, καὶ ἀπεκάλυψας αὐτὰ νηπίοις. ναί * ὁ πατήρ, ὅτι οὕτως
27 ἐγένετο εὐδοκία ἔμπροσθέν σου*. πάντα μοι παρεδόθη ὑπὸ τοῦ
πατρός μου· καὶ οὐδεὶς ἐπιγινώσκει τὸν υἱόν, εἰ μὴ ὁ πατήρ· οὐδὲ
τὸν πατέρα τις ἐπιγινώσκει, εἰ μὴ ὁ υἱός, καὶ ᾧ ἐὰν βούληται
28 ὁ υἱὸς ἀποκαλύψαι. Δεῦτε πρός με πάντες οἱ κοπιῶντες καὶ
29 πεφορτισμένοι, κἀγὼ ἀναπαύσω ὑμᾶς. ἄρατε τὸν ζυγόν μου ἐφ᾽
ὑμᾶς, καὶ μάθετε ἀπ᾽ ἐμοῦ, ὅτι πρᾶύς εἰμι καὶ ταπεινὸς [τῇ
30 καρδίᾳ] καὶ εὑρήσετε ἀνάπαυσιν ταῖς ψυχαῖς ὑμῶν. ὁ γὰρ ζυ-
Cap. γός μου [χρηστός,] καὶ τὸ φορτίον μου ἐλαφρόν ἐστιν.
12 Ἐν ἐκείνῳ τῷ καιρῷ ἐπορεύθη ὁ Ἰησοῦς τοῖς σάββασιν διὰ
τῶν σπορίμων· οἱ δὲ μαθηταὶ αὐτοῦ ἐπείνασαν, καὶ ἤρξαντο τίλ-

τῇ ἀδικίᾳ, συγχαίρει δὲ τῇ ἀληθείᾳ. 2 Thess. ii. 10, 12, ἐν τέρασι ψεύδους καὶ ἐν πάσῃ ἀπάτῃ τῆς ἀδικίας; and οἱ μὴ πιστεύσαντες τῇ ἀληθείᾳ ἀλλ᾽ εὐδοκήσαντες ἐν τῇ ἀδικίᾳ. 1 John ii. 4, we should expect ἄδικος for ψεύστης, and δικαιοσύνη for ἀλήθεια: and similarly 3 John 4, περιπατεῖς ἐν ἀληθείᾳ, and 12, Δημητρίῳ μεμαρτύρηται ὑπ᾽ αὐτῆς τῆς ἀληθείας: may this possibly mean "by his holy life itself?"

25. ἐξομολογοῦμαι] is almost universally used by V.A. for הוֹדָה Hiph. of יָדָה, in sense of "praise, give thanks:" and so ἐξομολόγησις stands in V.A. for תּוֹדָה "praise." Pss. xli. 5, xcix. 1, 3. For the Hithp., which always means "confess," they use ἐξαγορεύω (Trommii Concord.), as also once, when the Hiph. means "confess," Ps. xxxii. 5. In Liddell and Scott the word is rendered solely by "to confess in full," "to agree or promise."

26. εὐδοκία] ("vox profanis incognita." Grimm) in V.A. = רָצוֹן "appro-

bation, favor: active or passive: approving or being approved." (Lee.) Ps. lxix. 14 עֵת רָצוֹן καιρὸς εὐδοκίας. Ps. xix. 15 יִהְיוּ לְרָצוֹן אִמְרֵי־פִי ἔσονται εἰς εὐδοκίαν, i.e. γενήσονται εὐδοκία (or δεκτόν, which is sometimes given for רָצוֹן) "let the words of my mouth be acceptable" (supra v. 48). Here and L. x. 21 ἐγένετο εὐδοκία = הָיָה לְרָצוֹן.

30. χρηστός] = "mitis: gentle, kind, tender:" from which it seems to have slid into "easy." Vulgate "jugum meum suave est;" = almost "pleasant, soft, delightful."

Cap. XII. 1. τοῖς σάββασι] one of the few instances in M. of dative alone, without preposition, to express the time when, or place where, or manner or instrument, or cause.
τοῖς σάββασιν, ἐν σαββάτῳ.] We should have expected the article just different. "(1) On a certain sabbath... (2) not lawful on *the* sabbath day."

λειν στάχυας καὶ ἐσθίειν. οἱ δὲ Φαρισαῖοι ἰδόντες εἶπαν αὐτῷ, 2
Ἰδοὺ οἱ μαθηταί σου ποιοῦσιν, ὃ οὐκ ἔξεστι ποιεῖν ἐν σαββάτῳ.
ὁ δὲ εἶπεν αὐτοῖς, Οὐκ ἀνέγνωτε [τί] ἐποίησε Δαυὶδ, ὅτε ἐπεί- 3
νασεν καὶ οἱ μετ' αὐτοῦ; [πῶς] εἰσῆλθεν εἰς τὸν οἶκον τοῦ 4
θεοῦ, καὶ *τοὺς ἄρτους τῆς προθέσεως* ἔφαγεν, ὃ οὐκ ἐξὸν
ἦν αὐτῷ φαγεῖν, οὐδὲ τοῖς μετ' αὐτοῦ, εἰ μὴ τοῖς ἱερεῦσιν μόνοις;
ἢ οὐκ ἀνέγνωτε ἐν τῷ νόμῳ, ὅτι τοῖς σάββασιν οἱ ἱερεῖς ἐν τῷ 5
ἱερῷ τὸ σάββατον βεβηλοῦσι, καὶ [ἀναίτιοί] εἰσιν; λέγω δὲ ὑμῖν, 6
ὅτι τοῦ ἱεροῦ μεῖζον ἐστὶν ὧδε. εἰ δὲ ἐγνώκειτε τί ἐστιν, Ἔλεος 7
θέλω καὶ οὐ θυσίαν, οὐκ ἂν κατεδικάσατε τοὺς ἀναιτίους. κύριος 8
γάρ ἐστι καὶ τοῦ σαββάτου ὁ υἱὸς τοῦ ἀνθρώπου.

Καὶ μεταβὰς ἐκεῖθεν, ἦλθεν εἰς τὴν συναγωγὴν αὐτῶν. καὶ 9
ἰδοὺ ἄνθρωπος χεῖρα ἔχων ξηράν· καὶ ἐπηράτησαν αὐτὸν λέ- 10
γοντες, *Εἰ ἔξεστιν* τοῖς σάββασι θεραπεύειν; ἵνα [κατηγο-
ρήσωσιν] αὐτοῦ. ὁ δὲ εἶπεν αὐτοῖς, Τίς ἐξ ὑμῶν ἄνθρωπος, 11
ὃς ἕξει πρόβατον ἕν, καὶ ἐὰν ἐμπέσῃ τοῦτο τοῖς σάββασιν
εἰς βόθυνον, οὐχὶ κρατήσει αὐτὸ καὶ ἐγερεῖ; πόσῳ οὖν διαφέρει 12
ἄνθρωπος προβάτου; ὥστε ἔξεστιν τοῖς σάββασι καλῶς ποιεῖν.
τότε λέγει τῷ ἀνθρώπῳ, Ἔκτεινον τὴν χεῖρά σου· καὶ ἐξέτεινεν, 13
καὶ ἀπεκατεστάθη ὑγιὴς ὡς ἡ ἄλλη. οἱ δὲ Φαρισαῖοι [συμβού- 14
λιον ἔλαβον] κατ' αὐτοῦ ἐξελθόντες, ὅπως αὐτὸν [ἀπολέσωσιν.]
Ὁ δὲ Ἰησοῦς γνοὺς ἀνεχώρησεν ἐκεῖθεν· καὶ ἠκολούθησαν αὐτῷ 15
ὄχλοι πολλοὶ, καὶ ἐθεράπευσεν αὐτοὺς πάντας· καὶ [ἐπετίμησεν] 16
αὐτοῖς, ἵνα μὴ φανερὸν αὐτὸν ποιήσωσιν· ἵνα [πληρωθῇ] τὸ 17
ῥηθὲν διὰ Ἡσαΐου τοῦ προφήτου λέγοντος, Ἰδοὺ ὁ παῖς μου, ὃν 18
ᾑρέτισα· ὁ ἀγαπητός μου, εἰς [ὃν εὐδόκησεν] ἡ ψυχή μου· θήσω
τὸ πνεῦμά μου ἐπ' αὐτὸν, καὶ κρίσιν τοῖς ἔθνεσιν ἀπαγγελεῖ·
οὐκ ἐρίσει, οὐδὲ κραυγάσει· οὐδὲ ἀκούσει τις ἐν ταῖς πλατείαις 19
τὴν φωνὴν αὐτοῦ. κάλαμον συντετριμμένον οὐ κατεάξει, καὶ 20

---

4. εἰ μή]="but only," "but on the contrary." Compare Mk. xiii. 32, L. iv. 26, 27, Gal. ii. 16.
10. εἰ] for אִם interrogative : xix. 3, Mk. x. 2, L. xiii. 23, xiv. 3. In 1 Kings i. 27 V.A. has εἰ for אִם: but in 1 Sam. xiv. 45, εἰ θανατωθήσεται stands for הֲיָמוּת and 1 Kings xxii. 15 εἰ ἀναβῶ for הֲאֵלֵךְ, leading us to infer that εἰ was a common form of interrogation in Macedonian Greek. But Gen. xvii. 7 אִם... הַיִלֵּד, V.A. εἰ γενήσεται υἱὸς...καὶ εἰ and Job vi. 6 אִם... הֲ, as above, by εἰ twice.

They knew אִם = εἰ generally : and so rendered it by εἰ, even in interrogations and in other constructions, very awkwardly. 1 Kings i. 51, 52 אִם יְמִיתֵנִי, ὁμοσάτω εἰ θανατώσει, and אִם יִהְיֶה לְבֶן־חַיִל לֹא יִפֹּל, ἐὰν γένηται εἰς υἱὸν δυνάμεως, εἰ πεσεῖται, where εἰ is put for לֹא, apparently to correspond with εἰ in previous verse. I quote this latter passage as an instance of the startling translations so often found in V.A., which in all probability had their effect on the phraseology of N.T.

λίνον τυφόμενον οὐ σβέσει· ἕως ἂν ἐκβάλῃ [εἰς νῖκος] τὴν κρίσιν.
21 καὶ [τῷ ὀνόματι αὐτοῦ ἔθνη ἐλπιοῦσιν.]
22 Τότε προσηνέχθη αὐτῷ δαιμονιζόμενος τυφλὸς καὶ κωφός· καὶ ἐθεράπευσεν αὐτόν, ὥστε τὸν τυφλὸν καὶ κωφὸν καὶ λαλεῖν καὶ
23 βλέπειν. καὶ ἐξίσταντο πάντες οἱ ὄχλοι καὶ ἔλεγον, Μήτι οὗτός
24 ἐστιν ὁ υἱὸς Δαυίδ; οἱ δὲ Φαρισαῖοι ἀκούσαντες εἶπον, Οὗτος οὐκ ἐκβάλλει τὰ δαιμόνια, εἰ μὴ *ἐν τῷ Βεελζεβοὺλ* ἄρχοντι
25 τῶν δαιμονίων. Εἰδὼς δὲ τὰς ἐνθυμήσεις αὐτῶν, εἶπεν αὐτοῖς, Πᾶσα βασιλεία μερισθεῖσα καθ᾽ ἑαυτῆς, ἐρημοῦται· καὶ πᾶσα
26 πόλις ἢ οἰκία μερισθεῖσα καθ᾽ ἑαυτῆς, οὐ σταθήσεται. καὶ εἰ ὁ σατανᾶς τὸν σατανᾶν ἐκβάλλει, ἐφ᾽ ἑαυτὸν ἐμερίσθη· πῶς
27 οὖν σταθήσεται ἡ βασιλεία αὐτοῦ; καὶ εἰ ἐγὼ ἐν Βεελζεβοὺλ ἐκβάλλω τὰ δαιμόνια, οἱ υἱοὶ ὑμῶν ἐν τίνι ἐκβάλλουσι; διὰ
28 τοῦτο αὐτοὶ ὑμῶν ἔσονται κριταί. εἰ δὲ ἐγὼ ἐν Πνεύματι Θεοῦ ἐκβάλλω τὰ δαιμόνια, ἄρα ἔφθασεν ἐφ᾽ ὑμᾶς ἡ βασιλεία τοῦ Θεοῦ.
29 ἢ πῶς δύναταί τις εἰσελθεῖν εἰς τὴν οἰκίαν τοῦ ἰσχυροῦ καὶ τὰ σκεύη αὐτοῦ ἁρπάσαι, ἐὰν μὴ πρῶτον δήσῃ τὸν ἰσχυρόν, καὶ
30 τότε τὴν οἰκίαν αὐτοῦ ἁρπάσει; ὁ μὴ ὢν μετ᾽ ἐμοῦ, κατ᾽ ἐμοῦ
31 ἐστιν· καὶ ὁ μὴ συνάγων μετ᾽ ἐμοῦ, σκορπίζει. Διὰ τοῦτο λέγω ὑμῖν, Πᾶσα ἁμαρτία καὶ βλασφημία ἀφεθήσεται τοῖς ἀνθρώποις· ἡ δὲ [τοῦ Πνεύματος] βλασφημία οὐκ ἀφεθήσεται τοῖς ἀνθρώ-
32 ποις. καὶ ὃς ἂν εἴπῃ λόγον κατὰ τοῦ υἱοῦ τοῦ ἀνθρώπου, ἀφεθήσεται αὐτῷ· ὃς δ᾽ ἂν εἴπῃ κατὰ τοῦ Πνεύματος τοῦ ἁγίου, οὐκ ἀφεθήσεται αὐτῷ, οὔτε ἐν τούτῳ τῷ αἰῶνι οὔτε ἐν τῷ μέλλοντι.
33 ἢ ποιήσατε τὸ δένδρον καλόν, καὶ τὸν καρπὸν αὐτοῦ καλόν· ἢ ποιήσατε τὸ δένδρον σαπρόν, καὶ τὸν καρπὸν αὐτοῦ σαπρόν· ἐκ
34 γὰρ τοῦ καρποῦ τὸ δένδρον γινώσκεται. *γεννήματα ἐχιδνῶν,* πῶς δύνασθε ἀγαθὰ λαλεῖν, πονηροὶ ὄντες; ἐκ γὰρ τοῦ περισ-
35 σεύματος τῆς καρδίας τὸ στόμα λαλεῖ. ὁ ἀγαθὸς ἄνθρωπος ἐκ τοῦ ἀγαθοῦ θησαυροῦ ἐκβάλλει ἀγαθά· καὶ ὁ πονηρὸς ἄνθρωπος ἐκ τοῦ πονηροῦ θησαυροῦ ἐκβάλλει πονηρά. λέγω δὲ ὑμῖν,
36 ὅτι πᾶν ῥῆμα ἀργόν, ὃ λαλήσουσιν οἱ ἄνθρωποι, ἀποδώσουσιν

20. See xiii. 52. V.A. εἰς ἀλήθειαν ἐξοίσει κρίσιν: much more exact; though it also renders וּלְתוֹרָתוֹ אִיִּים יְיַחֵלוּ, as in N.T., putting ὄνομα for תּוֹרָה.

יָחַל = ἐλπίζω and may = πέποιθα, as תִּקְוָה, ἐλπίς = πίστις;—but our English Version is more true to sense of the original; "The isles shall wait for His Law:" i.e. "The Gentiles shall look onward in hope to His new rule of life and holiness."

28. ἔφθασεν] "has come on you unawares."

33. ποιήσατε] "suppose it," "set it down as."

35. ἐκβάλλει] See ix. 38.

περὶ αὐτοῦ λόγον ἐν ἡμέρᾳ κρίσεως. ἐκ γὰρ τῶν λόγων σου 37
δικαιωθήσῃ, καὶ ἐκ τῶν λόγων σου καταδικασθήσῃ.

Τότε ἀπεκρίθησαν αὐτῷ τινες τῶν γραμματέων καὶ Φαρισαίων 38
λέγοντες, Διδάσκαλε, θέλομεν ἀπὸ σοῦ σημεῖον ἰδεῖν. ὁ δ᾽ ἀπο- 39
κριθεὶς εἶπεν αὐτοῖς, Γενεὰ πονηρὰ καὶ μοιχαλὶς σημεῖον ἐπιζη-
τεῖ· καὶ σημεῖον οὐ δοθήσεται αὐτῇ, εἰ μὴ τὸ σημεῖον Ἰωνᾶ τοῦ
προφήτου. ὥσπερ γὰρ ἦν Ἰωνᾶς ἐν τῇ κοιλίᾳ τοῦ κήτους τρεῖς 40
ἡμέρας καὶ τρεῖς νύκτας· οὕτως ἔσται ὁ υἱὸς τοῦ ἀνθρώπου ἐν
τῇ καρδίᾳ τῆς γῆς τρεῖς ἡμέρας καὶ τρεῖς νύκτας. Ἄνδρες Νι- 41
νευῖται ἀναστήσονται ἐν τῇ κρίσει μετὰ τῆς γενεᾶς ταύτης, καὶ
κατακρινοῦσιν αὐτήν· ὅτι μετενόησαν *εἰς τὸ κήρυγμα* Ἰωνᾶ·
καὶ ἰδοὺ [πλεῖον Ἰωνᾶ] ὧδε. βασίλισσα νότου ἐγερθήσεται ἐν 42
τῇ κρίσει μετὰ τῆς γενεᾶς ταύτης, καὶ κατακρινεῖ αὐτήν· ὅτι
ἦλθεν ἐκ τῶν περάτων τῆς γῆς [ἀκοῦσαι] τὴν σοφίαν Σολο-
μῶνος· καὶ ἰδοὺ πλεῖον Σολομῶνος ὧδε. Ὅταν δὲ τὸ ἀκάθαρ- 43
τον πνεῦμα ἐξέλθῃ ἀπὸ τοῦ ἀνθρώπου, διέρχεται δι᾽ ἀνύδρων
τόπων, ζητοῦν ἀνάπαυσιν, καὶ οὐχ εὑρίσκει. τότε λέγει, Ἐπι- 44
στρέψω εἰς τὸν οἶκόν μου, ὅθεν ἐξῆλθον· καὶ ἐλθὸν εὑρίσκει
[σχολάζοντα,] σεσαρωμένον καὶ κεκοσμημένον. τότε πορεύεται 45
καὶ παραλαμβάνει μεθ᾽ ἑαυτοῦ ἑπτὰ ἕτερα πνεύματα πονηρότερα
ἑαυτοῦ, καὶ εἰσελθόντα κατοικεῖ ἐκεῖ. καὶ γίνεται τὰ ἔσχατα
τοῦ ἀνθρώπου ἐκείνου χείρονα τῶν πρώτων. οὕτως ἔσται καὶ
τῇ γενεᾷ ταύτῃ τῇ πονηρᾷ.

Ἔτι δὲ αὐτοῦ λαλοῦντος τοῖς ὄχλοις, ἰδοὺ ἡ μήτηρ καὶ οἱ 46
ἀδελφοὶ αὐτοῦ εἱστήκεισαν ἔξω, ζητοῦντες αὐτῷ λαλῆσαι. εἶπεν 47
δέ τις αὐτῷ, Ἰδοὺ ἡ μήτηρ σου καὶ οἱ ἀδελφοί σου ἔξω ἑστή-
κασιν, ζητοῦντές σοι λαλῆσαι. ὁ δὲ ἀποκριθεὶς εἶπεν τῷ λέγοντι 48
αὐτῷ, Τίς ἐστιν ἡ μήτηρ μου; καὶ τίνες εἰσὶν οἱ ἀδελφοί μου;
καὶ ἐκτείνας τὴν χεῖρα αὐτοῦ ἐπὶ τοὺς μαθητὰς αὐτοῦ, εἶπεν, 49
Ἰδοὺ ἡ μήτηρ μου καὶ οἱ ἀδελφοί μου. ὅστις γὰρ ἂν ποιῇ τὸ 50
θέλημα τοῦ πατρός μου τοῦ ἐν οὐρανοῖς, αὐτός μου· ἀδελφὸς καὶ
ἀδελφὴ καὶ μήτηρ ἐστίν.

CAP. 13.
Ἐν δὲ τῇ ἡμέρᾳ ἐκείνῃ ἐξελθὼν ὁ Ἰησοῦς ἀπὸ τῆς οἰκίας,
ἐκάθητο παρὰ τὴν θάλασσαν· καὶ συνήχθησαν πρὸς αὐτὸν ὄχλοι 2
πολλοί, ὥστε αὐτὸν εἰς πλοῖον ἐμβάντα καθῆσθαι· καὶ πᾶς
ὁ ὄχλος [ἐπὶ τὸν αἰγιαλὸν] εἱστήκει. καὶ ἐλάλησεν αὐτοῖς πολλὰ 3
ἐν παραβολαῖς λέγων, Ἰδοὺ ἐξῆλθεν ὁ σπείρων [τοῦ σπείρειν.]
καὶ ἐν τῷ σπείρειν αὐτόν, [ἃ μὲν] ἔπεσεν παρὰ τὴν ὁδόν· καὶ 4

41. εἰς τὸ κ.] Ps. xviii. 44 לְשֵׁמַע אֹזֶן יִשָּׁמְעוּ לִי, εἰς ἀκοὴν ὠτίου ὑπήκουσάν μοι.

5 ἐλθόντα τὰ πετεινὰ, κατέφαγεν αὐτά. ἄλλα δὲ ἔπεσεν ἐπὶ τὰ πετρώδη, ὅπου οὐκ εἶχεν γῆν πολλήν· καὶ εὐθέως ἐξανέτειλεν, διὰ 6 τὸ μὴ ἔχειν βάθος γῆς· ἡλίου δὲ ἀνατείλαντος ἐκαυματίσθη, καὶ 7 διὰ τὸ μὴ ἔχειν ῥίζαν, ἐξηράνθη. ἄλλα δὲ ἔπεσεν ἐπὶ τὰς ἀκάν-8 θας, καὶ ἀνέβησαν αἱ ἄκανθαι, καὶ ἀπέπνιξαν αὐτά. ἄλλα δὲ ἔπεσεν ἐπὶ τὴν γῆν τὴν καλὴν, καὶ ἐδίδου καρπὸν, ὃ μὲν ἑκα-9 τὸν, ὃ δὲ ἑξήκοντα, ὃ δὲ τριάκοντα. *ὁ ἔχων ὦτα,* ἀκουέτω.
10 Καὶ προσελθόντες οἱ μαθηταὶ εἶπαν αὐτῷ, Διατί ἐν παραβολαῖς 11 λαλεῖς αὐτοῖς; ὁ δὲ ἀποκριθεὶς εἶπεν αὐτοῖς, Ὅτι ὑμῖν δέδοται γνῶναι τὰ μυστήρια τῆς βασιλείας τῶν οὐρανῶν, ἐκείνοις δὲ οὐ 12 δέδοται. ὅστις γὰρ ἔχει, δοθήσεται αὐτῷ, καὶ περισσευθήσεται· 13 ὅστις δὲ οὐκ ἔχει, καὶ ὃ ἔχει, ἀρθήσεται ἀπ' αὐτοῦ. διὰ τοῦτο ἐν παραβολαῖς αὐτοῖς λαλῶ, ὅτι βλέποντες οὐ βλέπουσι, καὶ 14 ἀκούοντες οὐκ ἀκούουσιν, οὐδὲ συνιοῦσι. καὶ ἀναπληροῦται αὐτοῖς ἡ προφητεία Ἡσαΐου ἡ λέγουσα, Ἀκοῇ ἀκούσετε, καὶ οὐ 15 μὴ συνῆτε· καὶ βλέποντες βλέψετε, καὶ οὐ μὴ ἴδητε. ἐπαχύνθη γὰρ ἡ καρδία τοῦ λαοῦ τούτου, καὶ τοῖς ὠσὶν βαρέως ἤκουσαν, καὶ τοὺς ὀφθαλμοὺς αὐτῶν ἐκάμμυσαν· μήποτε ἴδωσι τοῖς ὀφθαλμοῖς, καὶ τοῖς ὠσὶν ἀκούσωσι, καὶ τῇ καρδίᾳ συνῶσι 16 καὶ ἐπιστρέψωσι, καὶ ἰάσομαι αὐτούς. Ὑμῶν δὲ μακάριοι οἱ ὀφθαλμοὶ, ὅτι βλέπουσιν· καὶ τὰ ὦτα ὑμῶν, ὅτι ἀκούουσιν. 17 ἀμὴν γὰρ λέγω ὑμῖν, ὅτι πολλοὶ προφῆται καὶ δίκαιοι ἐπεθύ-

Cap. XIII. 14, 15, 16. Acts xxviii. 26, 27. In both we have the exact words of V.A., except ἰάσωμαι for ἰάσομαι. I need scarcely say that it is not an accurate rendering. The Vulgate and English Version come close to the original. The first two clauses are imperative: the judgment of God passing sentence on those who resist Him, a heavy present penalty, lightened by hope of its remission. The "lest," פֶּן, μήποτε, is not *exclusive*, prohibitory, preventive, but *provisional*; "in case that at some future time," "ne forte," Vulg., "if so be, perchance." It is not a doom of hopeless condemnation, but of temporary suspension of blessings, lost for a time by apathy and disobedience, but recoverable upon repentance and conversion to God. The original certainly admits of this interpretation; and it seems most in accordance with the context in N.T. Our Lord spoke to the people at large in parables; dark sayings beyond their present comprehension—each with its hidden esoteric meaning. Short, striking, impressive lessons, to be stored up in their memories, wondered at, pondered over, till possibly the day of divine illumination should shine upon their hearts and reveal the mysteries of the kingdom of heaven. The μήποτε in 15 is the apodosis of the διὰ τοῦτο in 13. "Because they see not what is before their eyes and hear not what is spoken in their ears, and do not understand; and so in them is fulfilled...;" "therefore speak I to them in parables, in case that, at some future time, they may see...." καὶ ἰάσωμαι αὐτούς, וְרָפָא לוֹ. May not this possibly be רֹפֵא לוֹ, (participle); "And there may be a Healer for them:" "and that they may find a Saviour," "a Physician for their Souls"? Or possibly the subject of שָׁב and רָפָא may be the same, as change of tense seems to indicate: "and God may return and heal them."
The free paraphrase of the passage from Isaiah in Mk. iv. 12 carries out this idea, and seems to justify, on our Lord's authority and in His own words, the application or explanation suggested above.

μησαν ἰδεῖν ἃ βλέπετε, καὶ οὐκ εἶδον· καὶ ἀκοῦσαι ἃ ἀκούετε καὶ οὐκ ἤκουσαν. Ὑμεῖς οὖν ἀκούσατε τὴν παραβολὴν τοῦ σπεί- 18 ροντος. [παντὸς] ἀκούοντος τὸν λόγον τῆς βασιλείας καὶ μὴ 19 συνιέντος, ἔρχεται ὁ πονηρὸς καὶ ἁρπάζει τὸ ἐσπαρμένον ἐν τῇ καρδίᾳ αὐτοῦ· οὗτός ἐστιν [ὁ παρὰ τὴν ὁδὸν σπαρείς.] ὁ δὲ 20 ἐπὶ τὰ πετρώδη σπαρείς, οὗτός ἐστιν ὁ τὸν λόγον ἀκούων καὶ εὐθὺς μετὰ χαρᾶς λαμβάνων αὐτόν· οὐκ ἔχει δὲ ῥίζαν ἐν ἑαυτῷ, 21 ἀλλὰ πρόσκαιρός ἐστι· γενομένης δὲ θλίψεως ἢ διωγμοῦ διὰ τὸν λόγον, εὐθὺς σκανδαλίζεται. ὁ δὲ εἰς τὰς ἀκάνθας σπαρείς, οὗτός 22 ἐστιν ὁ τὸν λόγον ἀκούων, καὶ ἡ μέριμνα *τοῦ αἰῶνος* καὶ ἡ ἀπάτη τοῦ πλούτου συμπνίγει τὸν λόγον, καὶ ἄκαρπος γίνεται. 23 ὁ δὲ ἐπὶ τὴν γῆν τὴν καλὴν σπαρείς, οὗτός ἐστιν ὁ τὸν λόγον ἀκούων καὶ συνιείς. ὃς δὴ καρποφορεῖ, καὶ ποιεῖ ὁ μὲν ἑκατόν, ὁ δὲ ἑξήκοντα, ὁ δὲ τριάκοντα.

Ἄλλην παραβολὴν παρέθηκεν αὐτοῖς λέγων, Ὡμοιώθη ἡ βα- 24 σιλεία τῶν οὐρανῶν ἀνθρώπῳ σπείροντι καλὸν σπέρμα ἐν τῷ ἀγρῷ αὐτοῦ· ἐν δὲ τῷ καθεύδειν τοὺς ἀνθρώπους, ἦλθεν αὐτοῦ 25 ὁ ἐχθρὸς καὶ ἐπέσπειρεν ζιζάνια ἀνὰ μέσον τοῦ σίτου, καὶ ἀπῆλθεν. ὅτε δὲ ἐβλάστησεν ὁ χόρτος, καὶ καρπὸν ἐποίησεν, τότε ἐφάνη 26 καὶ τὰ ζιζάνια. προσελθόντες δὲ οἱ δοῦλοι τοῦ οἰκοδεσπότου, 27 εἶπον αὐτῷ, Κύριε, οὐχὶ καλὸν σπέρμα ἔσπειρας ἐν τῷ σῷ ἀγρῷ; πόθεν οὖν ἔχει ζιζάνια; ὁ δὲ ἔφη αὐτοῖς, Ἐχθρὸς ἄνθρωπος 28 τοῦτο ἐποίησεν. οἱ δὲ δοῦλοι λέγουσιν, Θέλεις οὖν ἀπελθόντες συλλέξωμεν αὐτά; ὁ δὲ ἔφη, Οὔ· μήποτε συλλέγοντες τὰ 29 ζιζάνια, ἐκριζώσητε ἅμα αὐτοῖς τὸν σῖτον. ἄφετε συναυξάνεσθαι 30 ἀμφότερα ἕως τοῦ θερισμοῦ· καὶ ἐν καιρῷ τοῦ θερισμοῦ ἐρῶ τοῖς θερισταῖς, Συλλέξατε πρῶτον τὰ ζιζάνια, καὶ δήσατε αὐτὰ δέσμας πρὸς τὸ κατακαῦσαι αὐτά· τὸν δὲ σῖτον συναγάγετε εἰς τὴν ἀποθήκην μου.

Ἄλλην παραβολὴν παρέθηκεν αὐτοῖς λέγων, Ὁμοία ἐστὶν ἡ 31 βασιλεία τῶν οὐρανῶν κόκκῳ σινάπεως, ὃν λαβὼν ἄνθρωπος ἔσπειρεν ἐν τῷ ἀγρῷ αὐτοῦ· ὃ μικρότερον μέν ἐστιν πάντων τῶν 32 σπερμάτων· ὅταν δὲ αὐξηθῇ, [μεῖζον τῶν λαχάνων] ἐστὶν, καὶ γίνεται δένδρον, ὥστε ἐλθεῖν τὰ πετεινὰ τοῦ οὐρανοῦ, καὶ κατασκηνοῦν ἐν τοῖς κλάδοις αὐτοῦ.

Ἄλλην παραβολὴν ἐλάλησεν αὐτοῖς, Ὁμοία ἐστὶν ἡ βασι- 33 λεία τῶν οὐρανῶν ζύμῃ, ἣν λαβοῦσα γυνὴ ἐνέκρυψεν εἰς ἀλεύρου σάτα τρία, ἕως οὗ ἐζυμώθη ὅλον.

19—23. Hopeless intricacy of subjects, genders, and relations.

25. ἀνὰ μέσον] V.A. for בְּתוֹךְ "in the midst of."

MATTHEW, XIII. 34—48.

34 Ταῦτα πάντα ἐλάλησεν ὁ Ἰησοῦς ἐν παραβολαῖς τοῖς ὄχλοις,
35 καὶ χωρὶς παραβολῆς οὐδὲν ἐλάλει αὐτοῖς· [ὅπως πληρωθῇ] τὸ ῥηθὲν διὰ τοῦ προφήτου λέγοντος, Ἀνοίξω ἐν παραβολαῖς τὸ στόμα μου· [ἐρεύξομαι κεκρυμμένα ἀπὸ καταβολῆς].
36 Τότε ἀφεὶς τοὺς ὄχλους, ἦλθεν εἰς τὴν οἰκίαν· καὶ προσῆλθον αὐτῷ οἱ μαθηταὶ αὐτοῦ λέγοντες, Φράσον ἡμῖν τὴν παραβολὴν
37 τῶν ζιζανίων τοῦ ἀγροῦ. ὁ δὲ ἀποκριθεὶς εἶπεν αὐτοῖς, Ὁ
38 σπείρων τὸ καλὸν σπέρμα, ἐστὶν ὁ υἱὸς τοῦ ἀνθρώπου· ὁ δὲ ἀγρός ἐστιν ὁ κόσμος· τὸ δὲ καλὸν σπέρμα, οὗτοί εἰσιν *οἱ
39 υἱοὶ τῆς βασιλείας·* τὰ δὲ ζιζάνιά εἰσιν* οἱ υἱοὶ τοῦ πονηροῦ·* ὁ δὲ ἐχθρὸς ὁ σπείρας αὐτὰ ἔστιν ὁ διάβολος· ὁ δὲ θερισμὸς, *συν-
40 τέλεια τοῦ αἰῶνός* ἐστιν· οἱ δὲ θερισταὶ ἄγγελοί εἰσιν. ὥσπερ οὖν συλλέγεται τὰ ζιζάνια, καὶ πυρὶ κατακαίεται, οὕτως ἔσται
41 ἐν τῇ συντελείᾳ τοῦ αἰῶνος. ἀποστελεῖ ὁ υἱὸς τοῦ ἀνθρώπου τοὺς ἀγγέλους αὐτοῦ, καὶ συλλέξουσιν ἐκ τῆς βασιλείας αὐτοῦ
42 πάντα *τὰ σκάνδαλα* καὶ τοὺς ποιοῦντας τὴν ἀνομίαν, καὶ βαλοῦσιν αὐτοὺς *εἰς τὴν κάμινον τοῦ πυρός· ἐκεῖ ἔσται ὁ
43 κλαυθμὸς καὶ ὁ βρυγμὸς τῶν ὀδόντων.* τότε οἱ δίκαιοι ἐκλάμψουσιν ὡς ὁ ἥλιος, ἐν τῇ βασιλείᾳ τοῦ πατρὸς αὐτῶν. *ὁ ἔχων ὦτα,* ἀκουέτω.

44 Ὁμοία ἐστὶν ἡ βασιλεία τῶν οὐρανῶν θησαυρῷ κεκρυμμένῳ [ἐν τῷ ἀγρῷ,] ὃν εὑρὼν ἄνθρωπος ἔκρυψεν· καὶ *ἀπὸ τῆς χαρᾶς* αὐτοῦ ὑπάγει καὶ πάντα ὅσα ἔχει πωλεῖ, καὶ ἀγοράζει τὸν ἀγρὸν ἐκεῖνον.

45 Πάλιν ὁμοία ἐστὶν ἡ βασιλεία τῶν οὐρανῶν ἀνθρώπῳ ἐμπόρῳ,
46 ζητοῦντι καλοὺς μαργαρίτας· εὑρὼν δὲ ἕνα πολύτιμον μαργαρίτην, ἀπελθὼν πέπρακεν πάντα ὅσα εἶχεν, καὶ ἠγόρασεν αὐτόν.

47 Πάλιν ὁμοία ἐστὶν ἡ βασιλεία τῶν οὐρανῶν σαγήνῃ βλη-
48 θείσῃ εἰς τὴν θάλασσαν, καὶ ἐκ παντὸς γένους συναγαγούσῃ· ἣν

---

35. Ps. lxxviii. 2 חִידוֹת מִנִּי־קֶדֶם, "dark sayings from time-of-old:" V.A. προβλήματα ἀπ' ἀρχῆς.

39. συντέλεια] "Confinium quod duo extrema jungit," Schl.; e.g. עוֹלָם הַבָּא and עוֹלָם הַזֶּה, and so in strict exactness requiring Pl. αἰώνων, as in Heb. ix. 26, where it expresses the confluence, or meeting, of the extremities of the two ages, æras, or dispensations; i. e. the Ante-Christian and Christian. Compare 1 Cor. x. 11, εἰς οὓς τὰ τέλη τῶν αἰώνων κατήντησεν, "upon whom the extremities," the end and beginning, "of the two æras have come down and met together." From this close, precise sense, it easily passed into "end;" as here and vv. 40, 49; and Cap. xxiv. 3, xxviii. 20. V.A. renders by it כָּלָה, קֵץ and אַחֲרִית. Dan. ix. 27, xii. 4, xii. 13, with καιρῶν or ἡμερῶν. And from hence is probably derived its use in N.T. Classical authors do not employ it in this above sense. Grimm gives one passage from Polybius, where it stands for "completion, fulfilment."

42. In parallel passage, v. 22, γέεννα corresponds to κάμινος here.

ὅτε ἐπληρώθη ἀναβιβάσαντες αὐτὴν ἐπὶ τὸν αἰγιαλὸν, καθίσαντες συνέλεξαν τὰ καλὰ εἰς ἄγγη, [τὰ δὲ σαπρὰ] ἔξω ἔβαλον. οὕτως 49 ἔσται ἐν τῇ συντελείᾳ τοῦ αἰῶνος· ἐξελεύσονται οἱ ἄγγελοι, καὶ ἀφοριοῦσιν τοὺς πονηροὺς ἐκ μέσου τῶν δικαίων, καὶ βαλοῦσιν 50 αὐτοὺς *εἰς τὴν κάμινον τοῦ πυρός·* ἐκεῖ ἔσται ὁ κλανθμὸς καὶ ὁ βρυγμὸς τῶν ὀδόντων. Συνήκατε ταῦτα πάντα; λέγουσιν 51 αὐτῷ, Ναί. Ὁ δὲ εἶπεν αὐτοῖς, Διὰ τοῦτο πᾶς γραμματεὺς 52 [μαθητευθεὶς] τῇ βασιλείᾳ τῶν οὐρανῶν, ὅμοιός ἐστιν ἀνθρώπῳ οἰκοδεσπότῃ, ὅστις ἐκβάλλει ἐκ τοῦ θησαυροῦ αὐτοῦ καινὰ καὶ παλαιά.

Καὶ ἐγένετο ὅτε ἐτέλεσεν ὁ Ἰησοῦς τὰς παραβολὰς ταύτας, 53 μετῆρεν ἐκεῖθεν· καὶ ἐλθὼν εἰς τὴν πατρίδα αὐτοῦ, ἐδίδασκεν 54 αὐτοὺς ἐν τῇ συναγωγῇ αὐτῶν, ὥστε ἐκπλήσσεσθαι αὐτοῖς καὶ λέγειν, Πόθεν τούτῳ ἡ σοφία αὕτη καὶ αἱ δυνάμεις; οὐχ οὗτός 55 ἐστιν ὁ τοῦ τέκτονος υἱός; οὐχὶ ἡ μήτηρ αὐτοῦ λέγεται Μαριὰ, καὶ οἱ ἀδελφοὶ αὐτοῦ Ἰάκωβος καὶ Ἰωσὴφ καὶ Σίμων καὶ Ἰούδας; καὶ αἱ ἀδελφαὶ αὐτοῦ οὐχὶ πᾶσαι *πρὸς ἡμᾶς* εἰσιν; πόθεν οὖν 56· τούτῳ ταῦτα πάντα; καὶ *ἐσκανδαλίζοντο ἐν αὐτῷ.* ὁ δὲ 57 Ἰησοῦς εἶπεν αὐτοῖς, Οὐκ ἔστιν προφήτης ἄτιμος, εἰ μὴ ἐν τῇ πατρίδι καὶ ἐν τῇ οἰκίᾳ αὐτοῦ. καὶ οὐκ ἐποίησεν ἐκεῖ δυνάμεις 58 πολλὰς διὰ τὴν ἀπιστίαν αὐτῶν.

ΕΝ ἐκείνῳ τῷ καιρῷ ἤκουσεν Ἡρώδης ὁ τετράρχης τὴν CAP. 14 ἀκοὴν Ἰησοῦ, καὶ εἶπεν [τοῖς παισὶν] αὐτοῦ, Οὗτός ἐστιν Ἰω- 2 άννης ὁ βαπτιστής· [αὐτὸς] ἠγέρθη ἀπὸ τῶν νεκρῶν, καὶ διὰ τοῦτο αἱ δυνάμεις ἐνεργοῦσιν ἐν αὐτῷ. Ὁ γὰρ Ἡρώδης κρα- 3 τήσας τὸν Ἰωάννην, ἔδησεν αὐτὸν ἐν τῇ φυλακῇ, διὰ Ἡρωδι- άδα τὴν γιναῖκα τοῦ ἀδελφοῦ αὐτοῦ. ἔλεγεν γὰρ αὐτῷ ὁ 4 Ἰωάννης, Οὐκ ἔξεστίν σοι ἔχειν αὐτήν. καὶ θέλων αὐτὸν ἀπο- 5 κτεῖναι, ἐφοβήθη τὸν ὄχλον, ὅτι ὡς προφήτην αὐτὸν εἶχον. [γενεσίοις δὲ γενομένοις] τοῦ Ἡρώδου, ὠρχήσατο ἡ θυγάτηρ τῆς 6 Ἡρωδιάδος ἐν τῷ μέσῳ, καὶ ἤρεσεν τῷ Ἡρώδῃ· ὅθεν μεθ᾽ ὅρκου 7 ὡμολόγησεν αὐτῇ δοῦναι [ὃ ἂν αἰτήσηται.] Ἡ δὲ [προβιβασθεῖσα] 8 ὑπὸ τῆς μητρὸς αὐτῆς, Δός μοι φησίν, ὧδε ἐπὶ πίνακι τὴν κε- φαλὴν Ἰωάννου τοῦ βαπτιστοῦ. καὶ λυπηθεὶς ὁ βασιλεὺς διὰ 9

56. πρὸς ἡμᾶς] Mk. vi. 3, John i. 1. In V.A. πρὸς stands for לְ, "apud" or "inter," Jerem. xli. 12; and εἰς for אֶל frequently. Deut. xvi. 6, 1 Kings viii. 30. Hence in N.T. Mk. i. 39, ii. 1, xiii. 9, 16, εἰς συναγωγὰς δαρήσεσθε, and ὁ εἰς τὸν ἀγρὸν ὤν. Acts vii. 53 εἰς διαταγὰς ἀγγέ- λων, "inter angelorum ordines," Deut. xxxiii. 2. εἰς also, in its almost universal use for לְ, in V.A., is put for it occasion- ally when it means "apud." Ps. xvi. 10 לֹא־תַעֲזֹב נַפְשִׁי לִשְׁאוֹל, εἰς ᾅδου.

MATTHEW, XIV. 10—31.

10 τοὺς ὅρκους καὶ τοὺς συνανακειμένους ἐκέλευσεν δοθῆναι· καὶ
11 πέμψας ἀπεκεφάλισεν τὸν Ἰωάννην ἐν τῇ φυλακῇ. καὶ ἠνέχθη
ἡ κεφαλὴ αὐτοῦ ἐπὶ πίνακι, καὶ ἐδόθη τῷ κορασίῳ· καὶ ἤνεγκεν
12 τῇ μητρὶ αὐτῆς. καὶ προσελθόντες οἱ μαθηταὶ αὐτοῦ ἦραν τὸ
σῶμα, καὶ ἔθαψαν αὐτόν· καὶ ἐλθόντες ἀπήγγειλαν τῷ Ἰησοῖ.
13 ἀκούσας δὲ ὁ Ἰησοῦς, ἀνεχώρησεν ἐκεῖθεν ἐν πλοίῳ εἰς ἔρημον
τόπον κατ' ἰδίαν. καὶ ἀκούσαντες οἱ ὄχλοι ἠκολούθησαν αὐτῷ
πεζῇ ἀπὸ τῶν πόλεων.
14 Καὶ ἐξελθὼν εἶδεν πολὺν ὄχλον, καὶ ἐσπλαγχνίσθη ἐπ' αὐ-
15 τοὺς, καὶ ἐθεράπευσεν τοὺς ἀρρώστους αὐτῶν. Ὀψίας δὲ γενομένης, προσῆλθον αὐτῷ οἱ μαθηταὶ λέγοντες, Ἐρημός ἐστιν
ὁ τόπος, καὶ ἡ ὥρα ἤδη παρῆλθεν· ἀπόλυσον οὖν τοὺς ὄχλους,
16 ἵνα ἀπελθόντες εἰς τὰς κώμας, ἀγοράσωσιν ἑαυτοῖς βρώματα. ὁ
δὲ Ἰησοῦς εἶπεν αὐτοῖς, Οὐ χρείαν ἔχουσιν ἀπελθεῖν· [δότε αὐ-
17 τοῖς ὑμεῖς φαγεῖν.] οἱ δὲ λέγουσιν αὐτῷ, Οὐκ ἔχομεν ὧδε εἰ μὴ
18 πέντε ἄρτους καὶ δύο ἰχθύας. ὁ δὲ εἶπε, Φέρετέ μοι αὐτοὺς ὧδε.
19 καὶ κελεύσας τοὺς ὄχλους ἀνακλιθῆναι [ἐπὶ τοὺς χόρτους,] λαβὼν τοὺς πέντε ἄρτους καὶ τοὺς δύο ἰχθύας, ἀναβλέψας εἰς τὸν
οὐρανὸν, [ηὐλόγησεν·] καὶ κλάσας ἔδωκεν τοῖς μαθηταῖς τοὺς
20 ἄρτους, οἱ δὲ μαθηταὶ τοῖς ὄχλοις. καὶ ἔφαγον πάντες, καὶ
ἐχορτάσθησαν· καὶ ἦραν τὸ περισσεῦον τῶν κλασμάτων δώδεκα
21 κοφίνους πλήρεις. οἱ δὲ ἐσθίοντες ἦσαν ἄνδρες ὡσεὶ πεντακισχί-
22 λιοι, χωρὶς γυναικῶν καὶ παιδίων. καὶ εὐθέως ἠνάγκασεν τοὺς
μαθητὰς ἐμβῆναι εἰς πλοῖον, καὶ [προάγειν αὐτὸν] εἰς τὸ πέραν,
23 [ἕως οὗ ἀπολύσῃ] τοὺς ὄχλους. καὶ ἀπολύσας τοὺς ὄχλους,
ἀνέβη εἰς τὸ ὄρος κατ' ἰδίαν προσεύξασθαι. Ὀψίας δὲ γενο-
24 μένης, μόνος ἦν ἐκεῖ. τὸ δὲ πλοῖον ἤδη μέσον τῆς θαλάσσης
ἦν, βασανιζόμενον ὑπὸ τῶν κυμάτων· ἦν γὰρ ἐναντίος ὁ ἄνεμος.
25 Τετάρτῃ δὲ φυλακῇ τῆς νυκτὸς ἦλθεν πρὸς αὐτοὺς περιπατῶν
26 ἐπὶ τὴν θάλασσαν. καὶ ἰδόντες αὐτὸν οἱ μαθηταὶ [ἐπὶ τῆς θα-
λάσσης] περιπατοῦντα, ἐταράχθησαν λέγοντες, *Ὅτι* φάν-
27 τασμά ἐστιν· καὶ *ἀπὸ τοῦ φόβου* ἔκραξαν. εὐθέως δὲ ἐλάλησεν αὐτοῖς ὁ Ἰησοῦς λέγων, Θαρσεῖτε· ἐγώ εἰμι, μὴ φοβεῖσθε.
28 Ἀποκριθεὶς δὲ αὐτῷ ὁ Πέτρος εἶπεν, Κύριε, εἰ σὺ εἶ, κέλευσόν με
πρός σε ἐλθεῖν ἐπὶ τὰ ὕδατα. ὁ δὲ εἶπεν, Ἐλθέ. καὶ καταβὰς
29 ἀπὸ τοῦ πλοίου Πέτρος, περιεπάτησεν ἐπὶ τὰ ὕδατα, καὶ ἦλθεν
30 πρὸς τὸν Ἰησοῦν. βλέπων δὲ τὸν ἄνεμον ἰσχυρὸν, ἐφοβήθη· καὶ
31 ἀρξάμενος καταποντίζεσθαι, ἔκραξεν λέγων, Κύριε σῶσόν με. εὐ-

Cap. XIV. 26. Compare vii. 23, xix. two very strong instances in point.
8, Acts xxviii. 25, I., iv. 41, 43 and vi 5,

θέως δὲ ὁ Ἰησοῦς ἐκτείνας τὴν χεῖρα, ἐπελάβετο αὐτοῦ, καὶ λέγει αὐτῷ, Ὀλιγόπιστε, *εἰς τί* ἐδίστασας; Καὶ ἀναβάντων αὐτῶν εἰς 32 τὸ πλοῖον, ἐκόπασεν ὁ ἄνεμος. οἱ δὲ ἐν τῷ πλοίῳ ἐλθόντες προσ- 33 εκύνησαν αὐτῷ, λέγοντες, Ἀληθῶς Θεοῦ υἱὸς εἶ. Καὶ διαπεράσαντες ἦλθον εἰς τὴν γῆν Γεννησαρέτ. καὶ ἐπι- 34 γνόντες αὐτὸν οἱ ἄνδρες τοῦ τόπου ἐκείνου, ἀπέστειλαν εἰς ὅλην 35 τὴν περίχωρον ἐκείνην, καὶ προσήνεγκαν αὐτῷ πάντας τοὺς κακῶς ἔχοντας, καὶ παρεκάλουν αὐτὸν, ἵνα μόνον ἅψωνται τοῦ κρασ- 36 πέδου τοῦ ἱματίου αὐτοῦ· καὶ ὅσοι ἥψαντο, *διεσώθησαν.*

ΤΟΤΕ προσέρχονται τῷ Ἰησοῦ οἱ ἀπὸ Ἱεροσολύμων γραμ- CAP. ματεῖς καὶ Φαρισαῖοι λέγοντες, Διατί οἱ μαθηταί σου παραβαί- 2 νουσιν τὴν παράδοσιν τῶν πρεσβυτέρων; οὐ γὰρ νίπτονται τὰς χεῖρας αὐτῶν, ὅταν ἄρτον ἐσθίωσιν. Ὁ δὲ ἀποκριθεὶς εἶπεν αὐ- 3 τοῖς, Διατί καὶ ὑμεῖς παραβαίνετε τὴν ἐντολὴν τοῦ Θεοῦ διὰ τὴν παράδοσιν ὑμῶν; Ὁ γὰρ Θεὸς εἶπεν, Τίμα τὸν πατέρα καὶ τὴν 4 μητέρα· καὶ, Ὁ κακολογῶν πατέρα ἢ μητέρα, θανάτῳ τελευτάτω· ὑμεῖς δὲ λέγετε, Ὃς ἂν εἴπῃ τῷ πατρὶ ἢ τῇ μητρί, Δῶρον ὃ 5 ἐὰν ἐξ ἐμοῦ ὠφεληθῇς· *καὶ οὐ μὴ τιμήσει* τὸν πατέρα αὐτοῦ 6 ἢ τὴν μητέρα αὐτοῦ· καὶ ἠκυρώσατε τὸν νόμον τοῦ Θεοῦ διὰ τὴν 7 παράδοσιν ὑμῶν. ὑποκριταὶ, καλῶς ἐπροφήτευσεν περὶ ὑμῶν 8 Ἡσαΐας λέγων, Ὁ λαὸς οὗτος τοῖς χείλεσίν με τιμᾷ· ἡ δὲ καρδία αὐτῶν πόρρω ἀπέχει ἀπ᾽ ἐμοῦ. μάτην δὲ σέβονταί με, διδάσκοντες 9 διδασκαλίας ἐντάλματα ἀνθρώπων. Καὶ προσκαλεσάμενος τὸν 10 ὄχλον εἶπεν αὐτοῖς, Ἀκούετε καὶ συνίετε. οὐ τὸ εἰσερχόμενον εἰς 11 τὸ στόμα *κοινοῖ* τὸν ἄνθρωπον· ἀλλὰ τὸ ἐκπορευόμενον ἐκ τοῦ

---

31. εἰς τί = לָמָה literally rendered.
36. διεσώθησαν] ix. 21.
Cap. XV. 4. θαν. τελ.] V. A. for יוּמָת מוֹת, Ex. xxi. 17. The translation of ὁ κακολογῶν, "he that curseth," is incongruous with the context. It was, rather, heartless indifference, want of due respect for parents, that led to the evading of the plain duty of supporting them. Now κακολογέω is used by V.A. several times for Pihel or Hiphil of קלל, "levis, vilis fuit;" in sense of *vilipendit*, "lightly regarded," "treated with disrespect:" viz. Ex. xxii. 28, Ez. xxii. 7, אָב וָאֵם הֵקַל Auth. V. "they have set light by." Prov. xx. 20. 1 Sam. iii. 13, כִּי מְקַלְלִים לָהֶם בָּנָיו, which may perhaps mean "had no respect for themselves." Now in other similar passages the same verb, and the cognate הקל, are rendered ἀτιμάζω in V. A., e.g. Deut. xxvii. 16, מַקְלֶה אָבִיו וְאָמּוֹ, the exact counterpart of Exod. xxi. 17, quoted by S. Matthew here, is ἀτιμάζων. Gen. xvi. 4, 5, Is. xvi. 14, and 2 Sam. xix. 44, מַדּוּעַ הֲקִלֹּתַנִי, "why hast thou despised us?" Hence we see that κακολογέω = ἀτιμάζω in V. A. But קלל Pi. means "curse" also; Gen. viii. 21, xii. 3. And so the two senses have been confounded together and a wrong interpretation given. Better to translate "he that makes light of," "disregards the claims of" his father and mother, so as to refuse to assist them, on the plea of a previous offering of his money to God's service. For κορβᾶν see M. xxvii. 6.
11. See Mk. vii. 2, 15, Acts x. 14, 28, xi. 8, Rom. xiv. 14. κοινὸς = "unclean." No such use of word in

12 στόματος, τοῦτο κοινοῖ τὸν ἄνθρωπον. Τότε προσελθόντες οἱ μαθηταὶ λέγουσιν αὐτῷ, Οἶδας ὅτι οἱ Φαρισαῖοι ἀκούσαντες τὸν
13 λόγον ἐσκανδαλίσθησαν; ὁ δὲ ἀποκριθεὶς εἶπεν, Πᾶσα [φυτεία]
14 ἣν οὐκ ἐφύτευσεν ὁ πατήρ μου ὁ οὐράνιος, ἐκριζωθήσεται. ἄφετε αὐτούς· τυφλοί εἰσιν ὁδηγοὶ τυφλῶν· τυφλὸς δὲ τυφλὸν ἐὰν ὁδηγῇ,
15 ἀμφότεροι εἰς βόθυνον πεσοῦνται. Ἀποκριθεὶς δὲ ὁ Πέτρος εἶπεν
16 αὐτῷ, Φράσον ἡμῖν τὴν παραβολήν. ὁ δὲ εἶπεν, [Ἀκμὴν] καὶ
17 ὑμεῖς ἀσύνετοί ἐστε; οὐ νοεῖτε, ὅτι πᾶν τὸ εἰσπορευόμενον εἰς τὸ
18 στόμα εἰς τὴν κοιλίαν χωρεῖ, καὶ εἰς ἀφεδρῶνα ἐκβάλλεται; τὰ δὲ ἐκπορευόμενα ἐκ τοῦ στόματος, ἐκ τῆς καρδίας ἐξέρχεται, κἀ-
19 κεῖνα κοινοῖ τὸν ἄνθρωπον. ἐκ γὰρ τῆς καρδίας ἐξέρχονται διαλογισμοὶ πονηροί, φόνοι, μοιχεῖαι, πορνεῖαι, κλοπαί, ψευδομαρτυ-
20 ρίαι, βλασφημίαι. ταῦτά ἐστιν τὰ κοινοῦντα τὸν ἄνθρωπον· τὸ δὲ ἀνίπτοις χερσὶ φαγεῖν, οὐ κοινοῖ τὸν ἄνθρωπον.
21 Καὶ ἐξελθὼν ἐκεῖθεν ὁ Ἰησοῦς, ἀνεχώρησεν εἰς τὰ μέρη Τύρου
22 καὶ Σιδῶνος. καὶ ἰδοὺ γυνὴ Χαναναία ἀπὸ τῶν ὁρίων ἐκείνων ἐξελθοῦσα ἐκραύγασεν λέγουσα, Ἐλέησόν με, Κύριε *υἱὸς* Δαυίδ·
23 ἡ θυγάτηρ μου κακῶς δαιμονίζεται. ὁ δὲ *οὐκ ἀπεκρίθη αὐτῇ λόγον.* καὶ προσελθόντες οἱ μαθηταὶ αὐτοῦ [ἠρώτουν] αὐτὸν
24 λέγοντες, [Ἀπόλυσον] αὐτήν, ὅτι κράζει ὄπισθεν ἡμῶν. ὁ δὲ ἀποκριθεὶς εἶπεν, Οὐκ ἀπεστάλην εἰ μὴ *εἰς τὰ πρόβατα τὰ ἀπο-
25 λωλότα οἴκου Ἰσραήλ.* ἡ δὲ ἐλθοῦσα προσεκύνει αὐτῷ λέγουσα,
26 Κύριε, βοήθει μοι. ὁ δὲ ἀποκριθεὶς εἶπεν, Οὐκ ἔξεστιν λαβεῖν
27 τὸν ἄρτον τῶν τέκνων καὶ βαλεῖν τοῖς κυναρίοις. ἡ δὲ εἶπεν, Ναί, Κύριε· καὶ γὰρ τὰ κυνάρια ἐσθίει ἀπὸ τῶν ψιχίων τῶν πιπτόντων
28 ἀπὸ τῆς τραπέζης τῶν κυρίων αὐτῶν. τότε ἀποκριθεὶς ὁ Ἰησοῦς εἶπεν αὐτῇ, Ὦ γύναι, μεγάλη σου ἡ πίστις· γενηθήτω σοι ὡς θέλεις. καὶ ἰάθη ἡ θυγάτηρ αὐτῆς ἀπὸ τῆς ὥρας ἐκείνης.
29 Καὶ μεταβὰς ἐκεῖθεν ὁ Ἰησοῦς ἦλθεν παρὰ τὴν θάλασσαν
30 τῆς Γαλιλαίας, καὶ ἀναβὰς εἰς τὸ ὄρος ἐκάθητο ἐκεῖ. καὶ προσῆλθον αὐτῷ ὄχλοι πολλοὶ ἔχοντες μεθ' ἑαυτῶν χωλούς, κωφούς, τυφλούς, κυλλοὺς καὶ ἑτέρους πολλούς, καὶ ἔρριψαν αὐτοὺς παρὰ
31 τοὺς πόδας αὐτοῦ· καὶ ἐθεράπευσεν αὐτούς, ὥστε τὸν ὄχλον θαυμάσαι βλέποντας κωφοὺς λαλοῦντας, κυλλοὺς ὑγιεῖς καὶ

V.A.: but it stands for מָבֹא in 1 Macc. i. 50, 65, θύειν ὕεια καὶ κτήνη κοινὰ and μὴ φαγεῖν κοινά, and Josephus *A. J.* XII. 12, 13, κοινοὺς ἀνθρώπους and κοινὸν βίον, as in Acts x. 28, ἄνθρ. κ. = "gentilis, homo profanus."

23. שָׁאַל = αἰτέω and ἐρωτάω. V.A. constantly misplaces the two, putting one for the other: as also N.T. writers, L. iv. 38, J. iv. 31, 1 Thess. v. 12, 1 John v. 16.

χωλοὺς περιπατοῦντας καὶ τυφλοὺς βλέποντας· καὶ ἐδόξασαν τὸν Θεὸν Ἰσραήλ.

Ὁ δὲ Ἰησοῦς προσκαλεσάμενος τοὺς μαθητὰς αὐτοῦ εἶπεν, 32 Σπλαγχνίζομαι ἐπὶ τὸν ὄχλον, ὅτι ἤδη ἡμέραι τρεῖς προσμένουσίν μοι καὶ οὐκ ἔχουσιν [τί] φάγωσιν· καὶ [ἀπολῦσαι] αὐτοὺς νήστεις οὐ θέλω, μή ποτε ἐκλυθῶσιν ἐν τῇ ὁδῷ. καὶ λέγουσιν αὐτῷ οἱ 33 μαθηταί, Πόθεν ἡμῖν ἐν ἐρημίᾳ ἄρτοι τοσοῦτοι ὥστε χορτάσαι ὄχλον τοσοῦτον; καὶ λέγει αὐτοῖς ὁ Ἰησοῦς, Πόσους ἄρτους ἔχετε; 34 οἱ δὲ εἶπον, Ἑπτά, καὶ ὀλίγα ἰχθύδια. καὶ ἐκέλευσεν τοῖς ὄχλοις 35 ἀναπεσεῖν ἐπὶ τὴν γῆν. καὶ λαβὼν τοὺς ἑπτὰ ἄρτους καὶ τοὺς 36 ἰχθύας εὐχαριστήσας ἔκλασεν καὶ ἔδωκεν τοῖς μαθηταῖς, οἱ δὲ μαθηταὶ τοῖς ὄχλοις. καὶ ἔφαγον πάντες καὶ ἐχορτάσθησαν, καὶ 37 τὸ περισσεῦον τῶν κλασμάτων ἦραν ἑπτὰ σπυρίδας πλήρεις. οἱ δὲ ἐσθίοντες ἦσαν τετρακισχίλιοι ἄνδρες χωρὶς γυναικῶν καὶ 38 παιδίων. καὶ ἀπολύσας τοὺς ὄχλους ἀνέβη εἰς τὸ πλοῖον, καὶ 39 ἦλθεν εἰς τὰ ὅρια Μαγαδάν.

Καὶ προσελθόντες οἱ Φαρισαῖοι καὶ Σαδδουκαῖοι πειράζοντες 16 ἐπηρώτησαν αὐτὸν σημεῖον ἐκ τοῦ οὐρανοῦ ἐπιδεῖξαι αὐτοῖς. ὁ δὲ 2 ἀποκριθεὶς εἶπεν αὐτοῖς, Ὀψίας γενομένης λέγετε, Εὐδία, πυρράζει γὰρ ὁ οὐρανός. καὶ πρωΐ, Σήμερον χειμών, πυρράζει γὰρ στυγνά- 3 ζων ὁ οὐρανός. τὸ μὲν πρόσωπον τοῦ οὐρανοῦ γινώσκετε διακρί- νειν, τὰ δὲ σημεῖα τῶν καιρῶν οὐ δύνασθε; γενεὰ πονηρὰ καὶ 4 *μοιχαλὶς* σημεῖον ἐπιζητεῖ, καὶ σημεῖον οὐ δοθήσεται αὐτῇ εἰ μὴ τὸ σημεῖον Ἰωνᾶ. καὶ καταλιπὼν αὐτοὺς ἀπῆλθεν.

Καὶ ἐλθόντες οἱ μαθηταὶ εἰς τὸ πέραν ἐπελάθοντο ἄρτους 5 λαβεῖν. ὁ δὲ Ἰησοῦς εἶπεν αὐτοῖς, *Ὁρᾶτε καὶ προσέχετε ἀπὸ 6 τῆς ζύμης* τῶν Φαρισαίων καὶ Σαδδουκαίων. οἱ δὲ διελογίζοντο 7 ἐν ἑαυτοῖς λέγοντες ὅτι ἄρτους οὐκ ἐλάβομεν. γνοὺς δὲ ὁ Ἰησοῦς 8 εἶπεν, Τί διαλογίζεσθε ἐν ἑαυτοῖς, ὀλιγόπιστοι, ὅτι ἄρτους οὐκ ἐλάβετε; οὔπω νοεῖτε, οὐδὲ μνημονεύετε τοὺς πέντε ἄρτους τῶν 9 πεντακισχιλίων καὶ πόσους κοφίνους ἐλάβετε; οὐδὲ τοὺς ἑπτὰ 10 ἄρτους τῶν τετρακισχιλίων καὶ πόσας σπυρίδας ἐλάβετε; πῶς 11 οὐ νοεῖτε ὅτι οὐ περὶ ἄρτων εἶπον ὑμῖν; προσέχετε δὲ ἀπὸ τῆς ζύμης τῶν Φαρισαίων καὶ Σαδδουκαίων. τότε συνῆκαν ὅτι οὐκ 12 εἶπεν προσέχειν ἀπὸ τῆς ζύμης τῶν ἄρτων ἀλλὰ ἀπὸ τῆς διδαχῆς τῶν Φαρισαίων καὶ Σαδδουκαίων.

Ἐλθὼν δὲ ὁ Ἰησοῦς εἰς τὰ μέρη Καισαρείας τῆς Φιλίππου 13 ἠρώτα τοὺς μαθητὰς αὐτοῦ λέγων, Τίνα λέγουσιν οἱ ἄνθρωποι εἶναι τὸν υἱὸν τοῦ ἀνθρώπου; οἱ δὲ εἶπον, Οἱ μὲν Ἰωάννην τὸν 14 βαπτιστήν, ἄλλοι δὲ Ἡλίαν, ἕτεροι δὲ Ἰερεμίαν ἢ ἕνα τῶν προ-

15 φητῶν. λέγει αὐτοῖς, Ὑμεῖς δὲ τίνα με λέγετε εἶναι; ἀποκριθεὶς
16 δὲ Σίμων Πέτρος εἶπεν, Σὺ εἶ ὁ Χριστὸς ὁ υἱὸς τοῦ Θεοῦ τοῦ
17 ζῶντος. ἀποκριθεὶς δὲ ὁ Ἰησοῦς εἶπεν αὐτῷ, Μακάριος εἶ, Σίμων
Βαριωνᾶ, ὅτι *σὰρξ καὶ αἷμα* οὐκ ἀπεκάλυψέν σοι ἀλλ' ὁ πατήρ
18 μου ὁ ἐν οὐρανοῖς. κἀγὼ δέ σοι λέγω ὅτι σὺ εἶ Πέτρος, καὶ ἐπὶ
ταύτῃ τῇ πέτρᾳ οἰκοδομήσω μου τὴν ἐκκλησίαν, καὶ *πύλαι ᾅδου*
19 οὐ κατισχύσουσιν αὐτῆς. καὶ δώσω σοι τὰς κλεῖδας τῆς βασιλείας
τῶν οὐρανῶν, καὶ ὃ ἂν δήσῃς ἐπὶ τῆς γῆς ἔσται δεδεμένον ἐν τοῖς
οὐρανοῖς, καὶ ὃ ἐὰν λύσῃς ἐπὶ τῆς γῆς ἔσται λελυμένον ἐν τοῖς
20 οὐρανοῖς. τότε διεστείλατο τοῖς μαθηταῖς ἵνα μηδενὶ εἴπωσιν ὅτι
αὐτός ἐστιν ὁ Χριστός.
21 Ἀπὸ τότε ἤρξατο ὁ Ἰησοῦς δεικνύειν τοῖς μαθηταῖς αὐτοῦ
ὅτι δεῖ αὐτὸν εἰς Ἱεροσόλυμα ἀπελθεῖν καὶ πολλὰ παθεῖν *ἀπὸ*
τῶν πρεσβυτέρων καὶ ἀρχιερέων καὶ γραμματέων καὶ ἀποκταν-
22 θῆναι καὶ τῇ τρίτῃ ἡμέρᾳ ἐγερθῆναι. καὶ προσλαβόμενος αὐτὸν
ὁ Πέτρος λέγει αὐτῷ ἐπιτιμῶν, *Ἵλεώς σοι,* Κύριε· [οὐ μὴ ἔσται
23 σοι τοῦτο.] ὁ δὲ στραφεὶς εἶπεν τῷ Πέτρῳ, Ὕπαγε ὀπίσω μου,
Σατανᾶ· σκάνδαλον εἶ μου, ὅτι οὐ φρονεῖς τὰ τοῦ Θεοῦ ἀλλὰ τὰ
τῶν ἀνθρώπων.
24 Τότε ὁ Ἰησοῦς εἶπεν τοῖς μαθηταῖς αὐτοῦ, Εἴ τις θέλει ὀπίσω
μου ἐλθεῖν, ἀπαρνησάσθω ἑαυτὸν καὶ ἀράτω τὸν σταυρὸν αὐτοῦ,
25 καὶ ἀκολουθείτω μοι. ὃς γὰρ ἐὰν θέλῃ τὴν ψυχὴν αὐτοῦ σῶσαι,
ἀπολέσει αὐτήν· ὃς δ' ἂν ἀπολέσῃ τὴν ψυχὴν αὐτοῦ ἕνεκεν ἐμοῦ,
26 εὑρήσει αὐτήν. τί γὰρ ὠφεληθήσεται ἄνθρωπος, ἐὰν τὸν κόσμον
ὅλον κερδήσῃ, τὴν δὲ ψυχὴν αὐτοῦ ζημιωθῇ; ἢ τί δώσει ἄν-
27 θρωπος ἀντάλλαγμα τῆς ψυχῆς αὐτοῦ; μέλλει γὰρ ὁ υἱὸς τοῦ
ἀνθρώπου ἔρχεσθαι *ἐν τῇ δόξῃ* τοῦ πατρὸς αὐτοῦ μετὰ τῶν
ἀγγέλων αὐτοῦ, καὶ τότε ἀποδώσει ἑκάστῳ κατὰ τὴν πρᾶξιν
28 αὐτοῦ. ἀμὴν λέγω ὑμῖν, εἰσίν τινες ὧδε ἑστῶτες οἵτινες οὐ μὴ

Cap. XVI. 18. πύλαι ᾅδου] i.e. "the Powers of Hades:" the gate of the city was, on fit occasions, the place of the tribunal, or throne of the judge or chief ruler. Deut. xxi. 19, Jerem. xxxviii. 7, Lam. v. 14, Esth. iv. 2, v. 13, Dan. ii. 49, Amos v. 15. Hence it came to be a term for "the king's court;" "the central seat of empire;" as with the Turks at this day; "the Porta Sublimis," "the Sublime Porte."

22. For חָלִילָה, ("vox indignantis, detestantis," Gesen.,) "profanum habeatur tibi," V. A. once has μηδαμῶς, 1 Sam.

xii. 23, חָלִילָה לִּי מֵחֲטֹא לַיהוָה, ἐμοὶ μηδαμῶς τοῦ ἁμαρτεῖν τῷ Κυρίῳ (an instance of strange obscuration of all meaning by literal translation): but generally ἵλεώς σοι, 1 Chr. xi. 19, 2 Sam. xx. 20. Supposed to be a form of "God be merciful to you," "God forbid." Schl. and Grimm quote Ælian for ἵλεως as an adjective.

26. "What will he-have-to-give-in-exchange-for his lost soul," at the last day? The different meanings of ψυχή (life and soul) in 25 and 26 make the passage difficult to translate. See x. 39.

MATTHEW, XVII. 1—20.

γεύσωνται θανάτου ἕως ἂν ἴδωσιν τὸν υἱὸν τοῦ ἀνθρώπου ἐρχόμενον ἐν τῇ βασιλείᾳ αὐτοῦ.

Καὶ μεθ' ἡμέρας ἓξ παραλαμβάνει ὁ Ἰησοῦς τὸν Πέτρον καὶ Ἰάκωβον καὶ Ἰωάννην τὸν ἀδελφὸν αὐτοῦ, καὶ ἀναφέρει αὐτοὺς εἰς ὄρος ὑψηλὸν κατ' ἰδίαν. καὶ μετεμορφώθη ἔμπροσθεν αὐτῶν, καὶ ἔλαμψεν τὸ πρόσωπον αὐτοῦ ὡς ὁ ἥλιος, τὰ δὲ ἱμάτια αὐτοῦ ἐγένετο λευκὰ ὡς τὸ φῶς. καὶ ἰδοὺ ὤφθη αὐτοῖς Μωυσῆς καὶ Ἠλίας μετ' αὐτοῦ συλλαλοῦντες. ἀποκριθεὶς δὲ ὁ Πέτρος εἶπεν τῷ Ἰησοῦ, Κύριε, καλόν ἐστιν ἡμᾶς ὧδε εἶναι· εἰ θέλεις, ποιήσω ὧδε τρεῖς σκηνάς, σοὶ μίαν καὶ Μωυσεῖ μίαν καὶ Ἠλίᾳ μίαν. ἔτι αὐτοῦ λαλοῦντος, ἰδοὺ νεφέλη φωτεινὴ ἐπεσκίασεν αὐτούς, καὶ ἰδοὺ φωνὴ ἐκ τῆς νεφέλης λέγουσα, Οὗτός ἐστιν ὁ υἱός μου ὁ ἀγαπητός, *ἐν ᾧ εὐδόκησα·* ἀκούετε αὐτοῦ. καὶ ἀκούσαντες οἱ μαθηταὶ ἔπεσαν *ἐπὶ πρόσωπον αὐτῶν* καὶ ἐφοβήθησαν σφόδρα. καὶ προσελθὼν ὁ Ἰησοῦς ἥψατο αὐτῶν καὶ εἶπεν, Ἐγέρθητε καὶ μὴ φοβεῖσθε. ἐπάραντες δὲ τοὺς ὀφθαλμοὺς αὐτῶν οὐδένα εἶδον εἰ μὴ τὸν Ἰησοῦν μόνον. καὶ καταβαινόντων αὐτῶν ἐκ τοῦ ὄρους ἐνετείλατο αὐτοῖς ὁ Ἰησοῦς λέγων, Μηδενὶ εἴπητε τὸ ὅραμα [ἕως οὗ] ὁ υἱὸς τοῦ ἀνθρώπου ἐκ νεκρῶν [ἐγερθῇ]. καὶ ἐπηρώτησαν αὐτὸν οἱ μαθηταὶ αὐτοῦ λέγοντες, Τί οὖν οἱ γραμματεῖς λέγουσιν ὅτι Ἠλίαν δεῖ ἐλθεῖν πρῶτον; ὁ δὲ ἀποκριθεὶς εἶπεν, Ἠλίας μὲν ἔρχεται καὶ ἀποκαταστήσει πάντα· λέγω δὲ ὑμῖν ὅτι Ἠλίας ἤδη ἦλθεν, καὶ οὐκ ἐπέγνωσαν αὐτόν, ἀλλὰ *ἐποίησαν ἐν αὐτῷ* ὅσα ἠθέλησαν· οὕτως καὶ *ὁ υἱὸς τοῦ ἀνθρώπου* μέλλει πάσχειν ὑπ' αὐτῶν. τότε συνῆκαν οἱ μαθηταὶ ὅτι περὶ Ἰωάννου τοῦ βαπτιστοῦ εἶπεν αὐτοῖς.

Καὶ ἐλθὼν πρὸς τὸν ὄχλον, προσῆλθεν αὐτῷ ἄνθρωπος γονυπετῶν αὐτὸν καὶ λέγων, Κύριε, ἐλέησόν μου τὸν υἱόν, ὅτι σεληνιάζεται καὶ κακῶς πάσχει· πολλάκις γὰρ πίπτει εἰς τὸ πῦρ καὶ πολλάκις εἰς τὸ ὕδωρ. καὶ προσήνεγκα αὐτὸν τοῖς μαθηταῖς σου, καὶ οὐκ ἠδυνήθησαν αὐτὸν θεραπεῦσαι. ἀποκριθεὶς δὲ ὁ Ἰησοῦς εἶπεν, Ὦ γενεὰ ἄπιστος καὶ διεστραμμένη, ἕως πότε μεθ' ὑμῶν ἔσομαι; ἕως πότε ἀνέξομαι ὑμῶν; φέρετέ μοι αὐτὸν ὧδε. καὶ ἐπετίμησεν αὐτῷ ὁ Ἰησοῦς, καὶ ἐξῆλθεν ἀπ' αὐτοῦ τὸ δαιμόνιον· καὶ ἐθεραπεύθη ὁ παῖς ἀπὸ τῆς ὥρας ἐκείνης. Τότε προσελθόντες οἱ μαθηταὶ τῷ Ἰησοῦ κατ' ἰδίαν εἶπον, Διὰ τί ἡμεῖς οὐκ ἠδυνήθημεν ἐκβαλεῖν αὐτό; ὁ δὲ λέγει αὐτοῖς, Διὰ τὴν ἀπιστίαν ὑμῶν· ἀμὴν

Cap. XVII. 2. See v. 16.
12. ἐποίησαν ἐν αὐτῷ] Is. v. 4 מַה לַּעֲשׂוֹת לְכַרְמִי וְלֹא עָשִׂיתִי בּוֹ

38 MATTHEW, XVII. 21—XVIII. 7.

γὰρ λέγω ὑμῖν, ἐὰν ἔχητε πίστιν ὡς κόκκον σινάπεως, ἐρεῖτε τῷ ὄρει τούτῳ, Μετάβα ἔνθεν ἐκεῖ, καὶ μεταβήσεται, καὶ οὐδὲν [ἀδυνα-
21 τήσει] ὑμῖν. τοῦτο δὲ τὸ γένος οὐκ ἐκπορεύεται εἰ μὴ *ἐν προσευχῇ καὶ νηστείᾳ.*
22 Ἀναστρεφομένων δὲ αὐτῶν ἐν τῇ Γαλιλαίᾳ εἶπεν αὐτοῖς ὁ Ἰησοῦς, Μέλλει ὁ υἱὸς τοῦ ἀνθρώπου παραδίδοσθαι εἰς χεῖρας
23 ἀνθρώπων, καὶ ἀποκτενοῦσιν αὐτὸν, καὶ τῇ τρίτῃ ἡμέρᾳ ἐγερθήσεται. καὶ ἐλυπήθησαν σφόδρα.
24 Ἐλθόντων δὲ αὐτῶν εἰς Καφαρναοὺμ προσῆλθον οἱ τὰ δίδραχμα λαμβάνοντες τῷ Πέτρῳ καὶ εἶπαν, Ὁ διδάσκαλος ὑμῶν
25 οὐ τελεῖ τὰ δίδραχμα; λέγει, Ναί. καὶ ἐλθόντα εἰς τὴν οἰκίαν προέφθασεν αὐτὸν ὁ Ἰησοῦς λέγων, Τί σοι δοκεῖ, Σίμων; οἱ βασιλεῖς τῆς γῆς ἀπὸ τίνων λαμβάνουσιν τέλη ἢ κῆνσον; ἀπὸ τῶν
26 υἱῶν αὐτῶν ἢ ἀπὸ τῶν ἀλλοτρίων; λέγει αὐτῷ, Ἀπὸ τῶν ἀλλοτρίων. ἔφη αὐτῷ ὁ Ἰησοῦς, Ἄρα γε ἐλεύθεροί εἰσιν οἱ υἱοί.
27 ἵνα δὲ μὴ σκανδαλίσωμεν αὐτοὺς, πορευθεὶς εἰς θάλασσαν βάλε ἄγκιστρον καὶ τὸν ἀναβάντα πρῶτον ἰχθὺν ἆρον, καὶ ἀνοίξας τὸ στόμα αὐτοῦ εὑρήσεις στατῆρα· ἐκεῖνον λαβὼν δὸς αὐτοῖς [ἀντὶ] ἐμοῦ καὶ σοῦ.

CAP.
18 Ἐν ἐκείνῃ τῇ ὥρᾳ προσῆλθον οἱ μαθηταὶ τῷ Ἰησοῦ λέγοντες,
2 Τίς ἄρα μείζων ἐστὶν ἐν τῇ βασιλείᾳ τῶν οὐρανῶν; καὶ προσ-
3 καλεσάμενος παιδίον ἔστησεν αὐτὸ ἐν μέσῳ αὐτῶν καὶ εἶπεν, Ἀμὴν λέγω ὑμῖν, ἐὰν μὴ [στραφῆτε] καὶ γένησθε ὡς τὰ παιδία,
4 οὐ μὴ εἰσέλθητε εἰς τὴν βασιλείαν τῶν οὐρανῶν. ὅστις οὖν ταπεινώσει ἑαυτὸν ὡς τὸ παιδίον τοῦτο, οὗτός ἐστιν [ὁ μείζων]
5 ἐν τῇ βασιλείᾳ τῶν οὐρανῶν. καὶ ὃς ἂν δέξηται ἓν παιδίον τοι-
6 οῦτον *ἐπὶ τῷ ὀνόματί* μου, ἐμὲ δέχεται. ὃς δ᾿ ἂν σκανδαλίσῃ ἕνα τῶν μικρῶν τούτων *τῶν πιστευόντων εἰς ἐμὲ,* συμφέρει αὐτῷ ἵνα κρεμασθῇ μύλος ὀνικὸς *εἰς τὸν τράχηλον* αὐτοῦ καὶ κατα-
7 ποντισθῇ ἐν τῷ πελάγει τῆς θαλάσσης. Οὐαὶ τῷ κόσμῳ *ἀπὸ τῶν σκανδάλων·* ἀνάγκη γὰρ ἐλθεῖν τὰ σκάνδαλα, πλὴν οὐαὶ τῷ

---

27. Strange use of ἀντὶ: not found in V.A.: in which the word very rarely occurs.

Cap. XVIII. 3, v. 18. ἀμὴν only found three times in V.A., 1 Chr. xvi. 36, Neh. v. 13, viii. 8; and in these only to show the very word used. Elsewhere it is rendered by ἀληθῶς and γένοιτο, which comprise its two meanings as used by us severally at the end of Creed or Prayer, Ps. xli. 14, Jerem. xxviii. 6, Jerem. xi. 5.

5. ἐπὶ τῷ ὀνόματί μου] = עַל שְׁמִי.
7. σκάνδαλον V.A. passim for מוֹקֵשׁ from כָּשַׁל, "to stumble," e.g. Lev. xix. 14, and for מוֹקֵשׁ, "a springe," Judges viii. 27, "anything that catches the feet and upsets a man," or "makes him stumble." Lexicographers limit the use of the word to V.A. and N.T. ἀπὸ τ. σκ. for מִן "in consequence of:" or "because of." (vii. 16.)

MATTHEW, XVIII. 8—21.

ἀνθρώπῳ ἐκείνῳ δι' οὗ τὸ σκάνδαλον ἔρχεται. εἰ δὲ ἡ χείρ σου 8
ἢ ὁ πούς σου σκανδαλίζει σε, ἔκκοψον αὐτὸν καὶ βάλε ἀπὸ σοῦ·
καλόν σοι ἐστιν εἰσελθεῖν εἰς τὴν ζωὴν χωλὸν ἢ κυλλόν, ἢ δύο
χεῖρας ἢ δύο πόδας ἔχοντα βληθῆναι εἰς τὸ πῦρ τὸ αἰώνιον. καὶ 9
εἰ ὁ ὀφθαλμός σου σκανδαλίζει σε, ἔξελε αὐτὸν καὶ βάλε ἀπὸ
σοῦ· καλόν σοί ἐστιν μονόφθαλμον εἰς τὴν ζωὴν εἰσελθεῖν, ἢ δύο
ὀφθαλμοὺς ἔχοντα βληθῆναι *εἰς τὴν γέενναν τοῦ πυρός.* Ὁρᾶτε 10
μὴ καταφρονήσητε ἑνὸς τῶν μικρῶν τούτων· λέγω γὰρ ὑμῖν ὅτι
οἱ ἄγγελοι αὐτῶν διὰ παντὸς βλέπουσιν τὸ πρόσωπον τοῦ πατρός
μου τοῦ ἐν οὐρανοῖς. τί ὑμῖν δοκεῖ; ἐὰν γένηταί τινι ἀνθρώπῳ 12
ἑκατὸν πρόβατα καὶ πλανηθῇ ἓν ἐξ αὐτῶν, οὐχὶ ἀφήσει τὰ ἐνενήκοντα ἐννέα ἐπὶ τὰ ὄρη καὶ πορευθεὶς ζητεῖ τὸ πλανώμενον; καὶ 13
ἐὰν γένηται εὑρεῖν αὐτό, ἀμὴν λέγω ὑμῖν ὅτι χαίρει ἐπ' αὐτῷ
μᾶλλον ἢ ἐπὶ τοῖς ἐνενήκοντα ἐννέα τοῖς μὴ πεπλανημένοις.
οὕτως *οὐκ ἔστιν θέλημα ἔμπροσθεν* τοῦ πατρός μου τοῦ ἐν 14
οὐρανοῖς ἵνα ἀπόληται ἓν τῶν μικρῶν τούτων. Ἐὰν δὲ ἁμαρ- 15
τήσῃ ὁ ἀδελφός σου, ὕπαγε ἔλεγξον αὐτὸν *μεταξὺ σοῦ καὶ αὐτοῦ μόνου·* ἐάν σου ἀκούσῃ, ἐκέρδησας τὸν ἀδελφόν σου. ἐὰν 16
δὲ μὴ ἀκούσῃ, παράλαβε μετὰ σοῦ ἔτι ἕνα ἢ δύο, ἵνα ἐπὶ στόματος
δύο μαρτύρων ἢ τριῶν [σταθῇ πᾶν ῥῆμα]. ἐὰν δὲ παρακούσῃ 17
αὐτῶν, εἰπὲ τῇ ἐκκλησίᾳ· ἐὰν δὲ καὶ τῆς ἐκκλησίας παρακούσῃ,
ἔστω σοι ὥσπερ [ὁ ἐθνικὸς καὶ ὁ τελώνης]. Ἀμὴν λέγω ὑμῖν, 18
ὅσα ἂν δήσητε ἐπὶ τῆς γῆς ἔσται δεδεμένα ἐν οὐρανῷ, καὶ ὅσα ἐὰν
λύσητε ἐπὶ τῆς γῆς ἔσται λελυμένα ἐν οὐρανῷ. Πάλιν λέγω ὑμῖν 19
ὅτι ἐὰν δύο συμφωνήσουσιν ἐξ ὑμῶν ἐπὶ τῆς γῆς περὶ [παντὸς]
πράγματος οὗ ἐὰν αἰτήσωνται, γενήσεται αὐτοῖς παρὰ τοῦ πατρός
μου τοῦ ἐν οὐρανοῖς. οὗ γάρ εἰσιν δύο ἢ τρεῖς *συνηγμένοι εἰς τὸ 20
ἐμὸν ὄνομα,* ἐκεῖ εἰμὶ ἐν μέσῳ αὐτῶν.

Τότε προσελθὼν ὁ Πέτρος εἶπεν αὐτῷ, Κύριε, ποσάκις ἁμαρ- 21
τήσει εἰς ἐμὲ ὁ ἀδελφός μου καὶ ἀφήσω αὐτῷ; ἕως ἑπτάκις;

---

8. As the Hebrews had no compara-
tive form, so we meet the same omission
in V.A. as here. καλόν...ἢ = טוֹב מִן.
Ps. cxviii. 8, ἀγαθὸν πεποιθέναι ἐπὶ Κύριον ἢ ἐπ' ἄνθρωπον. Tob. iii. 6, λυσιτελεῖ
μοι ἀποθανεῖν ἢ ζῆν, which exactly parallels L. xvii. 2, L. xviii. 14, οὗτος κατέβη
δεδικαιωμένος ἢ ἐκεῖνος.

12. ἀφίημι, "send away, let go, quit
hold of, let alone," easily slides into
"leave," a constant sense of it in V.A.
and N.T., e.g. xxiii. 38, xxiv. 2, Mk. xii.
19, 21, xiv. 50, John x. 12. In Exod. ix.
21 V.A. has ἀφῆκε for וַיַּעֲזֹב and Ruth ii.

16, 2 Sam. xx. 3 אֲשֶׁר הִנִּיחַ, ἃς ἀφῆκε,
"which he had left to keep the house."

14. θέλημα = εὐδοκία = δεκτὸν = רָצוֹן,
xi. 26. Ps. xix. 15, יִהְיוּ לְרָצוֹן לְפָנֶיךָ,
ἔσονται εἰς εὐδοκίαν (i.e. ἔσονται δεκτὸν or
θέλημα) ἔμπροσθέν σου, V.A. Hence
we may infer the process by which the
expression οὐκ ἔστι θελ. ἔμπρ. τ. πατρὸς
came into our text.

16. Every thing may be settled.

20. The exact parallel to this is found
in the Hebrew יְהִי לְשֵׁם יְיָ, Isai. lx. 9
(V.A. διὰ τὸ ὄνομα) and Jerem. iii. 17.

22 λέγει αὐτῷ ὁ Ἰησοῦς, Οὐ λέγω σοι ἕως ἑπτάκις, ἀλλὰ ἕως ἑβ-
23 δομηκοντάκις ἑπτά. διὰ τοῦτο ὡμοιώθη ἡ βασιλεία τῶν οὐρανῶν
ἀνθρώπῳ βασιλεῖ, ὃς ἠθέλησεν συνᾶραι λόγον μετὰ τῶν δούλων
24 αὐτοῦ. ἀρξαμένου δὲ αὐτοῦ συναίρειν, προσήχθη αὐτῷ εἷς ὀφει-
25 λέτης μυρίων ταλάντων. [μὴ] ἔχοντος δὲ αὐτοῦ ἀποδοῦναι ἐκέλευσεν αὐτὸν ὁ κύριος πραθῆναι καὶ τὴν γυναῖκα αὐτοῦ καὶ τὰ
26 τέκνα καὶ πάντα ὅσα ἔχει, καὶ ἀποδοθῆναι. πεσὼν οὖν ὁ δοῦλος
προσεκύνει αὐτῷ λέγων, Μακροθύμησον ἐπ᾽ ἐμοὶ, καὶ πάντα
27 ἀποδώσω. σπλαγχνισθεὶς δὲ ὁ κύριος τοῦ δούλου ἐκείνου ἀπέ-
28 λυσεν αὐτὸν, καὶ τὸ δάνειον ἀφῆκεν αὐτῷ. ἐξελθὼν δὲ ὁ δοῦλος
ἐκεῖνος εὗρεν ἕνα τῶν συνδούλων αὐτοῦ ὃς ὤφειλεν αὐτῷ ἑκατὸν
δηνάρια, καὶ κρατήσας αὐτὸν ἔπνιγεν λέγων, Ἀπόδος εἴ τι ὀφεί-
29 λεις. πεσὼν οὖν ὁ σύνδουλος αὐτοῦ παρεκάλει αὐτὸν λέγων,
30 Μακροθύμησον ἐπ᾽ ἐμὲ, καὶ ἀποδώσω σοι. ὁ δὲ οὐκ ἤθελεν, ἀλλὰ
ἀπελθὼν ἔβαλεν αὐτὸν εἰς φυλακὴν ἕως ἀποδῷ τὸ ὀφειλόμενον.
31 ἰδόντες οὖν οἱ σύνδουλοι αὐτοῦ τὰ γενόμενα ἐλυπήθησαν σφόδρα,
32 καὶ ἐλθόντες διεσάφησαν τῷ κυρίῳ πάντα τὰ γενόμενα. τότε
προσκαλεσάμενος αὐτὸν ὁ κύριος αὐτοῦ λέγει αὐτῷ, Δοῦλε πονηρὲ,
πᾶσαν τὴν ὀφειλὴν ἐκείνην ἀφῆκά σοι, ἐπεὶ παρεκάλεσάς με·
33 οὐκ ἔδει καὶ σὲ ἐλεῆσαι τὸν σύνδουλόν σου, ὡς κἀγὼ σὲ ἠλέησα;
34 καὶ ὀργισθεὶς ὁ κύριος αὐτοῦ παρέδωκεν αὐτὸν τοῖς βασανισταῖς
35 ἕως οὗ ἀποδῷ πᾶν τὸ ὀφειλόμενον. οὕτως καὶ ὁ πατήρ μου ὁ
οὐράνιος ποιήσει ὑμῖν, ἐὰν μὴ ἀφῆτε ἕκαστος τῷ ἀδελφῷ αὐτοῦ
ἀπὸ τῶν καρδιῶν ὑμῶν.

CAP. 19

Καὶ ἐγένετο ὅτε ἐτέλεσεν ὁ Ἰησοῦς τοὺς λόγους τούτους, μετῆρεν ἀπὸ τῆς Γαλιλαίας καὶ ἦλθεν εἰς τὰ ὅρια τῆς Ἰουδαίας πέραν
2 τοῦ Ἰορδάνου. καὶ ἠκολούθησαν αὐτῷ ὄχλοι πολλοί, καὶ ἐθεράπευσεν αὐτοὺς ἐκεῖ.

3 Καὶ προσῆλθον αὐτῷ Φαρισαῖοι πειράζοντες αὐτὸν καὶ λέγοντες, *Εἰ ἔξεστιν* ἀπολῦσαι τὴν γυναῖκα αὐτοῦ κατὰ πᾶσαν
4 αἰτίαν; ὁ δὲ ἀποκριθεὶς εἶπεν, Οὐκ ἀνέγνωτε ὅτι ὁ ποιήσας
5 ἀπ᾽ ἀρχῆς ἄρσεν καὶ θῆλυ ἐποίησεν αὐτούς; καὶ εἶπεν, Ἕνεκα
τούτου καταλείψει ἄνθρωπος τὸν πατέρα καὶ τὴν μητέρα καὶ
κολληθήσεται τῇ γυναικὶ αὐτοῦ, καὶ *ἔσονται οἱ δύο εἰς σάρκα
6 μίαν.* ὥστε οὐκέτι εἰσὶν δύο ἀλλὰ σὰρξ μία. ὃ οὖν ὁ Θεὸς
7 συνέζευξεν, ἄνθρωπος μὴ χωριζέτω. λέγουσιν αὐτῷ, Τί οὖν Μω-
8 σῆς ἐνετείλατο δοῦναι βιβλίον ἀποστασίου καὶ ἀπολῦσαι; λέγει
αὐτοῖς, *Ὅτι* Μωσῆς *πρὸς* τὴν σκληροκαρδίαν ὑμῶν ἐπέ-
τρεψεν ὑμῖν ἀπολῦσαι τὰς γυναῖκας ὑμῶν· ἀπ᾽ ἀρχῆς δὲ οὐ

Cap. XIX. 8. πρ. τ. σκ.] As we say, "for the hardness of your heart."

γέγονεν οὕτως. λέγω δὲ ὑμῖν, ὃς ἂν ἀπολύσῃ τὴν γυναῖκα αὐτοῦ 9
μὴ ἐπὶ πορνείᾳ καὶ γαμήσῃ ἄλλην, μοιχᾶται, καὶ ὁ ἀπολελυμένην
γαμήσας μοιχᾶται. λέγουσιν αὐτῷ οἱ μαθηταί, Εἰ οὕτως ἐστὶν 10
[ἡ αἰτία] τοῦ ἀνθρώπου μετὰ τῆς γυναικὸς, οὐ συμφέρει γαμῆσαι.
ὁ δὲ εἶπεν αὐτοῖς, Οὐ πάντες [χωροῦσιν] τὸν λόγον ἀλλ' οἷς δέ- 11
δοται. εἰσὶν γὰρ εὐνοῦχοι οἵτινες ἐκ κοιλίας μητρὸς ἐγεννήθησαν 12
οὕτως, καί εἰσιν εὐνοῦχοι οἵτινες εὐνουχίσθησαν ὑπὸ τῶν ἀνθρώπων, καί εἰσιν εὐνοῦχοι οἵτινες εὐνούχισαν ἑαυτοὺς διὰ τὴν βασιλείαν τῶν οὐρανῶν. ὁ δυνάμενος χωρεῖν χωρείτω.

Τότε προσηνέχθησαν αὐτῷ παιδία, ἵνα τὰς χεῖρας ἐπιθῇ αὐτοῖς 13
καὶ προσεύξηται· οἱ δὲ μαθηταὶ ἐπετίμησαν αὐτοῖς. ὁ δὲ Ἰησοῦς 14
εἶπεν, Ἄφετε τὰ παιδία καὶ μὴ κωλύετε αὐτὰ ἐλθεῖν πρός μέ·
τῶν γὰρ τοιούτων ἐστὶν ἡ βασιλεία τῶν οὐρανῶν. καὶ ἐπιθεὶς τὰς 15
χεῖρας αὐτοῖς ἐπορεύθη ἐκεῖθεν.

Καὶ ἰδοὺ [εἷς] προσελθὼν αὐτῷ εἶπεν, Διδάσκαλε, τί ἀγαθὸν 16
ποιήσω ἵνα σχῶ ζωὴν αἰώνιον; ὁ δὲ εἶπεν αὐτῷ, Τί με ἐρωτᾷς 17
περὶ τοῦ ἀγαθοῦ; εἷς ἐστιν ὁ ἀγαθός. εἰ δὲ θέλεις εἰς τὴν ζωὴν
εἰσελθεῖν, τήρει τὰς ἐντολάς. λέγει αὐτῷ, Ποίας; ὁ δὲ Ἰησοῦς 18
εἶπεν, Τὸ * οὐ φονεύσεις, οὐ μοιχεύσεις, οὐ κλέψεις, οὐ ψευδο-
μαρτυρήσεις,* τίμα τὸν πατέρα καὶ τὴν μητέρα, καὶ ἀγαπήσεις 19
τὸν πλησίον σου ὡς σεαυτόν. λέγει αὐτῷ ὁ νεανίσκος, Πάντα 20
ταῦτα ἐφύλαξα· τί ἔτι ὑστερῶ; ἔφη αὐτῷ ὁ Ἰησοῦς, Εἰ θέλεις 21
τέλειος εἶναι, ὕπαγε πώλησόν σου τὰ ὑπάρχοντα καὶ δὸς τοῖς
πτωχοῖς, καὶ ἕξεις θησαυρὸν ἐν οὐρανοῖς, καὶ δεῦρο ἀκολούθει μοι.
ἀκούσας δὲ ὁ νεανίσκος ἀπῆλθεν λυπούμενος· ἦν γὰρ ἔχων κτή- 22
ματα πολλά.

Ὁ δὲ Ἰησοῦς εἶπεν τοῖς μαθηταῖς αὐτοῦ, Ἀμὴν λέγω ὑμῖν ὅτι 23
πλούσιος δυσκόλως εἰσελεύσεται εἰς τὴν βασιλείαν τῶν οὐρανῶν.
πάλιν δὲ λέγω ὑμῖν, εὐκοπώτερόν ἐστιν κάμηλον διὰ τρυπήματος 24
ῥαφίδος εἰσελθεῖν ἢ πλούσιον εἰς τὴν βασιλείαν τῶν οὐρανῶν.
ἀκούσαντες δὲ οἱ μαθηταὶ ἐξεπλήσσοντο σφόδρα λέγοντες, Τίς ἄρα 25
δύναται σωθῆναι; ἐμβλέψας δὲ ὁ Ἰησοῦς εἶπεν αὐτοῖς, Παρὰ 26
ἀνθρώποις τοῦτο ἀδύνατόν ἐστιν, παρὰ δὲ Θεῷ πάντα δυνατά.

10. αἰτία] Only instance of this sense in N.T. None in V.A.

18. לֹא תִרְצָח. Same in LXX. A strong example of Hebr. use of Future for Imperative: as in English also, "Thou shalt not kill:" apparently, but not really: for "*shall*" *there* is not *future* at all. But the Greek future form has no possibility of such double meaning as Hebr. and Engl. have. The expression in text is a Hebrew idiom turned word for word into Greek, intelligible to Orientals, but at variance with the grammar and genius of the language.

23. δυσκόλως, "with hard effort," "with reluctance," fits in with the young man's sorrow.

27 Τότε ἀποκριθεὶς ὁ Πέτρος εἶπεν αὐτῷ, Ἰδοὺ ἡμεῖς ἀφήκαμεν
28 πάντα καὶ ἠκολουθήσαμέν σοι· τί ἄρα ἔσται ἡμῖν; ὁ δὲ Ἰησοῦς
εἶπεν αὐτοῖς, Ἀμὴν λέγω ὑμῖν ὅτι ὑμεῖς οἱ ἀκολουθήσαντές μοι,
ἐν τῇ παλιγγενεσίᾳ, ὅταν καθίσῃ ὁ υἱὸς τοῦ ἀνθρώπου [ἐπὶ
θρόνου] δόξης αὐτοῦ, καθίσεσθε καὶ ὑμεῖς ἐπὶ δώδεκα θρόνους
29 κρίνοντες τὰς δώδεκα φυλὰς τοῦ Ἰσραήλ. καὶ πᾶς ὅστις ἀφῆκεν
ἀδελφοὺς ἢ ἀδελφὰς ἢ πατέρα ἢ μητέρα ἢ τέκνα ἢ ἀγροὺς ἢ οἰκίας
ἕνεκεν τοῦ ὀνόματός μου, πολλαπλασίονα λήμψεται καὶ ζωὴν
30 αἰώνιον κληρονομήσει. πολλοὶ δὲ ἔσονται πρῶτοι ἔσχατοι καὶ
CAP. ἔσχατοι πρῶτοι.
20 Ὁμοία γαρ ἐστιν ἡ βασιλεία τῶν οὐρανῶν ἀνθρώπῳ οἰκοδεσπότῃ,
ὅστις ἐξῆλθεν [ἅμα πρωὶ] μισθώσασθαι ἐργάτας εἰς τὸν ἀμπελῶνα
2 αὐτοῦ. συμφωνήσας δὲ μετὰ τῶν ἐργατῶν [ἐκ δηναρίου] τὴν
3 ἡμέραν ἀπέστειλεν αὐτοὺς εἰς τὸν ἀμπελῶνα αὐτοῦ. καὶ ἐξελθὼν
περὶ τρίτην ὥραν εἶδεν ἄλλους ἑστῶτας ἐν τῇ ἀγορᾷ ἀργούς·
4 κἀκείνοις εἶπεν, Ὑπάγετε καὶ ὑμεῖς εἰς τὸν ἀμπελῶνα, καὶ [ὃ ἐὰν ᾖ]
5 δίκαιον δώσω ὑμῖν. οἱ δὲ ἀπῆλθον. πάλιν δὲ ἐξελθὼν περὶ ἕκτην
6 καὶ ἐνάτην ὥραν ἐποίησεν ὡσαύτως. περὶ δὲ τὴν ἑνδεκάτην ἐξελθὼν
εὗρεν ἄλλους ἑστῶτας, καὶ λέγει αὐτοῖς, Τί ὧδε ἑστήκατε ὅλην τὴν
7 ἡμέραν ἀργοί; λέγουσιν αὐτῷ, Ὅτι οὐδεὶς ἡμᾶς ἐμισθώσατο. λέγει
8 αὐτοῖς, Ὑπάγετε καὶ ὑμεῖς εἰς τὸν ἀμπελῶνα. ὀψίας δὲ γενομένης
λέγει ὁ κύριος τοῦ ἀμπελῶνος τῷ ἐπιτρόπῳ αὐτοῦ, Κάλεσον τοὺς
ἐργάτας καὶ ἀπόδος αὐτοῖς τὸν μισθὸν ἀρξάμενος ἀπὸ τῶν ἐσχάτων
9 ἕως τῶν πρώτων. καὶ ἐλθόντες οἱ περὶ τὴν ἑνδεκάτην ὥραν ἔλαβον
10 ἀνὰ δηνάριον. καὶ ἐλθόντες οἱ πρῶτοι ἐνόμισαν ὅτι πλεῖον
11 [λήμψονται] καὶ ἔλαβον τὸ ἀνὰ δηνάριον καὶ αὐτοί. λαβόντες δὲ
12 ἐγόγγυζον κατὰ τοῦ οἰκοδεσπότου λέγοντες, Οὗτοι οἱ ἔσχατοι μίαν
ὥραν ἐποίησαν, καὶ ἴσους ἡμῖν αὐτοὺς ἐποίησας τοῖς βαστάσασιν
13 τὸ βάρος τῆς ἡμέρας καὶ τὸν καύσωνα; ὁ δὲ ἀποκριθεὶς εἶπεν ἑνὶ
14 αὐτῶν, Ἑταῖρε, οὐκ ἀδικῶ σε· οὐχὶ δηναρίου συνεφώνησάς μοι; ἆρον
τὸ σὸν καὶ ὕπαγε. θέλω δὲ τούτῳ τῷ ἐσχάτῳ δοῦναι ὡς καὶ σοί.
15 οὐκ ἔξεστίν μοι ὃ θέλω ποιῆσαι ἐν τοῖς ἐμοῖς; *εἰ ὁ ὀφθαλμός σου

28. Note change of case after ἐπί.
Cap. XX. 2. "With the men he found there who worked-at-a-denarius per day." ἐργ. ἐκ δ.] Have we any authority for such a rendering in class. authors? Schleusner cites cap. xxvii. 7, Acts i. 18. I see no parallel to this passage in them.
12. W. & W. suggest "have made one hour:" as if by an idiom, corresponding to our own in English: and cite Acts xv.

33, xviii. 23, xx. 3, and James iv. 13. Schl. quotes Ruth ii. 19 אָנָה עָשִׂית, τοῦ ἐποίησας; Semel in N.T.
15. Deut. xv. 9, רָעָה עֵינְךָ בְּאָחִיךָ. V.A. πονηρεύσηται ὀφθαλμός σου τῷ ἀδελφῷ σοῦ, "envy, grudge." Tobit iv. 7, I find no instances of πονηρὸς with this force in V.A. but in Apocr. Sir. xiv. 10, xxxi. 14.

πονηρός ἐστιν ὅτι ἐγὼ ἀγαθός εἰμι*; οὕτως ἔσονται οἱ ἔσχατοι 16 πρῶτοι καὶ οἱ πρῶτοι ἔσχατοι.

Καὶ ἀναβαίνων ὁ Ἰησοῦς εἰς Ἱεροσόλυμα παρέλαβεν τοὺς 17 δώδεκα κατ' ἰδίαν, καὶ ἐν τῇ ὁδῷ εἶπεν αὐτοῖς, Ἰδοὺ ἀναβαίνομεν 18 εἰς Ἱεροσόλυμα, καὶ ὁ υἱὸς τοῦ ἀνθρώπου παραδοθήσεται τοῖς ἀρχιερεῦσιν καὶ γραμματεῦσιν, καὶ κατακρινοῦσιν [αὐτὸν θανάτῳ] καὶ παραδώσουσιν αὐτὸν τοῖς ἔθνεσιν εἰς τὸ ἐμπαῖξαι καὶ μαστι- 19 γῶσαι καὶ σταυρῶσαι, καὶ τῇ τρίτῃ ἡμέρᾳ ἐγερθήσεται.

Τότε προσῆλθεν αὐτῷ ἡ μήτηρ τῶν υἱῶν Ζεβεδαίου μετὰ τῶν 20 υἱῶν αὐτῆς, προσκυνοῦσα καὶ αἰτοῦσά τι ἀπ' αὐτοῦ. ὁ δὲ 21 εἶπεν αὐτῇ, Τί θέλεις; λέγει αὐτῷ, [Εἰπὲ] ἵνα καθίσωσιν οὗτοι οἱ δύο υἱοί μου εἷς ἐκ δεξιῶν σου καὶ εἷς ἐξ εὐωνύμων σου ἐν τῇ βασιλείᾳ σου. ἀποκριθεὶς δὲ ὁ Ἰησοῦς εἶπεν, Οὐκ οἴδατε 22 [τί] αἰτεῖσθε. δύνασθε πιεῖν τὸ ποτήριον ὃ ἐγὼ μέλλω πίνειν; λέγουσιν αὐτῷ, Δυνάμεθα. λέγει αὐτοῖς, Τὸ μὲν ποτήριόν μου 23 πίεσθε, τὸ δὲ καθίσαι ἐκ δεξιῶν μου καὶ ἐξ εὐωνύμων, οὐκ ἔστιν ἐμὸν τοῦτο δοῦναι, ἀλλ' οἷς ἡτοίμασται ὑπὸ τοῦ πατρός μου. ἀκούσαντες δὲ οἱ δέκα ἠγανάκτησαν περὶ τῶν δύο ἀδελφῶν. ὁ 24 δὲ Ἰησοῦς προσκαλεσάμενος αὐτοὺς εἶπεν, Οἴδατε ὅτι οἱ ἄρχοντες 25 τῶν ἐθνῶν κατακυριεύουσιν αὐτῶν καὶ οἱ μεγάλοι κατεξουσιάζουσιν αὐτῶν. οὐχ οὕτως ἔσται ἐν ὑμῖν· ἀλλ' [ὃς ἐὰν] θέλῃ ὑμῶν 26 μέγας γενέσθαι, ἔστω ὑμῶν διάκονος, καὶ ὃς ἐὰν θέλῃ ἐν ὑμῖν 27 εἶναι πρῶτος, ἔστω ὑμῶν δοῦλος· ὥσπερ ὁ υἱὸς τοῦ ἀνθρώπου 28 οὐκ [ἦλθεν διακονηθῆναι,] ἀλλὰ διακονῆσαι καὶ δοῦναι τὴν ψυχὴν αὐτοῦ λύτρον ἀντὶ πολλῶν.

Καὶ ἐκπορευομένων αὐτῶν ἀπὸ Ἱεριχὼ ἠκολούθησεν αὐτῷ 29 ὄχλος πολύς. καὶ ἰδοὺ δύο τυφλοὶ καθήμενοι παρὰ τὴν ὁδόν, 30 ἀκούσαντες ὅτι Ἰησοῦς παράγει, ἔκραξαν λέγοντες, Κύριε, ἐλέησον ἡμᾶς, υἱὸς Δαυίδ. ὁ δὲ ὄχλος ἐπετίμησεν αὐτοῖς ἵνα [σιωπήσωσιν]· 31 οἱ δὲ μεῖζον ἔκραξαν λέγοντες, Κύριε, ἐλέησον ἡμᾶς, υἱὸς Δαυίδ. καὶ στὰς ὁ Ἰησοῦς [ἐφώνησεν] αὐτοὺς καὶ εἶπεν, Τί θέλετε 32 ποιήσω ὑμῖν; λέγουσιν αὐτῷ, Κύριε, ἵνα ἀνοιγῶσιν οἱ ὀφθαλμοὶ 33 ἡμῶν. σπλαγχνισθεὶς δὲ ὁ Ἰησοῦς ἥψατο τῶν ὀμμάτων αὐτῶν, 34 καὶ εὐθέως ἀνέβλεψαν καὶ ἠκολούθησαν αὐτῷ.

Καὶ ὅτε ἤγγισαν εἰς Ἱεροσόλυμα καὶ ἦλθον εἰς Βηθσφαγῆ CAP. 21 εἰς τὸ ὄρος τῶν ἐλαιῶν, τότε ὁ Ἰησοῦς ἀπέστειλεν δύο μαθητὰς λέγων αὐτοῖς, Πορεύεσθε εἰς τὴν κώμην τὴν ἀπέναντι ὑμῶν, καὶ 2

---

24. "About the two brothers."
25. "Lord it over them." "Keep them under and down by arbitrary power."
28. Extreme instance of inf. after verb intrans., answering to inf. with ל in Hebr.

εὐθέως εὑρήσετε ὄνον δεδεμένην καὶ πῶλον μετ' αὐτῆς· λύσαντες
3 ἀγετέ μοι. καὶ ἐάν τις ὑμῖν εἴπῃ τι, ἐρεῖτε ὅτι ὁ Κύριος αὐτῶν
4 χρείαν ἔχει· εὐθέως δὲ ἀποστελεῖ αὐτούς. [τοῦτο δὲ γέγονεν
5 ἵνα πληρωθῇ] τὸ ῥηθὲν διὰ τοῦ προφήτου λέγοντος, Εἴπατε τῇ
θυγατρὶ Σιών, Ἰδοὺ ὁ βασιλεύς σου ἔρχεταί σοι πραΰς, ἐπιβε-
6 βηκὼς ἐπὶ ὄνον καὶ ἐπὶ πῶλον υἱὸν ὑποζυγίου. πορευθέντες δὲ
οἱ μαθηταὶ καὶ ποιήσαντες καθὼς συνέταξεν αὐτοῖς ὁ Ἰησοῦς,
7 ἤγαγον τὴν ὄνον καὶ τὸν πῶλον, καὶ ἐπέθηκαν ἐπ' αὐτῶν τὰ
8 ἱμάτια, καὶ ἐπεκάθισεν ἐπάνω αὐτῶν. [ὁ δὲ πλεῖστος ὄχλος]
ἔστρωσαν ἑαυτῶν τὰ ἱμάτια ἐν τῇ ὁδῷ, ἄλλοι δὲ ἔκοπτον κλάδους
9 ἀπὸ τῶν δένδρων καὶ ἐστρώννυον ἐν τῇ ὁδῷ. οἱ δὲ ὄχλοι οἱ
προάγοντες αὐτὸν καὶ οἱ ἀκολουθοῦντες ἔκραζον λέγοντες, *Ὡσαννὰ*
τῷ υἱῷ Δαυίδ, εὐλογημένος ὁ ἐρχόμενος ἐν ὀνόματι Κυρίου,

Cap. XXI. 5. Quotation from V.A. יָבוֹא לָךְ, not אֵלַיִךְ, which may possibly account for σοι; literally "Thy King shall come for thee," "Thou shalt see thy King come." לָךְ is generally rendered by σοι in V.A., whether it express "motion towards," or not.

9. Ps. cxviii. 25, אָנָּא יְהוָה הוֹשִׁיעָה נָּא. V.A. ὦ Κύριε σῶσον δή. "Hosanna" = "O save us, we pray Thee;" "O be Thou our Saviour." They applied to Jesus, whether consciously or not, the words of the Messianic Psalm, and hailed Him "Son of David," "King," "Saviour." How are we to account for the dative τῷ υἱῷ Δ.? We are expressly told they used *these very words*. Can it be, as it were, an ascription to Jesus—recognized as the Son of David, the true Messiah—of his Attribute of Saviour? Or were they possibly, in their ignorance of Hebrew, unaware of the exact force of the word, and thought of it only as an Act of Adoration, a Form of Praise—as unlearned Christians generally now-a-days—equivalent to "Honour," "Glory," "Praise," to the Son of David? Grimm translates ὡσ., σῶσον δή, by "propitius sis." And then, forgetting that both הוֹשִׁיעָה and σῶσον are transitive, and require an accusative after them, renders ὡσ. τῷ υἱῷ Δ. "propitius sis filio Davidis," i. e. "Messiæ," which is untenable.

There is another difficulty in the words ἐν τοῖς ὑψ.; not very great if we adopt the suggestion above of ὡσαννὰ being used with no very distinct idea of its real meaning: for then the phrase, in their mouths, would be much the same as Ps. cxlviii. 1, הַלְלוּיָהּ בַּמְּרוֹמִים, αἰνεῖτε K. ἐν τοῖς ὑψίστοις, V.A.

If however we are to suppose them to have used the word with full understanding of its true meaning, then it becomes exceedingly difficult to connect ἐν τοῖς ὑψίστοις with it and explain it rightly. "Be Thou our Saviour in Heaven above," taking ἐ. τ. ὑ. = בַּמְּרוֹמִים, is scarcely satisfactory.

May we hazard the interpretation, "Save us by the Most High," i.e. "in the name of the Most High"? Ps. liv. 3, אֱלֹהִים בְּשִׁמְךָ הוֹשִׁיעֵנִי, Ὁ Θεός, ἐν τῷ ὀνόματί σου σῶσόν με, V.A. Now עֶלְיוֹן, V.A. ὕψιστος, "Most High," is one of the Names of God, by which He is addressed and invoked. Ps. ix. 2, lvi. 2, xcii. 1, xcvii. 9, עֶלְיוֹן יָהּ אַתָּה. In Dan. vii. 18, 22, 25, 27, we find עֶלְיוֹנִין in plural; V.A. ὕψιστος, without article, as Κύριος constantly: Eng. V. "The Most High;" corresponding in structure and character to אֱלֹהִים. Gesenius shows it to have been a name for God among the Phœnicians. If then the prayer הוֹשִׁיעָה בֵּאלֹהִים, "Save us in the name of God," "by the power of God," be possible; might not הוֹשִׁיעָה בָּעֶלְיוֹנִים be a possible form also, and ὡσαννὰ ἐν τοῖς ὑψίστοις its equivalent? I anticipate the obvious objection that we should, in that case, expect the singular and not the plural; and that עֶלְיוֹנִין is, in point of fact, rendered by ὕψιστος in V.A. But the frequency of literal word-for-word translations from Hebrew and Chaldee in

ὡσαννὰ ἐν τοῖς ὑψίστοις. καὶ εἰσελθόντος αὐτοῦ εἰς Ἱεροσόλυμα 10 ἐσείσθη πᾶσα ἡ πόλις λέγουσα, Τίς ἐστιν οὗτος; οἱ δὲ ὄχλοι 11 ἔλεγον, Οὗτός ἐστιν ὁ προφήτης Ἰησοῦς ὁ ἀπὸ Ναζαρὲθ τῆς Γαλιλαίας.

Καὶ εἰσῆλθεν Ἰησοῦς εἰς τὸ ἱερὸν τοῦ Θεοῦ, καὶ ἐξέβαλεν 12 πάντας τοὺς πωλοῦντας καὶ ἀγοράζοντας ἐν τῷ ἱερῷ, καὶ τὰς τραπέζας τῶν κολλυβιστῶν κατέστρεψεν καὶ τὰς καθέδρας τῶν πωλούντων τὰς περιστεράς, καὶ λέγει αὐτοῖς, Γέγραπται, Ὁ οἶκός 13 μου οἶκος προσευχῆς κληθήσεται, ὑμεῖς δὲ αὐτὸν ποιεῖτε σπήλαιον λῃστῶν. καὶ προσῆλθον αὐτῷ τυφλοὶ καὶ χωλοὶ ἐν τῷ ἱερῷ 14 καὶ ἐθεράπευσεν αὐτούς. ἰδόντες δὲ οἱ ἀρχιερεῖς καὶ οἱ γραμματεῖς 15 τὰ θαυμάσια ἃ ἐποίησεν καὶ τοὺς παῖδας τοὺς κράζοντας ἐν τῷ ἱερῷ καὶ λέγοντας, Ὡσαννὰ τῷ υἱῷ Δαυίδ, ἠγανάκτησαν καὶ εἶπαν 16 αὐτῷ, Ἀκούεις τί οὗτοι λέγουσιν; ὁ δὲ Ἰησοῦς λέγει αὐτοῖς, Ναί· οὐδέποτε ἀνέγνωτε ὅτι ἐκ στόματος νηπίων καὶ θηλαζόντων κατηρτίσω αἶνον; καὶ καταλιπὼν αὐτοὺς ἐξῆλθεν ἔξω τῆς πόλεως 17 εἰς Βηθανίαν, καὶ ηὐλίσθη ἐκεῖ.

Πρωΐας δὲ ἐπαναγαγὼν εἰς τὴν πόλιν ἐπείνασεν. καὶ ἰδὼν 18 συκῆν [μίαν] ἐπὶ τῆς ὁδοῦ ἦλθεν ἐπ' αὐτήν, καὶ οὐδὲν εὗρεν ἐν 19 αὐτῇ εἰ μὴ φύλλα μόνον, καὶ λέγει αὐτῇ, Οὐ μηκέτι ἐκ σοῦ καρπὸς γένηται *εἰς τὸν αἰῶνα.* καὶ ἐξηράνθη παραχρῆμα ἡ συκῆ. καὶ ἰδόντες οἱ μαθηταὶ ἐθαύμασαν λέγοντες, [Πῶς πα- 20 ραχρῆμα] ἐξηράνθη ἡ συκῆ; ἀποκριθεὶς δὲ ὁ Ἰησοῦς εἶπεν αὐτοῖς, 21 Ἀμὴν λέγω ὑμῖν, ἐὰν ἔχητε πίστιν καὶ μὴ διακριθῆτε, οὐ μόνον τὸ τῆς συκῆς ποιήσετε, ἀλλὰ κἂν τῷ ὄρει τούτῳ εἴπητε, Ἄρθητι καὶ βλήθητι εἰς τὴν θάλασσαν, γενήσεται· καὶ πάντα ὅσα ἐὰν 22 αἰτήσητε ἐν τῇ προσευχῇ πιστεύοντες λήμψεσθε.

Καὶ ἐλθόντι αὐτῷ εἰς τὸ ἱερόν, προσῆλθον αὐτῷ διδάσκοντι 23 οἱ ἀρχιερεῖς καὶ οἱ πρεσβύτεροι τοῦ λαοῦ λέγοντες, *Ἐν ποίᾳ ἐξουσίᾳ* ταῦτα ποιεῖς; καὶ τίς σοι ἔδωκεν τὴν ἐξουσίαν ταύτην; ἀποκριθεὶς δὲ ὁ Ἰησοῦς εἶπεν αὐτοῖς, Ἐρωτήσω ὑμᾶς κἀγὼ 24 *λόγον ἕνα,* ὃν ἐὰν εἴπητέ μοι, κἀγὼ ὑμῖν ἐρῶ *ἐν ποίᾳ ἐξουσίᾳ* ταῦτα ποιῶ. τὸ βάπτισμα τὸ Ἰωάννου πόθεν ἦν; ἐξ οὐρανοῦ 25 ἢ ἐξ ἀνθρώπων; οἱ δὲ διελογίζοντο ἐν ἑαυτοῖς λέγοντες, Ἐὰν 26 εἴπωμεν, Ἐξ οὐρανοῦ, ἐρεῖ ἡμῖν, Διὰ τί οὖν οὐκ ἐπιστεύσατε αὐτῷ;

the V.A.—the only witness to the practice of the time within our reach—suggests the possibility of such close clinging to the Hebrew form in a popular and ordinary Greek equivalent, even against analogy and strict preciseness and propriety of expression. See 1 Sam. xvii. 43 V.A. κατηράσατο τὸν Δαυὶδ ἐν τοῖς θεοῖς αὐτοῦ for יְקַלֵּל אֶת־דָּוִד בֵּאלֹהָיו, "he cursed David by (i.e. in the name of) his Gods."

12. τὸ ἱερόν] the sacred precinct; ὁ ναός, the Temple, the Sanctuary.

19. εἰς τὸν αἰῶνα = לְעוֹלָם.

ἐὰν δὲ εἴπωμεν, Ἐξ ἀνθρώπων, φοβούμεθα τὸν ὄχλον· πάντες γὰρ
27 ὡς προφήτην ἔχουσιν τὸν Ἰωάννην. καὶ ἀποκριθέντες τῷ Ἰησοῦ
εἶπον, Οὐκ οἴδαμεν. ἔφη αὐτοῖς καὶ αὐτός, Οὐδὲ ἐγὼ λέγω ὑμῖν
28 ἐν ποίᾳ ἐξουσίᾳ ταῦτα ποιῶ. Τί δὲ ὑμῖν δοκεῖ; ἄνθρωπος εἶχεν
δύο τέκνα, καὶ προσελθὼν τῷ πρώτῳ εἶπεν, Τέκνον, ὕπαγε σήμερον
29 ἐργάζου ἐν τῷ ἀμπελῶνι. ὁ δὲ ἀποκριθεὶς εἶπεν, Οὐ θέλω, ὕστερον
30 δὲ μεταμεληθεὶς ἀπῆλθεν. προσελθὼν δὲ τῷ ἑτέρῳ εἶπεν ὡσαύτως.
31 ὁ δὲ ἀποκριθεὶς εἶπεν, *Ἐγὼ* κύριε, καὶ οὐκ ἀπῆλθεν. τίς ἐκ τῶν
δύο ἐποίησεν τὸ θέλημα τοῦ πατρός; λέγουσιν, Ὁ πρῶτος. λέγει
αὐτοῖς ὁ Ἰησοῦς, Ἀμὴν λέγω ὑμῖν ὅτι οἱ τελῶναι καὶ αἱ πόρναι
32 προάγουσιν ὑμᾶς εἰς τὴν βασιλείαν τοῦ Θεοῦ. ἦλθεν γὰρ
Ἰωάννης πρὸς ὑμᾶς ἐν ὁδῷ δικαιοσύνης, καὶ οὐκ ἐπιστεύσατε
αὐτῷ· οἱ δὲ τελῶναι καὶ αἱ πόρναι ἐπίστευσαν αὐτῷ· ὑμεῖς
33 δὲ ἰδόντες οὐδὲ μετεμελήθητε ὕστερον [τοῦ πιστεῦσαι] αὐτῷ. Ἄλλην παραβολὴν ἀκούσατε. ἄνθρωπος ἦν οἰκοδεσπότης ὅστις
ἐφύτευσεν ἀμπελῶνα, καὶ φραγμὸν αὐτῷ περιέθηκεν καὶ ὤρυξεν
ἐν αὐτῷ ληνὸν καὶ ᾠκοδόμησεν πύργον, καὶ ἐξέδετο αὐτὸν γεωργοῖς,
34 καὶ ἀπεδήμησεν. ὅτε δὲ ἤγγισεν ὁ καιρὸς τῶν καρπῶν, ἀπέστειλεν
τοὺς δούλους αὐτοῦ πρὸς τοὺς γεωργοὺς λαβεῖν τοὺς καρποὺς αὐτοῦ.
35 καὶ λαβόντες οἱ γεωργοὶ τοὺς δούλους αὐτοῦ [ὃν μὲν] ἔδειραν, [ὃν
36 δὲ] ἀπέκτειναν, [ὃν δὲ] ἐλιθοβόλησαν. πάλιν ἀπέστειλεν ἄλλους
δούλους πλείονας τῶν πρώτων, καὶ ἐποίησαν αὐτοῖς ὡσαύτως.
37 ὕστερον δὲ ἀπέστειλεν πρὸς αὐτοὺς τὸν υἱὸν αὐτοῦ λέγων,
38 Ἐντραπήσονται τὸν υἱόν μου. οἱ δὲ γεωργοὶ ἰδόντες τὸν υἱὸν
εἶπον ἐν ἑαυτοῖς, Οὗτός ἐστιν ὁ κληρονόμος· δεῦτε ἀποκτείνωμεν
39 αὐτὸν καὶ σχῶμεν τὴν κληρονομίαν αὐτοῦ. καὶ λαβόντες
40 αὐτὸν ἐξέβαλον ἔξω τοῦ ἀμπελῶνος καὶ ἀπέκτειναν. ὅταν
οὖν ἔλθῃ ὁ κύριος τοῦ ἀμπελῶνος, τί ποιήσει τοῖς γεωργοῖς
41 ἐκείνοις; λέγουσιν αὐτῷ, Κακοὺς κακῶς ἀπολέσει αὐτούς,
καὶ τὸν ἀμπελῶνα ἐκδώσεται ἄλλοις γεωργοῖς, οἵτινες ἀποδώσουσιν
42 αὐτῷ τοὺς καρποὺς ἐν τοῖς καιροῖς αὐτῶν. λέγει αὐτοῖς ὁ Ἰησοῦς,
Οὐδέποτε ἀνέγνωτε ἐν ταῖς γραφαῖς, Λίθον ὃν ἀπεδοκίμασαν οἱ
οἰκοδομοῦντες, οὗτος ἐγενήθη *εἰς κεφαλὴν γωνίας* παρὰ Κυρίου

---

30. Probably = הִנֵּנִי = ἰδοὺ ἐγώ V.A. Gen. xxii. 1, 1 Sam. iii. 8.

42. κεφαλὴ γωνίας, V.A. for ראש פנה, Ps. cxviii. 22: ἀκρογωνιαῖον λίθον, Is. xxviii. 16. Can it mean "the keystone of the arch," "the top or head of the angle," "the crown of the pointed arch," that binds all together? See Eph. ii. 20, iv. 16, where the picture and description is quite that of a key-stone, συναρμολογοῦντα καὶ συμβιβάζοντα the whole structure. Warburton, in his *Crescent and Cross*, speaks of very ancient arches in Egypt, supposed to be as old as Joseph's time. Hence we may suppose the Jews not altogether unacquainted with the use and properties of the arch.

αὕτη] V.A. for זאת fem.

ἐγένετο *αὕτη,* καὶ ἔστιν θαυμαστὴ ἐν ὀφθαλμοῖς ἡμῶν; διὰ 43 τοῦτο λέγω ὑμῖν ὅτι ἀρθήσεται ἀφ' ὑμῶν ἡ βασιλεία τοῦ Θεοῦ καὶ δοθήσεται ἔθνει *ποιοῦντι τοὺς καρποὺς* αὐτῆς. καὶ ἀκούσαντες 45 οἱ ἀρχιερεῖς καὶ οἱ Φαρισαῖοι τὰς παραβολὰς αὐτοῦ ἔγνωσαν ὅτι περὶ αὐτῶν λέγει· καὶ ζητοῦντες αὐτὸν κρατῆσαι ἐφοβήθησαν 46 τοὺς ὄχλους, ἐπεὶ εἰς προφήτην αὐτὸν εἶχον.

CAP.
Καὶ ἀποκριθεὶς ὁ Ἰησοῦς πάλιν εἶπεν *ἐν παραβολαῖς* αὐ- 22 τοῖς λέγων, Ὡμοιώθη ἡ βασιλεία τῶν οὐρανῶν ἀνθρώπῳ βασιλεῖ, 2 ὅστις ἐποίησεν γάμους τῷ υἱῷ αὐτοῦ. καὶ ἀπέστειλεν τοὺς δούλους 3 αὐτοῦ [καλέσαι] τοὺς κεκλημένους εἰς τοὺς γάμους, καὶ οὐκ ἤθελον ἐλθεῖν. πάλιν ἀπέστειλεν ἄλλους δούλους λέγων, Εἴπατε τοῖς 4 κεκλημένοις, Ἰδοὺ τὸ ἄριστόν μου ἡτοίμακα, οἱ ταῦροί μου καὶ τὰ σιτιστὰ τεθυμένα, καὶ πάντα ἕτοιμα· δεῦτε εἰς τοὺς γάμους. οἱ δὲ 5 ἀμελήσαντες ἀπῆλθον, ὃς μὲν εἰς τὸν ἴδιον ἀγρόν, ὃς δὲ ἐπὶ τὴν ἐμπορίαν αὐτοῦ· οἱ δὲ λοιποὶ κρατήσαντες τοὺς δούλους αὐτοῦ 6 ὕβρισαν καὶ ἀπέκτειναν. ὁ δὲ βασιλεὺς ὠργίσθη, καὶ πέμψας τὰ 7 στρατεύματα αὐτοῦ ἀπώλεσεν τοὺς φονεῖς ἐκείνους καὶ τὴν πόλιν αὐτῶν ἐνέπρησεν. τότε λέγει τοῖς δούλοις αὐτοῦ, Ὁ μὲν γάμος 8 ἕτοιμός ἐστιν, οἱ δὲ κεκλημένοι οὐκ ἦσαν ἄξιοι. πορεύεσθε οὖν ἐπὶ 9 τὰς διεξόδους τῶν ὁδῶν, καὶ ὅσους ἐὰν εὕρητε καλέσατε εἰς τοὺς γάμους. καὶ ἐξελθόντες οἱ δοῦλοι ἐκεῖνοι εἰς τὰς ὁδοὺς συνήγαγον 10 πάντας ὅσους εὗρον, πονηρούς τε καὶ ἀγαθούς· καὶ ἐπλήσθη ὁ γάμος ἀνακειμένων. [εἰσελθὼν δὲ ὁ βασιλεὺς θεάσασθαι] τοὺς ἀνακει- 11 μένους εἶδεν ἐκεῖ ἄνθρωπον οὐκ ἐνδεδυμένον ἔνδυμα γάμου. καὶ 12 λέγει αὐτῷ, Ἑταῖρε, πῶς εἰσῆλθες ὧδε [μὴ] ἔχων ἔνδυμα γάμου; ὁ δὲ ἐφιμώθη. τότε ὁ βασιλεὺς εἶπεν τοῖς διακόνοις, Δήσαντες αὐτοῦ 13 πόδας καὶ χεῖρας ἐκβάλετε αὐτὸν εἰς τὸ σκότος τὸ ἐξώτερον· ἐκεῖ ἔσται ὁ κλαυθμὸς καὶ ὁ βρυγμὸς τῶν ὀδόντων. πολλοὶ γάρ εἰσιν 14 κλητοί, ὀλίγοι δὲ ἐκλεκτοί.

Τότε πορευθέντες οἱ Φαρισαῖοι [συμβούλιον ἔλαβον] ὅπως 15 αὐτὸν [παγιδεύσωσιν] ἐν λόγῳ. καὶ ἀποστέλλουσιν [αὐτῷ] τοὺς 16 μαθητὰς αὐτῶν μετὰ τῶν Ἡρωδιανῶν λέγοντες, Διδάσκαλε, οἴδαμεν ὅτι ἀληθὴς εἶ καὶ τὴν ὁδὸν τοῦ Θεοῦ ἐν ἀληθείᾳ διδάσκεις, καὶ οὐ μέλει σοι περὶ οὐδενός· οὐ γὰρ *βλέπεις εἰς πρόσωπον* ἀνθρώπων· εἰπὲ οὖν ἡμῖν τί σοι δοκεῖ· ἔξεστιν δοῦναι κῆνσον Καίσαρι ἢ οὔ; 17 γνοὺς δὲ ὁ Ἰησοῦς τὴν πονηρίαν αὐτῶν εἶπεν, Τί με πειράζετε, ὑπο- 18 κριταί; ἐπιδείξατέ μοι τὸ νόμισμα τοῦ κήνσου. οἱ δὲ προσήνεγκαν 19 αὐτῷ δηνάριον. καὶ λέγει αὐτοῖς, Τίνος ἡ εἰκὼν αὕτη καὶ ἡ ἐπι- 20 γραφή; λέγουσιν αὐτῷ, Καίσαρος. τότε λέγει αὐτοῖς, Ἀπόδοτε οὖν 21

Cap. XXII. 9. "Outlets or byways" (strict and minute details).

22 τὰ Καίσαρος Καίσαρι καὶ τὰ τοῦ Θεοῦ τῷ Θεῷ. καὶ ἀκούσαντες ἐθαύμασαν, καὶ ἀφέντες αὐτὸν ἀπῆλθαν.

23 Ἐν ἐκείνῃ τῇ ἡμέρᾳ προσῆλθον αὐτῷ Σαδδουκαῖοι, οἱ λέγοντες
24 [μὴ] εἶναι ἀνάστασιν, καὶ ἐπηρώτησαν αὐτὸν λέγοντες, Διδάσκαλε, Μωυσῆς εἶπεν, Ἐάν τις ἀποθάνῃ μὴ ἔχων τέκνα, ἐπιγαμβρεύσει ὁ ἀδελφὸς αὐτοῦ τὴν γυναῖκα αὐτοῦ καὶ ἀναστήσει σπέρμα τῷ
25 ἀδελφῷ αὐτοῦ. ἦσαν δὲ παρ' ἡμῖν ἑπτὰ ἀδελφοί· καὶ ὁ πρῶτος γήμας ἐτελεύτησεν, καὶ [μὴ] ἔχων σπέρμα ἀφῆκεν τὴν γυναῖκα
26 αὐτοῦ τῷ ἀδελφῷ αὐτοῦ. ὁμοίως καὶ ὁ δεύτερος καὶ ὁ τρίτος, ἕως
27 τῶν ἑπτά. ὕστερον δὲ πάντων ἀπέθανεν καὶ ἡ γυνή. ἐν τῇ ἀνα-
28 στάσει οὖν τίνος τῶν ἑπτὰ ἔσται γυνή; πάντες γὰρ ἔσχον αὐτήν.
29 ἀποκριθεὶς δὲ ὁ Ἰησοῦς εἶπεν αὐτοῖς, Πλανᾶσθε, [μὴ] εἰδότες τὰς
30 γραφὰς [μηδὲ] τὴν δύναμιν τοῦ Θεοῦ. ἐν γὰρ τῇ ἀναστάσει οὔτε γαμοῦσιν οὔτε γαμίζονται, ἀλλ' ὡς ἄγγελοι ἐν τῷ οὐρανῷ εἰσίν.
31 περὶ δὲ τῆς ἀναστάσεως τῶν νεκρῶν οὐκ ἀνέγνωτε τὸ ῥηθὲν ὑμῖν
32 ὑπὸ τοῦ Θεοῦ λέγοντος, Ἐγώ εἰμι ὁ Θεὸς Ἀβραὰμ καὶ ὁ Θεὸς Ἰσαὰκ
33 καὶ ὁ Θεὸς Ἰακώβ; οὐκ ἔστιν ὁ Θεὸς Θεὸς νεκρῶν ἀλλὰ ζώντων. καὶ ἀκούσαντες οἱ ὄχλοι ἐξεπλήσσοντο ἐπὶ τῇ διδαχῇ αὐτοῦ.

34 Οἱ δὲ Φαρισαῖοι ἀκούσαντες ὅτι ἐφίμωσεν τοὺς Σαδδουκαίους
35 συνήχθησαν ἐπὶ τὸ αὐτό, καὶ ἐπηρώτησεν εἷς ἐξ αὐτῶν νομικὸς πει-
36 ράζων αὐτόν, Διδάσκαλε, ποία ἐντολὴ μεγάλη ἐν τῷ νόμῳ; ὁ δὲ ἔφη
37 αὐτῷ, Ἀγαπήσεις Κύριον τὸν Θεόν σου *ἐν* ὅλῃ τῇ καρδίᾳ σου καὶ
38 *ἐν* ὅλῃ τῇ ψυχῇ σου καὶ *ἐν* ὅλῃ τῇ διανοίᾳ σου. αὕτη ἐστὶν ἡ
39 μεγάλη καὶ πρώτη ἐντολή. δευτέρα δὲ ὁμοία αὐτῇ, Ἀγαπήσεις τὸν
40 πλησίον σου ὡς σεαυτόν. ἐν ταύταις ταῖς δυσὶν ἐντολαῖς ὅλος ὁ νόμος κρέμαται καὶ οἱ προφῆται.

41 Συνηγμένων δὲ τῶν Φαρισαίων ἐπηρώτησεν αὐτοὺς ὁ Ἰησοῦς
42 λέγων, Τί ὑμῖν δοκεῖ περὶ τοῦ Χριστοῦ; τίνος υἱός ἐστιν; λέγουσιν
43 αὐτῷ, Τοῦ Δαυίδ. λέγει αὐτοῖς, Πῶς οὖν Δαυὶδ *ἐν* πνεύματι καλεῖ
44 αὐτὸν κύριον λέγων, Εἶπεν Κύριος τῷ κυρίῳ μου, Κάθου ἐκ δεξιῶν
45 μου ἕως ἂν θῶ τοὺς ἐχθρούς σου ὑποκάτω τῶν ποδῶν σου. εἰ οὖν
46 Δαυὶδ καλεῖ αὐτὸν κύριον, πῶς υἱὸς αὐτοῦ ἐστίν; καὶ οὐδεὶς ἐδύνατο ἀποκριθῆναι αὐτῷ *λόγον,* οὐδὲ ἐτόλμησέν τις ἀπ' ἐκείνης τῆς ἡμέρας ἐπερωτῆσαι αὐτὸν οὐκέτι.

CAP. 23 Τότε ὁ Ἰησοῦς ἐλάλησεν τοῖς ὄχλοις καὶ τοῖς μαθηταῖς αὐτοῦ
2 λέγων, Ἐπὶ τῆς Μωυσέως καθέδρας ἐκάθισαν οἱ γραμματεῖς καὶ οἱ
3 Φαρισαῖοι. πάντα οὖν ὅσα ἂν εἴπωσιν ὑμῖν ποιήσατε καὶ τηρεῖτε, κατὰ δὲ τὰ ἔργα αὐτῶν μὴ ποιεῖτε· λέγουσιν γὰρ καὶ οὐ ποιοῦσιν.

---

25. ἀφῆκεν] xviii. 12, xxiii. 38, xxiv. 2.   34. ἐπὶ τὸ αὐτό]=יַחְדָּו, "together," V.A. Deut. xxii. 5, Ps. ii. 2.

[δεσμεύουσιν] δὲ φορτία βαρέα καὶ ἐπιτιθέασιν ἐπὶ τοὺς ὤμους 4
τῶν ἀνθρώπων, τῷ δὲ δακτύλῳ αὐτῶν οὐ θέλουσιν κινῆσαι
αὐτά. πάντα δὲ τὰ ἔργα αὐτῶν ποιοῦσιν πρὸς τὸ θεαθῆναι τοῖς 5
ἀνθρώποις. πλατύνουσιν γὰρ τὰ φυλακτήρια αὐτῶν καὶ μεγαλύ-
νουσιν τὰ κράσπεδα, φιλοῦσιν δὲ τὴν πρωτοκλισίαν ἐν τοῖς δείπνοις 6
καὶ τὰς πρωτοκαθεδρίας ἐν ταῖς συναγωγαῖς καὶ τοὺς ἀσπασμοὺς ἐν 7
ταῖς ἀγοραῖς καὶ καλεῖσθαι ὑπὸ τῶν ἀνθρώπων ῥαββί. ὑμεῖς δὲ μὴ 8
κληθῆτε ῥαββί· εἷς γάρ ἐστιν ὑμῶν ὁ διδάσκαλος, πάντες δὲ ὑμεῖς
ἀδελφοί ἐστε. καὶ πατέρα μὴ καλέσητε ὑμῶν ἐπὶ τῆς γῆς· εἷς γάρ 9
ἐστιν ὁ πατὴρ ὑμῶν ὁ οὐράνιος. μηδὲ κληθῆτε καθηγηταί, ὅτι 10
καθηγητὴς ὑμῶν ἐστὶν εἷς ὁ Χριστός. [ὁ δὲ μείζων] ὑμῶν ἔσται 11
ὑμῶν διάκονος. ὅστις δὲ ὑψώσει ἑαυτὸν ταπεινωθήσεται, καὶ ὅστις 12
ταπεινώσει ἑαυτὸν ὑψωθήσεται.

Οὐαὶ δὲ ὑμῖν, γραμματεῖς καὶ Φαρισαῖοι ὑποκριταί, ὅτι κλείετε 13
τὴν βασιλείαν τῶν οὐρανῶν ἔμπροσθεν τῶν ἀνθρώπων· ὑμεῖς γὰρ
οὐκ εἰσέρχεσθε, οὐδὲ τοὺς εἰσερχομένους ἀφίετε εἰσελθεῖν. οὐαὶ ὑμῖν, 15
γραμματεῖς καὶ Φαρισαῖοι ὑποκριταί, ὅτι [περιάγετε τὴν θάλασσαν
καὶ τὴν ξηρὰν ποιῆσαι] ἕνα προσήλυτον, καὶ ὅταν γένηται, ποιεῖτε
αὐτὸν *υἱὸν γεέννης* διπλότερον ὑμῶν. οὐαὶ ὑμῖν, ὁδηγοὶ τυφλοὶ, 16
οἱ λέγοντες, Ὃς ἂν ὀμόσῃ *ἐν τῷ ναῷ,* οὐδέν ἐστιν· ὃς δ' ἂν ὀμόσῃ
ἐν τῷ χρυσῷ τοῦ ναοῦ ὀφείλει. μωροὶ καὶ τυφλοί, τίς γὰρ μείζων 17
ἐστίν, ὁ χρυσὸς ἢ ὁ ναὸς ὁ ἁγιάσας τὸν χρυσόν; καί, Ὃς ἂν ὀμόσῃ 18
ἐν τῷ θυσιαστηρίῳ, οὐδέν ἐστιν· ὃς δ' ἂν ὀμόσῃ *ἐν τῷ δώρῳ*
τῷ ἐπάνω αὐτοῦ, ὀφείλει. τυφλοί, τί γὰρ μεῖζον, τὸ δῶρον ἢ τὸ 19
θυσιαστήριον τὸ ἁγιάζον τὸ δῶρον; ὁ οὖν ὀμόσας ἐν τῷ θυσι- 20
αστηρίῳ ὀμνύει ἐν αὐτῷ καὶ ἐν πᾶσιν τοῖς ἐπάνω αὐτοῦ·
καὶ ὁ ὀμόσας ἐν τῷ ναῷ ὀμνύει ἐν αὐτῷ καὶ ἐν τῷ κατοι- 21
κήσαντι αὐτόν· καὶ ὁ ὀμόσας ἐν τῷ οὐρανῷ ὀμνύει ἐν τῷ 22
θρόνῳ τοῦ Θεοῦ καὶ ἐν τῷ καθημένῳ ἐπάνω αὐτοῦ. οὐαὶ ὑμῖν, 23
γραμματεῖς καὶ Φαρισαῖοι ὑποκριταί, ὅτι ἀποδεκατοῦτε τὸ ἡδύοσμον
καὶ τὸ ἄνηθον καὶ τὸ κύμινον, καὶ ἀφήκατε τὰ βαρύτερα τοῦ νόμου,
τὴν κρίσιν καὶ τὸ ἔλεος καὶ τὴν πίστιν. ταῦτα δὲ ἔδει ποιῆσαι
κἀκεῖνα μὴ ἀφεῖναι. ὁδηγοὶ τυφλοί, οἱ διϋλίζοντες τὸν κώνωπα, τὴν 24

Cap. XXIII. 11. Future for imperative, v. 48.
13. ἔμπροσθεν here for ἐναντίον, v. 16, and vice versâ, Mk. ii. 12. Gen. xxx. 30, לְפָנַי, "ante me," "ante meum adventum," V.A. ἐναντίον ἐμοῦ. L. i. 17, ἐνώπιον for ἔμπροσθεν; and vice versâ M. xxv. 32.

15. υἱὸν γ.] "Criminal," "reprobate," "felon." v. 22, "one of the Gehenna brood," "one of those who represent it and incur its penalties." בְּנֵי גֵּיהִנֹּם. Compare viii. 12, οἱ υ. τῆς βασιλείας, L. x. 6, υ. εἰρήνης. xx. 36, ἀναστάσεως, 2 Thess. ii. 3, ἀπωλείας.

G.

25 δὲ κάμηλον καταπίνοντες. οὐαὶ ὑμῖν, γραμματεῖς καὶ Φαρισαῖοι ὑποκριταί, ὅτι καθαρίζετε τὸ ἔξωθεν τοῦ ποτηρίου καὶ τῆς παρο-
26 ψίδος, ἔσωθεν δὲ γέμουσιν [ἐξ] ἁρπαγῆς καὶ ἀκρασίας. Φαρισαῖε τυφλέ, καθάρισον πρῶτον τὸ ἐντὸς τοῦ ποτηρίου, ἵνα γένηται καὶ τὸ
27 ἐκτὸς αὐτοῦ καθαρόν. οὐαὶ ὑμῖν, γραμματεῖς καὶ Φαρισαῖοι ὑποκριταί, ὅτι παρομοιάζετε τάφοις κεκονιαμένοις, οἵτινες ἔξωθεν μὲν φαίνονται ὡραῖοι, ἔσωθεν δὲ γέμουσιν ὀστέων νεκρῶν καὶ πάσης ἀκαθαρσίας.
28 οὕτως καὶ ὑμεῖς ἔξωθεν μὲν φαίνεσθε τοῖς ἀνθρώποις δίκαιοι, ἔσωθεν
29 δέ ἐστε μεστοὶ ὑποκρίσεως καὶ ἀνομίας. οὐαὶ ὑμῖν, γραμματεῖς καὶ Φαρισαῖοι ὑποκριταί, ὅτι οἰκοδομεῖτε τοὺς τάφους τῶν προφητῶν
30 καὶ κοσμεῖτε τὰ μνημεῖα τῶν δικαίων, καὶ λέγετε, Εἰ ἤμεθα ἐν ταῖς ἡμέραις τῶν πατέρων ἡμῶν, οὐκ ἂν ἤμεθα [αὐτῶν κοινωνοὶ ἐν τῷ
31 αἵματι] τῶν προφητῶν. ὥστε μαρτυρεῖτε ἑαυτοῖς ὅτι υἱοί ἐστε τῶν
32 φονευσάντων τοὺς προφήτας. καὶ ὑμεῖς πληρώσατε τὸ μέτρον τῶν
33 πατέρων ὑμῶν. ὄφεις, γεννήματα ἐχιδνῶν, πῶς φύγητε ἀπὸ τῆς
34 κρίσεως τῆς γεέννης; διὰ τοῦτο ἰδοὺ ἐγὼ ἀποστέλλω πρὸς ὑμᾶς προφήτας καὶ σοφοὺς καὶ γραμματεῖς· ἐξ αὐτῶν ἀποκτενεῖτε καὶ σταυρώσετε, καὶ ἐξ αὐτῶν μαστιγώσετε ἐν ταῖς συναγωγαῖς ὑμῶν
35 καὶ διώξετε ἀπὸ πόλεως εἰς πόλιν· ὅπως ἔλθῃ ἐφ᾽ ὑμᾶς πᾶν αἷμα δίκαιον ἐκχυννόμενον ἐπὶ τῆς γῆς ἀπὸ τοῦ αἵματος Ἄβελ τοῦ δικαίου ἕως τοῦ αἵματος Ζαχαρίου υἱοῦ Βαραχίου, ὃν ἐφονεύσατε
36 μεταξὺ τοῦ ναοῦ καὶ τοῦ θυσιαστηρίου. ἀμὴν λέγω ὑμῖν, ἥξει πάντα
37 ταῦτα ἐπὶ τὴν γενεὰν ταύτην. Ἰερουσαλὴμ Ἰερουσαλήμ, ἡ ἀποκτείνουσα τοὺς προφήτας καὶ λιθοβολοῦσα τοὺς ἀπεσταλμένους πρὸς αὐτήν, ποσάκις ἠθέλησα ἐπισυναγαγεῖν τὰ τέκνα σου, ὃν τρόπον ὄρνις ἐπισυνάγει τὰ νοσσία ὑπὸ τὰς πτέρυγας αὐτῆς, καὶ οὐκ
38 ἠθελήσατε. ἰδοὺ ἀφίεται ὑμῖν ὁ οἶκος ὑμῶν ἔρημος. λέγω γὰρ ὑμῖν,
39 οὐ μή με ἴδητε ἀπ᾽ ἄρτι ἕως ἂν εἴπητε, Εὐλογημένος ὁ ἐρχόμενος ἐν ὀνόματι Κυρίου.

CAP.
24 Καὶ ἐξελθὼν ὁ Ἰησοῦς ἀπὸ τοῦ ἱεροῦ ἐπορεύετο, καὶ [προσῆλθον
2 οἱ μαθηταὶ αὐτοῦ ἐπιδεῖξαι] αὐτῷ τὰς οἰκοδομὰς τοῦ ἱεροῦ. ὁ δὲ ἀποκριθεὶς εἶπεν αὐτοῖς, Οὐ βλέπετε ταῦτα πάντα; ἀμὴν λέγω ὑμῖν, οὐ μὴ ἀφεθῇ ὧδε λίθος ἐπὶ λίθον ὃς οὐ καταλυθήσεται.

25. γέμουσιν ἐξ ἁ. κ. ἀκ.] Not "full of" (as 27), but "filled from or by," extortion or excess. But compare L. xi. 39. The ποτήριον and παροψίς, though not used in such special sense by V.A., may perhaps mean here bowls and dishes, the cup and platter, in which the drink-offering and meat-offering were presented before God: the *externals of worship*.

26. ἵνα expresses not "the means," but "the preparation:" not "in order that," but "so that afterwards:" "cleanse the inside (the heart) first, as preliminary to cleansing the outside." And as one element in the process, L. xi. 41, τὰ ἐνόντα δότε ἐλεημοσύνην, "give all you can in works of mercy."

καθημένου δὲ αὐτοῦ ἐπὶ τοῦ ὄρους τῶν ἐλαιῶν προσῆλθον αὐτῷ 3
οἱ μαθηταὶ κατ' ἰδίαν λέγοντες, Εἰπὲ ἡμῖν πότε ταῦτα ἔσται;
καὶ τί τὸ σημεῖον τῆς σῆς παρουσίας καὶ *συντελείας τοῦ αἰῶνος;*
καὶ ἀποκριθεὶς ὁ Ἰησοῦς εἶπεν αὐτοῖς, Βλέπετε μή τις ὑμᾶς 4
πλανήσῃ. πολλοὶ γὰρ ἐλεύσονται *ἐπὶ τῷ ὀνόματί* μου λέγοντες, 5
Ἐγώ εἰμι ὁ Χριστός, καὶ πολλοὺς πλανήσουσιν. [μελλήσετε] 6
δὲ ἀκούειν πολέμους καὶ [ἀκοὰς] πολέμων· ὁρᾶτε μὴ θροεῖσθε·
δεῖ γὰρ πάντα γενέσθαι, ἀλλ' οὔπω ἐστὶν τὸ τέλος. ἐγερθήσεται 7
γὰρ ἔθνος ἐπὶ ἔθνος καὶ βασιλεία ἐπὶ βασιλείαν, καὶ ἔσονται
λιμοὶ καὶ σεισμοὶ [κατὰ τόπους]. πάντα δὲ ταῦτα ἀρχὴ ὠδίνων. 8
τότε παραδώσουσιν ὑμᾶς εἰς θλῖψιν καὶ ἀποκτενοῦσιν ὑμᾶς, καὶ 9
ἔσεσθε μισούμενοι ὑπὸ πάντων τῶν ἐθνῶν διὰ τὸ ὄνομά μου. καὶ 10
τότε σκανδαλισθήσονται πολλοὶ καὶ ἀλλήλους παραδώσουσιν καὶ
μισήσουσιν ἀλλήλους. καὶ πολλοὶ ψευδοπροφῆται ἐγερθήσονται 11
καὶ πλανήσουσιν πολλούς. καὶ διὰ τὸ πληθυνθῆναι τὴν ἀνομίαν 12
ψυγήσεται ἡ ἀγάπη τῶν πολλῶν. ὁ δὲ ὑπομείνας εἰς τέλος, 13
οὗτος σωθήσεται. καὶ κηρυχθήσεται τοῦτο τὸ εὐαγγέλιον τῆς 14
βασιλείας ἐν ὅλῃ τῇ οἰκουμένῃ εἰς μαρτύριον πᾶσιν τοῖς ἔθνεσιν,
καὶ τότε ἥξει τὸ τέλος. "Ὅταν οὖν ἴδητε *τὸ βδέλυγμα τῆς 15
ἐρημώσεως* τὸ ῥηθὲν διὰ Δανιὴλ τοῦ προφήτου ἑστὸς ἐν τόπῳ
ἁγίῳ, ὁ ἀναγινώσκων νοείτω, τότε οἱ ἐν τῇ Ἰουδαίᾳ φευγέτωσαν 16
ἐπὶ τὰ ὄρη, ὁ ἐπὶ τοῦ δώματος μὴ καταβαινέτω ἆραι τὰ ἐκ τῆς 17
οἰκίας αὐτοῦ, καὶ ὁ ἐν τῷ ἀγρῷ μὴ [ἐπιστρεψάτω ὀπίσω ἆραι] 18
τὰ ἱμάτια αὐτοῦ. οὐαὶ δὲ ταῖς ἐν γαστρὶ ἐχούσαις καὶ ταῖς 19
θηλαζούσαις ἐν ἐκείναις ταῖς ἡμέραις. προσεύχεσθε δὲ ἵνα μὴ 20
γένηται ἡ φυγὴ ὑμῶν χειμῶνος μηδὲ σαββάτῳ. ἔσται γὰρ τότε 21
θλῖψις μεγάλη, οἵα οὐ γέγονεν ἀπ' ἀρχῆς κόσμου ἕως τοῦ νῦν
οὐδ' οὐ μὴ γένηται. καὶ εἰ μὴ [ἐκολοβώθησαν] αἱ ἡμέραι ἐκεῖναι, 22
οὐκ ἂν ἐσώθη πᾶσα σάρξ· διὰ δὲ τοὺς ἐκλεκτοὺς κολοβωθήσονται
αἱ ἡμέραι ἐκεῖναι. τότε ἐάν τις ὑμῖν εἴπῃ, Ἰδοὺ ὧδε ὁ Χριστός, ἢ 23
ὧδε, μὴ πιστεύσητε. ἐγερθήσονται γὰρ ψευδόχριστοι καὶ ψευδο- 24
προφῆται, καὶ [δώσουσιν σημεῖα] μεγάλα καὶ τέρατα ὥστε πλανῆ- 25
σαι, εἰ δυνατόν, καὶ τοὺς ἐκλεκτούς. ἰδοὺ προείρηκα ὑμῖν. ἐὰν οὖν 26
εἴπωσιν ὑμῖν, Ἰδοὺ ἐν τῇ ἐρήμῳ ἐστίν, μὴ ἐξέλθητε· Ἰδοὺ ἐν τοῖς

Cap. XXIV. 15. βδ. τ. ἐρημ.] V.A. for שִׁקּוּץ שֹׁמֵם, Dan. xi. 31, the qualifying genitive, borrowed from Hebr., "detestabile illud quo desolatio efficitur." "The desolating abomination" or "idol" (Engl. Vn. passim), i.e. "the Eagle of the Roman legions," which was sacrosanct, "an idolatrous emblem, and the very symbol of desolation." W. & W.

18. אִי, οὐαί, væ: all the same sound probably, or nearly so.

22. לֹא...כָּל = "nullus, nihil," is rendered in V.A. πᾶς...οὐκ, universally: e.g. Ex. xii. 16, copied in N.T. as L. i. 38.

27 ταμείοις, μὴ πιστεύσητε. ὥσπερ γὰρ ἡ ἀστραπὴ ἐξέρχεται ἀπ᾽ ἀνατολῶν καὶ φαίνεται ἕως δυσμῶν, οὕτως ἔσται ἡ παρουσία τοῦ
28 υἱοῦ τοῦ ἀνθρώπου. [ὅπου ἐὰν] ᾖ τὸ πτῶμα, ἐκεῖ συναχθήσονται οἱ
29 ἀετοί. Εὐθέως δὲ μετὰ τὴν θλῖψιν τῶν ἡμερῶν ἐκείνων ὁ ἥλιος σκοτισθήσεται, καὶ ἡ σελήνη οὐ δώσει τὸ φέγγος αὐτῆς, καὶ οἱ ἀστέρες πεσοῦνται ἀπὸ τοῦ οὐρανοῦ, καὶ αἱ δυνάμεις τῶν οὐρανῶν
30 σαλευθήσονται. καὶ τότε φανήσεται τὸ σημεῖον τοῦ υἱοῦ τοῦ ἀνθρώπου ἐν οὐρανῷ, καὶ τότε κόψονται πᾶσαι αἱ φυλαὶ τῆς γῆς καὶ ὄψονται τὸν υἱὸν τοῦ ἀνθρώπου ἐρχόμενον ἐπὶ τῶν νεφελῶν τοῦ
31 οὐρανοῦ [μετὰ δυνάμεως καὶ δόξης πολλῆς]. καὶ ἀποστελεῖ τοὺς ἀγγέλους αὐτοῦ [μετὰ σάλπιγγος φωνῆς μεγάλης], καὶ ἐπισυνάξουσιν τοὺς ἐκλεκτοὺς αὐτοῦ ἐκ τῶν τεσσάρων ἀνέμων ἀπ᾽ ἄκρων ογρανῶν
32 ἕως ἄκρων αγτῶν. Ἀπὸ δὲ τῆς συκῆς μάθετε τὴν παραβολήν. ὅταν ἤδη ὁ κλάδος αὐτῆς γένηται ἀπαλὸς καὶ τὰ φύλλα ἐκφύῃ,
33 γινώσκετε ὅτι ἐγγὺς τὸ θέρος· οὕτως καὶ ὑμεῖς ὅταν ἴδητε πάντα
34 ταῦτα, γινώσκετε ὅτι ἐγγύς ἐστιν ἐπὶ θύραις. ἀμὴν λέγω ὑμῖν, οὐ
35 μὴ παρέλθῃ ἡ γενεὰ αὕτη ἕως ἂν πάντα ταῦτα γένηται. ὁ οὐρανὸς
36 καὶ ἡ γῆ παρελεύσεται, οἱ δὲ λόγοι μου οὐ μὴ παρέλθωσιν. Περὶ δὲ τῆς ἡμέρας ἐκείνης καὶ ὥρας οὐδεὶς οἶδεν, οὐδὲ οἱ ἄγγελοι τῶν
37 οὐρανῶν, εἰ μὴ ὁ πατήρ μου μόνος. ὥσπερ δὲ αἱ ἡμέραι τοῦ Νῶε,
38 οὕτως ἔσται ἡ παρουσία τοῦ υἱοῦ τοῦ ἀνθρώπου. ὡς γὰρ ἦσαν ἐν ταῖς ἡμέραις τοῦ κατακλυσμοῦ τρώγοντες καὶ πίνοντες, γαμοῦντες καὶ ἐκγαμίζοντες, [ἄχρι ἧς ἡμέρας] εἰσῆλθεν Νῶε εἰς τὴν κιβωτὸν,
39 καὶ οὐκ ἔγνωσαν ἕως ἦλθεν ὁ κατακλυσμὸς καὶ ἦρεν ἅπαντας, οὕτως
40 ἔσται ἡ παρουσία τοῦ υἱοῦ τοῦ ἀνθρώπου. τότε δύο ἔσονται ἐν τῷ
41 ἀγρῷ, εἷς παραλαμβάνεται καὶ εἷς ἀφίεται· δύο ἀλήθουσαι ἐν τῷ
42 μύλῳ, μία παραλαμβάνεται καὶ μία ἀφίεται. γρηγορεῖτε οὖν, ὅτι
43 οὐκ οἴδατε ποίᾳ ἡμέρᾳ ὁ κύριος ὑμῶν ἔρχεται. Ἐκεῖνο δὲ γινώσκετε, ὅτι εἰ ᾔδει ὁ οἰκοδεσπότης ποίᾳ φυλακῇ ὁ κλέπτης ἔρχεται, ἐγρηγόρησεν ἂν καὶ οὐκ ἂν εἴασεν διορυγῆναι τὴν οἰκίαν αὐτοῦ.
44 διὰ τοῦτο καὶ ὑμεῖς γίνεσθε ἕτοιμοι, ὅτι ᾗ [οὐ δοκεῖτε] ὥρᾳ ὁ υἱὸς
45 τοῦ ἀνθρώπου ἔρχεται. Τίς ἄρα ἐστὶν ὁ πιστὸς δοῦλος καὶ

---

31. Μετὰ with gen. has so essentially the idea of "societas," that except with persons, or things personified, it is rarely found in classical authors. Hence its use in V.A. and N.T. is often perplexing. Ps. xvi. 11 for את, quoted Acts ii. 28, πληρώσεις με εὐφροσύνης μετὰ τοῦ προσώπου σου. L. xiv. 9, κατέχειν τὸν ἔσχατον τόπον μετ᾽ αἰσχύνης. Acts xv. 33 ἀπελύθησαν μετ᾽ εἰρήνης. Hebr. x. 22, προσερχώμεθα μετ᾽ ἀληθινῆς καρδίας. We must not be misled by the coincidence between our idiom and the Hebrew, to think the use of μετὰ natural and grammatical in Greek, because "with," in these and similar phrases, is so in English.—Compare Mk. xiii. 27, ἀπ᾽ ἄκρου γῆς ἕως ἄκρ. οὐρανοῦ. V. A. for קָצֶה = "finis, extremitas." Deut. iv. 32, xxviii. 64, ἀπ᾽ ἄκρ...ἕως ἄκρου.

φρόνιμος, ὃν κατέστησεν ὁ κύριος ἐπὶ τῆς οἰκετείας αὐτοῦ τοῦ δοῦναι αὐτοῖς τὴν τροφὴν ἐν καιρῷ; μακάριος ὁ δοῦλος ἐκεῖνος ὃν 46 ἐλθὼν ὁ κύριος αὐτοῦ εὑρήσει οὕτως ποιοῦντα. ἀμὴν λέγω ὑμῖν 47 ὅτι ἐπὶ πᾶσιν τοῖς ὑπάρχουσιν αὐτοῦ καταστήσει αὐτόν. ἐὰν δὲ 48 εἴπῃ ὁ κακὸς δοῦλος ἐκεῖνος ἐν τῇ καρδίᾳ αὐτοῦ, Χρονίζει μου ὁ κύριος ἐλθεῖν, καὶ ἄρξηται τύπτειν τοὺς συνδούλους αὐτοῦ, ἐσθίῃ δὲ 49 καὶ πίνῃ μετὰ τῶν μεθυόντων· ἥξει ὁ κύριος τοῦ δούλου ἐκείνου 50 ἐν ἡμέρᾳ ᾗ οὐ προσδοκᾷ καὶ ἐν ὥρᾳ ᾗ οὐ γινώσκει, καὶ διχοτομήσει 51 αὐτὸν καὶ τὸ μέρος αὐτοῦ μετὰ τῶν ὑποκριτῶν θήσει· ἐκεῖ ἔσται *ὁ κλαυθμὸς καὶ ὁ βρυγμὸς τῶν ὀδόντων.*

CAP.
Τότε ὁμοιωθήσεται ἡ βασιλεία τῶν οὐρανῶν δέκα παρθένοις, 25 αἵτινες λαβοῦσαι τὰς λαμπάδας ἑαυτῶν ἐξῆλθον εἰς ὑπάντησιν τοῦ νυμφίου. πέντε δὲ ἐξ αὐτῶν ἦσαν μωραὶ καὶ πέντε φρόνιμοι. 2 [αἵτινες μωραὶ,] λαβοῦσαι τὰς λαμπάδας αὐτῶν οὐκ ἔλαβον μεθ᾽ 3 ἑαυτῶν ἔλαιον· αἱ δὲ φρόνιμοι ἔλαβον ἔλαιον ἐν τοῖς ἀγγείοις μετὰ 4 τῶν λαμπάδων αὐτῶν. χρονίζοντος δὲ τοῦ νυμφίου ἐνύσταξαν πᾶσαι 5 καὶ ἐκάθευδον. μέσης δὲ νυκτὸς κραυγὴ γέγονεν, Ἰδοὺ ὁ νυμφίος, 6 ἐξέρχεσθε εἰς ἀπάντησιν. τότε ἠγέρθησαν πᾶσαι αἱ παρθένοι 7 ἐκεῖναι καὶ ἐκόσμησαν τὰς λαμπάδας ἑαυτῶν. αἱ δὲ μωραὶ ταῖς 8 φρονίμοις εἶπαν, Δότε ἡμῖν ἐκ τοῦ ἐλαίου ὑμῶν, ὅτι αἱ λαμπάδες ἡμῶν σβέννυνται. ἀπεκρίθησαν δὲ αἱ φρόνιμοι λέγουσαι, Μή ποτε 9 οὐ μὴ ἀρκέσῃ ἡμῖν καὶ ὑμῖν. πορεύεσθε [μᾶλλον] πρὸς τοὺς πωλοῦντας καὶ ἀγοράσατε ἑαυταῖς. [ἀπερχομένων δὲ αὐτῶν 10 ἀγοράσαι] ἦλθεν ὁ νυμφίος, καὶ αἱ ἕτοιμοι εἰσῆλθον μετ᾽ αὐτοῦ εἰς τοὺς γάμους, καὶ ἐκλείσθη ἡ θύρα. ὕστερον δὲ ἔρχονται καὶ αἱ 11 λοιπαὶ παρθένοι λέγουσαι, Κύριε κύριε, ἄνοιξον ἡμῖν· ὁ δὲ ἀπο- 12 κριθεὶς εἶπεν, Ἀμὴν λέγω ὑμῖν, οὐκ οἶδα ὑμᾶς. γρηγορεῖτε οὖν, ὅτι 13 οὐκ οἴδατε τὴν ἡμέραν οὐδὲ τὴν ὥραν. Ὥσπερ γὰρ ἄνθρωπος 14 ἀποδημῶν ἐκάλεσεν τοὺς ἰδίους δούλους καὶ παρέδωκεν αὐτοῖς τὰ ὑπάρχοντα αὐτοῦ, καὶ [ᾧ μὲν] ἔδωκεν πέντε τάλαντα, ᾧ δὲ δύο, 15 ᾧ δὲ ἕν, ἑκάστῳ κατὰ τὴν ἰδίαν δύναμιν, καὶ ἀπεδήμησεν εὐθέως.. πορευθεὶς δὲ ὁ τὰ πέντε τάλαντα λαβὼν εἰργάσατο *ἐν αὐτοῖς* 16 καὶ ἐποίησεν ἄλλα πέντε τάλαντα. ὡσαύτως καὶ ὁ τὰ δύο ἐκέρδησεν 17 ἄλλα δύο. ὁ δὲ τὸ ἓν λαβὼν ἀπελθὼν ὤρυξεν γῆν καὶ ἔκρυψεν τὸ 18 ἀργύριον τοῦ κυρίου αὐτοῦ. μετὰ δὲ πολὺν χρόνον ἔρχεται ὁ κύριος 19 τῶν δούλων ἐκείνων καὶ συναίρει λόγον μετ᾽ αὐτῶν. καὶ προσελθὼν 20 ὁ τὰ πέντε τάλαντα λαβὼν προσήνεγκεν ἄλλα πέντε τάλαντα λέγων, Κύριε, πέντε τάλαντά μοι παρέδωκας, ἴδε ἄλλα πέντε τάλαντα ἐκέρδησα. ἔφη αὐτῷ ὁ κύριος αὐτοῦ, Εὖ, δοῦλε ἀγαθὲ καὶ πιστέ, [ἐπὶ 21

ὀλίγα] ἧς πιστός, ἐπὶ πολλῶν σε καταστήσω· εἴσελθε εἰς τὴν
22 χαρὰν τοῦ κυρίου σου. προσελθὼν δὲ καὶ ὁ τὰ δύο τάλαντα εἶπεν,
Κύριε, δύο τάλαντά μοι παρέδωκας, ἴδε ἄλλα δύο τάλαντα ἐκέρδησα.
23 ἔφη αὐτῷ ὁ κύριος αὐτοῦ, Εὖ, δοῦλε ἀγαθὲ καὶ πιστέ, ἐπὶ ὀλίγα ἧς
πιστός, ἐπὶ πολλῶν σε καταστήσω· εἴσελθε εἰς τὴν χαρὰν τοῦ κυρίου
24 σου. προσελθὼν καὶ ὁ τὸ ἓν τάλαντον εἰληφὼς εἶπεν, Κύριε, ἔγνων
σε ὅτι σκληρὸς εἶ ἄνθρωπος, θερίζων ὅπου οὐκ ἔσπειρας, καὶ
25 συνάγων ὅθεν οὐ διεσκόρπισας· καὶ φοβηθεὶς ἀπελθὼν ἔκρυψα
26 τὸ τάλαντόν σου ἐν τῇ γῇ· ἴδε ἔχεις τὸ σόν. ἀποκριθεὶς δὲ ὁ
κύριος αὐτοῦ εἶπεν αὐτῷ, Πονηρὲ δοῦλε καὶ ὀκνηρέ, ᾔδεις ὅτι θερίζω
27 ὅπου οὐκ ἔσπειρα, καὶ συνάγω ὅθεν οὐ διεσκόρπισα; ἔδει σε οὖν
Βαλεῖν τὸ ἀργύριόν μου τοῖς τραπεζίταις, καὶ ἐλθὼν ἐγὼ ἐκομισάμην
28 ἂν τὸ ἐμὸν σὺν τόκῳ. ἄρατε οὖν ἀπ' αὐτοῦ τὸ τάλαντον καὶ δότε
29 τῷ ἔχοντι τὰ δέκα τάλαντα. τῷ γὰρ ἔχοντι παντὶ δοθήσεται καὶ
περισσευθήσεται· τοῦ δὲ μὴ ἔχοντος, καὶ ὃ ἔχει ἀρθήσεται ἀπ'
30 αὐτοῦ. καὶ τὸν ἀχρεῖον δοῦλον ἐκβάλετε εἰς τὸ σκότος τὸ ἐξώτερον·
ἐκεῖ ἔσται ὁ κλαυθμὸς καὶ ὁ βρυγμὸς τῶν ὀδόντων.
31 Ὅταν δὲ ἔλθῃ ὁ υἱὸς τοῦ ἀνθρώπου ἐν τῇ δόξῃ αὐτοῦ καὶ πάντες
32 οἱ ἄγγελοι μετ' αὐτοῦ, τότε καθίσει ἐπὶ θρόνου δόξης αὐτοῦ· καὶ
συναχθήσονται ἔμπροσθεν αὐτοῦ πάντα τὰ ἔθνη, καὶ ἀφοριεῖ
αὐτοὺς ἀπ' ἀλλήλων, ὥσπερ ὁ ποιμὴν ἀφορίζει τὰ πρόβατα
33 ἀπὸ τῶν ἐρίφων, καὶ στήσει τὰ μὲν πρόβατα ἐκ δεξιῶν αὐτοῦ,
34 τὰ δὲ ἐρίφια ἐξ εὐωνύμων. τότε ἐρεῖ ὁ βασιλεὺς τοῖς ἐκ
δεξιῶν αὐτοῦ, Δεῦτε *οἱ εὐλογημένοι τοῦ πατρός* μου, κληρο-
νομήσατε [τὴν ἡτοιμασμένην ὑμῖν βασιλείαν ἀπὸ καταβολῆς
35 κόσμου]. ἐπείνασα γὰρ καὶ ἐδώκατέ μοι φαγεῖν, ἐδίψησα καὶ
36 ἐποτίσατέ με, ξένος ἤμην καὶ συνηγάγετέ με, γυμνὸς καὶ περιεβάλετέ με, ἠσθένησα καὶ ἐπεσκέψασθέ με, ἐν φυλακῇ ἤμην

Cap. XXV. 21. Mark change of case, without any apparent reason.
27. βαλεῖν] See ix. 38.
34. יְהֹוָה בָּרַךְ, V.A. εὐλογητὸς Κυρίου (1), Gen. xxiv. 31, Vulg. "Benedictus Domini," and xxvi. 29, εὐλογημένος ὑπὸ Κυρίου. The general form is בָּ֯ יְהֹוָה. (2) εὐλογημένος τῷ Κυρίῳ. The two are practically identical [though V.A. puts the latter in dative on account of לְ, which is here "possessoris;" as 1 Sam. xvi. 18, לוֹ בֵּן, and xiv. 16, הַפִּצָה לְאִשְׁתּוֹ], and signify "Jehovah's blessed one," or, more correctly, "one of Jehovah's blessed ones." These terms of expression are as unnatural in English, as (1) and (2) are in Greek. In our "blessed of the Lord," of = ὑπό: and we have translated according to the spirit, and not the letter, as V.A. in εὐλογ. ὑπὸ Κ. As also in translating εὐλ. τοῦ πατρός μου, we have evaded the stiffness of the literal rendering "My Father's blessed ones," by turning it "Ye blessed of my Father." The irregular syntax of the latter portion of the verse has many parallels in N.T., e.g. Gal. iii. 23, Eph. ii. 3, τέκνα φύσει ὀργῆς, and has prototypes, possibly, in Hebrew: e.g. 2 Sam. xiii. 16.

καὶ ἤλθατε πρὸς μέ. τότε ἀποκριθήσονται αὐτῷ οἱ δίκαιοι 37
λέγοντες, Κύριε, πότε σε εἴδομεν πεινῶντα καὶ ἐθρέψαμεν; ἢ
διψῶντα καὶ ἐποτίσαμεν; πότε δέ σε εἴδομεν ξένον καὶ συνηγά- 38
γομεν; ἢ γυμνὸν καὶ περιεβάλομεν; πότε δέ σε εἴδομεν ἀσθενοῦντα 39
ἢ ἐν φυλακῇ καὶ ἤλθομεν πρὸς σέ; καὶ ἀποκριθεὶς ὁ βασιλεὺς 40
ἐρεῖ αὐτοῖς, Ἀμὴν λέγω ὑμῖν, ἐφ' ὅσον ἐποιήσατε ἑνὶ τούτων τῶν
ἀδελφῶν μου τῶν ἐλαχίστων, ἐμοὶ ἐποιήσατε. τότε ἐρεῖ καὶ τοῖς 41
ἐξ εὐωνύμων, Πορεύεσθε ἀπ' ἐμοῦ οἱ κατηραμένοι εἰς τὸ πῦρ τὸ
αἰώνιον τὸ ἡτοιμασμένον τῷ διαβόλῳ καὶ τοῖς ἀγγέλοις αὐτοῦ.
ἐπείνασα γὰρ καὶ οὐκ ἐδώκατέ μοι φαγεῖν, ἐδίψησα καὶ οὐκ 42
ἐποτίσατέ με, ξένος ἤμην καὶ οὐ συνηγάγετέ με, γυμνὸς καὶ οὐ 43
περιεβάλετέ με, ἀσθενὴς καὶ ἐν φυλακῇ καὶ οὐκ ἐπεσκέψασθέ με.
τότε ἀποκριθήσονται καὶ αὐτοὶ λέγοντες, Κύριε, πότε σε εἴδομεν 44
πεινῶντα ἢ διψῶντα ἢ ξένον ἢ γυμνὸν ἢ ἀσθενῆ ἢ ἐν φυλακῇ, καὶ
οὐ διηκονήσαμέν σοι; τότε ἀποκριθήσεται αὐτοῖς λέγων, Ἀμὴν 45
λέγω ὑμῖν, ἐφ' ὅσον οὐκ ἐποιήσατε ἑνὶ τούτων τῶν ἐλαχίστων,
οὐδὲ ἐμοὶ ἐποιήσατε. καὶ ἀπελεύσονται οὗτοι εἰς κόλασιν αἰώνιον, 46
οἱ δὲ δίκαιοι εἰς ζωὴν αἰώνιον.

CAP.
Καὶ ἐγένετο ὅτε ἐτέλεσεν ὁ Ἰησοῦς πάντας τοὺς λόγους τούτους, **26**
εἶπεν τοῖς μαθηταῖς αὐτοῦ, Οἴδατε ὅτι μετὰ δύο ἡμέρας τὸ 2
πάσχα γίνεται, καὶ ὁ υἱὸς τοῦ ἀνθρώπου παραδίδοται εἰς τὸ
σταυρωθῆναι.

Τότε συνήχθησαν οἱ ἀρχιερεῖς καὶ οἱ πρεσβύτεροι τοῦ λαοῦ 3
εἰς τὴν αὐλὴν τοῦ ἀρχιερέως τοῦ λεγομένου Καϊάφα, καὶ συνε- 4
βουλεύσαντο ἵνα τὸν Ἰησοῦν δόλῳ κρατήσωσιν καὶ ἀποκτείνωσιν.
ἔλεγον δέ, Μὴ ἐν τῇ ἑορτῇ ἵνα μὴ θόρυβος γένηται ἐν τῷ λαῷ. 5

Τοῦ δὲ Ἰησοῦ γενομένου ἐν Βηθανίᾳ ἐν οἰκίᾳ Σίμωνος τοῦ 6
λεπροῦ, προσῆλθεν αὐτῷ γυνὴ ἀλάβαστρον μύρου ἔχουσα βα- 7
ρυτίμου καὶ κατέχεεν ἐπὶ τὴν κεφαλὴν αὐτοῦ ἀνακειμένου. ἰδόν- 8
τες δὲ οἱ μαθηταὶ ἠγανάκτησαν λέγοντες, Εἰς τί [ἡ ἀπώλεια] αὕτη;
ἠδύνατο γὰρ τοῦτο πραθῆναι πολλοῦ καὶ δοθῆναι τοῖς πτωχοῖς. 9
γνοὺς δὲ ὁ Ἰησοῦς εἶπεν αὐτοῖς, Τί κόπους παρέχετε τῇ γυναικί; 10
ἔργον γὰρ καλὸν εἰργάσατο εἰς ἐμέ. πάντοτε γὰρ τοὺς πτωχοὺς 11
ἔχετε μεθ' ἑαυτῶν, ἐμὲ δὲ οὐ πάντοτε ἔχετε. Βαλοῦϲα γὰρ αὕτη 12

Cap. XXVI. 4. δόλῳ] Dative of manner: very rare in M. I have noted it only in iii. 12, iv. 24, vii. 22, xv. 8, 20, xxiii. 4, xxvii. 59.
8. ἀπώλεια] "profusio," Grimm. No quotations from any class. author, except one from Polybius, given by Schl., VI. 59.

5, where it is opposed to τήρησις. It corresponds probably to מִשְׁחָת = "perditio," active (a) and passive (b), (a) Prov. xviii. 9, xxviii. 24 and here; and (b) Is. i. 4, with which compare John xvii. 12.
12. Two things to be noted here: βα-

τὸ μύρον τοῦτο ἐπὶ τοῦ σώματός μου πρὸς τὸ ἐνταφιάσαι με
13 ἐποίησεν. ἀμὴν λέγω ὑμῖν, ὅπου ἐὰν κηρυχθῇ τὸ εὐαγγέλιον τοῦτο ἐν ὅλῳ τῷ κόσμῳ, λαληθήσεται καὶ ὃ ἐποίησεν αὕτη εἰς μνημόσυνον αὐτῆς.
14 Τότε πορευθεὶς εἷς τῶν δώδεκα, ὁ λεγόμενος Ἰούδας Ἰσκα-
15 ριώτης, πρὸς τοὺς ἀρχιερεῖς εἶπεν, Τί θέλετέ μοι δοῦναι, κἀγὼ ὑμῖν παραδώσω αὐτόν; οἱ δὲ ἔστησαν αὐτῷ τριάκοντα ἀργύρια.
16 καὶ ἀπὸ τότε ἐζήτει εὐκαιρίαν ἵνα αὐτὸν παραδῷ.
17 Τῇ δὲ πρώτῃ τῶν ἀζύμων προσῆλθον οἱ μαθηταὶ τῷ Ἰησοῦ
18 λέγοντες, Ποῦ θέλεις ἑτοιμάσωμέν σοι φαγεῖν τὸ πάσχα; ὁ δὲ εἶπεν, Ὑπάγετε εἰς τὴν πόλιν πρὸς τὸν δεῖνα καὶ εἴπατε αὐτῷ, Ὁ διδάσκαλος λέγει, Ὁ καιρός μου ἐγγύς ἐστιν, *πρὸς σὲ*
19 ποιῶ τὸ πάσχα μετὰ τῶν μαθητῶν μου. καὶ ἐποίησαν οἱ μαθηταὶ
20 ὡς συνέταξεν αὐτοῖς ὁ Ἰησοῦς, καὶ ἡτοίμασαν τὸ πάσχα. Ὀψίας
21 δὲ γενομένης ἀνέκειτο μετὰ τῶν δώδεκα. καὶ ἐσθιόντων αὐτῶν
22 εἶπεν, Ἀμὴν λέγω ὑμῖν ὅτι εἷς ἐξ ὑμῶν παραδώσει με. καὶ λυπούμενοι σφόδρα ἤρξαντο λέγειν αὐτῷ εἷς ἕκαστος, Μήτι ἐγώ εἰμι,
23 κύριε; ὁ δὲ ἀποκριθεὶς εἶπεν, Ὁ ἐμβάψας μετ' ἐμοῦ τὴν χεῖρα
24 ἐν τῷ τρυβλίῳ, οὗτός με παραδώσει. ὁ μὲν υἱὸς τοῦ ἀνθρώπου ὑπάγει καθὼς γέγραπται περὶ αὐτοῦ· οὐαὶ δὲ τῷ ἀνθρώπῳ ἐκείνῳ δι' οὗ ὁ υἱὸς τοῦ ἀνθρώπου παραδίδοται· καλὸν ἦν αὐτῷ εἰ οὐκ
25 ἐγεννήθη ὁ ἄνθρωπος ἐκεῖνος. ἀποκριθεὶς δὲ Ἰούδας ὁ παραδιδοὺς αὐτὸν εἶπεν, Μήτι ἐγώ εἰμι, ῥαββί; λέγει αὐτῷ, [Σὺ εἶπας].
26 Ἐσθιόντων δὲ αὐτῶν λαβὼν ὁ Ἰησοῦς τὸν ἄρτον καὶ εὐλογήσας ἔκλασεν καὶ ἐδίδου τοῖς μαθηταῖς καὶ εἶπεν, Λάβετε φάγετε· τοῦτό
27 ἐστιν τὸ σῶμά μου. καὶ λαβὼν ποτήριον καὶ εὐχαριστήσας
28 ἔδωκεν αὐτοῖς λέγων, Πίετε ἐξ αὐτοῦ πάντες· τοῦτο γάρ ἐστιν τὸ αἷμά μου τῆς διαθήκης τὸ περὶ πολλῶν ἐκχυννόμενον εἰς ἄφεσιν

λοῦσα expressing too violent an action, and ἐπὶ with gen. where we should expect acc. But βάλλειν is constantly used in N.T. for "pono, impono;" ix. 38, xxv. 27, Mk. j. 43, vii. 30, J. x. 4, as in V.A. for שִׂים, Gen. xxxi. 34, Deut. x. 2, Gen. xliv. 1, ἐμβάλετε τὸ ἀργύριον ἐπὶ τοῦ στόματος τοῦ μαρσίππου (marsupium), a similar construction to our passage.

18. πρὸς σὲ] xiii. 56.
ποιῶ] "let me offer;" in sacrificial sense, as Heb. xi. 28. Compare Ex. xii. 45, פֶּסַח יַעֲשֶׂה, V. A. ποιήσει τὸ πάσχα. xii. 21, θύειν τὸ πάσχα. Also xxix. 36, 38, 39, עָשָׂה, meaning θύειν, is rendered by ποιεῖν. τὸ μοσχάριον...τὸν ἀμνόν... ποιήσεις.

25 and 64. σὺ εἶπας] Not found in V.A. Possibly later Greek. It seems akin to φημὶ ἐγώ and aio, of classical authors. In xxvii. 11, Mk. xv. 2, L. xxiii. 3, J. xviii. 37, we have σὺ λέγεις. Lightfoot is cited by Schl. as showing a similar form of affirmation to be found in the Talmud. Hierosol.

26. Εὐλογεῖν includes the idea of giving thanks. L. ii. 28. In the other accounts of the institution of the Holy Eucharist, we find, Mk. xiv. 22, εὐλογήσας, L. xxii. 19, εὐχαριστήσας: 1 Cor. x. 16, εὐλογίας. In 1 Cor. xiv. 16 the two seem interchanged: as indeed here, verses 26 and 27.

ἁμαρτιῶν. λέγω δὲ ὑμῖν ὅτι οὐ μὴ πίω ἀπ' ἄρτι ἐκ τούτου τοῦ 29
γενηματοϲ τῆς ἀμπέλου ἕως τῆς ἡμέρας ἐκείνης ὅταν ' αὐτὸ πίνω
μεθ' ὑμῶν καινὸν ἐν τῇ βασιλείᾳ τοῦ πατρός μου.

Καὶ ὑμνήσαντες ἐξῆλθον εἰς τὸ ὄρος τῶν ἐλαιῶν. τότε λέγει 30
αὐτοῖς ὁ Ἰησοῦς, Πάντες ὑμεῖς σκανδαλισθήσεσθε * ἐν ἐμοὶ * 31
ἐν τῇ νυκτὶ ταύτῃ· γέγραπται γάρ, Πατάξω τὸν ποιμένα, καὶ
διασκορπισθήσονται τὰ πρόβατα τῆς ποίμνης. μετὰ δὲ τὸ 32
ἐγερθῆναί με προάξω ὑμᾶς εἰς τὴν Γαλιλαίαν. ἀποκριθεὶς δὲ 33
ὁ Πέτρος εἶπεν αὐτῷ, Εἰ πάντες σκανδαλισθήσονται ἐν σοί, ἐγὼ
οὐδέποτε σκανδαλισθήσομαι. ἔφη αὐτῷ ὁ Ἰησοῦς, Ἀμὴν λέγω 34
σοι ὅτι ἐν ταύτῃ τῇ νυκτὶ πρὶν ἀλέκτορα φωνῆσαι τρὶς ἀπαρνήσῃ
με. λέγει αὐτῷ ὁ Πέτρος, Κἂν δέῃ με σὺν σοὶ ἀποθανεῖν [οὐ μή 35
σε ἀπαρνήσομαι]. ὁμοίως καὶ πάντες οἱ μαθηταὶ εἶπον.

Τότε ἔρχεται μετ' αὐτῶν ὁ Ἰησοῦς εἰς χωρίον λεγόμενον 36
Γεθσημανεῖ, καὶ λέγει τοῖς μαθηταῖς, Καθίσατε αὐτοῦ [ἕως ἂν
ἀπελθὼν ἐκεῖ προσεύξωμαι]. καὶ παραλαβὼν τὸν Πέτρον καὶ τοὺς 37
δύο υἱοὺς Ζεβεδαίου ἤρξατο λυπεῖσθαι καὶ ἀδημονεῖν. τότε λέγει 38
αὐτοῖς, Περίλυπός ἐστιν ἡ ψυχή μου ἕως θανάτου· μείνατε ὧδε
καὶ γρηγορεῖτε μετ' ἐμοῦ. καὶ προελθὼν μικρὸν ἔπεσεν ἐπὶ 39
πρόσωπον αὐτοῦ προσευχόμενος καὶ λέγων, Πάτερ, εἰ δυνατόν
ἐστιν, παρελθάτω ἀπ' ἐμοῦ τὸ ποτήριον τοῦτο· πλὴν οὐχ ὡς ἐγὼ
θέλω ἀλλ' ὡς σύ. καὶ ἔρχεται πρὸς τοὺς μαθητὰς καὶ εὑρίσκει 40
αὐτοὺς καθεύδοντας, καὶ λέγει τῷ Πέτρῳ, Οὕτως οὐκ ἰσχύσατε
μίαν ὥραν γρηγορῆσαι μετ' ἐμοῦ; γρηγορεῖτε καὶ προσεύχεσθε ἵνα 41
μὴ εἰσέλθητε εἰς πειρασμόν· τὸ μὲν πνεῦμα πρόθυμον, ἡ δὲ σὰρξ
ἀσθενής. πάλιν ἐκ δευτέρου ἀπελθὼν προσηύξατο λέγων, Πάτερ 42
μου, εἰ οὐ δύναται τοῦτο παρελθεῖν ἐὰν μὴ αὐτὸ πίω, γενηθήτω τὸ
θέλημά σου. καὶ ἐλθὼν πάλιν εὗρεν αὐτοὺς καθεύδοντας· ἦσαν 43
γὰρ αὐτῶν οἱ ὀφθαλμοὶ βεβαρημένοι. καὶ ἀφεὶς αὐτοὺς πάλιν 44
ἀπελθὼν προσηύξατο τὸν αὐτὸν λόγον εἰπών. τότε ἔρχεται πρὸς 45
τοὺς μαθητὰς καὶ λέγει αὐτοῖς, Καθεύδετε λοιπὸν καὶ ἀναπαύεσθε·
ἰδοὺ ἤγγικεν ἡ ὥρα καὶ ὁ υἱὸς τοῦ ἀνθρώπου παραδίδοται εἰς χεῖρας
ἁμαρτωλῶν. ἐγείρεσθε [ἄγωμεν]· ἰδοὺ ἤγγικεν ὁ παραδιδούς με. 46

Καὶ ἔτι αὐτοῦ λαλοῦντος, ἰδοὺ Ἰούδας εἷς τῶν δώδεκα ἦλθεν, 47
καὶ μετ' αὐτοῦ ὄχλος πολὺς [μετὰ μαχαιρῶν καὶ ξύλων] ἀπὸ τῶν
ἀρχιερέων καὶ πρεσβυτέρων τοῦ λαοῦ. ὁ δὲ παραδιδοὺς αὐτὸν 48

---

29. γέννημα V. A. very frequently for any fruit or produce of field or tree, as well as the young of animals, e.g. רִי, Deut. xxvi. 10, and תְּנוּבָה, Gen. xlvii. 23; indeed the latter use, for "fœtus, progenies," is rare: Josh. xv. 14, Apocrypha, Sir. x. 18, γενν. γυναικῶν.

ἔδωκεν αὐτοῖς σημεῖον λέγων, Ὃν ἐὰν φιλήσω, αὐτός ἐστιν· κρατή-
49 σατε αὐτόν. καὶ εὐθέως προσελθὼν τῷ Ἰησοῦ εἶπεν, Χαῖρε, ῥαββί·
50 καὶ κατεφίλησεν αὐτόν. ὁ δὲ Ἰησοῦς εἶπεν αὐτῷ, Ἑταῖρε, [ἐφ᾽ ὃ]
πάρει; τότε προσελθόντες ἐπέβαλον τὰς χεῖρας ἐπὶ τὸν Ἰησοῦν καὶ
51 ἐκράτησαν αὐτόν. καὶ ἰδοὺ εἷς τῶν μετὰ Ἰησοῦ ἐκτείνας τὴν χεῖρα
ἀπέσπασεν τὴν μάχαιραν αὐτοῦ, καὶ πατάξας τὸν δοῦλον τοῦ
52 ἀρχιερέως ἀφεῖλεν αὐτοῦ τὸ ὠτίον. τότε λέγει αὐτῷ ὁ Ἰησοῦς,
Ἀπόστρεψον τὴν μάχαιράν σου εἰς τὸν τόπον αὐτῆς· πάντες γὰρ οἱ
53 λαβόντες μάχαιραν *ἐν μαχαίρῃ* ἀπολοῦνται. ἢ δοκεῖς ὅτι οὐ
δύναμαι ἄρτι παρακαλέσαι τὸν πατέρα μου, καὶ παραστήσει μοι
54 πλείω δώδεκα λεγεῶνας ἀγγέλων; πῶς οὖν πληρωθῶσιν αἱ γραφαὶ
55 ὅτι οὕτως δεῖ γενέσθαι; Ἐν ἐκείνῃ τῇ ὥρᾳ εἶπεν ὁ Ἰησοῦς τοῖς
ὄχλοις, Ὡς ἐπὶ λῃστὴν ἐξήλθατε [μετὰ μαχαιρῶν καὶ ξύλων] συλλαβεῖν με· καθ᾽ ἡμέραν ἐν τῷ ἱερῷ ἐκαθεζόμην διδάσκων, καὶ οὐκ
56 ἐκρατήσατέ με. τοῦτο δὲ [ὅλον] γέγονεν ἵνα πληρωθῶσιν αἱ γραφαὶ
τῶν προφητῶν. τότε οἱ μαθηταὶ πάντες [ἀφέντες] αὐτὸν ἔφυγον.
57 Οἱ δὲ κρατήσαντες τὸν Ἰησοῦν ἀπήγαγον πρὸς Καϊάφαν τὸν
ἀρχιερέα, ὅπου οἱ γραμματεῖς καὶ οἱ πρεσβύτεροι συνήχθησαν.
58 ὁ δὲ Πέτρος ἠκολούθει αὐτῷ ἀπὸ μακρόθεν ἕως τῆς αὐλῆς τοῦ
ἀρχιερέως, καὶ εἰσελθὼν ἔσω ἐκάθητο μετὰ τῶν ὑπηρετῶν ἰδεῖν τὸ
59 τέλος. οἱ δὲ ἀρχιερεῖς καὶ τὸ συνέδριον ὅλον ἐζήτουν ψευδομαρτυ-
60 ρίαν κατὰ τοῦ Ἰησοῦ, ὅπως αὐτὸν θανατώσουσιν, καὶ οὐχ εὗρον
πολλῶν προσελθόντων ψευδομαρτύρων. ὕστερον δὲ προσελθόντες
61 δύο εἶπον, Οὗτος ἔφη, Δύναμαι καταλῦσαι τὸν ναὸν τοῦ Θεοῦ καὶ διὰ
62 τριῶν ἡμερῶν οἰκοδομῆσαι. καὶ ἀναστὰς ὁ ἀρχιερεὺς εἶπεν αὐτῷ,
63 Οὐδὲν ἀποκρίνῃ τί οὗτοί σου καταμαρτυροῦσιν; ὁ δὲ Ἰησοῦς ἐσιώπα.
καὶ ἀποκριθεὶς ὁ ἀρχιερεὺς εἶπεν αὐτῷ, Ἐξορκίζω σε κατὰ
τοῦ Θεοῦ τοῦ ζῶντος, ἵνα ἡμῖν εἴπῃς εἰ σὺ εἶ ὁ Χριστός, ὁ υἱὸς τοῦ
64 Θεοῦ. λέγει αὐτῷ ὁ Ἰησοῦς, [Σὺ εἶπας·] πλὴν λέγω ὑμῖν, ἀπ᾽
ἄρτι ὄψεσθε τὸν υἱὸν τοῦ ἀνθρώπου καθήμενον ἐκ δεξιῶν *τῆς
65 δυνάμεως* καὶ ἐρχόμενον ἐπὶ τῶν νεφελῶν τοῦ οὐρανοῦ. τότε ὁ
ἀρχιερεὺς διέρρηξεν τὰ ἱμάτια αὐτοῦ λέγων, Ἐβλασφήμησεν· τί
ἔτι χρείαν ἔχομεν μαρτύρων; ἴδε νῦν ἠκούσατε τὴν βλασφημίαν.
66 τί ὑμῖν δοκεῖ; οἱ δὲ ἀποκριθέντες εἶπον, Ἔνοχος θανάτου ἐστίν.
67 Τότε ἐνέπτυσαν εἰς τὸ πρόσωπον αὐτοῦ καὶ ἐκολάφισαν αὐτόν, οἱ δὲ
68 ἐράπισαν, λέγοντες, Προφήτευσον ἡμῖν, Χριστέ, τίς ἐστιν ὁ παίσας σε;

50. ἐφ᾽ ὃ] for ἐπὶ τίνι, = עַל־מָה, led?"
Numb. xxii. 32 and Jer. ix. 11.
52. ἐν μαχαίρῃ] See iii. 11.
54. "How are the Scr. to be fulfil-
64. τῆς δυνάμεως] "Buxtorf shows
(Lex. Talm. p. 385) that the Jews applied
the term גְּבוּרָה to God." Schl.

MATTHEW, XXVI. 69—XXVII. 12.

Ὁ δὲ Πέτρος ἐκάθητο ἔξω ἐν τῇ αὐλῇ· καὶ προσῆλθεν αὐτῷ 69 [μία] παιδίσκη λέγουσα, Καὶ σὺ ἦσθα μετὰ Ἰησοῦ τοῦ Γαλιλαίου. ὁ δὲ ἠρνήσατο ἔμπροϲθεν πάντων λέγων, Οὐκ οἶδα [τί] λέγεις. 70 ἐξελθόντα δὲ αὐτὸν εἰς τὸν πυλῶνα, εἶδεν αὐτὸν ἄλλη καὶ 71 λέγει αὐτοῖς ἐκεῖ, Καὶ οὗτος ἦν μετὰ Ἰησοῦ τοῦ Ναζωραίου. καὶ πάλιν ἠρνήσατο μετὰ ὅρκου *ὅτι* οὐκ οἶδα τὸν ἄνθρωπον. 72 μετὰ μικρὸν δὲ προσελθόντες οἱ ἑστῶτες εἶπον τῷ Πέτρῳ, Ἀληθῶς 73 καὶ σὺ ἐξ αὐτῶν εἶ· καὶ γὰρ [ἡ λαλιά] σου δῆλόν σε ποιεῖ. τότε 74 ἤρξατο καταθεματίζειν καὶ ὀμνύειν *ὅτι* οὐκ οἶδα τὸν ἄνθρωπον· καὶ εὐθέως ἀλέκτωρ ἐφώνησεν. καὶ ἐμνήσθη ὁ Πέτρος τοῦ ῥήματος 75 Ἰησοῦ εἰρηκότος *ὅτι* πρὶν ἀλέκτορα φωνῆσαι τρὶς ἀπαρνήσῃ με· καὶ ἐξελθὼν ἔξω ἔκλαυσεν πικρῶς.

CAP.
Πρωίας δὲ γενομένης [συμβούλιον ἔλαβον] πάντες οἱ ἀρχιερεῖς 27 καὶ οἱ πρεσβύτεροι τοῦ λαοῦ κατὰ τοῦ Ἰησοῦ, ὥστε θανατῶσαι αὐτόν. καὶ δήσαντες αὐτὸν ἀπήγαγον καὶ παρέδωκαν Πιλάτῳ τῷ 2 ἡγεμόνι.

Τότε ἰδὼν Ἰούδας ὁ παραδιδοὺς αὐτὸν ὅτι κατεκρίθη, μετα- 3 μεληθεὶς [ἔστρεψεν] τὰ τριάκοντα ἀργύρια τοῖς ἀρχιερεῦσιν καὶ πρεσβυτέροις λέγων, Ἥμαρτον παραδοὺς αἷμα ἀθῷον. οἱ δὲ εἶπον, 4 Τί πρὸς ἡμᾶς; *σὺ ὄψῃ.* καὶ ῥίψας τὰ ἀργύρια ἐν τῷ ναῷ 5 ἀνεχώρησεν, καὶ ἀπελθὼν ἀπήγξατο. οἱ δὲ ἀρχιερεῖς λαβόντες τὰ 6 ἀργύρια εἶπαν, Οὐκ ἔξεστιν βαλεῖν αὐτὰ εἰς τὸν *κορβανᾶν,* ἐπεὶ τιμὴ αἵματός ἐστιν. συμβούλιον δὲ λαβόντες ἠγόρασαν [ἐξ αὐτῶν] 7 τὸν ἀγρὸν τοῦ κεραμέως εἰς ταφὴν τοῖς ξένοις. διὸ ἐκλήθη ὁ ἀγρὸς 8 ἐκεῖνος ἀγρὸς αἵματος ἕως τῆς σήμερον. τότε ἐπληρώθη τὸ ῥηθὲν 9 διὰ τοῦ προφήτου Ἰερεμίου λέγοντος, Καὶ ἔλαβον τὰ τριάκοντα ἀργύρια, τὴν τιμὴν τοῦ τετιμημένου ὃν ἐτιμήσαντο ἀπὸ υἱῶν Ἰσραήλ, καὶ ἔδωκαν ἀүτὰ εἰϲ τὸν ἀγρὸν τοῦ κεραμέως, καθὰ συνέταξέν 10 μοι Κύριος.

· Ὁ δὲ Ἰησοῦς ἐστάθη ἔμπροσθεν τοῦ ἡγεμόνος· καὶ ἐπηρώτησεν 11 αὐτὸν ὁ ἡγεμὼν λέγων, Σὺ εἶ ὁ βασιλεὺς τῶν Ἰουδαίων; ὁ δὲ Ἰησοῦς ἔφη αὐτῷ, [Σὺ λέγεις]. καὶ ἐν τῷ κατηγορεῖσθαι αὐτὸν ὑπὸ τῶν 12

72, 74, 75. ὅτι] asseverandi = כִּי or אַךְ, supra vii. 23, and xxvii. 43, 47.

Cap. XXVII. 4. רָאָה has force of "look out for," "take care of," in 1 Kings xii. 16, רְאֵה בֵיתְךָ דָוִד, and Ps. xxxvii. 37, רְאֵה יָשָׁר Ide εὐθύτητα, V.A.

σὺ ὄψῃ] Future for imp., infra 24, and see v. 48, vi. 33.

6. קָרְבָּן, Lev. vii. 38, xiii. 15, and elsewhere, = "oblatio." Mark vii. 11, κορβᾶν. Hence קָרְבָּנָא, "locus oblationum."

7. ἐξ] in this sense "quite unknown to class. authors." Schl.: Acts i. 18.

9. Zech. xi. 13, וָאַשְׁלִיךְ אֹתוֹ בֵּית יְהוָה אֶל־הַיּוֹצֵר V.A. καὶ ἐνέβαλον αὐτοὺς εἰς τὸν οἶκον Κυρίου εἰς τὸ χωνευτήριον (foundry). אֶל = "apud," which seems to be the explanation of εἰς-τὸν-ἀγρὸν-τοῦ in text. Our English Version of Zech. is accurate, "I cast them to the potter." Gesenius suggests אוֹצָר = "ærarium." 1 Kings vii. 51, xiv. 26.

13 ἀρχιερέων καὶ τῶν πρεσβυτέρων οὐδὲν ἀπεκρίνατο. τότε λέγει
14 αὐτῷ ὁ Πιλᾶτος, Οὐκ ἀκούεις πόσα σου καταμαρτυροῦσιν; καὶ οὐκ ἀπεκρίθη αὐτῷ *πρὸς οὐδὲ ἓν ῥῆμα,* ὥστε θαυμάζειν τὸν ἡγεμόνα
15 λίαν. Κατὰ δὲ ἑορτὴν εἰώθει ὁ ἡγεμὼν ἀπολύειν ἕνα τῷ ὄχλῳ δέσ-
16 μιον ὃν ἤθελον. εἶχον δὲ τότε δέσμιον ἐπίσημον, λεγόμενον Ἰησοῦν
17 Βαραββᾶν. συνηγμένων οὖν αὐτῶν εἶπεν αὐτοῖς ὁ Πιλᾶτος, Τίνα
18 θέλετε ἀπολύσω ὑμῖν, Ἰησοῦν Βαραββᾶν ἢ Ἰησοῦν τὸν λεγόμενον Χριστόν; ᾔδει γὰρ ὅτι διὰ φθόνον παρέδωκαν αὐτόν. καθημένου
19 δὲ αὐτοῦ ἐπὶ τοῦ βήματος ἀπέστειλεν πρὸς αὐτὸν ἡ γυνὴ αὐτοῦ λέγουσα, *Μηδὲν σοὶ καὶ τῷ δικαίῳ ἐκείνῳ·* πολλὰ γὰρ ἔπαθον
20 σήμερον κατ' ὄναρ δι' αὐτόν. οἱ δὲ ἀρχιερεῖς καὶ οἱ πρεσβύτεροι ἔπεισαν τοὺς ὄχλους ἵνα αἰτήσωνται τὸν Βαραββᾶν, τὸν δὲ Ἰησοῦν
21 ἀπολέσωσιν. ἀποκριθεὶς δὲ ὁ ἡγεμὼν εἶπεν αὐτοῖς, Τίνα θέλετε
22 *ἀπὸ τῶν δύο* ἀπολύσω ὑμῖν; οἱ δὲ εἶπον, Βαραββᾶν. λέγει αὐτοῖς ὁ Πιλᾶτος, Τί οὖν ποιήσω Ἰησοῦν τὸν λεγόμενον Χριστόν;
23 λέγουσιν πάντες, Σταυρωθήτω. ὁ δὲ ἔφη, Τί γὰρ κακὸν ἐποίησεν;
24 οἱ δὲ περισσῶς ἔκραζον λέγοντες, Σταυρωθήτω. ἰδὼν δὲ ὁ Πιλᾶτος ὅτι οὐδὲν ὠφελεῖ ἀλλὰ μᾶλλον θόρυβος γίνεται, λαβὼν ὕδωρ ἀπενίψατο τὰς χεῖρας ἀπέναντι τοῦ ὄχλου λέγων, *Ἀθῷός εἰμι ἀπὸ* τοῦ
25 αἵματος τούτου· *ὑμεῖς ὄψεσθε.* καὶ ἀποκριθεὶς πᾶς ὁ λαὸς εἶπεν,
26 Τὸ αἷμα αὐτοῦ ἐφ' ἡμᾶς καὶ ἐπὶ τὰ τέκνα ἡμῶν. τότε ἀπέλυσεν αὐτοῖς τὸν Βαραββᾶν, τὸν δὲ Ἰησοῦν φραγελλώσας *παρέδωκεν ἵνα σταυρωθῇ.*
27 Τότε οἱ στρατιῶται τοῦ ἡγεμόνος παραλαβόντες τὸν Ἰησοῦν εἰς
28 τὸ πραιτώριον συνήγαγον ἐπ' αὐτὸν ὅλην τὴν σπεῖραν. καὶ ἐκδύ-
29 σαντες αὐτὸν χλαμύδα κοκκίνην περιέθηκαν αὐτῷ, καὶ πλέξαντες στέφανον ἐξ ἀκανθῶν ἐπέθηκαν ἐπὶ τῆς κεφαλῆς αὐτοῦ καὶ κάλαμον ἐν τῇ δεξιᾷ αὐτοῦ, καὶ γονυπετήσαντες ἔμπροσθεν αὐτοῦ ἐνέπαιζον
30 αὐτῷ λέγοντες, Χαῖρε *ὁ βασιλεὺς* τῶν Ἰουδαίων, καὶ ἐμπτύσαντες εἰς αὐτὸν ἔλαβον τὸν κάλαμον καὶ ἔτυπτον [εἰς τὴν κεφαλὴν]
31 αὐτοῦ. καὶ ὅτε ἐνέπαιξαν αὐτῷ, ἐξέδυσαν αὐτὸν τὴν χλαμύδα

14. πρός] seems here = לְ in Deut. xxiv. 5, לֹא יַעֲבֹר לוֹ לְכָל־דָּבָר, "ne minima quidem res, non adeo ulla." Eccl. ix. 4, כִּי לְכֶלֶב חַי, "even a living dog," "down to a dog," ὁ κύων ὁ ζῶν αὐτός, V.A., where αὐτός = "even." Or perhaps πρός = עַד, rendered by ἕως in Judg. iv. 16, οὐ κατελείφθη ἕως ἑνός, V.A. לֹא נִשְׁאַר עַד־אֶחָד, 2 Sam. xvii. 22.

19. Same sort of expression as τί σοὶ κἀμοί; L. viii. 28, J. ii. 4, מַה־לִּי וָלָךְ, Judg. xi. 12.

21. Τίνα ἀπὸ τ. δ.] Job v. 1, מִי מִקְּדֹשִׁים.

24. Ἀθ. ἀπὸ] Gen. xxiv. 41, וְהָיִיתָ נָקִי מֵאָלָתִי, V.A. ἀθῷος ἔσῃ ἀπὸ τῆς ἀρᾶς μου.

25. Josh. ii. 19, דָּמוֹ בְרֹאשׁוֹ, i.e. "the guilt is his."

29. ὁ βασιλεύς] See i. 20, xi. 26.

καὶ ἐνέδυσαν αὐτὸν τὰ ἱμάτια αὐτοῦ, καὶ ἀπήγαγον αὐτὸν εἰς τὸ σταυρῶσαι.

Ἐξερχόμενοι δὲ εὗρον ἄνθρωπον Κυρηναῖον, ὀνόματι Σίμωνα· 32 τοῦτον *ἠγγάρευσαν* ἵνα ἄρῃ τὸν σταυρὸν αὐτοῦ. καὶ ἐλθόντες 33 εἰς τόπον λεγόμενον Γολγοθὰ, [ὅ ἐστιν κρανίου τόπος λεγόμενος,] ἔδωκαν αὐτῷ πιεῖν οἶνον μετὰ χολῆς μεμιγμένον· καὶ γευσάμενος 34 οὐκ ἠθέλησεν πιεῖν. σταυρώσαντες δὲ αὐτὸν διεμερίσαντο τὰ 35 ἱμάτια αὐτοῦ βαλόντες κλῆρον, καὶ καθήμενοι ἐτήρουν αὐτὸν ἐκεῖ. 36 καὶ ἐπέθηκαν ἐπάνω τῆς κεφαλῆς αὐτοῦ τὴν αἰτίαν αὐτοῦ γεγραμ- 37 μένην, Οὗτός ἐστιν Ἰησοῦς ὁ βασιλεὺς τῶν Ἰουδαίων. Τότε σταυ- 38 ροῦνται σὺν αὐτῷ δύο λῃσταί, εἷς ἐκ δεξιῶν καὶ εἷς ἐξ εὐωνύμων. οἱ δὲ παραπορευόμενοι ἐβλασφήμουν αὐτὸν, κινοῦντες τὰς κεφαλὰς 39 αὐτῶν καὶ λέγοντες, *Ὁ καταλύων* τὸν ναὸν καὶ ἐν τρισὶν ἡμέραις 40 οἰκοδομῶν, σῶσον σεαυτόν· εἰ υἱὸς εἶ τοῦ Θεοῦ, κατάβηθι ἀπὸ τοῦ σταυροῦ. ὁμοίως δὲ καὶ οἱ ἀρχιερεῖς ἐμπαίζοντες μετὰ τῶν γραμ- 41 ματέων καὶ πρεσβυτέρων ἔλεγον, Ἄλλους ἔσωσεν, ἑαυτὸν οὐ δύνα- 42 ται σῶσαι· βασιλεὺς Ἰσραήλ ἐστιν, καταβάτω νῦν ἀπὸ τοῦ σταυ- ροῦ καὶ πιστεύσομεν ἐπ' αὐτόν· *πέποιθεν ἐπὶ τὸν Θεόν,* ῥυσάσθω 43 νῦν αὐτὸν εἰ θέλει αὐτόν· εἶπεν γὰρ *ὅτι* Θεοῦ εἰμὶ υἱός. τὸ δ' 44 αὐτὸ καὶ οἱ λῃσταὶ οἱ συνσταυρωθέντες σὺν αὐτῷ ὠνείδιζον αὐτόν. Ἀπὸ δὲ ἕκτης ὥρας σκότος ἐγένετο ἐπὶ πᾶσαν τὴν γῆν ἕως ὥρας 45 ἐνάτης. περὶ δὲ τὴν ἐνάτην ὥραν ἀνεβόησεν ὁ Ἰησοῦς φωνῇ με- 46 γάλῃ λέγων, Ἡλὶ ἡλὶ λεμὰ σαβαχθανί; τοῦτ' ἔστιν, Θεέ μου Θεέ μου, ἵνα τί με ἐγκατέλιπες; τινὲς δὲ τῶν ἐκεῖ ἑστηκότων ἀκούσαν- 47 τες ἔλεγον *ὅτι* Ἡλίαν [φωνεῖ] οὗτος. καὶ εὐθέως δραμὼν εἷς ἐξ 48 αὐτῶν καὶ λαβὼν σπόγγον πλήσας τε ὄξους καὶ περιθεὶς καλάμῳ ἐπότιζεν αὐτόν. οἱ δὲ λοιποὶ ἔλεγον, Ἄφες ἴδωμεν εἰ ἔρχεται 49 Ἡλίας σώσων αὐτόν. Ὁ δὲ Ἰησοῦς πάλιν κράξας φωνῇ μεγάλῃ 50 ἀφῆκεν τὸ πνεῦμα. καὶ ἰδοὺ τὸ καταπέτασμα τοῦ ναοῦ ἐσχίσθη 51 ἀπὸ ἄνωθεν ἕως κάτω εἰς δύο, καὶ ἡ γῆ ἐσείσθη, καὶ αἱ πέτραι ἐσχίσθησαν, καὶ τὰ μνημεῖα ἀνεῴχθησαν καὶ πολλὰ σώματα τῶν 52 κεκοιμημένων ἁγίων ἠγέρθησαν· καὶ ἐξελθόντες ἐκ τῶν μνημείων 53 μετὰ τὴν ἔγερσιν αὐτοῦ εἰσῆλθον εἰς τὴν ἁγίαν πόλιν καὶ ἐνεφα- νίσθησαν πολλοῖς. ὁ δὲ ἑκατόνταρχος καὶ οἱ μετ' αὐτοῦ τηροῦντες 54

32. See Gesenius and Grimm sub voce: ἀγγαρεύω= "to press into the king's service;" primarily as a "cursor" or "tabellarius," secondarily for any public use, and so generally to "compel," a word of Persian origin. 2 Chr. xxx. 1, Neh. ii. 7, אִגְּרוֹת = ἐπιστολαί.

43. עַל בָּטַח. In 2 Kings xviii. 20, 21, we have in succession, τίνι πεποιθὼς πέποιθας σαυτῷ ἐπὶ τὴν ῥάβδον; "בְּ עַל לְךָ, and πεποιθόσιν ἐπ' αὐτόν.

46. Ps. xxii. 2, V.A. "Ὁ Θεός μου," as Mk. xv. 34, L. xviii. 11. Θεέ, unusual.

τὸν Ἰησοῦν ἰδόντες τὸν σεισμὸν καὶ τὰ γινόμενα ἐφοβήθησαν σφό-
55 δρα, λέγοντες, Ἀληθῶς Θεοῦ υἱὸς ἦν οὗτος. Ἦσαν δὲ ἐκεῖ γυναῖκες
πολλαὶ ἀπὸ μακρόθεν θεωροῦσαι, αἵτινες ἠκολούθησαν τῷ Ἰησοῦ
56 ἀπὸ τῆς Γαλιλαίας διακονοῦσαι αὐτῷ· ἐν αἷς ἦν Μαρία ἡ Μαγδα-
ληνή, καὶ Μαρία ἡ τοῦ Ἰακώβου καὶ Ἰωσῆ μήτηρ, καὶ ἡ μήτηρ τῶν
υἱῶν Ζεβεδαίου.
57 Ὀψίας δὲ γενομένης ἦλθεν ἄνθρωπος πλούσιος ἀπὸ Ἀριμαθαίας,
58 τοὔνομα Ἰωσήφ, ὃς καὶ αὐτὸς [ἐμαθήτευσεν] τῷ Ἰησοῦ· οὗτος προσελθὼν τῷ Πιλάτῳ ᾐτήσατο τὸ σῶμα τοῦ Ἰησοῦ. τότε ὁ Πιλᾶτος
59 ἐκέλευσεν ἀποδοθῆναι. καὶ λαβὼν τὸ σῶμα ὁ Ἰωσὴφ ἐνετύλιξεν
60 αὐτὸ ἐν σινδόνι καθαρᾷ, καὶ ἔθηκεν αὐτὸ ἐν τῷ καινῷ αὐτοῦ μνημείῳ
ὃ ἐλατόμησεν ἐν τῇ πέτρᾳ, καὶ προσκυλίσας λίθον μέγαν τῇ θύρᾳ
61 τοῦ μνημείου ἀπῆλθεν. ἦν δὲ ἐκεῖ Μαρία ἡ Μαγδαληνὴ καὶ ἡ ἄλλη
Μαρία, καθήμεναι ἀπέναντι τοῦ τάφου.
62 Τῇ δὲ ἐπαύριον, ἥτις ἐστὶν μετὰ τὴν παρασκευήν, συνήχθησαν
63 οἱ ἀρχιερεῖς καὶ οἱ Φαρισαῖοι πρὸς Πιλᾶτον λέγοντες, Κύριε, ἐμ-
νήσθημεν ὅτι ἐκεῖνος ὁ πλάνος εἶπεν ἔτι ζῶν, Μετὰ τρεῖς ἡμέρας
64 ἐγείρομαι. κέλευσον οὖν ἀσφαλισθῆναι τὸν τάφον ἕως τῆς τρίτης
ἡμέρας, μή ποτε ἐλθόντες οἱ μαθηταὶ αὐτοῦ κλέψωσιν αὐτὸν καὶ
εἴπωσιν τῷ λαῷ, Ἠγέρθη ἀπὸ τῶν νεκρῶν, καὶ ἔσται ἡ ἐσχάτη
65 πλάνη χείρων τῆς πρώτης. ἔφη αὐτοῖς ὁ Πιλᾶτος, Ἔχετε κουστω-
66 δίαν· ὑπάγετε ἀσφαλίσασθε ὡς οἴδατε. οἱ δὲ πορευθέντες ἠσφα-
λίσαντο τὸν τάφον σφραγίσαντες τὸν λίθον μετὰ τῆς κουστωδίας.

CAP.
28 Ὀψὲ δὲ σαββάτων, [τῇ ἐπιφωσκούσῃ εἰς μίαν σαββάτων,] ἦλθεν
2 Μαρία ἡ Μαγδαληνὴ καὶ ἡ ἄλλη Μαρία θεωρῆσαι τὸν τάφον. καὶ
ἰδοὺ σεισμὸς ἐγένετο μέγας· ἄγγελος γὰρ Κυρίου καταβὰς ἐξ οὐρανοῦ προσελθὼν ἀπεκύλισεν τὸν λίθον καὶ ἐκάθητο ἐπάνω αὐτοῦ.
3 ἦν δὲ ἡ εἰδέα αὐτοῦ ὡς ἀστραπὴ καὶ τὸ ἔνδυμα αὐτοῦ λευκὸν ὡς
4 χιών. *ἀπὸ δὲ τοῦ φόβου* αὐτοῦ ἐσείσθησαν οἱ τηροῦντες καὶ
5 ἐγενήθησαν ὡς νεκροί. ἀποκριθεὶς δὲ ὁ ἄγγελος εἶπεν ταῖς γυναιξὶν,
Μὴ φοβεῖσθε ὑμεῖς· οἶδα γὰρ ὅτι Ἰησοῦν τὸν ἐσταυρωμένον ζητεῖτε.
6 οὐκ ἔστιν ὧδε· ἠγέρθη γὰρ καθὼς εἶπεν· δεῦτε ἴδετε τὸν τόπον ὅπου
7 ἔκειτο. καὶ ταχὺ πορευθεῖσαι εἴπατε τοῖς μαθηταῖς αὐτοῦ ὅτι
ἠγέρθη ἀπὸ τῶν νεκρῶν, καὶ ἰδοὺ προάγει ὑμᾶς εἰς τὴν Γαλιλαίαν,
8 ἐκεῖ αὐτὸν ὄψεσθε. ἰδοὺ εἶπον ὑμῖν. καὶ ἀπελθοῦσαι ταχὺ ἀπὸ
τοῦ μνημείου μετὰ φόβου καὶ χαρᾶς μεγάλης [ἔδραμον ἀπαγγεῖλαι]
9 τοῖς μαθηταῖς αὐτοῦ. καὶ ἰδοὺ ὁ Ἰησοῦς ὑπήντησεν αὐταῖς λέγων,

Cap. XXVIII. 1. In Lev. xxiii. 15, שבת, ἑβδομὰς V. A., corresponds to שבע in parallel passage Deut. xvi. 9: it is apparently not used again in this sense: nor σάββατα in V.A.

Χαίρετε· αἱ δὲ προσελθοῦσαι ἐκράτησαν αὐτοῦ τοὺς πόδας καὶ προσεκύνησαν αὐτῷ. τότε λέγει αὐταῖς ὁ Ἰησοῦς, Μὴ φοβεῖσθε· 10 ὑπάγετε ἀπαγγείλατε τοῖς ἀδελφοῖς μου ἵνα ἀπέλθωσιν εἰς τὴν Γαλιλαίαν, κἀκεῖ με ὄψονται.

Πορενομένων δὲ αὐτῶν, ἰδού τινες τῆς κουστωδίας ἐλθόντες εἰς 11 τὴν πόλιν ἀπήγγειλαν τοῖς ἀρχιερεῦσιν ἅπαντα τὰ γενόμενα. καὶ 12 συναχθέντες μετὰ τῶν πρεσβυτέρων [συμβούλιόν τε λαβόντες] ἀργύρια ἱκανὰ ἔδωκαν τοῖς στρατιώταις, λέγοντες, Εἴπατε ὅτι οἱ 13 μαθηταὶ αὐτοῦ νυκτὸς ἐλθόντες ἔκλεψαν αὐτὸν ἡμῶν κοιμωμένων. καὶ ἐὰν ἀκουσθῇ τοῦτο *ἐπὶ τοῦ ἡγεμόνος,* ἡμεῖς πείσομεν αὐτὸν 14 καὶ ὑμᾶς ἀμερίμνους ποιήσομεν. οἱ δὲ λαβόντες τὰ ἀργύρια ἐποίη- 15 σαν ὡς ἐδιδάχθησαν· καὶ διεφημίσθη ὁ λόγος οὗτος παρὰ Ἰουδαίοις μέχρι τῆς σήμερον ἡμέρας.

Οἱ δὲ ἕνδεκα μαθηταὶ ἐπορεύθησαν εἰς τὴν Γαλιλαίαν εἰς τὸ 16 ὄρος οὗ ἐτάξατο αὐτοῖς ὁ Ἰησοῦς, καὶ ἰδόντες αὐτὸν προσεκύνησαν, 17 οἱ δὲ ἐδίστασαν. καὶ προσελθὼν ὁ Ἰησοῦς ἐλάλησεν αὐτοῖς λέγων, 18 Ἐδόθη μοι πᾶσα ἐξουσία ἐν οὐρανῷ καὶ ἐπὶ τῆς γῆς. πορευθέντες 19 μαθητεύσατε πάντα τὰ ἔθνη, βαπτίσαντες αὐτοὺς εἰς τὸ ὄνομα τοῦ πατρὸς καὶ τοῦ υἱοῦ καὶ τοῦ ἁγίου Πνεύματος, διδάσκοντες αὐτοὺς 20 τηρεῖν πάντα ὅσα ἐνετειλάμην ὑμῖν. καὶ ἰδοὺ ἐγὼ μεθ᾽ ὑμῶν εἰμι πάσας τὰς ἡμέρας ἕως τῆς συντελείας τοῦ αἰῶνος.

14. ἐπί=עַל, "juxta, apud." Is. xix. 7. Gen. xvi. 7, V.A. εὗρεν αὐτὴν ἐπὶ τῆς πηγῆς.

19. Does εἰς here = לְ or בְּ? The latter, in its frequent sense of "into," is rendered in V.A. by εἰς generally: though occasionally by ἐν, e.g. Ex. iv. 21.

20. ἕως τῆς σ. τ. α.] See xiii. 39, xxiv. 3.

S. MARK.

CHAPTER I.

HEBRAISMS. 2. πρὸ π. σ. 9. ἐν ἐκ. τ. ἡ. 11. ἐν ᾧ εὐδόκ. M. 3. 17, note. 15. π. ἐν. 28. ἡ ἀκοὴ, M. 4. 24, note. 39. εἰς ὅλ. τ. Γ. Also 8. 14. 15. 23. 24. 37. 40.

NON-CLASSICAL. 16. ἐν τ. θ. 24. ἦ. ἀπ. and τίς εἶ. 25. φιμ. 35. ἔνν. λ. 38. ἄγ. 43. ἐμβρ. 45. ἤρχ.

SEPTUAGINT. 7. ἰσχυρ. M. 3. 11, note. 18. ἀφέντες, M. 18. 12. 21. τὰ σάββατα for "the Sabbath," M. 28. 1. 34. ἐξέβαλε. 34. ἤφιε, see L. 18. 16.

CHAP. I. 2. πρὸ προσώπου] = לִפְנֵי as Amos 9. 4, and V. A. passim: an Hebraic idiom unknown in pure Greek.

12. ἐκβάλλει] See M. 9. 38, note, and infra 43.

15. π. ἐν τῷ εὐαγγ.] בְּ הֶאֱמִין = "fidem habuit," "trusted in," "put confidence in." V. A. render generally by πιστεύειν ἐν; but לְ הֶ"ן = "credidit," "believed," by same verb with dative. But this distinction is sometimes neglected in V. A., e.g. Gen. 15. 6, Ps. 78. 36, 119. 66. In N. T. we have some few instances of πιστεύειν ἐν and πίστις ἐν: one here; and Rom. 3. 25, Eph. 1. 15, Col. 1. 4, Phil. 3. 3, 1 Tim. 3. 13, 2 Tim. 3. 15; which are probably due to the Hebrew use of בְּ, as the more frequent forms, with εἰς, ἐπὶ and πρὸς, to the Hebrew לְ. The *very rare* occurrence of the verb with *any such prepositions* in Classical Authors, or in any Greek books except N. T., lends weight to this suggestion.

21. τοῖς σάββ.] V. A. generally Plural; Hebr. Singular. This is one of the rare instances of dative of point of time. M. 12. 1. Mc. 3. 2, 4; 6. 21.

23. ἐν πν. ἀκαθ.] a very startling instance of ἐν for בְּ. M. 3. 11, note: and also infra 2. 8.

24. τί ἡμῖν καὶ σοί] M. 27. 19, note.

CHAPTER II.

HEBR. 2. εἰς οἰκ. and ἐλ. αὐ. τ. λ. 10. υἱ. τ. ἀνθ. 14. ἐπὶ τ. τ. 15. καὶ ἐγ....καὶ. 19. υἱ. τ. ν. 20. ἐλ. δ. ἡμ. 23. ὁδ. π. 26. τ. ἄρτ. τ. προθ.

NON-C. 1. δι' ἡμ. 2. χ. μ. τ. πρ. 4. μὴ. 5. τ. ἀφέ. 11. σοὶ λ. 13. ἤρχ. 14. παράγ. 17. ἦλθ. κ. 25. τί ἐπ. 26. πῶς.

SEPT. 12. ἐναντίον. 22. βάλλ. οἱ. ν.

CHAPTER III.

HEBR. 17. Βοαν. 18. Καναν. 22. ἐν τ. ἄρχ. 23. ἐν παρ. 29. εἰς τ. αἰ. Also 11. 21. 22.

---

39. εἰς ὃ. τ. Γ.] 6. 3; 13. 9, 16; M. 13. 56, note.

43. ἐξέβ. α.] dimisit eum. V. A. have ἐκβάλλω for שָׁלַח Pihel, Exod. 12. 33, Ps. 43. 3, where the original means "to cast out." Hence the word being thus used as equivalent to שׁלח in one mood and sense, seems to have come to be taken as equivalent to it in all its moods and senses; and so to the general one of "*dimitto*." And this has passed on to the N. T., M. 9. 38, J. 10. 4.

CHAP. II. 8. τῷ πν.] dat. of instrument, or manner; very rare; about twelve times in the whole Gospel. 1. 34, 5. 29, 6. 32, 7. 2, 6, 13. 26, 8. 12, 12. 13.

12. ἐναντίον] See M. 23. 14; and 15. 23, for ὅτι.

15. καὶ ἐγ....καὶ] Common Hebrew form.

17. ἦλθον κ.] See M. 2. 26. In V. A. we sometimes find τοῦ before infinitive, sometimes not, in similar phrases. Gen. 27. 5, וַיֵּלֶךְ לָצוּד ἐπορεύθη θηρεῦσαι; and 28. 6, שָׁלַח אֹתוֹ לָקַחַת ἀπέστειλε λαβεῖν. 2 Ch. 20. 36, וַיְחַבְּרֵהוּ...לַעֲשׂוֹת אֳנִיּוֹת לָלֶכֶת ἐκοινώνησε...τοῦ ποιῆσαι τὰ πλοῖα τοῦ πορευθῆναι. 2 Sam. 21. 16, וַיֹּאמֶר לְהַכּוֹת διενοεῖτο τοῦ πατάξαι.

23. ὁδὸν π.] Judg. 17. 8, יָבֹא הַר לַעֲשׂוֹת דַּרְכּוֹ ἦλθεν ἕως ὄρους τοῦ ποιῆσαι ὁδὸν αὑτοῦ. Herod. 7. 42, ποιεῖσθαι ὁδόν. Schl. considers it a Latinism for "iter facere."

26. ἄρτους προθ.] V. A. for לֶחֶם מַעֲרֶכֶת (from עָרַךְ instruxit) Ex. 40. 23; 1 Chr. 9. 32, 23. 29: and also for לְפָּנִים Ex. 35. 13, 39. 36; rendered literally τοῦ προσώπου 1 Kings 21. 2, Neh. 10. 33. (In Ex. 25. 30, ἄρτους ἐνωπίους ἐναντίον μου.) The two expressions spring alike from Ex. 40. 23, בַּעֲרֹךְ עָרַךְ לֶחֶם לִפְנֵי יְהֹ׳ καὶ προέθηκεν ἄρτους τῆς προ-θέσεως. This is a good instance of the Hebr. gen. of qualification equivalent to an adjective: aptly rendered by the English idiomatic combination "shew-bread." M. 1. 11.

CHAP. III. 2. Syntax very irregular all through the Chapter.

3. ἐξ. ἔχ. τὴν χ.] "that had his hand withered."

NON-C. 3. ἔγ. εἰς τ. μ. 5. μετ' ὁ. 6. συμβ. ἐπ. 11. ὅτ. αὐ. ἐθ. 13. ἀπῆλ. 14. ἐπ. δ. 20. μήτε. 21. οἱ π. αὐ. ἐξ. κρ. 24. σταθ. 29. ἐν. ἐ. αἰ. κρ. 31. φων. αὐ. 34. ἴδε.

CHAPTER IV.

HEBR. 1. πρ. τ. θάλ. 9. ὁ ἔχ. ὦτα ἀκ. 24. ἐν ᾧ μ. 30. ἐν π. π. π.

---

6. *συμβ. ἐποίουν*] See 15. 1 and compare M. 12. 14, for σ. λαμβάνειν, of which there are five instances in M.

17. Βοανεργὲς] supposed = בְּנֵי רָגֶשׁ. Ps. 2. 1, רָגְשׁוּ, V. A. ἐφρύαξαν (A) : and 55. 14, נְהַלֵּךְ בְּרָגֶשׁ ἐπορεύθημεν ἐν ὁμονοίᾳ (B) : and 64. 3, מֵרִגְשַׁת פֹּעֲלֵי אָוֶן ἀπὸ πλήθους ἐργαζομένων ἀδικίαν (C) : and Dan. 6. 7, 12, 16, הַרְגִּישׁוּ "cum strepitu concurrerunt." The idea of the word seems to be, "the sound of many voices speaking together": and so it might come to be rendered by βροντή. Keble, in his close and admirable translation of the Psalms, renders (A) "gathering raged"; (B) "Together through the Courts of God, In Choir we sweetly passed"; (C) "When sinners shout and shout again." This passage is quoted by Westcott (Dict. of Bible) in proof of the supposition that our Lord used *Aramaic* in familiar discourse.

18. Βαρθολομαῖος] = בַּר תֹּלְמִי. Ps. 2. 12, Prov. 31. 2, בַּר = Son, constantly used in Proper Names.

Κανανίτην] Syr. קַנְאָא = Ζηλώτης, L. 6. 13, M. 10. 4.

21. *οἱ παρ' αὐτοῦ*] I find no instance of this in V. A.: but in 1 Macc. 13. 52 it occurs in same sense (a passage worth consulting for its use of ἐν, μετὰ, τοῦ). The nearest approach to it in N. T. is Mc. 5. 26, τὰ παρ' αὐτῆς, her property.

ἐξέστη] 2 Cor. 5. 13. No instance in V. A. of this sense of word : several of its meaning "terror, astonishment"; but not, "loss of reason."

29. *εἰς τ. αἰ.*] literal for לְעוֹלָם V. A.: Ps. 48. 8, 89. 37, 1 Kings 1. 31, and passim. See 1 Th. 4. 15. For ἔνοχος see M. 5. 21.

CHAP. IV. 1. *παρὰ τὴν θ.*] M. 13. 1, 20. 30, Mc. 5. 21, 10. 46, L. 8. 35, Acts 10. 6. These examples of παρὰ with acc., after verbs not signifying "motum ad locum," seem caught from V. A. usage, which gives παρὰ for אֵצֶל "juxta, apud," with acc. as often as with dative, after verbs of same kind : Lev. 10. 12, 1 Kings 10. 19, 13. 24, Ezek. 33. 30. For πρὸς τὴν θ. see M. 13. 56.

10. *ἠρώτ. αὐτὸν...τὴν π.*] Double acc. after ἐρωτάω : apparently arising from its constant confusion with αἰτέω, in N. T.: possibly to be traced to its representing שָׁאַל which has both meanings, "interrogo" and "peto"; John 14. 16, 12. 21, M. 15. 23, L. 14. 18. Other instances are L. 20. 3, J. 16. 23, M. 21. 24 : but these do not quite correspond

1—2

Non-C. 1. παρὰ and πρὸς τ. θάλ. 5. ἄλλο δὲ. 10. ἠρ. αὐ....
τ. π. 21. ἔρχ. 22. οὐ γάρ....ἔλθῃ. 24. βλ. τί ἀκ. 34. ἐπέλυε.
38. ἐπὶ τ. π. 39. πεφ.
SEPT. 29. ἀποστ. τ. δ.

CHAPTER V.

HEBR. 2. ἐν π. ἁ. 7. τί ἐ. κ. σ. 8. ἐξ. τ. πν. voc. 11. πρ.
τ. δ. 21. ἦν π. τ. θ. 25. οὖσα ἐ. ρ. αἵ. 28. ὅτι. 34. ὕ. εἰς εἰρ.
41. ταλ. κ. and τὸ κορ.
Non-C. 16. πῶς ἐ. τ. δ. 28. σωθ. 32. περιεβ. ἰδ. 43. διεστ.

---

to the phrase here. This confusion is more curious, as V. A. carefully distinguish the two meanings.

12. "So that they may see with their eyes open and not perceive, and hear with open ear, but not understand; in case they may at some future time turn to God and their sins be forgiven." This passage confirms my suggestions at M. 13. 14.

21. "Is the lamp brought in?"

22. The Greek here is very different from M. 10. 26 and L. 12. 2, usually quoted as parallel, and cannot bear the meaning of our A. V. Perhaps we may render thus: "For a thing is not necessarily hidden, which may have escaped manifestation hitherto; nor was it made to be a mystery, but to come to light." Present concealment does not prevent future manifestation (e.g. vv. 21, 27).

23. ὦτα ἀκούειν] M. 11. 15.

29. ἀποστέλλει τὸ δ.] Joel 3. 13, שִׁלְחוּ מַגָּל ἐξαποστείλατε δρέπανον V. A. Rev. 14. 15, 16.

30. "To what *are we to liken*?" or "with what comparison *are we* to compare it?" מָשָׁל = similitudo, παραβολή, Ez. 24. 3, 17. 2; or = proverb, παροιμία, Ez. 18. 2. In each case מָשָׁל מָשַׁל = παραβάλλε παραβολήν.

39. ἐκόπασεν] 6. 51, Jonah 1. 11, וְיִשְׁתֹּק לָךְ מַה נַּעֲשֶׂה τί ποιήσομέν σοι καὶ κοπάσει ἡ θάλασσα; V. A. (mark Hebraism in καί). The verb, originally = "to be tired out," is used as correlative of Hebr. verbs meaning "rest and quiet after labour": e.g. חָדַל, שָׁתַק. It bears this sense also in Class. Authors.

CHAP. V. 8. τὸ πν.] Hebraism for voc., infra 41, and 10. 47, and 14. 34, see note M. 1. 20, 11. 26, Luke 8. 54, 6. 20, Gal. 4. 6, Eph. 5. 22.

22, 23. See notes 4. 1 and M. 7. 23.

25. ἐν ρ. αἵμ.] Levit. 20. 18.

26. τὰ παρ' αὐτῆς] 3. 21. Grimm: "quæ ab ejus latere erant, ideoque ei suppetebant." Unsatisfactorily. We may strain it to mean, "everything out of her purse."

S. MARK.

Chapter VI.

HEBR. 2. δυν. 3. πρ. ἡ. κ. ἐσκ. ἐν αὐ. 7. δύο δύο. 14. 15. 23. 35. ὅτι. 39. συμπ. σ. 40. πρ. πρ. 48. ἐν τῷ ἑ.
NON-C. 19. ἐνεῖχε. 25. μετὰ σπ. 27. σπεκ. 31. ὑμ. αὐτ. 33. προῆλ. αὐ. 34. μὴ. 35. ὥρα π. 36. τί γ. φ. 45. ἕως αὐ. ἀπ. 51. ἐκόπ. 52. ἐπὶ τ. ἄ. 56. ἐσώζ.

---

28. σωθ.] M. 9. 21, note: for sense of "healing."

34. ὖ. εἰς εἰρήνην] L. 7. 50, 8. 48; V. A. for לְךָ לְשָׁלוֹם, 1 Sam. 1. 17, 20. 42. This use of לְ, and its literal rendering by εἰς in V. A. and N. T., is adverbial; Lev. 25. 18, 26. 5, יָשַׁב לָבֶטַח; V. A. μετὰ ἀσφαλείας = "securely," "safely" (as in Auth. V.); Ex. 26. 9, לְבָד, à part, apart; Job 36. 31, לְמַכְבִּיר, abundantly (Ges. "copiosè"); Is. 42. 3, לֶאֱמֶת, "according to truth," i.e. "righteousness" (see M. 11. 29, 12. 20); "uprightly." Compare Jerem. 6. 29 and 4. 30 for לַשָּׁוְא; V. A. εἰς κενὸν and εἰς μάταιον; Gal. 2. 2, εἰς κενὸν, adverb: and Rom. 12. 3, εἰς τὸ σωφρονεῖν, soberly, a very remarkable instance of the form, from containing the article, necessary to turn inf. into noun. The only classical authors cited by Grimm for this use of εἰς, are Diodorus 19. 9 and Heliodorus 10. 30, εἰς κενὸν, Josephus, Philo, Ælian (εἰς τὸ παντελὲς).

41. טְלִיתָא קוּמִי] Chaldee or Syriac. This is often cited in proof of our Lord speaking familiarly in Aramaic. Dr Roberts takes the opposite view, suggesting, that though he usually spoke Greek, he used Aramaic words on this occasion for the child's sake; who, from her youth and as being daughter of an ἀρχισυνάγωγος, a strict Jew probably, Ἑβραῖος ἐξ Ἑβραίων, and not an Ἑλληνιστὴς with foreign tendencies and sympathies, was likely to know Greek.

CHAP. VI. 7. δύο δύο] V. A. passim; Gen. 7. 9, 15, שְׁנַיִם שְׁנַיִם δύο δύο: and infra 39, συμπόσια συμπόσια.

8, 9. Syntax very irregular.

14. αἱ δυνάμεις] M. 7. 22, note.

19. ἐνεῖχεν αὐ.] Gen. 49. 23, semel in V. A., "were full of hate against, pressed fiercely on," Herod. 1. 118, 8. 27, χόλον ἐνέχειν τινι.

καὶ οὐκ ἠδύνατο] BUT could not: corresponding to what Ges. calls "vau adversativus" = "sed" or "et tamen," Gen. 17. 20, 21, Jud. 16. 15: V. A. passim. Infra 7. 24.

27. σπεκουλάτωρ] Latinism; possibly = spiculator, δορυφόρος.
31. αὐτοί] "by yourselves": alone.
35. ὥρα πολλή] Very strange phrase and baffling analysis.
40. πρασιαί] Beds in gardens, squares, plots, rows.
49. ἔδοξαν] M. 3. 9, note: for the various meanings of verb.

Chapter VII.

Hebr. 2. κοιναῖς. 5. περιπ. 22. ὀφθ. πον. 24. καὶ οὐκ ἠδ. Also 6. 15. 20.

Non-C. 3. πυγμῇ. 4. παρ. κρ. 19. καθαρ. 25. αὐτῆς. 26. ἠρώτα. 35. ἀκοαί.

Sept. 10. ὁ κακολογῶν θ. τελ. 30. βεβλημ. 33. ἔβαλε.

---

52. ἐπὶ τοῖς ἄρτοις] I find no satisfactory explanation of this form, and do not understand it: nor does any one seem to do so.

Chap. VII. 2. κοιναῖς χ.] κοινός = βέβηλος "profanus," "defiled, unclean": opp. to καθαρός, ἅγιος, ἡγιασμένος, ἀφωρισμένος. As the idea of ἅγιον was "separation," we have it and its derivatives in V. A. for נֵזֶר, Numb. 6. 12, Lev. 25. 5, 11, Zech. 7. 3. The exactly opposite is contained in κοινός. V. A. never use it in this sense; but in Apocr. 1 Macc. 1. 47, 62, θύειν ὕεια καὶ κτήνη κοινά and μὴ φαγεῖν κοινά = טָמֵא; and Joseph. Ann. Iud. xii. 12, 13, κοινοὺς ἀνθρώπους and κοινὸν βίον, "ex usu a nativis Græcis alieno," Grimm. Infra 15. See note M. 15. 11, Acts 10. 14, 28, and 11. 8, Rom. 14. 14.

3. πυγμῇ] thoroughly: *"fist-deep."*

5. περιπατοῦσι] I find only one passage in V. A., 2 Kings 20. 3, where this verb is used *alone* as here, to signify "go on," "conduct themselves," "live." But in N. T. there are many (e.g. Acts 21. 21): chiefly in S. John and S. Paul, Eph. 4. 1, Rom. 13. 13, 2 Cor. 5. 8, 2 J. 4, 6.

9. καλῶς ἀθετεῖτε] "'tis well of you to set at naught."

10. θαν. τελ.] = מוֹת יוּמָת, Ex. 21. 17, same in V. A. *See note, M.* 15. 4, for κακολογῶν.

19. καθαρίζον π. τ. β.] Possibly, "clearing away all that has been eaten." But there may be some special force in καθαρίζειν, as following κοινοῦν so closely; expressing, as it does, the exactly opposite idea.

22. ὀφθ. πον.] M. 20. 15 note.

26. Ἑλληνίς] = a Gentile, see Col. 3. 11. The term Ἕλλην includes all heathens. She was a Canaanite, M. 15. 21. ἠρώτα "she kept asking Him": mark confusion between this verb and αἰτέω, supra 4. 11, note.

30. βεβλημένην] βάλλω = "put," very common in N. T., from use in V. A., for שׂוּם *pono*, M. 26. 12, note, infra 33.

34. ἐφφαθά] for הִפָּתַח Niph., from פָּתַח *aperuit*: Aramaic form, 3. 17.

35. αἱ ἀκοαί] "His ears": L. 7. 1, Acts 17. 20, Heb. 5. 11; all like this, plural with article. None of these seems quite parallel to the Classical use, cited by L. and S., *of ἀκοή without article;* ἀκοαῖς δέχεσθαι, εἰς ἀκοὰς ἐλθεῖν, δι' ἀκοῆς.

Chapter VIII.

HEBR. 4. ἐπ' ἐρημ. 12. εἰ δοθ. 15. βλέπ. ἀπό. 19. εἰς τ. π. 31. ἀπὸ τ. π.

NON-C. 1. μὴ ἐχ. τί φ. 7. εἶπε π. 9. ἀπέλ. 12. τῷ πν. 22. φέρ. 30. ἐπετίμ.

SEPT. 32. παρρησίᾳ.

Chapter IX.

HEBR. 1. ἐν δ. 11. ὅτι λέγ. 19. πρὸς ὑ. ἔσ. 25. τὸ πν.

CHAP. VIII. 3. ἐκλυθήσονται] M. 15. 32, Hebr. 12. 3, 5, "unstrung, relaxed," as after fatigue. Frequent in V. A., to express weariness and exhaustion, for יָעֵף or עָיֵף, 2 Sam. 16. 14, 17. 29, Is. 46. 1, and for רָפָה, Is. 13. 7, and other words of similar meaning. And it has Classical authority.

4. ἐπ' ἐρημίας] Grimm defines "ἐπί, c. gen. de loco in quo; de loco in cujus superficie." Must not the latter condition always hold, for strict grammatical correctness? We may perhaps say here, "upon desert ground": but it is strained. But עַל, to which ἐπί corresponds, in V. A., seems to mean "apud, juxta," without any necessary notion of "super" involved (see Gesenius): and this has probably affected the use of ἐπί in N. T. 1 Cor. 6. 1, M. 28. 14, note.

12. εἰ δ.] εἰ negandi, for אִם, in elliptical expressions: V. A. passim, 1 Sam. 15. 45, חַי־יְהוָֹ"ה אִם יִפֹּל ζῇ Κύριος εἰ πεσεῖται; 2 Sam. 11. 11, חַיֶּךָ אִם אֶעֱשֶׂה ζῇ ἡ ψυχή σου εἰ ποιήσω; 1 Kin. 1. 51, יִשָּׁבַע לִי אִם יָמִית ὁμοσάτω μοι εἰ οὐ θανατώσει (mark here the insertion of οὐ). Ps. 94. 11, quoted Hebr. 3. 11, 4. 3.

15. διεστέλλετο] 5. 43, 7. 36, 9. 9, M. 16. 20, Acts 15. 24, Hebr. 12. 20. This middle voice is found in V. A. several times; chiefly in Ez.: for Hiph. הִזְהִיר monuit. Grimm names Aristotle and Polybius as using it.

βλέπετε ἀπό] 12. 38: these are the only instances of this form, which appears to be Hebraic.

20. "Fragment-fillings of how many baskets?"

30. ἐπετίμησεν] "sensu mitiore, severius admoneo = charge strictly": never so used, apparently, "apud Græcos" (to use Grimm's term for Classical writers) nor in V. A.

32. παρρησίᾳ] See John 7. 4 and 11. 54, παρρησίᾳ περιεπάτει, and Col. 2. 15; LXX. Lev. 26. 13 for קוֹמְמִיּוּת "with a high hand": rather "erecto corpore."

CHAP. IX. 11. This use of ὅτι here and verse 28 is very curious and unique. Are there not two Questions? the first, ὅτι λέγουσιν...: with

26. 31. ὅτι.   29. ἐν οὐδενὶ...ἐν πρ.   39. ἐπὶ τῷ ὀ.   41. ἐν τῷ ὀ.
43. εἰς τ. γ.   47. γέεν. τοῦ π.   50. ἐν τίνι.
NON-C.   6. ᾔδει τί λαλ.   12. ἐπὶ τ. υἱ.   21. πόσος χρ. ὡς.
35. ἐφών.   42. καλόν...βέβληται.
SEPT.   39. κακολογ.

CHAPTER X.

HEBR.   2. εἰ ἔξεστι, M. 12. 10, note.   8. ἔσ. οἱ δ. εἰς, M. 2. 6, note.   11. ἐπ' αὐ.   24. πεπ. ἐπὶ τ. χρ.   26. καὶ τίς.   33. ὅτι. 46. π. τ. ὀ.   47. ὁ υἱ. Δ.   51. ῾Ραβ.
NON-C.   11. ὃς ἐὰν ἀπ.   17. εἰς.   23. πῶς δ.   30. ἐὰν μὴ λ. 33. κατακρ. θαν.   38. τί.   42. οἱ δοκ. ἄρχειν.   45. ἦλθε δ.   49. εἶπε φ.

CHAPTER XI.

HEBR.   3. 17. ὅτι.   4. πρὸς τ. θ.   9. 10. ῾Ωσ. ἐν τ. ὑψ.   28. ἐν π. ἐξ.
NON-C.   8. εἰς τ. ὁ.   14. φάγοι.   22. ἔχ. π. Θ.   24. ἂν αἰτεῖσθε.
SEPT.   16. ἤφιε in sense of permitting: L. 18. 16.

---

its answer, Ἠλίας...πάντα: the second, καὶ πῶς..., answered verse 13.

12.   ἐπὶ τὸν υἱ.]   John 12. 16, we have ἐπ' αὐτῷ γεγρ. *dative.*

19.   πρὸς ὑμᾶς ἔσ.]   See notes M. 13. 56 and 2 Th. 3. 10: and compare infra 11. 4.

42.   Curious use of Tenses: baffling explanation.

44.   Quotation from LXX. Is. 66. 24, almost identical. See notes M. 5. 22, 29, for γέενναν τοῦ π. .

CHAP. X. 24.   πεποιθ.] with dative: see note M. 27. 43, and supra, cap. 1. 15.

33.   κατακρ. αὐτὸν θανάτῳ] a most strange construction, inexplicable by any ordinary rules of Greek syntax.

42.   οἱ δοκοῦντες ἄρχειν] Grimm renders "qui censentur imperare, qui agnoscuntur imperatores": but this is a very strained interpretation. It is very difficult to unravel the real force of the words.

46.   παρά] with acc., for אֵצֶל near: 4. 1, note.

49.   εἶπεν αὐ. φωνηθ.] a thoroughly ungrammatical and unclassical phrase: L. 19. 15, 2 Cor. 4. 6.

CHAP. XI. 10.   ὡσαννὰ ἐν τ. ὑψ.]   M. 21. 10, note.

22.   πίστιν Θ.]   The expression defies analysis: we see what it means, but cannot define how it gets the meaning.

S. MARK. 9

CHAPTER XII.

HEBR. 1. ἐν π. 6. 29. ὅτι. 10. εἰς κ. γ. 14. βλ. εἰς πρ. 14. 32. ἐπ' ἀλ. 36. ἐν τ. Πν. 38. βλ. ἀπὸ, supra 8. 15.
NON-C. 4. ἐκεφαλ. 13. λόγῳ. 18. 24. οἵτινες and μὴ. 28. ποία. 30. ἐξ ὅλ. 34. νουν. 37. ὁ π. ὄχ. 41. πῶς ὁ ὅ. β. 42. μία.
SEPT. 12. 19. 20. ἀφίημι, in sense of "leave," M. 18. 12, note. 44. βίου = means of living, L. 15. 13, note.

CHAP. XII. 10, 11. See notes, M. 2. 6, 21. 42 : the passage is an exact quotation from V. A. The feminine αὕτη is literal rendering of the Hebr. feminine זֹאת.

12. πρὸς αὐτοὺς] "with a view to them," "in reference to them": Rom. 10. 21.

13. λόγῳ] The parallel passages M. 22. 15, L. 20. 20, have ἐν λόγῳ and λόγου. This use of λόγος, sing. where we should expect plural, is curious.

14. ἐπ' ἀληθείας] "on the side of truth." Or perhaps a strict literal translation of the Hebrew idiom (vide Gesen. עַל): e.g. עַל שֶׁקֶר LXX. ἀδίκως (i.e. ψευδῶς), see my note, Matt. 11. 19 ; Ps. 31. 24, עַל יֶתֶר περίσσως LXX. IN ADVERBIAL SENSE: see infra 32. And so ἐπ' ἀλ. = עַל אֱמֶת. But it has classical authority : Demosthenes passim.

30. Exact quotation from V. A. ; ἐξ for בְּ. For future ἀγαπήσεις see note M. 19. 18.

36. M. 22. 43 has ἐν πνεύματι = "by inspiration." Both forms are intensely Hebraic and furnish a good illustration of the perplexities that confront and bewilder any Student of the Sacred Text, acquainted with Classical Greek only, if he is truthfully and honestly striving to *understand* what he has before him : and not merely to turn it into English. If he is content with the bald, literal translation of our E. V., "*in spirit,*" or "*by the Holy Ghost,*" corresponding to the Vulgate, "*in spiritu*" and "*in spiritu sancto,*" on the plea that he fully understands what the phrases severally mean, and does not need any exact critical investigation of the original expression : we must deplore the introduction of such a spirit into so serious an enquiry. The first step towards any *profitable* study of G. T., is to divest oneself absolutely of all old memories of the familiar English Version, and of the associations popularly connected with its well remembered phraseology : and then to endeavour, without any à *priori* bias, to discover the real meaning. I need not say that "*in spirit,*" whatever sense may have been popularly connected with it in this particular passage, is widely different from the

Chapter XIII.

HEBR. 3. 9. 16. εἰς τ. ὅ. 14. βδ. τ. ἐρ. M. 24. 15, note. 20. οὐ...πᾶσα σ. 22. δώσ. σημ. 25. δυνάμεις.

NON-C. 6. ἐπὶ τῷ ὀνόμ. 19. ἀπ' ἀ. κτ. 33. πότε.

SEPT. 3. 9. 16. εἰς = *at*, or *near*: notes M. 13. 56, 26. 18. 25. αἱ δυνάμεις..., Is. 34. 4. 27. ἀπ' ἄκρ....οὐρ. 34. ἀφεὶς.

Chapter XIV.

HEBR. 4. εἰς τί ἡ ἀπ. 6. ἐν ἐμοί. 14. 27. 58. 69. 71. ὅτι. 27. ἐν ἐμοί. 36. 'Αβ. ὁ π. 49. ἤμ. πρ. ὑ. and 54. 60. εἰς τ. μ. 62. τῆς δ. 64. ἔνοχον θ. notes M. 5. 22, 1 Cor. 11. 27, Heb. 2. 15.

NON-C. 1. πῶς. 2. μήποτε...ἔσται. 5. ἠδ...πρ. and ἐνεβρ. 9. εἰς ὅ. τ. κ. 19. εἷς κ. εἷς and μήτι ἐγώ. 31. ἐκ π....μᾶλλον and οὐ...ἀπαρν. 32. ἕως πρ. 36. οὐ τί...σύ. 41. ἀπέχει. 42. ἄγ. 43. μετὰ μ. 44. σύσσ. 51. ἐπὶ γ. 56. 59. καὶ ἴσ...ἦσαν. 65. ἔβ. 72. ἐπιβ.

SEPT. 25. γεννήμ. 50. ἀφέντες.

---

more correct rendering of the Hebraic ἐν πνεύματι "by divine inspiration," more fully expressed by the form in Mc. ἐν τῷ πν. τῷ ἁγίῳ.

CHAP. XIII. 19. ἀπ' ἀρχῆς κτ.] The omission of article is simply Hebraic in its irregularity: and in this particular context may possibly be due to the opening words of Genesis. Read carefully J. 1. 1, note.

20. Observe Hebr. idiom: כָּל־לֹא, note, M. 24. 22, L. 1. 38, Apoc. 21. 27.

25. αἱ δυνάμεις...] L. 21. 26, note. The singular form is more frequent in V. A. as the equivalent of צָבָא.

27. ἀπ' ἄκρου] Note, M. 24. 31.

32. εἰ μή] *but, on the contrary*: M. 24. 36, L. 4. 26, 27, Gal. 2. 16.

CHAP. XIV. 4. ἀπώλεια] M. 26. 8, note.

41. ἀπέχει] W. and W. quote Herod. 3. 142 as using ἀπέχει for "licet." Schl. gives Anacr. Ode 28. 33. This is the only instance in N. T. Not found in V. A.

43. μετὰ μαχ.] M. 24. 31, note.

54. אוֹר in Hebrew occasionally means *fire*, Is. 44. 16, 47. 14, where V. A. has πῦρ: though almost always elsewhere φῶς. Hence φῶς may possibly have come to be taken in the same double sense as אוֹר, for which it so generally stands.

62. τῆς δυν.] Note, M. 26. 64.

65. ἔβαλλον] The only instance of this meaning of verb in N. T.; none occurs in V. A.

72. ἐπιβαλών] Some refer this to "covering up his face."

S. MARK.

Chapter XV.

HEBR. 21. ἀγγαρ. 34. Ὁ Θ....εἰς τί.
NON-C. 1. συμβ. π. 11. ἀνέσ. 15. τὸ ἱκ. π. 22. φέρ. 36. εἷς. 47. ποῦ.

Chapter XVI.

HEBR. 5. ἐν τ. δ. 17. ἐν τῷ ὄν.
NON-C. 6. ἴδε.

CHAP. XV. 1. ἐπὶ τὸ πρωΐ] לַבֹּקֶר. εἰς τὸ πρωΐ V. A., Ps. 30. 6, 59. 17.

2. σὺ λέγεις] M. 26. 25, note.

15. ἱκ. π.] satisfacere; suam dare satisfactionem. A. 17. 9.

34. ὁ Θεός...εἰς τί] M. 1. 20, 27, 46, notes: look out examples given there and supra Mc. 5. 8. Εἰς τί is simply the literal rendering of לָמָה why : *Hebrew* not *Greek*.

47. ἐθεώρ. ποῦ τίθ.] For non-sequence of Tenses, past followed by present, infra 16. 1, so common in N. T., see M. 1. 22, note.

CHAP. XVI. 5. V. A. always render יָמִין by plural: generally ἐκ δεξιῶν, as infra 19, answering to יָמִין.

S. LUKE.

Chapter I.

HEBR. 5. ἐν τ. ἡμ. 6. πορευόμ. 7. 18. προβ. ἐν τ. ἡ. αὐ. 15. ἐνώπ. 17. ἐν φρ. 18. κατὰ τί. 20. εἰς τ. κ. αὐ. 21. ἐν τ. χρ. 29. ἐπὶ τ. λ. 32. υἱ. ὑψ. 34. ἀνδ. οὐ γ. 37. οὐκ ἀδ....ῥῆμα. 44. ἐν ἀγ. 49. ἐπ. μ....δυν. 51. ἐπ. κ. ἐν β. 58. μετ' αὐ. 69. κ. σωτ. 76. πρὸ π. 77. ἐν ἀφ. 78. ἐν οἷς. 79. σκ. θ. Also 25. 46. 61.

NON-C. 15. ἔτι. 20. μὴ. 25. ἐν ἡμ....ἀφ. 39. μετὰ σ. 54. μνησθ. 57. ἐγένν.

SEPT. 17. ἐνώπ. for ἔμπροσθεν, see 5. 19 for contrary use. 20. ἀνθ' ὧν. 36. συνείληφ.

CHAP. I. 5. ἐν ταῖς ἡμέραις] M. 2. 1, note. See Esther 1. 1, where, to avoid the *non-Hellenic* ἡμέραι, V. A. puts βασιλεία; almost as bad; and no article, as if to correspond with Hebrew בִּימֵי.

7. προβ. ἐν τ. ἡμ. αὐτῶν] Genesis 24. 1, בָּא בַּיָּמִים: also Josh. 13. 1, in V. A. προβεβηκὼς ἡμερῶν.

17. ἐνώπιον instead of ἔμπροσθεν, M. 5. 16.

20. ἀνθ' ὧν] = מֵאֲשֶׁר, or אֲשֶׁר יַעַן, or עַל אֲ": 4. 18, 19. 44. Of course, the primary, original meaning is "wherefore"; and not "because."

32. υἱὸς ὑψ.] בֶּן הָעֶלְיוֹן. Daniel has עֶלְיָא by itself, as an Epithet and Name of God; 4. 21, 29, 31. The Hebrew עֶלְיוֹן is very common as an adjective combined with אֵל. Infra 6. 35.

34. V. A. always give this for יָדַע אִישׁ, Gen. 4. 1, 19. 8, Numb. 31. 17.

36. In V. A. συλλαμβάνω = concipio: but not in Classical Authors.

78. ἐν οἷς] Hebr. for בְּ, *causæ*.

79. σκιᾷ θανάτου] M. 4. 16, note.

S. LUKE.

Chapter II.

HEBR. 6. αἱ ἡμ. 10. π. τ. λ. 14. ἐν ὑψ. 15. καὶ ἐγ....καὶ εἶπον. 15. 19. ῥῆμα. 21. τοῦ π. and καὶ ἐκλ. 34. κεῖται εἰς. 38. ἀνθωμ. Also 27. 29. 36.

NON-C. 26. 45. μὴ ἰδ. 37. νύκτα κ. ἡμ.

Chapter III.

HEBR. 5. 16. 20. καὶ = ὅτι.
NON-C. 14. ὀψ. 23. ἀρχ.
SEPT. 7. γενν. ἐχ. 16. ὁ ἰσχ.

Chapter IV.

HEBR. 4. ὅτι...Θεοῦ. 22. τῆς χ. 25. ἐπ' ά. 34. τί ἡ. καὶ σ. 38. ἠρώτ. Mc. 4. 10, note. Also 1. 7. 12. 19. 21. 32. 41. 43.

CHAP. II. 4. In V. A. πατριά everywhere = בֵּית אָב, or מִשְׁפָּחָה, "the Father's house."

10. "All *the people*": i.e. the Jews.

14. ἐν ὑψ.] (See M. 21. 9, note.) V. A. for בַּמְּרוֹמִים, Job 16. 19, "in Heaven": Ps. 92. 9, מָרוֹם is an epithet of Jehovah. V. A. σὺ δὲ ὕψιστος, K.

εὐδοκία] Note, M. 11. 26. Can it mean here, "the power of pleasing God"; "acceptance with God"?

15. ῥῆμα] = דָּבָר = thing, passim: V. A. Gen. 15. 1.

21. Here τοῦ περιτ. = לְמוּל; note M. 1. 6. Mark Hebraism in καὶ ἐκλήθη.

34. Double notion of *a stone* set up for (1) a *Stumbling Block*, an object to knock against and fall over, and (2) *a Sign*.

38. ἀνθωμ.] M. 11. 25, note.

41. Dative of *time when*, "point of time": very rare in N. T. Mk. 1. 21, note.

CHAP. III. 5. ἔσται εἰς] = γενήσεται = הָיָה לְ : M. 1. 6, note. We have here a quotation from memory: not exactly agreeing with V. A.

7. τ. ἐκπ. ὀ. βαπτ.] Irregular construction: common both in Hebrew and V. A.

16. ἰσχυρ.] Note, M. 3. 11; a word not forcible enough for the idea, to our notions, as derived from its Classical use.

21. ἐν τῷ β.] This is almost, but not quite, equivalent to gen. absolute. καὶ 'Ι. β.] Here καὶ is not "*and*" but "*also*."

CHAP. IV. 4. οὐκ ἐπ' ά. μ. ζ.] M. 4. 4, note: *important*.

7. ἐνώπιόν μου] = לְפָנַי. The Greek words do not carry the meaning.

NON-C. 13. ἄχ. κ.   14. καθ' ὅ. τ. π.   33. φ. μεγ. Also 16. 34.
SEPT. 7. ἐνώπιον.   18. οὗ ἕνεκεν.

CHAPTER V.

HEBR. 1. 12. ἐγ....κ. αὐ. ἦν.   3. ἠρώτ.   17. δ. Κυρ.   26. 36. ὅτι.   34. υἱ. τ. νυμφ.
NON-C. 7. τ' ἐλθ. σ.   19. μὴ.   36. εἰ δὲ μή.   37. βάλλει.
SEPT. 11. ἀφ.   19. ἔμπρ. for ἐνώπιον, infra 12. 8.

CHAPTER VI.

HEBR. 4. τ' ἄρτ. τ. προθ.   8. εἰς τ. μ.   12. ἐγέν....ἐξῆλθε.
15. Ζηλ.   20. οἱ πτωχοί, see note, M. 5. 3.   35. ὑ. τ. ὑψ. supra 1. 32 and M. 21. 9, notes.
NON-C. 7. παρετ. ἵνα εὕρωσι.   12. ἐν τῇ πρ. τοῦ Θ.   15. Ἰούδαν Ἰακώβου.   17. ἦλθον ἀκοῦσαι.   18. ὀχλ.   35. ἐπὶ τοὺς ἀ. 43. οὐκ ἐ....ποιοῦν.

---

12. This passage shows clearly that ὅτι is not used for Quotations *alone*, nor *always*; for in v. 10 it forms part of V. A. text: whereas, in the Quotation in v. 11, there is no ὅτι in V. A.

13. ἄχρι κ.] "till opportunity offered."

14. Curious use of gen. with κατά in this sense: whence obtained?

18. In Gen. 22. 16, יַעַן אֲשֶׁר is, in V. A., οὗ εἵνεκεν, and is equivalent to ἀνθ' ὧν, L. 1. 20, 19. 44, being its *literal basis*. The *latter* is good Greek, the *former* bad: but to the V. A. Translators they seemed, apparently, identical. πτωχός] M. 5. 3, note. Our English Version gives "meek" in this passage of Isaiah.

23. παραβ.] = *proverb* here: as V. A. 1 Sam. 10. 12, Ez. 18. 2.

CHAP. V. 34. ποιῆσαι ν.] M. 8. 25, J. 6. 10, Acts 17. 26. Whence is this use of ποιεῖν derived? It suits English idiom exactly, and so does not startle us, but it is not *Greek*: I trace it in V. A., but not often, e.g. Ps. 104. 32, Jerem. 32. 23, Job 5. 18, gen. for Hiphil, but it is not a Hebrew idiom.

35. "But *a time will* come: and, when the Bridegroom shall have been taken from them, then shall they fast."

CHAP. VI. 5. A strong instance for ὅτι in asseveration: M. 7. 23, note, Acts 28. 25.

20. Nom. *plural* for Voc. is rare.

24. ἀπέχω seems to carry notion of sufficiency, M. 6.·2, 5. In Gen. 43. 23, שָׁלוֹם לָכֶם אַל, τὸ ἀργύριον ὑμῶν εὐδοκιμοῦν ἀπέχω, V. A. whatever it may mean.

32. 1 Pet. 2. 19, τοῦτο χάρις παρὰ Θεῷ.

S. LUKE.

Chapter VII.

HEBR. 1. εἰς τ. ἀ. Mc. 7. 35, note. 4. 16. ὅτι. 11. ἐγέν.... ἐπορ. 12. καὶ ἰδού. 21. ἀπό ν. 23. σκ. ἐν ἐμοί. 27. πρὸ προσ. 28. ἐν γ. γυν. M. 11. 11, note. 35. κ. ἐδικ. ἠ. σ. ἀπό... M. 11. 19, note. 50. πορ. εἰς εἰρήνην M. 5. 34, note.

NON-C. 3. ἐρωτῶν...διασώσῃ. 6. σκ. 7. εἰπὲ λ. 23. ὃς ἐὰν μή. 24. ἐξελ....θεάσ. 28. ὁ μικρ. 33. 42. μήτε. 36. ἠρ....φάγῃ. *Past* indic. followed by Subj. infra 9. 45. 37. ἥτις. 39. ποταπή. 40. ἔχω σ. τι εἰπ. 42. μὴ for οὐ.

Chapter VIII.

HEBR. 1. καὶ ἐγ....καὶ αὐ. δ. 8. ὁ ἔχ. ὦτα ἀκ. 15. ἐν κ. κ. and ἐν ὑπομ. 28. τί ἐ. κ. σ. 35. παρὰ τ. π. 43. οὖσα...δώδεκα. Also 48. 49. 54, Mc. 5. 8.

NON-C. 4. τῶν κ. π. 5. ὁ μὲν. 13. πρὸς καιρὸν. 17. καὶ εἰς φ. ἔ. 27. ἐκ χ. ἱ. 29. π. γ. χρ.

Chapter IX.

HEBR. 18. ἐγέν....συνῆσαν. 22. ὅτι asseverandi. 41. ἔσ. πρὸς ὑ. M. 13. 56, Mc. 9. 19, notes. 49. ἐπὶ τῷ ὀ. 51. ἐγέν. δὲ...

CHAP. VII. 21. ἐθεράπ. ἀπὸ μαστίγων] V. A. use μάστιξ for נגע, one of the meanings of which is leprosy (Lev. 13. 3), and elsewhere *macula, nævus*. Hence possibly our English Translators, Ps. 90. 10, render μ. by "plague": and so the sense of "disease" may have become connected with it, as in Mc. 3. 10, 5. 29, and here.

32. π. τοῖς καθ.] For this construction, see supra 3. 7.

45. Mark emphasis in καταφ., M. 26. 48.

CHAP. VIII. 10. Compare M. 13. 14, Mc. 4. 12. This passage of S. Luke is much the plainest and clearest.

21. ποιεῖν λόγον] A very singular usage.

27. V. A. use ἱκανὸς for *multus*, Ez. 1. 24, φωνὴν ὕδατος ἱκανοῦ, and this is common in Apocrypha, 1 Macc. 13. 11, δύναμιν ἱκανὴν, see Xenophon Cyrop. 2. 1. 8, Anab. 4. 8. 18, Polyb. Hist. 2. 12. As we use "plenty" and "enough," in sense of "many." Infra 23. 8, 9.

CHAP. IX. 28. ἐγ.... ἡμέραι...καὶ...ἀνέβη...προσ.] Most irregular construction; involving Hebraisms and non-classical anomalies.

καὶ αὐ. and τοῦ πορ. M. 2. 6, note. 52. πρὸ πρ. Mc. 1. 2. 61. τοῖς εἰς τὸν οἰ.

Non-C. 3. ἀνὰ δ. χ. 13. δότε φ. and εἰ μήτι...ἀγοράσωμεν. 14. κατακλ. αὐ. κ. 22. ἀποκτ. 31. ἔλεγον τ. ἕ. 33. μὴ...λέγει. 46. τὸ τίς...μείζων αὐ. 48. ὁ γ. μικρ. 52. εἰσ...ὥστε ἐτ. 54. εἶπ. π. κ. 57. ἀπέρχῃ. 60. ἄφες.

Chapter X.

Hebr. 2. οὖν. 10. εἰς τ. π. 13. αἱ δ. 21. ναὶ...σου. 27. ἀγαπήσεις, M. 6. 33, 19. 18, notes. 37. ὁ π. ἕ. μετ' ἁ. Also 1. 6. 17. 38.

Non-C. 21. ἐν αὐ. τ. ώ. 30. ἀφ....συγκυρίαν. 35. ἐπὶ τ. αὐ. 41. τυρβάζῃ Latinism.

Sept. 2. 35. ἐκβάλλῃ. 21. ἐξομολογοῦμαι and οὕτως...σου.

---

34. ἐν τῷ ἐκείνους εἰσ.] Strictly rendered, this means the exactly opposite of what took place, and limits the overshadowing by the cloud to our Lord and Moses and Elias. It is, of course, an instance of ungrammatical construction.

36. ἐν τῷ γεν.] "When the voice *had* past"; and yet Vulg. give "dum fieret vox."

39. μετὰ ἁ.] Notes, M. 24. 31, Mc. 14. 43, Acts 2. 28.

51. πρόσ. ἐστήριξε] So V. A. render שָׂם פָּנָיו, Jer. 21. 10, Ez. 21. 2, and נְתַן פָּנִים, Ez. 14. 8; *a merely literal rendering.*

Chap. X. 2. οὖν in V. A. often stands for וְ, because וְ often means "therefore": thus οὖν and καὶ are both equivalents of וְ: can they in consequence have come to be used *one for the other?* It looks so here.

6. υἱὸς εἰρ.] Common Hebr. idiom בֶּן שָׁלוֹם, passim in V. T. בֶּן חַיִל, 1 Kings 1. 52, υἱὸς δυνάμεως V. A.; Eph. 2. 2, υἱὸς ἀπειθείας, 1 Pet. 1. 14, τέκνα ὑπακοῆς, M. 8. 12, note.

7. τὰ παρ' α.] Grimm supplies δοθέντα, Phil. 4. 18.

10. πλατεῖα] V. A. always for רְחֹב, "wide place," or "street."

19. Compare Ps. 91. 13, "Thou shalt go upon the adder..."

21. ναὶ...εὐδοκία, M. 11. 26, note.

27. This *future* is most intensely *Hebraic* and not *Greek*, which has no such force of *command* connected with its future tense, as the Hebrew and English have (in *shall*). M. 5. 48, 19. 18, notes.

37. עָשָׂה חֶסֶד עִם] Literally rendered by V. A. passim: as here. 2 Sam. 10. 2, ποιήσω ἔλεος μετὰ Ἀννών.

S. LUKE.

Chapter XI.

Hebr. 4. ὀφειλ. 7. εἰς τ. κ. ἑ. M. 13. 56, J. 1. 1, notes. 22. ἐφ' ᾗ ἐπεπ. 32. εἰς τὸ κ. Also 20.

Non-C. 3. ἐπιούσιον. 5. πορεύσ....εἴπῃ. 36. τι. 37. ἠρ. 38. ἐβαπτ. 41. τὰ ἐν. 50. ἀπὸ κ. κ. 54. ἀποστ.

Sept. 34. ἁπλοῦς, M. 6. 22, note.

Chapter XII.

Hebr. 4. φοβ. ἀπὸ. 5. εἰς τ. γ. 8. ὁμολ. ἐν. 10. εἰς τ. ὑ. 31. προστεθ. 32. τὸ μ. π. voc. 56. ὅτι, M. 7. 23, note.

Non-C. 1. ἐν οἷς. 10. πᾶς ὃς ἐρεῖ λ. 33. μὴ. 36. πότε ἀ. 46. ἀπίστων. 47. πρὸς τ. θ. for κατά. 58. δὸς ἐργ. and πράκτορι.

Chap. XI. 4. ὀφειλ.] M. 6. 12, note.

5—8 and 11. Utterly irregular construction.

20. ἐν δ.] M. 3. 11, note, infra 14. 31. See note, L. 22. 49, Apoc. 13. 10, 19. 15. All palpable Hebraisms, adopted, no doubt, insensibly and unconsciously into the Greek of our Lord's time, from the familiar phraseology of V. A., in which בְּ is almost always rendered literally by ἐν. And just as V. A. followed Hebr. idiom, and N. T. authors followed V. A., so the Vulgate Translation has kept in the same track, and constantly puts *in* for ἐν in passages similar to the one before us, against Latin idiom, and the clear sense: e.g. here; "*in digito Dei*"; infra 22. 49, "*si percutimus in gladio?*" 1 Cor. 4. 21, "*in virgâ veniam ad vos?*" These instances of the way in which long and intimate acquaintance with V. A. and N. T. moulded the expressions of the *Latin* Translators, men of education and learning, illustrate and confirm the probability of the argument for referring all similar violations of *Greek* Idiom in N. T. to a *Hebrew* source. And it is remarkable how the phraseology of the Vulgate has affected the style even of the most learned Latin Fathers: e.g. S. Ambrose (De fide I. v. 42), "Non *in dialecticâ* complacuit Deo salvum facere populum suum." Just as our own popular theological terminology is coloured throughout by the forms of expression prevalent in our Authorised Version.

41. τὰ ἐνόντα] A remarkable phrase: not used, apparently, in Classical authors, and not found in V. A.

Chap. XII. 8. M. 10. 32, note. Trommius gives no instance of ὁμολογεῖν ἐν from V. A. Schleusner gives some of הוֹדָה with עַל and לְ.

29. "Be not unsettled and worried."

31. τ. π. προστεθ. ὑ.] A very difficult and important passage. M. 6. 33, note; infra 20. 11.

SEPT. 1. προσέχ. ἑ. ἀπὸ, M. 6. 1, note. 8. ἔμπρ. for ἐνώπιον, 5. 19.

CHAPTER XIII.

HEBR. 4. ὀφειλ. supra 11. 4. 9. εἰς τὸ μ. 27. ἐργ. τ. ἀ. 33. πορεύ. Also 19. 23.

NON-C. 1. 31. ἐν ἀ. τ. κ. 2. δοκ. 11. μή. 25. ἀφ' οὗ.

CHAPTER XIV.

HEBR. 1. καὶ ἐγ....καὶ. 31. ἐν δ. χ. M. 3 11, Jude 14, notes. 34. μωρ. ἐν τ. ἀρτ. M. 5. 13, note. 35. ἐχ. ὦτα ἀ. Also 2. 3. 30.

NON-C. 7. ἐπέχων. 8. κατακλ. εἰς τ. πρ. 8. 9. μή....ἐρεῖ δὸς τ. τ. and μετ' α. 10. ἀνάπεσαι. 12. φώνει. 13. ποι. δοχ. 15. φάγ. ἄρτ. 17. τῇ ὥρᾳ. 18. ἀπὸ μ. and ἐρωτῶ. 19. 31. πορ. δ. 28. ψηφ.

---

42. M. 24. 45, θεραπεία = θεραπεύοντες. Herod. 5. 21.
53. Change of case after ἐπὶ, is utterly inexplicable.
58. δὸς ἐργ.] Probably a Latinism: "da operam."

CHAP. XIII. 23. Literal translation of אִם interrogative, 14. 3, copied literally in Vulgate: "si pauci sunt" and "si licet sabb. curare," and 22. 49, "si percutimus?"

25. Strange confusion of tenses and moods. Perhaps καὶ ἀποκρ. may be a Hebraism: "when once he has shut...then shall he answer."
27. 2 Macc. 3. 6, ἐργ. τῆς ἀνομίας: the word is not found in V. A.
28. ὁ κλ....] M. 8. 12, note.
29. The kingdom of Heaven spoken of as a Feast: as Is. 25. 6.
33. πορεύ.] "go on my way": as περιπατεῖν in same sense.
34. The mixture of Persons in this verse is very perplexing.

CHAP. XIV. 27. β. τ. στ.] It may be doubted whether the meaning of this expression is generally analysed and ascertained. It is assumed to be equivalent to "mortification," "self-denial," "crucifying the flesh"; and no doubt it *implies* this, though in a secondary not a primary sense. How then is the second idea involved in the first, and deducible from it? Because the man condemned to be crucified had to carry his cross to the place of execution: hence "to carry a cross" was an open sign, a demonstration, that some one was to be put to death: a symbol and emblem of death to be inflicted. Hence "to take up and carry one's own cross" voluntarily, came metaphorically to signify the willing-

S. LUKE.

Chapter XV.

Hebr. 16. ἀπὸ τ. κ. 18. εἰς τ. οὐ. κ. ἐ. σ. Also 2. 27.

Non-C. 4. 8. ἕως εὔ. 7. ἤ. 13. μακρὰν. 22. πρώτην. Also 1. 29.

Chapter XVI.

Hebr. 8. τὸν οἰ. τ. ἀ., οἱ υἱ. τ. αἰ. τ., and ὑπέρ...γενεὰν. 9. μ. τ. ἀ. 10. ἄδικος. 11. τῷ ἀ. μ....ἀληθινὸν. 26. ἐστήρ. 27. ἐρ.

Non-C. 2. φων. αὐ. 14. ἐξεμ. 20. ἐβέβλ. 24. βάψῃ... ὕδατος.

---

ness "to kill something deserving of death," "to mortify the evil deeds of the sinful body," "to crucify the flesh," and "to exhibit and avow openly the intention to do this:" and so has passed into the common sense of "a symbol of mortification," "an open profession of self-sacrifice and self-denial."

Chap. XV. 12. βίος] = "facultates vivendi, opes," Mc. 12. 44, L. 8. 43. V. A. Cant. 8. 7. The same sense seems common in Apocrypha.

ἐπιβάλλον] This phrase has classical authority, being found in Herodotus and Demosthenes, and occurs in Diodorus 14. 17, and Polybius. There are some instances in Apocrypha, Tob. 6. 11, 1 Macc. 10. 30, 2 Macc. 3. 3, 9. 16: but none in V. A.

16. ἀπὸ τ. κ.] For this use of ἀπὸ for מִן expressing cause or instrument, see M. 7. 16 and Heb. 5. 7, notes.

Chap. XVI. 4. "That people may receive me," "qu'on m'admette": so infra, 9, "that there may be some one to receive you": i.e. "that you may be received."

6. He gave them the bills, drawn out by himself in the correct amounts, and allowed them to alter the figures.

8. ὁ κ.] i.e. "the rich man, his master." *Our Lord's* remarks on the parable begin at "ὅτι οἱ υἱοὶ..."

9. M. 11. 19, note. Here ἄδικος = ψευδής, unreal, unreliable; δίκαιος = ἀληθινός. 1 Tim. 3. 16, ἐδικαιώθη "was authenticated, proclaimed to be true Christ, by the Holy Spirit," at his Baptism. S. John 3. 20, 7. 18.

20. ἐβέβλητο] A quasi-Imperfect; βέβληται] a quasi-Present: M. 8. 6.

22. κόλπον] In 23, κόλποις.

26. ἐστήρικται] Used in much the same sense as στερέωμα in Gen. 1. for רָקִיעַ "the wide expanse of Heaven."

2—2

CHAPTER XVII.

HEBR. 4. ἀφήσεις. 10. ὅτι δ. 11. ἐγ. καὶ...διήρχ. 20. ἡ βασ. τοῦ Θ. Μ. 3. 2, note.

NON-C. 1. ἀνένδ....τοῦ. 2. λυσιτ....ή. 3. πρ. ἑαυτ. Μ. 6. 1, note. 7. ἀνάπ. 8. ἐτ. τί δ. and φ. κ. π. 9. δοκῶ. 13. ἦρ. φ. 24. ἐκ τῆς...εἰς τ. 29. ἔβρ. 35. ἐπὶ τ. αὐ. Also 15. 20. 33.

SEPT. 1. σκάνδ. Μ. 18. 7, note. 21. ἐντός. 33. ζωογ. 35. ἐπὶ τὸ αὐ. and ἀφεθ.

CHAPTER XVIII.

HEBR. 6. ὁ κρ. τ. ἁ. 43. ἔδωκ. αἱ. Also 11. 13. Nomin.

NON-C. 2. μή. 4. ἐπὶ χ. 5. εἰς τ. ἑ. ὑπ. 6. τί. 10. ἀνέβ. πρ. 14. παρ' ἑ. 15. προσ....ἵνα ἅ. 24. πῶς δ. 31. γεγρ....τῷ υἱ. 39. προάγ. ἐπετ. ἵ. σιωπήσῃ.

SEPT. 16. ἄφετε.

CHAP. XVII. 1. ἀνενδεκτόν] (from ἐνδέχεται) = "an impossible thing," "an impossibility": "there is an impossibility of scandals not coming." Acts 3. 12 affords an almost parallel instance of a verbal adjective passing into and used as a Substantive.

3. προσ. ἑαυτ.] Acts 5. 35. V. A. render thus הִשָּׁמֶר, Gen. 24. 6, Ex. 10. 28. Infra 20. 46, M. 6. 1.

4. ἀφ. αὐτῷ] Fut. for Imper., M. 5. 48, 19. 18. Apoc. 4. 10.

9. δοκέω] = cogito, M. 3. 9. V. A. for חָשַׁב, Gen. 38. 15, ἔδοξεν αὐτὴν πόρνην εἶναι.

21. ἐντός] V. A for בְּקֶרֶב "in medio": Ps. 38. 3, 108. 21, and also for Plural of קֶרֶב, Ps. 102. 1, Is. 16. 11, as if it were equivalent, in their usage, to "*in the midst of*," as well as "inside."

29. ἔβρ. π.] = "on pleuvoit."

33. ζωογ.] Acts 7. 19. The only two instances in N. T. There are several in V. A. of the word in this sense "to keep alive," as equivalent to the Pihel or Hiphil of חָיָה, Ex. 1. 17, Judges 8. 19, 1 Kings 2. 6, 27. 9. It is probably peculiar to V. A.

35. ἐπὶ τὸ αὐ.] V.A. for יַחְדָּו, M. 22. 34, note, Acts 1. 15.

CHAP. XVIII. 16. ἄφετε] = "suffer, permit," very common use of verb in V. A.: the literal rendering of הַרְפֵּה, Hiphil of רָפָה, 2 Kings 4. 27, ἄφες αὐτήν for הַרְפֵּה לָהּ. Also for נָתַן, Gen. 20. 6, Judges 15. 1.

31. γεγρ. τῷ υἱῷ] A very unusual form in ordinary Greek.

33. τῇ ἡμ.] Dative of "time when": unusual in N. T. M. 12. 1, note: more frequent in L. than in the other Evangelists, as the other cognate forms; infra 20. 47, note.

35. ἐκαθῆτο π. τὴν ὁ.] Mc. 4. 1, 10. 46, notes.

Chapter XIX.

HEBR. 3. ἀπὸ τ. ὁ. 15. ἐγέν. καὶ εἶπε. 27. ἔμπρ. 37. δυν. 38. ἐν ὑψ. 43. ἤξ. ἡ...καὶ. Also 7. 9. 42.

NON-C. 2. καὶ ἀ....κ. οὗτ. 3. ἰδ. τίς ἐ. τῇ ἠλ. μ. dat. of part. 11. δοκεῖν. 12. χ. μακρὰν...λ. 13. ἕως ἔ. 15. εἶπε φ....ἵνα γνῷ. Mc. 10. 49, note. 20. ἐν σ. Latinism. 23. ἔπρ. 48. τὸ τί π.

SEPT. 44. ἀνθ' ὧν, supra 1. 20, note.

Chapter XX.

HEBR. 3. ἕνα λ. 11. πρ. π. M. 6. 33. 21. λαμβ. πρ. and ἐπ' ἀληθ. 28. ἐξαν. σπ. 36. ἀν. υἱοί. 42. ἐκ δ. 46. προσ. ἀπὸ. supra 17. 3. Also 2. 5. 8. 17.

NON-C. 7. μή. 9. χρ. ἱκ. 19. ἐν αὐτ. τ. ὤ.

SEPT. 26. ἐνάντιον for ἐνώπιον, infra 24. 19, M. 5. 16, note.

CHAP. XIX. 3. τῇ ἠλ. μικρὸς] Dat. of *part.*, where we should expect acc. J. 13. 21, note.

38. ὁ ἐρχ. β. ἐν ὀ. K.] For ὁ β. ὁ ἐρχ. ἐν ὀ. K. This form, so ungrammatical in Greek, is no doubt due to the frequent occurrence of the same construction in Hebrew, of which I have elsewhere given examples, e.g. infra 21. 1. In εἰρ. ἐν οὐρ. we have a curious variation from the Angels' Song, "Peace on *Earth*." They greeted Him as Messiah in words of Ps. 118. 26: see M. 21. 9, note.

48. τὸ τί π.] "The what-to-do"; "the course to take."

CHAP. XX. 17. κεφ. γων.] See M. 21. 42, for explanation of this metaphor.

21. λαμβ. πρ. is the exact literal rendering of נָשָׂא פָנִים, Lev. 19. 15, V. A. οὐ λήψῃ πρόσωπον πτωχοῦ. Fut. prohibitive with οὐ not Greek but Hebraic. M. 19. 18, note.

27. τινες...οἵ] "some," viz. "those who denied..."

28. ἐξαν. σπ.] = literally. V. A. הָקֵם זֶרַע, Gen. 38. 8, ἀναστ. σπ.

35. οἱ κατ....τυχ.] These words may possibly be quoted as justifying the notion of the annihilation of the wicked and the resurrection to life of the good alone.

38. Θ. οὐκ...] = "There is no God of dead people, but of living people: for all are alive for Him": to do Him service, as God and King, people must be *alive*.

47. προφ.] Dative of "cause or manner": very rare generally in N. T. (M. 26. 4, Mc. 2. 8, notes), though more frequent in S. Luke than any other writer: I have noted it 18 times in his Gospel, and

Chapter XXI.

Hebr. 6. ἐλ. ἡμ. 8. ὅτι ἐγώ εἰμι. 16. ἐξ ὑ. 18. καὶ = but. 22. τοῦ π. 26. ἀπὸ φ. and αἱ δυν. τ. οὐρ. 35. ἐπὶ π. Also 34. 37.

Non-C. 11. φόβ. 14. θ. εἰς τ. κ. 24. ἄχρι π. 30. ἀφ᾽ ἑ. 34. πρ. ἑαυτ. Also 27. 38.

Chapter XXII.

Hebr. 1. πάσχα. 15. ἐπιθ. ἑ. 30. δώδ. φ. 49. εἰ π. ἐν μ. 53. ἡ ἐξ. τ. σκ.

Non-C. 2. 4. τὸ π. αὐ. 6. ἐξωμ. 16. 18. Subj. without ἄν. 24. τὸ τίς... 35. μή τ. ὑ. 42. εἰ β. π. 47. προήρχ. αὐ. 69. ἀπὸ τ. ν.

Sept. 18. γεννήματος. M. 26. 29, note.

---

17 in the Acts. In S. Matthew it occurs, so far as I have marked, only 8 times, in S. Mark 12: in all S. Paul's epistles, under 50 times. The usual substitute for this form, so universal in Classical Authors, is ἐν with dative, *an evident Hebraism:* M. 3. 11, note.

Chap. XXI. 1. τοὺς β....πλ.] Curious construction: similar to 19. 38.

21. J. 4. 35, James 5. 4, have both, as here, plural of χώρα, in sense of *field :* a signification belonging to אֶרֶץ occasionally, for which V. A. generally give χώρα. Here it need not bear *that* meaning, but may mean "heathen lands," "foreign lands." It has no Classical authority.

26. δύναμις here seems equivalent to "forces" in the physical meaning, such as control the movements of what we call "the heavenly bodies": e.g. gravitation, attraction, &c.

Chap. XXII. 19. εἰς τ. ἐμ. ἀνάμν.] "as my memorial, the memorial I desire": or, in active sense, "my appointed way of reminding my Father." For ποιεῖτε see M. 26. 18, note.

25. κυρ.] "lord it over them": M. 20. 25, note.

30. τὰς δώδ. φυλ.] "the different divisions and portions of my people." The *diocese,* in the Church, is the equivalent of the *Tribe* among God's ancient People. κρίνειν, in Hebrew sense, "to govern."

49. πατ. ἐν μαχαίρᾳ] This phrase is very frequent in V. A. as literal translation of הִכָּה בְחֶרֶב, 2 Kings 19. 37, 2 Chr. 29. 9, Josh. 19. 47, Jerem. 26. 23, and a hundred other places. And it was consequently, no doubt, (see Apoc. 2. 16, 11. 7,) in common use in our Lord's

Chapter XXIII.

HEBR. 9. ἐν λ. ἐκ. 28. ἐπ' ἑ....τέκνα. 31. ὑγρῷ ξ....ξηρῷ. 43. ἐν τῷ π. Also 5. 9.

NON-C. 3. σὺ λέγ. M. 26. 25. 5. ἀνασ. 8. ἐξ ἐκ. supra 8. 27. 11. σὺν τ. στ....ἀνέπ. αὐ. τῷ Π. dative. 15. ἄξ. θ. 16. παιδ. 17. καθ' ἑ. no article. 33. ἀπῆλθ. 41. ἄτοπον. 51. συγκατατ.

Chapter XXIV.

HEBR. 1. τῇ μιᾷ τ. σ. 4. ἐν ἑ. ἀ. 22. ἐπὶ τ. μν. 25. βρ. τοῦ π. ἐπὶ, M. 2. 6, note. 34. ὅτι emphatic, M. 7. 23, note. 42. ἀπὸ μ. 47. ἐπὶ τῷ ὀν. 49. ἐξ ὕψ. Also 35.

NON-C. 12. πρὸς ἑ. 13. ἐν αὐτ. ἡμ. 18. σὺ μ. π. 21. ἀλλά γε σ. π. τ. 25. βρ. τῇ κ. dative. 35. ἐγνώσθη αὐτοῖς.

---

day. How familiar it was to the Authors of V. A. may be inferred by their rendering the idiomatic expression וַיְכוּ לְפִי חָרֶב, Josh. 19. 47, by ἐν στόματι μαχαίρας ἐπάταξαν in defiance of Greek grammar and idiom. For εἰ interrogative, see note, M. 12. 10.

CHAP. XXIII. 2. Χρ. β.] King Messiah.
28. ἐφ' ἑ. κλ....] Judges 11. 37, אֶבְכֶּה עַל, κλαύσομαι ἐπὶ τὰ παρθένια μου.
31. ἐν τῷ ὑγρῷ...ξηρῷ] Proverbial: Ez. 17. 24, 20. 47. Of course the use of ἐν is Hebraic.
54. ἡμ. παρασκευή] "The Preparation day": in J. 19. 42 it is called ἡ π. τῶν Ἰουδ., showing how completely it was looked on as a day of fixed and regular Jewish observance. σαββ. ἐπέφ.] "The sabbath was *dawning*": and yet it began at *Sunset*. The unnaturalness of their division of the day and its arbitrary commencement, is shown strikingly by this use of ἐπέφ.

CHAP. XXIV. 25. πιστ. ἐπὶ π.] See M. 27. 43, note, Mc. 10. 24. Or perhaps ἐπὶ πᾶσιν may not be connected with πιστ., but may mean "after all."
42. ἀπὸ μελ.] = "a part of," "some," for מִן. V. A. constantly translate this literally, and the Vulgate follows suit. Ex. 17. 5, ἀπὸ τῶν πρ., "de senioribus," Lev. 5. 9, מִדַּם, ῥανεῖ ἀπὸ τοῦ αἵμ.
47. κηρ....ἀρξ.] A very anomalous and ungrammatical construction, irreducible to any order.
49. ἐξ ὕψους] V. A. for מִמָּרוֹם, Ps. 18. 17, Thr. 1. 13.

Sept. 19. ἐναντίον, supra 20. 26. M. 23. 14, note.

---

52. μετὰ χαρᾶς] M. 24. 31, Acts 2. 28, notes: supra 9. 39. There is a curious example of its use for בְּ in V. A. Is. 48. 1, לֹא בֶאֱמֶת, οὐ μετ' ἀληθείας, exactly as *we* use *with*, and so also Is. 15. 3, בִּבְכִי, μετὰ κλαυθμῶν. Nah. 1. 2, μετὰ θυμοῦ. These are the only instances I find in V. A. of μετὰ with genitive of *thing*, as distinct from gen. of *person*. But these are sufficient, I think, to assign it to a Septuagint origin.

S. JOHN.

Chapter I.

Hebr. 1. πρὸς τ. θ. 6. ἐν. αὐτ. ʼl. 7. εἰς μ. 12. ἔλαβον, and πιστ. εἰς τὸ ὅ. 2. 11. 23. 13. ἐξ αἵμ.... 18. ὢν εἰς τ. κ. M. 13. 56, note. 23. εὐθύνατε τὴν ὁ. = פַּנּוּ דֶּרֶךְ, Is. 40. 3. Also 20. 26. 31. 32. 33.

CHAP. I. 1. *ἐν ἀρχῇ*] How are we to account for the absence of the definite article here, in a passage remarkable for its strict accordance with grammatical precision, and in a writer generally so exact in his use of it? Are we to resort to elaborate refinements of criticism, or strive to give a simpler and more natural, though possibly less philosophical, explanation of its omission? The account of the creation, Gen. 1. 1, opens with בְּרֵאשִׁית, V. A. *ἐν ἀρχῇ*: no article in either language. We know how familiar the Hebrew phrase was to the Jews in earlier time, as the title of the Book itself; we may well imagine the ideas associated with it, the sanctity (as it were) that environed it. May we not infer that equal honour would be paid, by the later Jews, to the phrase that literally rendered it in the Greek Version, embalming it for all future generations? Is it not probable that the Evangelist had the words of Moses in his mind, and deliberately and intentionally reproduced them? Mc. 13. 19, note.

ἦν πρὸς τὸν Θ.] For this sense of πρός with acc. = אֵל *apud, juxta*, see notes, M. 13. 56, Mc. 1. 39, 6. 3, 2 Th. 3. 10. It is a Hebraism and not a metaphysical refinement of Classical usage. It is superfluous, no doubt, to repeat here, what every Scholar knows, that πρός with acc. can only follow verbs implying *motion towards an object, movement* either (1) of body or other material substances, or (2) of mind or spirit, towards something outside it. It *cannot* follow any verb implying *stationariness*: with which the dative or genitive are *almost* invariably

Non-C. 14. μονογ. παρὰ Π. 15. 30. πρῶτός μου. 26. μέσος ὑ. 32. ἐπ' αὐτόν, acc.: we should expect αὐτῷ. 33. ὁ. π. μ. β. M. 2. 2, note. 40. εἶδον ποῦ. 42. πρῶτος for πρῶτον. 47. τι ἀγ. 48. εἶδε...καὶ λέγει, past coupled with present, M. 1. 22, note: infra 50. 49. πόθεν and φωνῆσαι.

Sept. 1. ἦν πρὸς τὸν Θ. 15. 27. 30. ἔμπρ. 18. ὁ ὢν εἰς τὸν κ. 29. αἴρων ἁμ.

---

found. I say *almost*, for some few instances of deviation from this general use may, of course, be cited: but such exceptions prove the rule. Πρὸς τὸν Θεὸν *cannot*, we may boldly say, in grammatical Greek, mean *apud Deum*, as it undoubtedly means here, and as the Vulgate has it, and our E. V. "with God." And yet it is abundantly clear, from the notes referred to above, that πρὸς, εἰς and παρὰ, with acc., *are* coupled with verbs involving no idea of *motion towards*, constantly in N. T., suggesting that such must have been the common vernacular usage among Hebrews speaking or writing Greek at the time. To what are we to assign this violation of Grammatical correctness? I venture to hope that the explanation offered by me, 2 Th. 3. 10, is reasonable and sufficient; and that the Septuagint Translators, men evidently possessing a very slight and inadequate acquaintance with Greek, having ascertained that אֶל *generally* was equivalent to πρὸς with acc., assumed it to be so *universally*, and rendered it accordingly: or they may only have carried out a misconception previously prevalent and adopted in the vulgar phraseology. In either case, the use, thus introduced, became probably imbedded, as so many other similar Hebraisms, in the Vernacular Greek of the Jews in Egypt, Palestine and Asia Minor. And hence the words stand for what S. John meant them to stand for, and not for what they mean in themselves, grammatically.

12. ἔλαβον] "received, accepted": an unusual sense of the word "apud Græcos," deducible possibly from παρέλαβον in 11; not found, I think, in V. A.; perhaps only a literal translation of the Chaldee קבל = "to hear and adopt," whence "cabala."

15, 30. ἔμπρ.] *de ordine*, Gen. 48. 20, ἔθηκεν Ἐφραιμ ἔμπρ. τοῦ Μανασσῆ for לִפְנֵי; Deut. 21. 6, for עַל פִּי, in same sense.

16. ἀντί] For תַּחַת, "in place of," one after another: Ps. 45. 17, תַּחַת אֲבֹתֶיךָ יִהְיוּ בָ", ἀντὶ τῶν πατέρων σου.

23. τὴν ὁ. Κ.] From V. A.: there is no def. article in the original, nor is one required; the contrast in our E. V., "prepare ye *the way*... make straight...*a highway*," is without any foundation: neither noun has the def. art. ה.

Chapter II.

HEBR. 3. πρὸς αὐ. 4. τί ἐμ. κ. σοί; Also 11. 23.

NON-C. 7. ἕως ἄνω. 10. ἐλάσσω = pejor, deterior. 19. λύω = diruo, destruo. 20. The construction τεσσ. ἔτεσιν ᾠκ. 25. ὁ ἄνθρ. generically, for οἱ ἄνθρ. unusual. There is a tinge of Hebraism about it.

Chapter III.

HEBR. 1. Νικ. ὄν. αὐτῷ. 15. ὁ πιστ. εἰς, Mc. 1. 15, note. 21. ἐν Θεῷ. 28. ὅτι ἀπ. εἰ. 29. χαρᾷ χ. Also 28.

NON-C. 3. 7. ἄνωθεν = δεύτερον = de novo. 25. ἐκ. 34. ἐκ μέτρου. 36. ἀπειθῶν as opposed to πιστεύων, Eph. 5. 6, note; and ἐπ' αὐτόν.

Chapter IV.

HEBR. 6. ἐκ τῆς ὁδ. ἐκ for מִן, used in sense of ὑπό. 14. εἰς τὸν αἰ. 17. 39. 42. ὅτι. 23. ἔρχ. ὤ. κ. νῦν ἐ. and ἐν πν.

NON-C. 7. ἔρχ....ἀντλῆσαι. 8. τροφὰς. 10. αἰτεῖν with acc. of person. 15. πρ. αὐτὸν for αὐτῷ. 16. φωνεῖν = call. 28. ἀπῆλθε = went away. 30. ἤρχοντο. 52. κομψ. ἔσχε, and ὥρ. ἑβδ. acc. of time *when*.

SEPT. 3. ἀφῆκε, M. 18. 12.

---

29. αἴρειν] = "recedere facio, removeo"; V. A. Is. 5. 23, Gen. 35. 2 and elsewhere.

43. Κηφᾶς] Aramaic, Mc. 3. 17.

44. τῇ ἑπ.] Dative of time when: L. 18. 33, note.

CHAP. II. 4. τί ἐμοὶ καὶ σοί] A pure Hebraism. מַה לִּי וָלָךְ, 2 Sam. 16. 10, 19. 22, V. A. Vulgate "quid mihi et tibi"; as much against Latin idiom, as τί ἐ. κ. σ. is against Greek. M. 27. 19, note, Mc. 1. 24.

25. περὶ τοῦ ἀ....ἐν τῷ ἀ.] This use of ὁ ἄνθρωπος for *mankind* is not grammatically correct: it is most probably derived from Hebrew: as Gen. 8. 21, יֵצֶר לֵב הָאָדָם, ἡ διάνοια τοῦ ἀνθ. V. A.

CHAP. III. 15, 18. πιστεύειν εἰς] Mc. 1. 15, note: supra 1. 12.

20, 21. Here φ. = רָשָׁע is opposed to ἀλήθ. = אֱמֶת, V. A. Ps. 119. 86, 151. L. 16. 9 and M. 11. 19, notes: infra 7. 18.

35. ἐν τῇ χ.] Ex. 4. 21, τὰ τέρατα ἃ δέδωκα ἐν ταῖς χερσί σου, אֲשֶׁר שַׂמְתִּי בְיָדֶךָ. It is the *literal* translation of בְּ.

CHAP. IV. 31. M. 15. 23, L. 4. 38.

35. τὰς χώρας] L. 21. 21, note, Jac. 5. 4.

S. JOHN.

CHAPTER V.

HEBR. 4. κατέβ. ἐν τῇ κ. for εἰς τήν. 19. 30. ἀφ' ἑαυτοῦ. 25. ἔρχ. ὥρα κ. ν. ἑ.

NON-C. 4. κατὰ κ. 6. πολὺν χρ. ἔχει. 18. ἔλυε τὸ σ. 19. 30. ἀφ' ἑαυτοῦ. 35. πρὸς ὥραν, 1 Th. 2. 17, note. 39. δοκεῖτε ἔχ. Μ. 3. 9. 44. δόξαν, "approval": infra 12. 43. 45. εἰς ὃν ἤλπ.

SEPT. 7. βάλῃ, Μ. 26. 12.

CHAPTER VI.

HEBR. 5. πρὸς τ. Φ. 8. εἶς ἐκ τῶν μ. and 11. ἐκ τῶν ὀψ. and 60. 35. ὁ ἄρτος τῆς ζωῆς. 39. ἵνα πᾶν...μὴ ἀπ. ἐξ αὐτοῦ. 51. εἰς τὸν αἰ. = לְעוֹלָם. 57. καὶ ὁ τρ. με κἀκεῖνος... Also 14. 42.

NON-C. 6. ᾔδει τί ἔμ. 7. διακ. δην. ἄρτοι. 9. παιδ. ἕν. 10. ποιήσ....ἀναπεσεῖν. 11. ὀψαρίων. 12. συναγ. τὰ π. 17. ἤρχοντο. 21. ἤθελον λαβεῖν. 25. ὧδε γέγ. 50. τὶς. 52. ἐμάχ. 57. διά with acc.: in sense of *through* or *by*. 66. ἐκ τούτου and εἰς τὰ ὀπίσω. 68. ἀπελεύσομαι. 71. ἔλεγε τὸν Ἰ. = "he spoke *of.*"

SEPT. 70. διάβολος = "adversarius, delator": (as Judas was): V. A. for צָר, hostis, Esther 7. 4, and שָׂטָן, Job 1. 6, 7, 9, Ps. 108. 6.

CHAP. V. 2. Βηθεσδά] = בֵּית חֶסֶד, home of mercy.

4. κατὰ κ.] "At times." κατέβ. ἐν τῇ κ.] One instance among many of ἐν for εἰς as literal rendering of בְּ, 1 Cor. 7. 15.

13. ἐξέν.] V. A. constantly for סוּר or פָּנָה, literally "enato," Schl.; Judges 4. 18, 18. 26, 2 K. 2. 24, 23. 16.

18. ἔλυσε τὸ σ.] In V. A. we find βεβηλοῦν τὸ σ. as opposed to ἁγιάζειν, but *not* λύειν, as opposed to φυλάσσειν, τὸ σ. In N. T. we have it with ἐντολήν, Μ. 5. 19, νόμον, J. 7. 23, γραφήν, 10. 35.

35. πρὸς ὥραν] See note, 1 Thess. 2. 17, Gal. 2. 5.

44. δόξα] = approval, good opinion: infra 12. 44, Rom. 3. 23.

CHAP. VI. 2. ἐπὶ τῶν ἀ.] "in the case of."

8. εἶς ἐκ τῶν μ.] Corresponding to the use of מִן *partitive*. Nch. 1. 2, εἷς ἀπὸ ἀδελφῶν μου, Ruth 4. 2. Also infra 60.

27. ἐργάζ....βρῶσιν] Compare Eph. 4. 28, ἐργαζ. τὸ ἀγαθόν... Herodotus 1. 24, χρήματα. It is a very rare application of the verb.

35. ὁ ἄρτος τῆς ζ.] Our English idiom corresponds with this Hebraism, which is utterly alien to the Greek: and the words here used cannot, of themselves, convey the idea required.

45. διδακτοὶ Θ.] V. A. for לִמּוּדֵי יְהוָה, "God's Pupils," "God's enlightened ones," "God's instructed ones": *not* "God-enlightened,"

S. JOHN.

Chapter VII.

Hebr. 1. περιεπάτει. 18. ἀληθής...ἀδικία, M. 11. 19, L. 16. 9. 19. 30. καὶ = but, yet. 25. ἐκ τῶν μ. 31. ὅτι emphatic. Also 12. 28. 29.

Non-C. 4. ἐν παρρησίᾳ. 15. μὴ μεμαθ. 41. μὴ γάρ.

Sept. 20. δαιμόνιον = evil spirit. Infra 10. 20: see M. 9. 33, 1 Tim 4. 1, notes.

Chapter VIII.

Hebr. 10. ἡ γυνή, vocative. 15. κατὰ τὴν σάρκα. 31. μένητε ἐν τῷ λ. Also 17. 35.

Non-C. 2. ἠρχόμην as imperfect of ἔρχομαι. 6. γῆν = ground. 9. εἷς καθ' εἷς and οἱ ἔσχατοι = youngest. 12. οὐ μὴ with future. 23. ἐκ τῶν κάτω...ἄνω. 25. τὴν ἀρχήν. 37. χωρεῖ.

Sept. 29. ἀφίημι = "leave," Mc. 12. 12.

Chapter IX.

Hebr. 9. ὅτι (thrice) emphatic, and 41 : M. 7. 23, note, and Cap. 10. 36, 41. 32. ἐκ τοῦ αἰ.

"God-instructed": Is. 54. 13, θήσω...πάντας...διδακτοὺς Θεοῦ, M. 25. 34, note. Our E. V. rendering "taught of God," which, no doubt, conveys the *spirit* of the words, seems to coincide so exactly with διδακτοὶ Θεοῦ, that a less careful student might suppose it gave the letter also, which it does not: this would require ὑπό.

Chap. VII. 4. ἐν παρρησίᾳ] Mark 8. 32: infra 11. 54. Here it seems to mean "a state in which every one talks of you."

18. ἀληθής] Opposed to ἀδικός, as L. 16. 9, 11, 2 Thess. 2. 10.

36. Ἑλλήνων] Vulg. "Gentium"; E. V. "Gentiles." So 1 Cor. 10. 32 and elsewhere. To the Jews, apparently, the term Ἕλλην took in all the rest of mankind : Ἰουδαῖοί τε καὶ Ἕλληνες.

38. ποταμοί...ζῶντος] There is *no such* passage, *word for word*, in the Old T. But the idea is fully conveyed by Is. 35. 1, 6, 7, describing the life-giving, renovating, effects of the Holy Spirit, consequent on the coming of Messiah, God Incarnate, vv. 2, 4.

39. "Nondum effusus erat": compare Acts 19. 2.

Chap. VIII. 44. Subaudi τις : "when a man speaks a lie, he speaks what is natural to him: for he is a liar, like his father the Devil": "he and his father" are alike.

58. πρὶν Ἀ. γεν.] "before A. *was born*."

Non-C. 2. ἥμαρτεν ἵνα γεννηθῇ. irregular sequence. 5. ὅταν = "so long as." 16. τηρεῖν τὸ σ. 18. αὐτοῦ τοῦ ἀναβλ. 25. ὤν.

CHAPTER X.

HEBR. 28. εἰς τὸν αἰ. 32. ἐκ τοῦ πατρός. 42. ἐπίστευσαν εἰς... Mc. 1. 15, note. Also 36. 41.
Non-C. 10. θύειν = "kill." 11. καλὸς for ἀγαθός. 12. ὁ...οὐκ ὤν, for ὁ μή. 15. γινώσκω = I know. 18. ἀπ' ἐμαυτοῦ and ἐντολή. 24. τὴν ψυχὴν αἴρεις = "suspensam tenes." 31. ἐβάστασαν.
SEPT. 12. ἀφίησι, supra 8. 29. 22. ἐγκαίνια, Ezr. 6. 17, Neh. 12. 27. Also 20.

CHAPTER XI.

HEBR. 26. 31.
Non-C. 3. ἴδε for ἰδού. 7. ἄγωμεν intrans. 9. προσκόπτει. 17. τ. ἡμ. ἔχοντα. 18. ἀπὸ σταδίων δ. infra 12. 1. 33. ἐτάραξεν ἑ. 44. ἡ ὄψις and ἄφετε ὑπ. 21. 28. 56. 57. 47. συνήγ....συνέδρ.

CHAPTER XII.

HEBR. 4. εἰς ἐκ. 11. 36. ἐπίστ. εἰς, infra 14. 1, 12. 13. ὡσαννὰ, M. 21. 10, note. 36. υἱὸν φ. 34.

CHAP. IX. 7. Σιλωάμ] שִׁלֹחַ, Is. 8. 7, from שָׁלַח, emisit: "fons emissionis," i.e. "fons aquæ se effundens in lacum": Grimm.

CHAP. X. 4. ἐκβάλῃ] M. 9. 38, Mc. 1. 43. Same use of verb in V. A. 2 Chr. 23. 14, ἐκβάλετε αὐτὴν ἐκτὸς τοῦ οἴκου, and 29. 5, ἐκβάλετε τὴν ἀκαθαρσίαν ἐκ τῶν ἁγίων, for הוֹצִיאוּ = "put out."

10. θύειν, for *occidere*, to slay, without any sacrificial meaning, is very seldom found in Classical Authors, and in V. A. apparently once only, Is. 22. 13: in Apocrypha Sir. 24. 32, 1 Macc. 7. 19: and in N. T. only in the present instance.

11. καλὸς as equivalent to ἀγαθός, is very rarely met with, in the best writers, except *in the neuter* and in the phrase καλὸς κἀγαθός.

15. κἀγὼ γινώσκω] "so I know": a common Hebraism, supra 6. 57.

17. τιθέναι] = "depono, abjicio," would seem to be confined to S. John: supra 11, and 13. 4, 37, 15. 13. 1 John 3. 16.

35. λυθῆναι] supra 5. 18.

CHAP. XI. 48. ἔθνος] Only *occasionally* used for the Jewish nation, instead of λαός, L. 7. 5, Acts 10. 22.

54. παρρησίᾳ] Mc. 8. 32, note, Col. 2. 15.

55. χώρα, in sense of *the country*, rus, has some Classical authority, Xen. Mem. 3. 6. 11.

CHAP. XII. 1. πρὸ ἓξ ἡμ.] A similar construction to ἀπὸ σταδίων δεκ. 11. 18, 21. 8.

Non-C. 6. τὸ γλ....and τὰ βαλλ. 8. μεθ' ἑαυτῶν with *you*. 15. καθημ. ἐπὶ πῶλον, acc. 32. ἐκ for ἀπὸ. 43. δίξα = good opinion : supra 5. 44. 48. λαμβάνων = receiving, assenting to.

Sept. 21. ἐρωτάω for αἰτέω, M. 15. 23, note : infra 14. 16. and 17. 9. 15. 37. ἔμπροσθεν, in presence of : note M. 5. 16.

Chapter XIII.

Hebr. 8. 33. 35.

Non-C. 4. τίθησι τὸ ἱμ. : supra 10. 17. 13. φων. = call : supra 9. 18. 21. ἐταρ. τῷ πν. dat. 22. ἀπορούμενοι and περὶ τίνος. 37.

Sept. 2. 5. βάλλειν = put : note M. 9. 38.

---

3. ἐπληρώθη ἐκ τῆς ὀ.] = מִן אָמְלָא, V. A. Ps. 127. 5, μακάριος ὃς πληρώσει τὴν ἐπιθυμίαν αὐτοῦ ἐξ αὐτῶν : Lev. 9. 17, προσήνεγκε τὴν θυσίαν καὶ ἔπλησε τὰς χεῖρας ἀπ' αὐτῆς.

7. ἄφες αὐ.] "allow her" : see L. 18. 16, and M. 18. 12, notes. Supra 11. 44.

20. Ἕλληνες here stands for Jews settled abroad : Greek-Jews.

22. Andrew and Philip, both Greek names : they may possibly have had Greek connexions, and so were naturally applied to by these *Greeks*, i.e. *foreign Jews*.

38. Strictly ἀκοή = "id quod audit." V. A. give it for שְׁמוּעָה, "id quod auditur" ; Is. 53. 1, "a message," R. 12. 16, Hebr. 4. 2. The whole passage is a quotation from V. A., as R. 10. 16.

40. See M. 13. 14, note, for the parallel passage.

Chap. XIII. 21. ἐταρ. τῷ πν.] Dat. of part. instead of acc., M. 5. 3, L. 19. 3, Acts 2. 37, 18. 25, R. 14. 1, Eph. 4. 18, 23, Col. 1. 21.

Chap. XIV. 16. παράκλ.] "Qui interpellat divinas aures pro nobis," Rom. 8. 27 : "advocationis implens officia et defensionis exhibens munera." The same word, 1 J. 2. 1, is applied to our Lord, "advocate." In the Fathers, "advocatio" and "consolatio" are used as equivalent terms : Pearson, Art. 8. But may not *our* Translation, "Comforter" = Strengthener (fortis), be a *prægnans interpretatio*, and really carry us back to the true meaning of Παράκλητος, as understood by Students of V. A., like S. John ; whose knowledge of Greek was probably gained originally from that Book ? Ps. 125. 1, הָיִינוּ כְּחֹלְמִים, ὡσεὶ παρακεκλημένοι, Is. 38. 16, הַחֲלִימֵנִי, παρακληθεὶς ἔζησα ("so wilt Thou recover me," E. V.) : where V. A. clearly connects notion of "strength, renewal, recovery," with παρακαλέω. חָלַם (generally "to

Chapter XV.

Non-C. 18. πρῶτον ὑ. 15. 16. ἔθηκα ὑ.

Chapter XVI.

Hebr. 2. ἔρχεται ὥρα. 26. ἐρωτήσω. 30. ἐν τούτῳ.
Non-C. 2. δόξῃ, M. 3. 8. 15. ἐκ τοῦ ἐμοῦ for ἐκ τῶν ἐμῶν.
17. εἶπον ἐκ τῶν μ. some of. 21. γεννᾷν, of the mother.

---

dream") means also to be strong: Job 39. 4, יַחְלְמוּ בְנֵיהֶם, "their young ones grow strong": Job 4. 3, יָדַיִם רָפוֹת תְּחַזֵּק, χείρας ἀσθενεῖς παρεκαλέσας: Is. 35. 3, אַמְּצוּ בִּרְכַּיִם בֹּשְׁלוֹת, γονάτα παραλελυμένα παρακαλέσατε: Deut. 3. 28, אַמְּצֵהוּ, παρακαλέσατε αὐτόν. In all these, the Hebrew is unmistakeably "*strengthen*": Acts 9. 31, πορευόμεναι τῇ παρακλ.

Chap. XV. 2, 3. καθαίρω = purgo, to prune. "Ye are already clean" (not as result of καθ. in 2, but of "the washing" 13. 10). διὰ τ. λ.] "for the reception of..." *not* as our E. V. "through the word..." nor *propter*, "on account of," as Vulgate.

6, 8. The whole construction of these two verses is most irregular; *the tense* in ἐβλήθη, ἐξηρ. and ἐδοξάσθη, *the article* in τὸ κλῆμα, the plural in αὐτὰ, and the change of subject in συνάγ. and καίεται, and the illative use of conjunction in καὶ γενήσεσθε.

Chap. XVI. 2. ἔρχ. ὥρα ἵνα] We *may* translate, almost grammatically with Vulgate, "venit hora, ut omnis...arbitretur," "an hour is coming for every one that killeth you to think": but this is, possibly, an undue refinement in the conception of the force of ἵνα, which may be meant to convey nothing more than "when."

8. ἐλέγξει] "will set the world right": *prove* its former notions *wrong*, give them correct opinions as to sin, and righteousness, and condemnation.

23, 26. ἐρωτήσ. οὐδέν] Ye shall not need to apply to me to explain your difficulties, having the full light of the H. S. Καὶ οὐ λ. ὑ., ὅτι ἐγὼ ἐρωτ. τ. π.] Can this perhaps mean "I shall not need to question the Father as to your acceptance with Him":—for I know He loves you?

25, 29. παρρησίᾳ] In its primary sense, "speaking everything out," "keeping nothing back," "disguising nothing," "plainly," "fully."

32. εἰς τὰ ἴδια] = εἰς οἶκον, 19. 27, rendered severally in Vulgate "in propria" and "in sua"; against Latin idiom: "to his own house," V. A. for אֶל־בֵּיתוֹ, Esth. 5. 10, 6. 12, Ἀμὰν εἰσελθὼν εἰς τὰ ἴδια and ὑπέστρεψεν... Same sense in Apocrypha.

S. JOHN.

Chapter XVII.
HEBR. 11. 17. ἐν. 9. 15. ἐρωτῶ. 12. ὁ υἱ. τῆς ἀπ.
NON-C. 2. πᾶν ὃ for πάντα ἅ. 23. τετ. εἰς ἕν.

Chapter XVIII.
NON-C. 2. συνήχθη. 11. οὐ μὴ interrog. 32. ἵνα πληρωθῇ in a *past* sense: as παραδ. in 36.

Chapter XIX.
HEBR. 3. ὁ βασ. voc. 13. εἰς τόπον, M. 13. 56, note.
SEPT. 27. εἰς τὰ ἴδια, supra 16. 32.

CHAP. XVII. 5. τῇ δόξῃ] Dat. of "manner," *very rare* in S. John, 11. 2, 33, 43, 21. 8.

11. ἐν τῷ ὀν. σου] "by Thy power, Thy attributes of might": involved in שֵׁם.

12. ὁ υἱ. τ. ἀπ.] Is. 1: 4, בֶּן מַשְׁחִית, υἱὸς ἄνομος, V. A. 57. 4, יַלְדֵי פֶשַׁע, τέκνα ἀπωλείας: in Apocrypha, Sir. 16. 9, ἔθνος ἀπ. "Homo perditus, de cujus salute planè desperandum est," Schl. Vulg. "filius perditionis," which *means* no more, in *real* Latin, than "Son of perdition" does in *true* English. All three translations, Greek, Latin, and English, of this common Hebrew form, are utterly against the idiom of the several languages: although a correct sense has been assigned to them by traditional explanation and general acceptation. M. 8. 12, 23. 15, L. 10. 6, notes.

CHAP. XVIII. 11. οὐ μὴ πίω] I cannot recal any instance of this equivalent for the future negative, *used interrogatively*.

31. ἡμ. οὐ. ἔ. ἀπ. οὐδ.] Not absolutely, but at this season of the Passover (perhaps): or on such a charge, political and not religious. They put Stephen to death: and our Lord recognises their power to do so, M. 33. 31—34.

CHAP. XIX. 3. ἐδίδουν αὐ. ῥαπ.] Supra 18. 22, Vulg. "dabant ei alapas": comp. 2 Th. 1. 8, διδόντος ἐκδίκησιν: Vulg. "dantis vindictam." It appears to be a Hebrew idiom; it is hardly Greek or Latin: but it falls naturally into English, as Hebrew idioms often do. See below, 11.

11. διὰ τοῦτο] is used by V. A. for לָכֵן, in *both* of its meanings: "*therefore*" and "*nevertheless*": "*for this*" and "*for all this.*" The latter, of course, is less common. Probably we should take it so here, "notwithstanding." Is. 7. 14, 10. 24, 30. 18, Jerem. 5. 2, 16. 14, 30. 16, Ez. 39. 25, in all of which V. A. has διὰ τοῦτο, and our

S. JOHN.

Chapter XX.

Hebr. 16. ῥαββ. 19. 26. εἰς τὸ μέσον. 21. εἰρήνη ὑ. 31. ἐν τῷ ὀ. αὐ.

Non-C. 7. ἕνα for τινα. 15. δοκοῦσα = cogitans, M. 3. 9, and ἐβάστ. = *taken away*. Also 1. 3.

Sept. 25. βάλω. 27. φέρε...ἴδε.

Chapter XXI.

Hebr. 4. εἰς τὸν αἰ. supra 1. 18, 4. 1. 6. ἀπὸ τοῦ πλ. for מִן causæ, M. 7. 16, Hob. 5. 7, notes. 23. καὶ = ἀλλά, a common sense of וְ.

Non-C. 3. ὑπάγω ἁλιεύειν. 8. ὡς ἀπὸ π. δ. 12. 1. 9. κειμένην. 12. ἐξέτασαι αὐτόν. 14. τοῦτο τρ. ἐφαν. 25. πολλὰ ὅσα ἐπ. and omission of ἂν before χωρῆσαι.

E. V. "*therefore*": although, "for all this," "nevertheless" is clearly required. Of course we find, as is to be expected, "propterea, propter hoc, ideo," in these passages in Vulgate: the indiscriminate, unreflecting rendering of לָכֵן, by the words *generally* expressing its meaning, as though *it had no other*. Any one who will take the trouble to examine the passages cited above, will be struck with the obvious inaccuracy of the Greek, Latin, and English translations, and the necessity of substituting the *adversative* for the *causal* adverb. Our English idiom "*for all this*" suits the Hebrew exactly.

Chap. XX. 10. πρὸς ἑαυτούς] Vulg. "ad semetipsos": both alike unintelligible to persons acquainted only with ordinary Greek and Latin, and apparently Hebraic. 1 Sam. 26. 12, וַיֵּלְכוּ לָהֶם, is exactly equivalent to our text. Prov. 15. 27, עֹכֵר בֵּיתוֹ, V. A. ἐξόλλυσιν ἑαυτόν. These two passages seem to suggest that πρὸς ἑαυτούς = לָהֶם = אֶל־בֵּיתָם = οἴκαδε.

20. εἰρήνη ὑ.] This very common Hebrew mode of greeting or blessing, שָׁלוֹם לָכֶם, corresponding to the Salaam Aleicum of the East of our day, is not often found in V. A., in *this*, the *simplest* form: instances are Judges 6. 23, 1 Chr. 12. 18. We are so familiar with it, from Scriptural and Liturgical use, that we are apt to forget that neither this, nor its Latin equivalent, "Pax vobiscum," are natural idiomatic expressions in Greek or Latin, or give a full and adequate idea of its Hebrew meaning.

THE ACTS.

Chapter I.

HEBR. 5. οὐ μετὰ π. ή. 6. εἰ...ἀποκ. M. 12. 10 and infra 19. 2. 10. καὶ ἰδού, Gen. 40. 9. 18. ἐκ μ. 19. Ἀκελδαμά. הֲקַל דְּמָא, Ch.: דָּם Hebr. = blood. 20. ἐν β. ψ. the omission of the article. Also 2. 3. 5.

NON-C. 4. συναλιζ. 7. ἔθετο ἐν τ. ἰ. ἑ. 18. ἐλάκησε μέσος. 21. συνελθόντων ἡ. in the sense here obviously required. 25. παρέβη πορευθῆναι.

SEPT. 15. ἐπὶ τὸ αὐτὸ for יַחַד or יַחְדָּיו, cap. 3. 1. Deut. 25. 5, 11, ἐὰν κατοικῶσιν and ἐὰν μάχωνται...ἐπὶ τ. αὐ.

CHAP. I. 4. τὴν ἐπαγ.] Comp. Eph. 1. 13, πνεῦμα τῆς ἐπ.
6. εἰ] M. 12. 10, note, and infra 19. 2 : L. 14. 3.
8. ἕως ἐσχάτου τῆς γ.] Infra 13. 47, where we have the phrase in text exactly quoted from V. A. for עַד־קְצֵה הָאָרֶץ.
10. καὶ ἰδού] M. 9. 10, note. For the apparently superfluous καὶ, see Gen. 40. 9, בַּחֲלוֹמִי וְהִנֵּה גֶפֶן לְפָנָי, where the ו is purely, to our notions, without force: so 39. 19, וַיִּחַר אַפּוֹ...כִּשְׁמֹעַ, ὡς ἤκουσε...καὶ ἐθυμώθη. It is a very common Hebr. idiom: impossible to render *literally* in Greek—as V. A. have done, and the N. T. writers, following in their track, and using the familiar phrase caught from them—without a solecism.
13. Ἀλφαίου...Ζηλωτής] M. 10. 4. Has the omission of the article in the patronymic genitive, any examples in Classical Greek?
14. σὺν γ.] "with certain women." Or are we to take this as an instance of an omitted article, so common in G. T.? Heb. 1. 1, ἐν υἱῷ.
15. ἐπὶ τὸ αὐτὸ] M. 22. 34, L. 17. 35, notes. It is constantly used by V. A. and seems peculiar to them. Ps. 2. 2, οἱ ἄρχοντες συνήχθησαν

Chapter II.

Hebr. 17. πᾶσα σάρξ = all mankind. 18. ἀπὸ τ. πν. 19. δάσω τ. 22. ἀπὸ τ. Θ. 24. ὠδῖνας. 25. εἰς αὐτόν. 27. 31. εἰς ᾅδου. 28. μετὰ τοῦ π. 30. ἐκ καρποῦ τῆς ὀσφ. 34. ἐκ δεξιῶν = מִימִין, Mc. 16. 5, note. 46. ἐν ἀγ. 47. πρὸς ὅ. τ. λ.

ἐπὶ τὸ αὐτό, Deut. 22. 10, οὐκ ἀροτριάσεις ἐν μόσχῳ καὶ ὄνῳ ἐπὶ τὸ αὐτό, which I cite to show that the phrase can be used without any idea implied of "*motion towards*," as simply meaning "*together*," as in the passage before us, and cap. 2. 1. Observe also the strange misuse of ἐν for בְּ, so common in V. A., M. 3. 11, note; which Vulgate has perpetuated, here as elsewhere, by its use of *in* for ἐν, against the very genius of the language: e.g. "non arabis *in* bove et asino simul," where the use of the future tense, in Greek and Latin alike, by way of *prohibition*, is as utterly wrong as the use of the preposition, M. 5. 48, 19. 18, notes. Ps. 42. 4, בְּקוֹל רִנָּה, ἐν φωνῇ ἀγαλλιάσεως, V. A., "*in voce* exsultationis," Vulg.: forced even into English, in our Prayer-Book Version, translated mainly from Vulg., by the absurdly literal "I went.. *in the voice* of joy and praise." A striking instance of the way in which the ignorance of the first translators has coloured the subsequent Versions, and affected the phraseology of all the authors of the N. T.

18, 19. Supposing these 2 verses to be parenthetical,—not really forming part of S. Peter's speech, but inserted by way of explanation by S. Luke,—how does this affect the argument based on the use of the Aramaic Aceldama?

20. ὁ κατοικῶν] V. A. also has ὁ; in the Hebr. there is no article.

Chap. II. 6. συνεχ.] Confer Is. 60. 5, וְנָהַרְתְּ, Vulg. "et affluet," "*and flow together*," E. V. which, of course, is equivalent to "be confounded": infra 19. 29, 32, 21. 31: it has the force of "disorder," "concursus tumultuarius." V. A. use the verb only twice, about Babel: Gen. 11. 7, 9, נָבְלָה שְׂפָתָם, συγχέωμεν τὴν γλῶσσαν αὐτῶν. It has Classical authority.

9. It seems more natural to refer the irregularities in the use of def. article in this passage, to Hebraic want of precision therein, as universally acknowledged, than to endeavour to account for them otherwise.

11. Was this, as usually supposed, the gift of a supernatural faculty of speaking, consciously and intelligently, languages unknown before, fitting them for future work in foreign lands; or only inspiration to utter, in foreign languages, statements of divine truth, without any conscious understanding? In short, *not a qualification* for work among the heathen, but a *sign to* the heathen? We certainly never have any allusion to any Apostle using any other language but the Greek, then

Non-C. 7. collocation of ἰδού. 8. ἐγεννήθημεν = "we were born." 16. διὰ τ. π. 30. ἀναστήσειν...καθίσαι. 37. κατ. τῇ κ. J. 13. 21, note. 39. εἰς μακράν. 45. καθότι ἄν τις...εἶχε.

Chapter III.

Hebr. 3. ἠρώτα. 6. ἐν τῷ ὁ. 21. ἄχρι χρ. ἀποκ. without def. article. 23. ἔσται...ἐξολοθ. 24. καὶ κατ.

---

universally prevalent: and so, probably, not mentioned as one used on the day of the miracle.

20. V. A. generally, as here, omit article before K. when it means Jah: as if a Proper Name, though it is really not so.

22. ἀπὸ τοῦ Θ. ἀποδεδ.] ἀπὸ = מִן, "auctoris, vel causæ efficientis, vel instrumenti": of which there are frequent examples in V. T., e.g. Is. 28. 7, תָּעוּ מִן־הַשֵּׁכָר, V. A. ἐσείσθησαν ἀπὸ τῆς μέθης.

24. ὠδ.] V. A. for חֶבֶל, "a cord": hence λύσας, "untied, loosed." Ps. 18. 5, ὠδῖνες ᾅδου περιεκύκλωσάν με, and 116. 3, περίεσχόν με ὠ. θανάτου; both of which contain the notion of "cords" or "bands."

25. εἰς] For אֶל, "looking to, with respect to, him." Gen. 20. 2, אֶל־שָׂרָה, "with respect to," as also 1 Sam. 1. 27, הַזֶּה אֶל־הַנַּעַר, and 4. 19, אֶת־הַשְּׁמוּעָה אֶל־הִלָּקַח אֲרוֹן, "the report with respect to the ark being taken." In all these cases אֶל exactly corresponds to the use of εἰς in this passage, and Eph. 5. 32, ἐγὼ λέγω εἰς Χριστόν.

27. εἰς ᾅδου] After *a verb of rest*: inexplicable, if it were not the literal rendering of לִשְׁאוֹל, V. A. εἰς ᾅδην. It is but one instance, out of hundreds, of their blindly taking the *general* equivalent for a Hebrew word, as *universally* appropriate; εἰς for לְ almost always.

28. μετὰ τ. πρ.] From V. A. for אֶת־פָּנֶיךָ, Ps. 15. 11. We have here the Septuagint word for word, and see how the μετὰ came: אֶת = "*near, with*": hence μετὰ, as the nearest literal equivalent, is employed by V. A.; conveying the true notion, doubtless, to minds accustomed to Oriental idioms, but utterly and entirely *non-Greek:* against Greek phraseology altogether. *We* understand it, from our English use of "*with*," to express "the instrument": but I venture to say it could not have been understood by any one accustomed only to pure Classical Greek. M. 24. 31, L. 24. 52, notes.

38. ἐπὶ τῷ ὀνόματι] Literal for עַל־שֵׁם, M. 18. 5.

47. πρὸς ὅλον τὸν λαόν] An instance of πρὸς = אֶל, apud: J. 1. 1, 2 Th. 3. 10, notes.

Chap. III. 1. ἐπὶ τὴν ὥρ.] ἐπὶ here and 4. 5 is *literal* for לְ. Mc. 15. 1, note.

NON-C. 2. τις ἀνήρ. 5. ἐπεῖχεν. 10. πρὸς τὴν ἐλ. 12. πεπ. τοῦ π. 16. ὁλόκληρ. 19. ἐξαλειφθ. the past tense. 21. ἀποκαταστ.

SEPT. 1. ἐπὶ τὸ αὐ. supra 1. 15, note.

CHAPTER IV.

HEBR. 2. ἐν τῷ 'I. 5. ἐπὶ τὴν αὐ. 3. 1. 12. ἐν ᾁ. οὐδενί. 17. ἀπειλῇ ἀπ. and ἐπὶ τῷ ὀν. τ. M. 18. 5. 19. ἐνώπιον τοῦ Θ. 27. ἐπ᾽ ἀληθείας, Mc. 12. 14. 36. υἱὸς π. 7. 9. 11.

---

5. ἐπεῖχεν αὐ.] Found in this sense in V. A., Job 27. 8, 30. 26, and in Apocrypha: Sir. 34. 2, 35. 11.

12. πεπ. τοῦ περιπ.] "the efficient cause of": as if participle had passed into a substantive, and ὁ πεπ. = ὁ ποιητής = ὁ αἴτιος. L. 17. 1, ἀνένδεκτον, infra 7. 10, ἡγούμενον ἐπί.

13. κατὰ πρ. II.] לְפָנַי: a pure Hebraism.

19. ὅπως] "in order that a time...may come...and that He may send...": their repentance and conversion would hasten and secure the coming of Jesus again.

25. πατριαί] Gen. 12. 3: V. A. here has ἔθνη. But πατριὰ generally stands for מִשְׁפָּחָה familia, "quarum plures una tribus comprehendebat; sicut una familia plures domos paternas, οἴκους, בֵּית אָבוֹת" Gesenius. ἐξ οἴκου καὶ πατριᾶς Δαυίδ (L. 2. 4) "non solum ex eâdem prosapiâ, sed etiam ex ipsius Davidis familiâ" Grimm.

CHAP. IV. 11. γεν. εἰς κεφ. γ.] M. 2. 6 and 21. 42, notes.

12. We can make this grammatical only by taking τὸ δεδομ. ἐν ἀνθ. as the subject to ἐστι. "And the salvation (of the world) is not by any one else: for the Name set forth and given out among men, by and through which we must be saved, is no other Name under Heaven." All three uses of ἐν in the verse are Hebraic.

21. "Finding the-way-to-punish-them none at all"; "not forthcoming."

23. τοὺς ἰδίους] J. 1. 11, 13. 1, 1 Tim. 5. 8, unusual "apud Græcos" as a noun, or adjective without a noun: J. 6. 32.

27. λαοῖς 'I.] Most unusual in plural, as applied to the Jews: Grimm explains its introduction here as due to the use of plural in verse 25, quoted from V. A. But this can hardly hold: for the word there refers not to Jews, but to heathen, and is put for לְאֻמִּים = ἔθνη.

30. εἰς ἴασιν καὶ σημεῖα...γίνεσθαι] We may take this either as if (1) all the nouns are connected with γίνεσθαι, or as if (2) the preposition is to be supplied again before σημεῖα: either (1) "for cures and signs...

ACTS. 39

Non-C. 2. διαπ. 3. ἔθεντο εἰς τ. 9. εὐεργ. ἀνθ. ἀσθ. 13. ἰδιῶται. 15. συνέβαλον. 16. τί π. τοῖς ἀ. τ. dative. 23. τοὺς ἰδ. and ὅσα. 33. μεγ. δυν. 34. κτήτορες. 35. καθ. ἄν τις εἶχε. 37. τὸ χρῆμα.

CHAPTER V.

HEBR. 8. εἰ, infra 7. 1, interrog. 9: τί ὅτι = מָה כִּי. 10. πρὸς τ. ἄ. 23. ὅτι emphatic, and ἐν π. ἀ. 28. παραγγ. παρηγγ. and ἐπὶ τῷ ὀ. 36. ἐγέν. εἰς οὐδ. 41. ἀπὸ πρ.

Non-C. 1. Ἀν. ὀνόματι. 3. ψεύσ. σε τὸ πν. 4. ἐψ. ἀνθρ. 5. ἐξέψυξε. 7. μὴ εἰδ. 16. ὄχλου. 17. ἡ οὖσα αἵ. 19. διὰ τῆς ν. 21. ἀπέστ....ἀχθ. 30. ἐπὶ ξ. 33. διεπρί. 34. τίμιος τῷ λ. 35. προσέχ. ἑ. L. 17. 3. 37. ἱκανὸν, L. 8. 27, note.

---

to be done," or (2) "for healing, and for the working of signs...". The difference is very slight: and in each case the strange construction of an infinitive, standing for a noun and governed by a preposition, *without an article*, εἰς...γίνεσθαι instead of εἰς τὸ...γίνεσθαι, has to be accounted for. This cannot be done on any principles of Greek syntax: but as לִהְיוֹת אֹרוֹת וּמוֹפְתִים would be correct in Hebrew, we see how its literal equivalent may have found its way into N. T. I cannot cite any instances from V. A., though I doubt not they abound.

36. Βαρ Νάβας] = בַּר נְבִיא, "filius interpretationis" or "vaticinationis": not "*consolation,*" but "*instruction, prophesying, preaching.*" "Sons of the Prophets," in V. T., means "persons trained to be Religious Teachers": and "Son of exposition" = "good expounder." M. 8. 12, 23. 15. Our Translators were influenced, probably, by *usual* meaning of παράκλησις, as if *universal;* but see infra 13. 15, 15. 31, which bear quite naturally the sense of "exhortation," "exposition."

37. τὸ χρῆμα] I find no instance of the *singular* in V. A. Grimm says, "raro in sing. pro pecuniâ apud profanos."

CHAP. V. 10. ἔθαψαν πρὸς τὸν ἄ.] Vulg. "ad virum ejus" against Latin idiom, for "apud" or "juxta." J. 1. 1, note.

17. ἡ οὖσα αἵρ.] This cannot be strictly translated, according to grammatical rules, so as to give the meaning required: it is altogether anomalous. Compare infra 13. 1, 28. 17.

18. τηρ.] Not the *place,* but the *act:* "put them up safe in public keeping."

28. The *Pharisees* brought about the death of Jesus, not the *Sadducees:* and these were naturally unwilling to have it ascribed to *them.*

Chapter VI.

Hebr. 1. ἐν ταῖς ἡμ. τ.   5. ἤρεσεν...ἐνώπιον.   11. ὅτι emph.
Non-C. 1. παρεθεωρ.   3. μαρτυρουμ.   7. ὁ λόγος ηὔξανε.

Chapter VII.

Hebr. 1. εἰ...ἔχει, L. 14. 3.   2. ὁ Θ. τῆς δόξης.   4. εἰς ἦν.   14. ἐν ψ. ἐβδ.   23. ἀνέβη ἐπὶ τ. κ. αὐ.   30. ἐν γῇ...ἐν ἐρ. θ. omission of

---

42. κατ' οἰ.] "at home." πᾶσαν ἡμ. seems to mean, strictly, "all the day long," rather than "every day."

Chap. VI. 1. Ἑλληνισταί, Ἑβραῖοι] Dr Roberts (Diss. on Gospels) argues that these terms indicate *principles* and not *birth-place*. Clearly, all in the Church as yet were Jews by birth. But the Jews, in Palestine and abroad, had long been divided into two parties: the old, strict, Jewish party (Ἑβρ.) and the innovators (Ἑλληνιστ.) Hellenizers, who adopted Greek names, habits, ideas. Ἑλληνίζειν is not merely to *speak Greek*, but to *imitate Greeks*: "to play the Greek." οἱ ἐκ περιτομῆς, 10. 45, 11. 2 = Ἑβραῖοι in above sense. Jews settled in Greek countries are called Ἕλληνες, J. 12. 20. But generally in G. T. Ἰουδαῖος is opposed to Ἕλλην, infra 18. 4, 19. 10, 17, R. 1. 16, 10. 12, 1 Cor. 1. 24, Col. 3. 11, and Ἑβραῖος to Ἑλληνιστής: and this may possibly illustrate the title of the Epistle πρὸς Ἑβραίους, as addressed, not to the Jews generally, nor even to the Jewish converts collectively, but to the strict Jewish party, the sticklers for the Law, in the Church.

5. ἤρεσεν...ἐνώπιον] = וַיִּיטַב הַדָּבָר, in V. A. generally: e.g. Deut. 1. 23, 2 Sam. 3. 36, ἤρ. ἐν. αὐτῶν πάντα. It is altogether Hebraic: "it seemed good in their eyes" our E. V. constantly: exactly corresponding with the Hebrew. It is worthy of note that the names of all the seven are Greek: as if selected on purpose to satisfy the Ἑλληνισταί.

7. ὁ λόγος...ηὔξανε] We must take the verb as applied *to the growth of a tree*, and the spread of its branches: "the word of the Lord"—*not* "increased" (which conveys no meaning, and is, in fact, necessarily impossible: for "the Gospel," "the Revealed Word of God," here alluded to, admits of no increase or addition), but—"spread abroad."

Chap. VII. 2. What is the bearing and scope of S. Stephen's speech? It seems as if he wanted to reply to the two accusations, cap. 6. 14: and so argues, (1) that while they talked so much of Moses and obedience to the Law, they had really rejected *him* (39) and many of the Prophets, showing thereby that they did not know God's messengers when among them, and so it was with the Christ when He came (51): and (2) that article. 37. ἀκούσεσθε, future-imperative, L. 17. 4. 42. τῇ στρατ. τοῦ οὐρ. and ἐν β. τῶν πρ. and οἶκος Ἰσρ. nom. for voc. 45. ἀπὸ πρ. 53. εἰς διατ. Also 29. 34. 35. 44. 55.

NON-C. 10. ἡγούμενον, supra 3. 12. 11. χορτ. 12. σῖτα. 19. κατασοφ. τὸ γ. 31. 32. κατανοῆσαι. 51. ἀπερίτμ. τῇ κ.... dative of part.: and ἀντιπίπτετε. Also 54.

SEPT. 10. ἐναντίον. 19. τοῦ π. for לְעַשׂוֹת and ζωογ.

CHAPTER VIII.

HEBR. ἐν ἐκ. τῇ ἡμέρᾳ for χρόνῳ. 10. ἀπὸ μ. ἕως μ. 17. 39. πν. ἅγ. without article: comp. 18. 20. εἴη εἰς ἀ. 23. whole verse. 40. εἰς Ἀ. Μ. 13. 56, J. 1. 18.

Jerusalem was not necessarily the only place of worship, nor the possession of Judæa essential to God's people, nor the Temple indispensable (38, 44, 48).

14. ἐν ψ. ἐβδ.] See M. 3. 11, note, for this use of ἐν.

19. τοῦ ποιεῖν] = לַעֲשׂוֹת, M. 2. 6, note, from V. A. Infra 13. 47. For ζωογονεῖν = " to preserve alive," see L. 17. 33.

20. ἀστ. τῷ Θ.] Compare Jon. 3. 3, עִיר גְּדוֹלָה לֵאלֹהִים, πόλις μεγάλη τῷ Θ. V. A. an evident Hebraism. 2 Cor. 10. 4, δυνατὰ τῷ Θ.

30. φ. π. β.] " a fire-flame of a bush"; " a bush-fire flame": " a bush-emitted fire-flame."

34. δεῦρο] " V. A. potissimum pro לָךְ and לְכָה" Grimm. 1 K. 16. 1, 20. 20, Jud. 4. 22, 2 K. 5. 19, לֵךְ לְשָׁלוֹם, " go in peace," δεῦρο εἰς εἰρήνην, a most startling instance of their slavish adherence to the use of one word, against the sense, much the same as supra, verse 3, where it means not "come," but "go": as 1 Kings 1. 53. The form had become familiar among the Jews of our Lord's day. M. 19. 21, Mc. 10. 21.

42. τῇ στρατιᾷ τοῦ οὐρ.] The literal translation by V. A. of צְבָא הַשָּׁמַיִם, "agmen cœleste," pl. " Sabaoth": " quod (1) nunc de angelorum, (2) nunc de siderum agmine dicitur" Grimm. (1) 1 K. 22. 19, Neh. 9. 6: in N. T., L. 2. 13 and possibly this verse: (2) 2 Chr. 33. 3, 5 and elsewhere.

53. εἰς διαταγὰς ἀ.] Deut. 33. 2, M. 13. 56, εἰς for אֶל "apud, inter": as Deut. 16. 6, אֶל הַמָּקוֹם...וְזָבַחְתָּ אֶת־הַפֶּסַח, θύσεις τὸ πάσχα...εἰς τὸν τόπον. 1 Kings 8. 30.

CHAP. VIII. 10. ἀπὸ μικροῦ ἕως μεγ.] 1 Sam. 30. 19, V. A. for מִן הַקָּטֹן וְעַד הַגָּדוֹל and also Ex. 22. 3, Deut. 29. 10, altogether Hebraic.

16. βεβαπτ. εἰς τὸ ὄν.] M. 18. 20, 28. 19, 1 Cor. 10. 2, Gal. 3. 27.

21. εὐθεῖα] V. A. for יָשָׁר, being its primary meaning. Judg. 17. 6,

NON-C. 1. κατὰ τὰς χώρας. 2. κοπετόν. 3. κατὰ τοὺς οἴ. εἰσ. 10. ἡ καλουμ. 11. ἐκ. χρόνῳ, dative of duration of time: and ἐξεστακέναι. 13. ἐξίστατο. 16. ἐπ' οὐδενὶ : dat. for acc. 22. εἰ ἄρα = "if anyhow," "if possibly." 27. δυνάστης. 30. γιγνώσκ. 32. περιοχή. 34. δέομαί σου.

SEPT. 21. εὐθεῖα for ὀρθή.

CHAPTER IX.

HEBR. 2. τῆς ὁδοῦ. 15. σκεῦος ἐ. 31. πορευ. τῷ φ. 42. ἐπ. ἐπὶ τὸν K. M. 27. 43, Mc. 1. 15, notes.

ἀνὴρ τὸ εὐθὲς ἐν ὀφθ. αὐτοῦ ἐποίει, הַיָּשָׁר בְּעֵינָיו. What is wanted for sense is ὀρθή, not *straight*, but *upright*: not *planum* but *rectum*. λόγῳ] literal for דָּבָר in its constant meaning of "res, negotium": E. V. "in this matter." Vulg. verbatim, "in sermone isto."

23. ὄντα εἰς] Supra 4. 11. "I see thou art becoming a deadly poison and a bundle of wickedness." χ. π.] "bile of bitterness": i.e. very, utter, mere, bile, or bitterness, which, in Hebrew, implies poison. Job 20. 25. Ges. sub voce מְרֹרָה and מֵי הַמָּרִים, of the adulterous wife, N. 5. 18 : Ps. 69. 22, יִתְּנוּ רֹאשׁ בְּבָרוּתִי : "they put poison into my food," V. A. εἰς τὸ βρῶμά μου ἔδωκαν χολὴν, Deut. 29. 18, ῥίζα φύουσα ἄνω ἐν χ. καὶ π. In margin of E. V. "a poisonful herb." Quoted at Hebr. 12. 15.

30. γιγνώσκω] in later Greek, seems to have meant "to understand": whence γνῶσις. Infra 21. 37.

31. πῶς γὰρ;] "*Why, how can I?*"

33. τ. γ. αὐ. τίς δ.] "Who will state his past history," i.e. "speak to his character"? V. A. give γενέαι for דֹּרוֹת, Gen. 6. 9, Is. 53. 8, in this sense: in the first passage it clearly = "history."

34. δέομαί σου] A unique and peculiar use of the words, by way of *adjuration and appeal*, standing alone, without an infinitive or accusative or dependent sentence expressing the object of the request. We ought, probably, to supply εἰπεῖν. Our English phrase "I pray thee" in E. V. is idiomatic, and conveys the idea naturally : which the Greek does not.

CHAP. IX. 2. τινας...ἄνδρας τε καὶ γ.] In *good* Greek this would be, εἴτε ἄ. εἴτε γ. For τῆς ὁδοῦ ὄντας, compare infra 19. 9, 23, 22. 4, 24. 22. In each case, of course, we must supply τοῦ Θεοῦ or τοῦ K. to complete the phrase as commonly found. In the Hebrew idiom, true religion is "the road to Heaven"; "God's way" as contrasted with "man's way": and this metaphor pervades and colours all the phraseology both of Old and New Test. Ps. 25. 8, 12, 67. 2, 139. 24 : M. 22.

NON-C. 1. ἐμπν. ἀπ. gen. 7. μηδένα. 9. 26. μή. 10. 11. ὀνόματι, a sort of dative of manner. 21. ἐξίσταντο and πορθήσας. 21. 24. Non-sequence of Tenses. 22. συνέχυνε. 27. πῶς. 31. 43. καθ᾽ ὅλης... 36. τις ἦν μαθ. ungrammatical order of words.

SEPT. 10. ἰδοὺ ἐγώ, Gen. 22. 1, 27. 1, for הִנֵּנִי.

CHAPTER X.

HEBR. 4. εἰς μν. Ex. 17. 14, κατάγραψον τοῦτο εἰς μνημ. 14. 28. οὐδ....πᾶν κοινόν. 17. καὶ ἰδού, and ἐπὶ τὸν π. = אֶל apud.

16, Acts 18. 25, 26. The special peculiarity in the passage before us, and those akin to it cited *first* above, is that they show implicitly, if not explicitly, that the Church from the very first assumed and proclaimed the Christian Religion to be emphatically and alone "*the* way," i.e. "*the* road to Heaven," "the way of life," "God's way."

15. σκ. ἐκλ.] Jer. 50. 25, כְּלִי זַעַם, σκ. ὀργῆς, R. 9. 22, σκ. ὀργῆς. βαστάσαι τὸ ὄ. μου ἐνώπιον] "to lift up," "to exalt" my name "in the presence of."

29. S. Paul had no sympathy with the Hellenizers, as being, possibly, many of them, Sadducees: he was Ἑβρ. ἐξ Ἑβρ. 6. 1, κατὰ νόμον Φαρισαῖος, Ph. 3. 5. Grimm narrows the meaning of Ἑλληνιστ.: "dicitur in N. T. de Judæis apud exteros natis et Græcè loquentibus": and Schl. takes the same inadequate view.

31, 42. καθ᾽ ὅλης...] I find no clue to this use of gen. in V. A. nor can I connect it with any Hebrew form. πορευόμ. τῷ φόβῳ] Possibly "dat. of manner," very rare in N. T., L. 20. 47, note: but the construction is unnatural. Of course πορευόμ. is a well-known *Hebrew* idiom literally rendered into Greek, to which it is utterly alien, and conveys no such idea as that of the original: no more than it would in English, if we were not habituated to its use in Holy Scripture. For παρακλήσει τοῦ ἁγ. πν. see J. 14. 16, note. If we retain here the rendering of E. V., "the *comfort* of the H. Gh.", it must be in its primary, natural, sense of *strength* (from fortis), or rather "strengthening"; "*encouragement*" exactly.

35. πάντες οἱ κ....οἵτινες ἐπ.] This can hardly mean, with our E. V., "all those who dwelt...saw him and turned" either in construction of sentence or in probability: rather "all the inhabitants, who had turned..., saw him."

CHAP. X. 14, 28. κοινόν] M. 15. 11, Mc. 7. 2, 15, note.

45. οἱ ἐκ π. π.] This shows there was a party *without* the Church not πιστοί but ἐκ περιτ.; as 11. 2 shows there were some of the same

28. καὶ = but, as ן constantly. 34. ἐπ' ἀληθ. Mc. 12. 14, *note*.
37. τὸ γ. ρ̇.

NON-C. 2. δεόμ. τοῦ Θ. 3. 30. ὥραν ἐνν. point of time: acc. instead of dat. 10. γεύσασθαι = eat. 11. ἀρχαῖς = corners. 13. θῦσον, J. 10. 10. 17. διερωτ. τὴν οἰκ. 30. ἀπὸ τετ. ἡμ. μέχρι. 37. τὸ γεν. ρ̇. order of words. καθ' ὅλης τῆς 'Ι. supra 9. 31, note. 38. καταδυν. 48. ἡρώτ.

SEPT. 6. 32. παρὰ θάλασσαν, Mc. 4. 1, note. 15. ἐκ δευτέρου, V. A. for שֵׁנִית, Josh. 5. 2, 2 Sam. 14. 29.

CHAPTER XI.

HEBR. 8. κοινόν. 19. ἀπὸ τ. θλ. and ἐπὶ Στ. ἐπὶ = עַל "super," "about." 3. 14. 16.

NON-C. 10. ἐπὶ τρὶς. 17. ἐγὼ δὲ and τίς ἤμην δ. κ. 22. ἦκ.... εἰς τὰ ὦ. 23. προθ. 26. χρηματ. 5. 13. 19. 24.

CHAPTER XII.

HEBR. 23. ἀνθ' ὧν, L. 1. 20, note.

NON-C. 2. τὸν ἀδ. 'Ι. collocation of words: and 12. 7. ἐν τάχει. 10. πρ. φ. καὶ δ. omission of article: as 11. ἐκ χ. and 12. Τ. κ. Σ. 15. ὁ ἄγγ. αὐ. the article. 23. ἐξέψ. 24. ὁ λόγος τοῦ Θ. ηὔξανε, supra 6. 7 note, and 19. 20. Also 17. 19.

---

party, ἐκ π., *in* the Church. The term implies that there was "a circumcision party"; sticklers for the whole principles of the old Jewish belief: Ἑβραῖοι as opposed to Ἑλληνισταί, 6. 1. If so, such a party would consist, in all probability, of Pharisees: how then could S. Paul, as an avowed Pharisee, be opposed to them? Is it not possible that, under one aspect, Ἑλληνιστής was equivalent to Sadducee? Supra 9. 29. We know that the latter were in many ways Hellenizers, imitators of the Greeks, in social habits, as in philosophical speculations.

CHAP. XII. 3. πρ. σ.] "He afterwards seized Peter," M. 6. 33, note: V. A. Gen. 4. 2, וַתֹּסֶף לָלֶדֶת, καὶ προσέθηκε τεκεῖν, Jud. 20. 28, הַאוֹסִף עוֹד ל, εἰ προσθῶ ἔτι... (where observe εἰ = הֲ interrogative, M. 12. 10): Gen. 8. 12, לֹא יָסְפָה שׁוּב, οὐ προσέθετο τοῦ ἐπιστρέψαι (where note the τοῦ, M. 2. 6; which V. A. use so universally for ל with infinitive, as to have inserted it here, though there is no ל in the Hebrew). L. 20. 11.

12. συνιδών] Used, apparently, as if = ξυνειδώς, "conscious, aware of the fact." 14. 6.

Chapter XIII.

HEBR. 10. τὰς ὁδοὺς Κ. τ. εὐ. 17. μετὰ β. ὑ. supra 2. 28. 22. 34. ὅτι. 39. 42. εἰς τὸ μ. for בְּ, as frequently in V. A., M. 28. 19, note. 47. εἰς φῶς...σωτηρίαν.

NON-C. 1. κατὰ τ. οὐ. ἑ. supra 5. 17. 2. ὁ προσκ. αὐ. 11. μὴ...καιροῦ. 16. ἄνδρες Ἰ. καὶ οἱ φ. supra 12. 12. 17. παροικίᾳ. 20. ὡς ἔτεσι τετρακ. dat. for acc. of continuance of time. 28. 34. μὴ for οὐ. 35. ἐν ἑτέρῳ.

SEPT. 34. ὅσια.

Chapter XIV.

HEBR. 3. μὲν οὖν = for all this. 23. εἰς ὃν, Mc. 1. 15, note.

NON-C. 1. κατὰ τὸ αὐτὸ. 6. συνιδόντες. 8. τις ἀνὴρ for ἀνήρ τις. 9. σώζειν = "to heal," M. 9. 21, note. 16. παρῳχημέναις.

CHAP. XIII. 9. Roman names often adopted : verse 1, and 1. 23.

10, 12. Strong instances of the irregular, arbitrary and apparently capricious way, in which, after Hebrew usage, the article is either omitted or inserted, in V. A. and N. T. By Greek rule, τὰς ὁδοὺς would require τοῦ Κ.

11. ἄχρι κ.] L. 4. 13, "up to a time that suits."

15. παρακλ.] 4. 36, 15. 31 : "teaching, instruction, exhortation"; as in the explanation of the name of Barnabas, supra 4. 36, בַּר נְבִיא, υἱὸς παρακλήσεως, where, from the derivation, it *must* mean as above, "a son of exposition": i.e. "an expounder."

18. ἐτροποφ.] Some MSS. ἐτροφ. Numb. 11. 12, Deut. 1. 31, V. A.

24. πρὸ προσ.] Mc. 1. 2 for "before."

33. ἀναστ.] "by raising up," R. 1. 4.

34. τὰ ὅσια] V. A. Is. 55. 3, 2 Ch. 6. 42, ἐλέη, for חַסְדֵי = mercies, both of them.

50. τὰς σεβ. γ. τὰς εὐσχ.] The women of rank and fashion, who were proselytes to Judaism. Infra 17. 4, 12.

CHAP. XIV. 3. μὲν οὖν] Here the sense seems much rather to require "nevertheless" than "therefore," "*for all this*" rather than "*for this*," or "therefore." I have shown before, J. 19. 11, that διὰ τοῦτο, to which μὲν οὖν is equivalent, is used indifferently, in each of the above meanings, for לָכֵן, which bears them both, and so it may be with μὲν οὖν, as here. Compare 7. 30, 28. 5, 1 Cor. 6. 4 : which seem to confirm this suggestion.

23. χειροτ.] Sensu ecclesiastico, "lay hands on." This, as the syntax shows (χειρ....παρέθεντο), was the act of the *Apostles, not of the*

SEPT. 9. π. τοῦ σωθ. τοῦ with inf. for לְ, infra 15. 20, ἐπιστεῖλαι αὐτοῖς τοῦ ἀπέχεσθαι, absolutely unintelligible to a Greek reader. R. 15. 22.

CHAPTER XV.

HEBR. 2. εἰς for אֶל or אֵת = apud, at. 13. ἀποκρίνομαι, V. A. for אָמַר, εἴπειν, Gen. 29. 26, Ex. 21. 5, 1 Kings 3. 26. 17. ἐφ' οὗς...αὐτοὺς. 21. ἐκ γ. ἀ. from מִן in this sense. 33. μετ' εἰρ. M. 24. 31.

NON-C. 1. τῷ ἔθει. 5. τινες...πεπιστ. 6. ἰδεῖν. 7. ἀρχαίων, as for so short a time. 11. πιστ. σωθ. 24. λέγοντες, in sense of "ordering," "commanding." 28. τῶν ἐπάν. τούτων. 29. ἔρρωσθε, Latinism = "valete." 30. τὸ πλῆθος. 33. ποι. χρ. and μετ' εἰρήνης, M. 24. 31, and supra 2. 28. 38. Order of words. 41. τὴν Σ. καὶ Κ. *one* article for *two* distinct nouns.

SEPT. 31. παράκλησις = "directions, instructions": supra 4. 36, 13. 15, notes.

CHAPTER XVI.

HEBR. 17. ὁδὸν σ., Ps. 67. 2. 31. πίστ. ἐπὶ, Mc. 1. 15. 36. ὅτι emphatic, and πορ. ἐν εἰρ.

NON-C. 2. ἐμαρτυρ. 4. κεκρ. 5. ἐπερίσσ. 7. ἐπείραζον, active. 16. προσευχή. 18. διαπ. καὶ ἐπιστρ. τῷ πν. 19. ἐξῆλθε, and ἐπιλαβ. with acc. 22. ἐκέλ. imp. 26. ἀνέθη. 29. φῶτα.

---

people, as the advocates of popular election pretend; τοῦτο χειροτονία καλεῖται· ἡ χεὶρ ἐπίκειται τοῦ ἀνδρὸς: Chrysostom. Alford claims this to be possible, from analogy of 6. 2—6, and says: "the Apostles ordained the Presbyters whom the churches elected." But how about the grammar of our sentence here, which cannot *possibly* be strained to that meaning?

CHAP. XV. 1. τῷ ἔθει] Possibly, "dat. of manner": but hard to force into the sense of "according to."

2. πρὸς τοὺς ἀπ. εἰς 'Ι.] εἰς = *at*: for אֶת or אֶל; V. A. and N. T. passim, Mc. 1. 39. Infra 23. 11, J. 1. 1.

12. Compare μετ' αὐτῶν, supra 4, and 14. 27, with δι' αὐτῶν here.

17. Is. 4. 1, עָלֵינוּ יִקָּרֵא שִׁמְךָ, κεκλήσθω τὸ ὄνομά σου ἐφ' ἡμᾶς, V. A. i. e. "let us be called thine." Here, "whom I have taken for my own."

24. ἀνασκ.] = turning up the foundations, upsetting. Thuc. 4. 116, λήκυθον καθελὼν καὶ ἀνασκευάσας.

CHAP. XVI. 13. "Where a meeting-for-prayer was wont to be held": a proseucha, Juv.

Sept. 37. ἐκβάλλ. M. 9. 38, Mc. 1. 43.

Chapter XVII.

Hebr. 6. 28. 31.

Non-C. 6. μή. 9. τὸ ἱκανὸν. 12. εὐσχ., supra 13. 50 and verse 4, πρώτων. 19. δυνάμ. γνῶναι. 20. ξενίζοντα. 21. εὐκ. and καινότ. comp.; in this sense. 31. πίστις = "assurance," "grounds of belief."

Sept. 12. μὲν οὖν, supra 14. 3, note.

Chapter XVIII.

Hebr. 15. ὄψεσθε αὐ. fut. for imper. M. 27. 4, 24, note. 21. εἰς 'Ι. 25. τὴν ὁδὸν τ. K. infra 19. 9, 23.

Non-C. 5. συνείχ. τῷ λ. 11. ἐκάθισε. 12. κατεπέστ. 18. εἶχε γ. εὐχ. 21. ἑορτ. ποι. 23. ποιεῖν χρ.

Chapter XIX.

Non-C. 9. σχολῇ. 11. δυνάμεις ἐπ. M. 7. 22, note. 12. σουδ. ἡ σιμικ. Latinisms. 13. ὁρκ. ὑ. τὸν 'Ι. 18. ἤρχοντο. 19. 26.

---

29. φῶτα] James 1. 17. Plural very unusual.

34. ἠγαλλ...πεπιστ.] "Rejoiced *for* his having...".

Chap. XVII. 4. Ἑλλήν.] = Gentile, supra 6. 1, *note*. Col. 3. 11.

9. "Quod satisfecit sibi": Mc. 15. 15.

23. We translate θυσιαστήριον the Jewish, and βωμὸς the Heathen, altar, by the same word. ἀγν. Θ.] "to *any* unknown God" perhaps: or it may be merely an instance of article omitted, more Hebraico.

26. ἐπὶ πᾶν τὸ πρόσ.] A thoroughly Hebrew idiom, startling in its Greek reproduction.

34. κολλ. αὐ. ἐπ.] "believed after close and intimate intercourse."

Chap. XVIII. 7. σεβ. τὸν Θ.] The usual name in N. T. for Gentile proselytes.

25. ζ. τ. πν.] "being in his spirit a fervent man": *dative of part,* ungrammatical: M. 5. 3.

Chap. XIX. 3, 4, 5. εἰς τί...εἰς τὸ 'Ι. β.] M. 18. 20, 28. 19, *notes*. Rom. 6. 3.

9. κακολ.] "speaking evil of": M. 15. 4, Mc. 7. 10, *notes*. τὴν ὁδὸν] supra 9. 2, and infra 23.

14. "And those who did this were certain men, sons..."

ἱκανοί. 26. πάσης τῆς 'Α. name of country, used for gen. of place where. 27. τὸ μέρος, for "profession, pursuit." 34. ἐπιγνόντες... φωνὴ ἐγέν.: comp. 20. 3.

Chapter XX.

HEBR. 9. ἀπὸ τοῦ ὕπν. literal for מִן = ὑπὸ. 13. 14. 16. εἰς 19. ἐν ταῖς ἑ. 25. τὴν β. τοῦ Θ. Μ. 3. 3, note. 32. τῷ λ. τῆς χ. αὐ.

Non-C. 2. λόγῳ π. sing. 3. Compare 17. 23 and 19. 24. 5. ἔμενον ἡμᾶς. 6. ἄχρις. 12. ἤγαγον. 14. 16. εἰς, Μ. 13. 56, note. 23. κατὰ πόλιν. 24. ὡς τελει. 29. βαρεῖς.

SEPT. 20. 27. τοῦ μὴ ά. and 21. 12.

Chapter XXI.

HEBR. 24. στοιχεῖς. 28. κεκοίν. τὸν ἅγιον, Μc. 7. 2, note. 37. εἰ ἔξ.

Non-C. 3. ἦν...ἀποφ. present for fut. 5. ὅτε ἐγ. ἡμ. ἐξ. 8. 10. ἐμείναμεν and ἐπιμενόντων, tense. 11. εἰς χ. ἑ. omission of article. 30. εἷλκον καὶ ἐκλείσθ. change of tense. 31. φάσις. 37. Ἑλλ. γιν. supra 8. 30, note.

SEPT. 6. εἰς τὰ ἴδια, J. 16. 32, note.

Chapter XXII.

HEBR. 4. τὴν ὁδὸν, supra 9. 2, 16. 17. 20. καὶ αὐτὸς. 22. καθῆκε. 23. ῥίπτεω for ῥίπτω. 24. εἰπὼν = commanding. 25.

Non-C. 17. Whole verse.

CHAP. XX. 7. ἐν τῇ μιᾷ τῶν σαβ.] σάββατα is used in G. T. apparently indifferently for (1) The Sabbath day; (2) The week: as in Matt. 28. 1 (where see note) (1) ὀψὲ σαββάτων and (2) εἰς μίαν σαββάτων. But in this latter sense, as equivalent to ἐβδομάς, שָׁבוּעַ, it is apparently never used again in V. A.

CHAP. XXI. 21. περιπ. τοῖς ἔθ.] Mc. 7. 5, note. The strange use of dative is possibly reducible to the rule of "dative of manner," of which, and its cognates "cause and instrument," S. Luke has more examples, in proportion, than any other of the Sacred Writers, L. 20. 47, note: infra 24. 4, 2 K. 17. 8, V. A. ἐπορεύθησαν δικαιώμασιν ἐθνῶν.

28. ὁ λαὸς] = עַמִּי, "God's people," as opposed to τὰ ἔθνη.

38. οὐκ ἄρα σὺ εἶ] "Thou art not then": *not a question.*

CHAP. XXIII. 1. πολιτεύεσθαι] Phil. 1. 27 = "to live in a state of society," "act as citizen of a commonwealth," "live in the world," in the abstract: as Joseph. Life, §§ 2 and 49, ἠρξάμην πολιτεύεσθαι, τῇ τῶν

Chapter XXIII.

HEBR. 6. π. ἐλπ. καὶ ἀναστ. = "the hope of the resurrection." Mark omission of article. 11. εἰς for אֶל. Also 18. 20.

NON-C. 12. λέγοντες μή. φ. 8. 23. ἀπὸ τρ. ὦ. 30. μηνυθ.... ἐπιβουλῆς...μέλλειν, and ἔρρωσο, Latinism for "vale."

Chapter XXIV.

HEBR. 21. ὅτι emph. 22. τῆς ὁδοῦ. 24. τῆς εἰς Χρ. πίστεως, Mc. 1. 5, note.

NON-C. 1. ἐνεφ. 3. κατ. γεν. 5. 6. εὑρόντες γάρ...ὂν καὶ ἐκράτησ.: syntax wrong. 7. μετὰ π. β. supra 2. 28, note. 12. ἐπισύστ., compare 2 Cor. 11. 28. 13. παραστῆσαι. 18. ἐν οἷς Vulg. "in quibus," literally, but unintelligibly: E. V. "whereupon": infra 26. 12. 21. τί...ἤ for τί ἄλλο ἤ. 25. δικ. καὶ ἐγκ. καὶ τοῦ κρί., arbitrary use and omission of article, borrowed possibly from Hebrew irregularity. And τὸ νῦν ἔχον. 26. ἅμα καὶ ἐλπίζων, violation of syntax: unless we connect with ἔμφ. γεν., as expressing two reasons for sending him away: "being alarmed..." "withal hoping also." 27. χάριτας plural.

Chapter XXV.

NON-C. 1. ἐπιβὰς. 16. οὐκ ἔστιν ἔθος...χαρ....πρὶν ἤ...ἔχοι, non-sequence of tenses. 17. 24. μηδεμίαν, strong instances of μή for οὐ, so common in G. T. 20. ἔλεγον εἰ β. 17. 21, 24. 25. 21. ἐπικαλ. τηρηθ. αὐτόν. 23. φαντασία, and τοῖς κατ' ἐξοχ. οὖσι τῆς π. 26. ἐφ' ὑμῶν: supra 9.

Φαρισαίων αἱρέσει ἀκολουθῶν, and μετὰ πάσης ἀρετῆς πεπολίτευμαι (where use of μετὰ corresponds with V. A. and N. T. usage). But 2 Macc. 6. 1 and 3 Macc. 3. 4, it is followed by a dative, as *of the manner*, τοῖς τοῦ Θ. νόμ. πολιτεύ. But here τῷ Θεῷ is a quasi-*dat. of person*: as ζῆν τῷ Θ. "To live for God."

6. γνοὺς...ὅτι] Vulg. "sciens *quia*": infra 24. 26, ἐλπίζων ὅτι... "sperans quod": I cite these two instances of the debased Latin of the Vulgate, through which our E. V. has been so frequently misguided: and much more, the Psalter in our Prayer-Book.

15, 20. τοῦ ἀνελεῖν] For לְ with inf. supra 7. 19, 13. 47.

CHAP. XXV. 9. ἐπ' ἐμοῦ] M. 28. 14, note. If ἀπ' ἐμοῦ is read, it is = לְפָנַי, coram me: 1 John 2. 28, as in V. A. Ecclesiasticus 41. 17, αἰσχύνεσθε ἀπὸ πατρός: and Lev. 19. 32, ἀπὸ προσώπου πολιοῦ ἐξαναστήσῃ, for לִפְנֵי in each case.

Chapter XXVI.

Hebr. 7. ἐν ἐ. 16. εἰς τ. ὤφθ. 20. εἰς π. χ. 22. μικρῷ τ. κ. μεγ. supra 8. 10. 31.

Non-C. 3. γνώστην: V. A. four times. "Accus. pendens": harsh and unusual construction, after ἐπὶ σοῦ. 12. ἐν οἷς, L. 12. 1, supra 24. 18. 14. τῇ 'Ε. δ. 22. ὧν ἐλάλ....μελλόντων γίν. 23. παθητός. 32. ἀπολελ. ἐδύνατο.

Chapter XXVII.

Non-C. 10. ὕβρεως. 20. 21. 33. ἄχρι οὗ. 41. ἐλύετο, J. 2. 19. 44. οὓς μὲν...

Sept. 1. ἐκρ. τοῦ ἀποπλεῖν, M. 2. 6, note.

Chapter XXVIII.

Hebr. 5. μὲν οὖν, supra 14. 3. 14. ἐπ' αὐτοῖς, Mc. 8. 4, note. 25. πρὸς τοὺς πατέρας and ὅτι.

---

16. τόπον] Eph 4. 27, μὴ δίδοτε τόπον τῷ διαβ. Latinism: "locum dare," Vulg. "opportunity, way": frequent in this sense.

20. ἔλεγον...εἰ βούλοιτο] Vulg. "dicebam si vellet": against Latin idiom. E. V. translates "asked": but on what grounds? May it possibly be explained by the common use of εἰ interrogative, borrowed from Hebr.? "I said: did he wish..."?

22. ἐβουλόμην...] E. V. "I would also..." does not give the force of imperfect. "I was anxious myself also..."

27. πέμποντα...μὴ σημ.] "for any one sending...not to signify": of course "apud Græcos," in correct construction, τὸ is required.

Chap. XXVI. 7. ὑπὸ 'Ι.] Indignantis: "accused by *Jews*."

8. εἰ] Infra 23, and Hebr. 7. 15: in sense of *that*.

9. πρὸς τὸ ὄ.] "with respect to..." ἔδοξα ἐμαυτῷ...δεῖν. "I thought that it was a binding duty for me": not ἔδ. ἐμ. but ἐμ. δεῖν. For δοκέω = cogito, see M. 3. 9, note.

26. λανθ....οὐδέν] "I do not at all believe that any of these things is unknown to him."

Chap. XXVIII. 7. ἐν τοῖς περὶ τὸν τόπον] τὰ περὶ...is, of course, an ordinary and grammatical form in Classical authors: but such an extension of it, as the above, ἐν τοῖς περὶ... seems very unusual. χωρία] = "estates," "farms," though rare, is used by Thucyd. 1. 106.

Two inscriptions are said by Dr Roberts to have been found in Malta, one in Greek, the other in Latin, giving the official name of the Governor, as πρῶτος Μελιταίων.

Non-C. 3. καθάπτω, act. for middle. 6. 7. ἐν δὲ τοῖς περὶ... χωρία. 9. προσήρχ. 15. ἔλαβε θ. 17. τοὺς ὄντας τῶν 'Ι. πρώτους. 25. ἀπελ. 31. μετὰ π. π. supra 2. 28, 24. 7.

---

17. This *conversation* was in all probability held in Greek; for S. Paul, we know, wrote to the Converts at Rome, both Jews and Gentiles, in that language.

23. ξενία] is not found, I believe, "apud Græcos," in the sense of a "lodging," as here and Philemon 22: nor in V. A. The order is, οἷς ἐξέτ. τὴν β. τοῦ Θ. διαμαρτυρ. πείθων τε... "with strong appeals and obtestations, and endeavours to persuade..."

25. πρὸς] "with respect to," Hebr. 1. 7, *note*. ὅτι *asseverandi*: M. 7. 23, L. 6. 5, James 1. 13.

26. ἀκούσετε καὶ οὐ μὴ συνῆτε] This combination seems to indicate two futures, "you shall hear and not understand": which is more grammatical and not less forcible than to suppose ἀκούσετε and βλέψετε as instances of Hebraic future for imperative, M. 5. 48, note, conveying a sentence, or command.

27. μή ποτε] = "in case that," "lest that," "at some future time": and thus the prophecy predicts a *temporary* suspension of blessings, M. 13. 14, Mc. 4. 12, note.—ἐπαχ....ἐκάμμ. is parenthetical.

ROMANS.

Chapter I.

Hebr. 1. 2. 3. 4. 5. 7. 17. omission of article. 3. κατὰ σάρκα. 9. ἐν τῷ πν. 10. 12. 25. 27.

Chap. I. 1. εἰς εὐαγγ. Θ.] The omission of the article here, and in the following verses, and all through the Epistle, is unquestionably Hebraic: and inexplicable on any other theory, except by very overstrained and forced and unnatural criticism.

4. ἐν δυν....] "marked clearly out as the Son of God with power answerable to ('in accordance with,' 'corresponding to') the Holy Spirit in Him, by His Resurrection." ἐξ] = מִן instrumenti, M. 7. 16, Heb. 5. 7, notes.

5. εἰς ὑπακοὴν πίστεως] Is this "gen. *objecti*" or "subjecti": "obedience *to* the faith"; or "the obedience of faith," "rendered *by* faith," "springing out of faith"? The latter agrees best with Classical usage, by analogy of ὑπακούω, generally found with dat. But ὑπακοή is *not* a Classical, and scarcely a Septuagint word: "neque apud profanos exstat neque apud LXX., præter 2 Sam. 22. 36." Grimm.

ὑπὲρ τοῦ ὀνόματος] Acts 9. 16, 15. 26, "for his *Name's* sake." What do we understand in these passages by *Name?* Alford suggests "for His glory." It is probably Hebraic.

6. κλητοὶ Ἰ. Χ. and 7. ἀγαπ. Θ.] M. 25. 34, note. V. A. Ps. 59. 5, οἱ ἀγαπητοί σου and Ps. 107. 6, 126. 2, for יְדִידְךָ. This is clearly a Hebraism. In the case of *substantives*, of course, the genitive of possession is intelligible: but ἀγαπητοὶ and κλητοὶ are *adjectives*.

12. "By the joint and mutual confidence in each other, both of you and of me."

13. καὶ ἐκ.] "*But* I was prevented." Hebraic.

16. δύναμις Θ.] "God's powerful agent for salvation."

CHAPTER II.

HEBR. 4. τοῦ πλ. τῆς χ.
NON-C. 12. ἀνόμως. 29. ἐκ for ἀπό.

---

17. Δικαιοσύνη Θ.] What do we understand by this, translated in E. V. "the righteousness of God"? Clearly not its literal meaning, as an attribute or quality of God: "the righteousness essentially inherent in Him." It is a genitive not of possession, but of "origination, institution, approval, appointment": "the way of justification ordained by God": "God's plan and law of righteousness," ἐκ πίστεως εἰς πίστιν "springing out of faith, and tending to its end in faith," "beginning in faith, and perfected by continuous development and confirmation of faith." Gesenius gives force of "liberatio, felicitas, salus," to צֶדֶק and צְדָקָה, generally rendered "righteousness": and makes them parallel to יְשׁוּעָה, salvation, Is. 46. 13, 51. 6, 8, 56. 1, in each of which the two words are put together, side by side, as equivalent terms.

23. ἤλλαξαν ἐν] Ps. 106. 20, יָמִירוּ...בְּתַבְנִית, ἠλλάξαντο τὴν δόξαν αὐτῶν ἐν ὁμοιώματι: i.e. "changed it *for*," a common Hebr. use of בְּ. Our E. V. interpretation is *false*. ὁμ. εἰκ. = "an image-likeness": "they exchanged the glory of God for an image-likeness of perishable man." And so 25: "exchanged the truth of God for the lie": "gave up the true God for the idol." 3rd Commandment, Ex. 20. 7, לֹא תִשָּׂא אֶת־שֵׁם יה' לַשָּׁוְא may possibly mean, "Thou shalt not give the name of the Lord to a false God." Otherwise, לַשָּׁוְא is taken *adverbially*, as Jer. 4. 30, V. A. εἰς μάταιον, and 6. 29, εἰς κενόν. V. A. translation of 3rd Commandment, Ex. 20. 7, οὐ λήψῃ...ἐπὶ ματαίῳ, is very obscure. שָׁוְא = ψεῦδος.

25, 32. οἵτινες] "as persons who had..." κτίσις "the act of creation" used here and elsewhere in N. T. for "the thing created."

32. δικαίωμα] V. A. passim, for all the Hebrew words that mean "decree," "command," "law." Infra 2. 26.

CHAP. II. 7. ὑπομ. ἔργου ἀγ.] Remark (1) the construction ὑπ. ἔργ. and (2) sing. for plural ἔργον for ἔργα: infra 15.

8. τοῖς ἐξ ἐρι.] The same form as οἱ ἐκ περιτομῆς, Acts 10. 45, and οἱ ἐκ πίστεως, infra 3. 26, 4. 11.

9. πᾶσ. ψ. ἀνθ.] Comp. R. 13. 1. Hebraic: derived possibly from the description of man, Gen. 2. 7, ἐγένετο ἄνθ. εἰς ψ. ζῶσαν. Hence "every soul" in Jewish phraseology, is equivalent to "every body" in our common English idiom: which is exactly opposite to the Hebrew.

27. διὰ γρ. καὶ π.] V. A. use διὰ for בְּקֶרֶב and בְּתוֹךְ *in medio*, Jos. 3. 2, 2 Chr. 23. 20, 32. 4. Here and infra 4. 11, 7. 5, 11, 13, 14. 20,

Chapter III.

HEBR. 5. Θ. δικ. no article. 7. 26. ἐν. 18. ἀπ. τῶν ὀφθ. 20. οὐ δικ. πᾶσα σ.

---

15. 4, Gal. 3. 19, 2 Tim. 2. 2, such an interpretation suits very well: "out of the very midst of." Dr Wordsworth, here and at 4. 11, suggests the notion of "*a barrier to be broken through.*" How to translate the διά in the above and corresponding passages, has always been a great perplexity. I venture to submit the above attempt at a solution.

CHAP. III. 1, 2. In this, the first distich of question and answer, occupying verses 1—9, (in which S. Paul suggests, and replies to, the probable arguments of an imaginary objector to the statements of Cap. 1 and 2,) there is no difficulty but γάρ; evaded by Vulg. and E. V., and by all the Commentators I have met with: "for, first of all," (the Jews have this advantage) "because that..."

3, 4. Before going further, I must refer to the Hebrew idiom, so often illustrated in these notes, M. 11. 19, L. 16. 19, 1 Cor. 13. 6, 2 Th. 2. 10, by which

$$\delta\text{ίκαιος} = \dot{α}ληθής = πιστός$$
$$\delta\text{ικαιοσύνη} = \dot{α}λήθεια = πίστις$$
$$\dot{α}δικία = ψεῦδος \text{ or } ψεῦσμα = \dot{α}πιστία.$$

Here, in 3, πίστις has, *not* its ordinary, but a special meaning, and = "trustworthiness, truthfulness, faithfulness," the characteristic of one who is πιστός, 1 Th. 5. 24, Hebr. 10. 23, πιστὸς ὁ καλῶν and ἐπαγγειλάμενος. Grimm, sub voce, translates "indoles ejus, cui confidi potest"; and cites Gal. 5. 22, Titus 2. 10. Here also ἀπιστία and ἀπιστέω describe severally the character and action of one, who is ἄπιστος: i.e. "unfaithful to his vows, false, disloyal, disobedient."

5, 6. "Well, but, if our (ἀδικία = ψεῦδος = ἀπιστία) commend and confirm the faithfulness (δικαιοσ. = ἀλήθ. = πίστις) of God," (as "keeping his promise for ever," notwithstanding all our unfaithfulness) "is God, who is thus bringing his wrath to bear upon us, (by rejecting the Jews from their privileges as exclusively His people) unfaithful to his pledged word after all?" "God forbid: for in that case how shall God judge the world?" (Gen. 18. 25).

7, 8. "I do not agree yet": urges the objector, "for if..." Or, more briefly, "If then the truthfulness of God has been more abundantly and triumphantly demonstrated, to His Glory, by my untruthfulness and violated pledges"; (if i.e. my ψεῦσμα = ἀδικία has tended only to the greater glory of God) "why, after this, am I even subject to condemnation as a sinner?" "O! stop there," pleads S. Paul in reply;

ROMANS. 55

Non-C. 1. τὸ περισσόν. 9. προεχόμεθα, middle. 26. 12. ἕως ἑνός.

CHAPTER IV.

HEBR. 3. 9. ἐλογ. εἰς δικ. 12. στοιχεῖν. 17. κατέναντι.
NON-C. 6. λέγει. 12. τοῖς ἴχνεσι: quasi-dat. of manner. 21. πληροφορ.

"and do not go on to say" (as the logical sequence of your last profane objection) "let us then, by all means" (ὅτι emphatic) "do evil..."

12. The very words of V. A. οὐκ ἐστὶν ἕως ἑνός אֶחָד גַּם אֵין, "not as much as one."

21. δικ. Θ.] "God's appointed method-of-justification."

22. πίστεως Ἰ. Χρ.] not "faith in Jesus Christ": but "the faith approved of and required by Jesus Christ": the corresponding term to δικ. Θ. in 21, Gal. 2. 16, 20, Phil. 1. 27, τῇ πίστει τοῦ εὐαγγ. 2 Th. 2. 13.

23. δόξης] = possibly, "good opinion," "approval": infra 5. 2, J. 5. 43, 12. 44.

26. τὸν ἐκ πίστ. Ἰ.] Compare A. 10. 45, 11. 2.

30. δικ. περιτ. ἐκ π.] Is it not possible that we may have here a blending of the two previous expressions, 1. 17, ὁ δικ. ἐκ π. ζήσ. and 26, δικαι. τὸν ἐκ π. Ἰ.? For the latter compare A. 10. 45, 11. 2, οἱ ἐκ περιτομῆς πιστοί, and infra 4. 12, 14, 16. The Jews, who believed on Jesus, were οἱ ἐκ πίστεως Ἰ., and were justified in consequence of *taking their stand on that side.* Is there not then, probably, a *constructio prægnans* in the words before us; and may not περιτομὴν ἐκ π. = τοὺς ἐκ πίστεως Ἰουδαίους, and ἐκ πίστεως be taken both with the *verb* and the *noun*, combining the promise of the old prophecy, and the later familiar form of expression? The very choice of ἐκ may perhaps be due to its occurrence in Habakkuk, V. A., where it stands simply for בְּ.

CHAP. IV. 11. σημ. περιτ.] Not a Greek construction, though correct in Hebrew and English: ἡ περιτομή was τὸ σημ. τῆς διαθήκης. Such expressions as "the sign of Circumcision," "the book of Genesis," suit *our* idiom: but are against Greek grammar. δι' ἀκρ.] "out of the midst of," "in spite of." Supra 2. 26.

16. τῷ ἐκ τοῦ...πίστεως Ἀ.] τῷ here is the dative, *not* of τὸ σπέρμα (as E. T. seems to imply), but of the abstract term τὸ ἐκ τοῦ νόμου = οἱ ἐκ τ. ν. "the law party." "The promise...sure to all the seed, not only to the "law-party, but to the faith-party": not only to those who-hold-on-to-the law of Moses, but to those who army themselves under the banner of faith.

Chapter V.

HEBR. 4. καταισχ. 5. πν. ἁγ. τοῦ δ. position of article: as also 15. 9. 11. 21. ἐν. 14. ἐπὶ τῷ ὁμ.

Chapter VI.

HEBR. 6. ὁ παλαιὸς...ἄνθρ.: and τὸ σῶμα τῆς ἁμ. 19. ἀσθέν. τῆς σαρκός.

---

17. κατέν.] "our father in the eyes of God": who seeth not as man: V. A. for לִפְנֵי. Supra 2. 18.

20. . Dative of instrument, twice in this verse: infra 5. 15.

Cπap. V. 4. οὐ καταισχ.] "never disappoints." Ps. 21. 5, 25. 3, 31. 1, 18, 34. 5, פְּנֵיהֶם אַל יֶחְפָּֽר, τὰ πρόσωπα αὐτῶν οὐ μὴ καταισχυνθῇ: Zech. 9. 5, הוֹבִישׁ מָבְטָח, "her expectation shall be disappointed." In Hebrew, "to blush," "to have the face ashamed," conveys this meaning. Jer. 14. 4, Is. 19. 9, בֹּשׁוּ עֹבְדֵי פִשְׁתִּים, αἰσχύνη λήψεται τοὺς ἐργαζ.

7. ὑπὲρ γάρ] כִּי elliptically taken, often means "but," and so is rendered in V. A. ἀλλά, Gen. 17. 15, 42. 12, et passim. Hence, from ἀλλά being thus frequently equivalent to γάρ, may not γάρ, possibly, have been looked on as an equivalent to ἀλλά: or rather, may not the literal γάρ have been used at times to express כִּי, instead of ἀλλά, which the sense requires; and may not this usage have become familiar to the *readers* of V. A., and so crept into N. T., as here?

11. This use of a participle *absolute*, as it were, without any grammatical connexion with what goes before or after, is not uncommon with S. Paul. Infra 12. 9, 13. 11.

12. ἐφ' ᾧ] = "because." Confer L. 1. 20, 19. 44, for similar use of ἀνθ' ὧν.

15. "For whereas, on the one hand, the penalty was in consequence of one offence resulting in condemnation; on the other hand, the free gift is after many offences, issuing in acquittal."

18. δικ. ζ.] Seems the correlative of κατάκρ. θάν. implied though not expressed in 17. For δικαίωμα in this sense, see Rev. 19. 8.

Chap. VI. 2. ἀπεθ. τῇ ἁμ.] Dat. of *person*: infra 10. 11; sin is *personified*, treated as a person, in both places, "dead for all claims of sin," "to all suggestions," "to all influences" of sin: 2 Cor. 5. 13, 1 Pet. 2. 24, ταῖς ἁμ. ἀπογενόμενοι, and so infra ἐθανατώθητε τῷ νόμῳ.

4. *Not* συνετάφ. εἰς τὸν θάνατον, but διὰ τοῦ β. εἰς τὸν θ., "the baptism-into-his-death" of 3. There are set before us here, verses 3, 4, 5, three things, which we share in common with Christ: (1) death,

NON-C. 5. ἀλλὰ καί. 10. ὃ ἀπέθανε. 11. ἑαυτούς. 23. ὀψώνια.

(2) burial, (3) resurrection : all typified and represented by baptism, as practised in primitive times : (1) the immersion *into*, (2) the momentary resting *beneath*, (3) the raising up *out of*, the water.

5. An argument, not for a natural consequence, but for a moral obligation on the ground of an admitted fact. "For if" (as every believer must allow) "we have been paired and matched" (as it were) "with Him," assimilated to Him, by baptism, which is "the representation," the perpetual shadowing forth and exhibition of His *death*, and is meant mystically to remind us thereof : and if, further, we have therein also sought to imitate his *descent into the grave*, claiming the spiritual and supernatural effects of both ; how much greater and stronger is the moral obligation, to reproduce in ourselves and imitate and exhibit in our lives the pattern supplied, the lesson taught, by His *resurrection* ? "seeing that we have been assimilated to Him in the likeness of His death, surely, much more shall we strive to be so in the imitation of His resurrection." Since we have claimed to set forth a copy of His death and burial, how much more are we bound to exhibit and exemplify His resurrection ?

6. τοῦτο γιγν.] Not so much *knowing*, as *considering :* "with this thought ever before us." τὸ σῶμα τῆς ἁμαρτίας] "our sin-bound," "sin-possessed," "sin-enslaved body." Infra 12, 14. "Our body, where sin reigns, is sin's." Wordsworth.

10. ὃ γὰρ ἀπέθανε...] "For, the death which He died, He died unto sin once for all : but the life which He liveth, He liveth unto God" : i.e. "by the death which He died," He showed "once for all" incontrovertibly, that "He was dead to sin," not drawn to it, nor swayed by it, nor alive to it, in any sense ; but *dead to it*, as a corpse is dead to any influence from without.

14. S. Paul appeals here again to moral obligation, to right feeling, to conscience, to generous impulses and the instinctive sense of duty based on gratitude for mercies received : to what those, who are not under stern, rigid law, but under a covenant of grace, must admit to be binding on them.

16. δοῦλοι.. ἁμ. εἰς θ.] "sin tending to, and ending in, death."

19. "I use a figure of speech common among men, on account of your natural incapacity for other treatment of the subject."

20. ἐλεύθεροι...τῇ δικ.] "Ye were *as free men* to righteousness": "rejecting the claims of," "repudiating the control of," "disdainful of all allegiance to" righteousness, treated here as a person.

Chapter VII.

HEBR. 3. ἐὰν γένηται ἀνδρὶ. 5. ἐν τῇ σαρκὶ: and τὰ παθ. τῶν ἁμ. 22. τὸν ἔσω ἄνθρ. 24. τοῦ σώμ. τοῦ θ.

Chapter VIII.

HEBR. 2. ὁ νόμ. τοῦ πν. 3. σαρκὸς ἁμ. 15. nom. for voc. 34. ἐν δεξιᾷ. 36. πρόβ. σφ.

---

22. εἰς ἁγιασμόν] "in continuous, progressive, advances toward sanctification"; as supra 19.

CHAP. VII. 3. ἐὰν γέν. ἀνδρὶ] So V. A. literally for Lev. 22. 12, בַּת כֹּהֵן כִּי תִהְיֶה לְאִישׁ. Ez. 23. 4, ἐγένοντό μοι: nubebant mihi. Jud. 14. 20, ἐγένετο ἡ γυνὴ Σαμψὼν ἐνὶ τῶν φίλων αὐτοῦ: Numb. 30. 7, ἐὰν γενομένη γένηται ἀνδρὶ, which shews γενομένη ἀνδρὶ = "nupta viro." τοῦ μὴ εἶναι...] A remarkable instance of τοῦ with inf. for לְ, M. 2. 6, "so as not to be..."

4. διὰ τοῦ σωμ. τοῦ Χρ.] "through *the death of* the body of Christ," our participation in the benefits of which, communicated to us at our admission into the Christian covenant, is illustrated and represented by the types and forms of Baptism": Col. 2. 12, συνταφέντες αὐτῷ ἐν τῷ βαπτίσματι ἐν ᾧ καὶ συνηγέρθητε, "dead and buried with Him in baptism" to sin and the law, "raised up with Him" to live for Him, as a wife for her husband, "to bring forth fruit for God."

5. ἐν τῇ σαρκὶ] In our natural state, before baptism. τὰ παθ. τῶν ἁμ.] Hebraism: "our sinful affections, cherished in despite of the law," τὰ διὰ τοῦ νόμου, "breaking through the barriers of the law."

6. κατηργήθ. ἀπὸ] The metaphor of verses 2 and 4 continued. The illustrations, borrowed from baptism and marriage, are inextricably mixed up together.

13. ἡ ἁμ. διὰ τῆς ἐντ.] "sin committed by people under the influence of," "in defiance of," "the commandment," "by breaking through the barriers of it," "out of the midst of it": supra 2. 27. This rendering of διὰ, justified, I hope, by the passages cited there, seems to lessen the difficulties connected with its use here, and supra 8, 11, and elsewhere.

24. τοῦ σώμ. τοῦ θ. τούτου] "*this* death-enslaved body." 6. 6.

CHAP. VIII. 2. ὁ νόμος-τοῦ-πν. τῆς ζωῆς-ἐν-Χρ.] The spiritual law of life-in-and-by-Christ Jesus.

9. S. Paul presupposes, assumes as an undoubted fact, that those to whom he was writing, were members of Christ, Christ's people, Χριστοῦ: and so necessarily, πνεῦμα Χρ. ἔχοντες: regenerate, having the Spirit dwelling in them: no longer ἐν σαρκὶ but ἐν πνεύματι. There is

ROMANS. 59

Non-C. 11. διά with acc. 18. τὴν μέλλ. δ. ἀποκ. A. 28. 17.
19. κτίσις for κτίσμα. 21.
Sept. 20. ματαιότης.

Chapter IX.

Hebr. 8. λογίζ. εἰς. 22. σκ. ὀργ. 33. λίθον προσκ. καὶ π. σκ. and πᾶς...οὐ.
Non-C. 6. οἷον ὅτι. 11. μήπω and τί ἀγ.
Sept. 3. ἀνάθεμα = הֵרֶם, res deo devota, sine spe redemtionis, Jos. 6. 17, 18. 1; Deut. 7. 26, res exitio destinata. Grimm and Schl.

---

no doubt implied by εἴπερ: it expresses an admitted fact: "*You are not in the flesh,*" left to yourselves in your inherited weakness of the old man, in your human nature unaided from above, "*but you are in the Spirit,*" taken up into,—adopted by,—interpenetrated by all the influences of,—within the sphere and realm of,—the Spirit; "if the Spirit of God dwelleth in you" (which cannot be questioned). "For if any man have not the Spirit of Christ, he is none of His"; not a Christian at all.

10. νεκρὸν δι' ἁμ....] "dead *for the work* of sin,...alive *for the work* of righteousness": "as (μὲν) the body is mortified..., so (δὲ) the soul is quickened..."

20. ματαιότης] V. A. for הֶבֶל, Job 7. 16. κενὸς and μάταιος are used, in translating this word, indifferently, as though equivalent, Jer. 10. 3, Threni 4. 17: see also James 2. 20, ὦ ἄνθρωπε κενέ. εἰς κενὸν = μάτην passim in V. A. and N. T. In this place ματ. = "corruption, dissolution, temporary annihilation": "the being emptied out." διὰ τὸν ὑποτ. = "for the purposes of..."

23. υἱοθεσίαν] The ἀπολύτρ. τοῦ σώμ., the full and complete redemption of the body,—by its deliverance from the δουλεία τῆς φθορᾶς, the enslavement and bonds of death and corruption, at the Resurrection,—will be the completion of our υἱοθεσία, our Adoption as God's children: our Lord calls it "our Regeneration." M. 19. 28.

Chap. IX. 1. ἐν Χρ.] Is this an Hebraic form of adjuration, the literal rendering of "בְּ יְבַעְיֶּ?, Gal. 1. 20? ἐν πν. ἁγ., "by the motion of the Holy Spirit."

10. κ. ἔ.] שָׁכְבָה, in V. A. κοίτη, literally, as if its only sense were "bed": whereas it means "effusio seminis." Lev. 15. 16, ἄνθρωπος ᾧ ἂν ἐξέλθῃ ἐξ αὐτοῦ κοίτη σπέρματος.

22. σκεύη ὀργῆς] "vasa in quæ ira effundatur": σκεύη ἐλέους "vasa apta in quæ conferatur benignitas," Grimm:—very remarkable Hebraisms.

CHAPTER X.

HEBR. 5. 9. 11.   SEPT. 1. εὐδοκία. 17. ἀκοή.

---

28. Exact from V. A. Compare with Hebrew, Is. 10. 22, 23: curious translation both of כָּלָה and כִּלָּיוֹן. "God bringeth his dispensations to an end, cutting them short in righteousness." Gesen. renders "interitus decretus est: affert inundando justitiam."

CHAP. X. 8. τὸ ῥῆμα] "The essential thing," "materies," "the sum and substance": = דָּבָר in its constant usage. Or "the message"; "it comes home to thee," "fits close to thee" in mouth and in heart; i.e. "the message of the faith..."

11, 13. These two Quotations are S. Paul's proofs from Scripture of his positions in 9 and 10: that in (11) asserting the reward of πίστις; that in (13) of στόματος ὁμολογία. Each γάρ is independent and distinct: the second not a *confirmation* of the first, but antithetical to it: as is so frequent in his use of γάρ: which we find repeated three or four times in succession, introducing each a fresh and separate reason. Cap. 8. 13, 14, 15: 13. 9, 12.

12. Ἰ. τε καὶ Ἕ.] Acts 6. 1, note.

16. ἀκοή] Quotation from V. A. John 12. 38, note, Heb. 4. 2. The sense that seems to lie in our translation of 17, "and hearing by the word of God," vanishes, if examined carefully. May we explain it thus? Isaiah says, in amazement, "*Who* hath believed our message-heard-by-him?" (as though all ought to have believed.) "Clearly then" (S. Paul argues from this astonishment of Isaiah) ἄρα "faith ought to have followed heedful-hearing-of-the-message, and that ought to have been given because of the word of God conveyed by it": was due to the message as being the word of God.

19. "Did not Israel know" that the Gentiles would hear the message and be admitted into God's family? Yes: for Moses and Isaiah had told them so. ἐπ᾽ οὐκ ἔθνει, V. A. for בְּלֹא עָם, "by them-that-are-no-people" of God. Could they have understood this, as if meaning "against"? or were they accustomed to render בְּ by ἐπί frequently, and did so here, blindly? Can ἐπί, by any possible contortion, mean "*by*," instrumentally?

21. πρὸς τ. Ἰ.] "with respect to," Hebr. 1. 7. For אֶל in this sense see Gen. 20. 2. "Abraham said *of* Sarah" E. V.; where V. A. have περί. 2 Kings 19. 32, πρός. This use of a wrong preposition is a strong instance of what has been said above, J. 1. 1, note.

ROMANS. 61

Chapter XI.

Hebr. 2. ἐν Ἡλίᾳ, by. 9. γεν. εἰς. 34. καὶ = in order that.

Chapter XII.

Non-C. 1. διὰ with gen. 5. ὁ δὲ καθ' εἷς. 16. φρον. παρ' ἑαυτ. 18. τὸ ἐξ ὑμῶν. 20. ψώμιζε.
Sept. 3. εἰς τὸ σωφρ.

Chapter XIII.

Hebr. 1. 3. 9. οὐ μ. M. 9. 18, note. 13. περιπ. Mc. 7. 5.
Non-C. 1. ἐξουσία. 3. φόβος τῶν ἀ. ἔ. 8. τὸν ἕτερον.

Chap. XI. 2. κατὰ for עַל, "with respect to," 1 Cor. 15. 15. עַל often has this meaning: Gen. 18. 19, Joel 1. 3, Is. 37. 9. And it is often rendered in V. A. by κατὰ: although not in the passages quoted. We may allowably infer that this meaning may have been attached to it, by the authors and readers of V. A. as an equivalent for עַל.

8. Not exactly as either in Hebrew or V. A.

12. ἥττημα] "fall and forfeiture," πλήρωμα, "final and full restoration."

25. ἀπὸ μέρους] Occurs only 5 times in N. T., and about as often in V. A.: where it stands twice for לְמִקְצָת, literally rendered: Dan. 1. 2, Neh. 7. 70. S. Paul alone uses it, R. 11. 25, 15. 15, 24, 2 Cor. 1. 14, 2. 5. It would seem to be never found in Classical Authors.

30. ἀπειθείᾳ] *not* "unbelief" but "disobedience": Grimm :—see note, Eph. 5. 6.

Chap. XII. 1. λογ. λ.] 1 Pet. 2. 1, "spiritual," perhaps, as opposed to λατρεία δι' ἀλογῶν, by sacrifices of animals without reason.

3. εἰς τὸ σ.] "soberly," E. V. and this is correct. But *how* do we get this from the Greek? It is apparently a phrase insensibly adopted from V. A., as a convenient adverbial formula, (see Mc. 5. 34) by those acquainted with that Version; and so seems to have got into N. T. as in εἰς κενὸν, 2 Cor. 6. 1, Gal. 2. 2, and here: where τὸ σωφρ. stands for a noun. Phil. 2. 13, 16.

19. δότε τόπον] = dare spatium: "make way for it," "let it pass by."

Chap. XIII. 1. πᾶσα ψυχή] = "every one, every body." Supra 2. 9.

10. πλήρωμα νόμου] "the whole-law-in-full."

Chapter XIV.

HEBR. 11. ζῶ ἐγώ. 14. 21. ἐν. 14. κοινόν.

NON-C. 1. τῇ π. dat. of *part.* 2. πιστεύει φ. 5. κρίνει. 6. φρονῶν.

Chapter XV.

HEBR. 5. 13. ὁ Θ. τῆς ὑπομονῆς... 6. 13. 19. ἐν. 11. nom. for voc.

NON-C. 1. ἀδύνατος in sense of *weak.* 8. τὰς ἐπαγγ. τῶν π. 15. ἀπὸ μ. 21. συνήσ. 26. κοινωνίαν.

CHAP. XIV. 4. τῷ ἰδ. κ.] Like ζῇ τῷ Θ., 6. 10 : and infra 6, 7, 8. All are instances of what used to be called "dative of the person."

11. ζῶ ἐγώ] Is. 45. 23. Hebr. 'חַי־אָנִי נְאֻם, V. A. κατ' ἐμαυτοῦ ὀμνύω: to which ζῶ ἐγώ is clearly equivalent in the mind of S. Paul : חַי אָנִי אִם לֹא ", Is. 49. 18, V. A. ζῶ ἐγώ...ὅτι. ἐξομόλ.] "shall give praise," "adore." M. 11. 25, note : and infra 15. 9.

14. εἰ μή] = ἀλλά, as so often in N. T.: note M. 12. 4 ; 24. 36, Mc. 13. 32 : and this corresponds exactly to the well-known use of כִּי אִם, which V. A. generally render by ἀλλά: Gen. 32. 29, 1 Sam. 8. 19, Ps. 1. 4, or by ὅτι ἀλλ' ἤ, 2 K. 23. 23, but occasionally also by εἰ μή, Gen. 32. 27, Lev. 22. 6.

19. τῆς οἰκοδομῆς τῆς εἰς ἀλλ.] A N. T. illustration and phrase altogether : not found in Hebrew. τῆς εἰς ἀ. οἰκ. *means* clearly "mutual edification": but *how* it comes to mean it, I cannot see.

20. διὰ πρ.] Note 2. 27 : 4. 11 ; "in spite of," "in disregard of," offence to his conscience : "breaking it down."

CHAP. XV. 2. ἀγ. πρ. οἰκ.] "with a view to that which is good-for-edification."

4. παρακλ.] = "Instruction, teaching, enlightenment": Note Acts 4. 36, 13. 15, 15. 31, "that we may hold our hope *in-combination-with, under the pervading influence of,* patience, and the teaching of the Holy Scriptures"; "maintain our own hope in combination with toleration and forbearance to others, and the direction and true interpretation of H. Scr.":—which is the best security under the blessing of ὁ Θ. τῆς ὑπ.... (5) for the τὸ αὐτὸ φρ. and ἐν ἑνὶ στ. δοξάζειν (6) : and gives the true force to the injunction of (7) προσλαμβάν. "accept," "welcome," others, notwithstanding minor differences and imperfections. I submit this interpretation as consistent with the whole context, confirming and summing up all the arguments of Cap. 14. "Patience and comfort of the Scriptures" are out of tune with the whole previous passage : which

Chapter XVI.

HEBR. 9. 10. 11. 12. 22. ἐν K. 20. ὁ Θ. τῆς εἰρ.
NON-C. 18. εὐλογία and ἀκάκων.

---

enjoins emphatically forbearance and submission to divine instruction, in our dealings with the tender consciences and scruples of weaker brethren. Possibly there may be no connexion between τὸ αὐτὸ φρονεῖν (5) and ἐν ἑνὶ στόματι δ. (6): and τὸ αὐτὸ may refer to ὁ Θεὸς and not to ἐν ἀλλήλοις. "May the God of forbearance and instruction grant to you to be *like-minded with Himself* in your conduct towards one another after the example of Jesus Christ"; "make you, in accordance with His revealed will and character, tolerant of the infirmities of others, as Jesus was, and ready and willing to teach them the truth in meekness; so that by His blessing, all may be won to *agree* in the faith, and so *with one mind* and *one mouth* glorify God."

9. τὰ δὲ ἔθνη] For εἰς δὲ τὸ τὰ ἔθνη... τῷ ὀν. σ. ψ.] V. A. for לִשְׁמֶךָ. The translators were aware of לְ giving signification of *dative of person* sometimes: and so rendered it here, by dative alone; *against Greek idiom altogether*. Hebr. 13. 15.

12. Exact quotation from V. A. ἡ ῥίζα שֹׁרֶשׁ (*surculus* not *radix*: "offshoot"): no article with either nominative in Hebrew: as required by the sense.

22. ἐνεκοπτ. τοῦ ἐ.] For לְ with inf. M. 2. 6.

30. διά] with gen. in this sense peculiar. 12. 1, 1 Cor. 1. 10.

CHAP. XVI. 2. ἐν κυρίῳ] Possibly here "because of," "for the Lord's sake," ἐν for בְּ "propter." 2 Kings 14. 6, אִישׁ בְּחֶטְאוֹ יָמוּת, V. A. ἕκαστος ἐν ταῖς ἁμ. αὐ. ἀποθ. Gen. 18. 28, reducible to class (C) in note M. 3. 11.

23. Acts 20. 4, Γάϊος was a Corinthian. 1 Cor. 1. 14.

25. Observe κατὰ first *with* and then *without* article: required by the sense in each case: omitted in the latter by common Hebraic usage, exhibited so frequently and so remarkably in this Epistle, notably in these last 3 verses, and not to be accounted for in any other way.

1 CORINTHIANS.

Chapter I.

HEBR. 1. 2. 3. 4. 5. 9. ἐν: and art. omitted. 4. ἐπὶ = עַל, infra 8. 11. 29. 30.

NON-C. 8. ἕως τέλους. 16. λοιπόν. ·25. ἰσχυρότερον.

Chapter II.

HEBR. 3. ἐγ. πρὸς, M. 13. 56. 4. 5. 8. 7. 16. omission of art. 14. ψυχικός.

NON-C. 2. τι. 12. εἰδῶμεν. 13. διδακτοῖς πνεύματος. 16. construction: τίς ἔγνω...ἵς.

Chapter III.

HEBR. 3. κατ' ἄνθρ. περιπατ.

NON-C. 2. γάλα ὑ. ἐπότ. 3. ὅπου. 8. ἕν. 17. οἵτινές ἐστε ὑ.

CHAP. I. 21. "When in the midst of the revelations of God's wisdom, the world recognised not God in that wisdom" (looked not through it to God): "it pleased God, by this despised and seemingly foolish announcement..."; "by the promulgation of a doctrine which they esteemed foolishness..."

30. ἐξ αὐτοῦ] This use of ἐξ is probably Hebraic, for מִן = ὑπὸ, R. 1. 4, 2 Cor. 2. 2, 7. 9, Rev. 2. 11. "Through Him you are in Christ." So also ἀπὸ Θ. = ὑπὸ Θ., recalls another V. A. rendering of מִן. Jude 23, note.

CHAP. II. 1. καθ' ὑπεροχὴν] "by way of any excellence." μαρτύριον] Hebr. idiom, applied to the *Law*, first, Ex. 25. 16: and afterwards to the *Gospel*.

5. πίστις ἐν] Note Mc. 1. 15.

CHAP. III. 8. ἕν εἰσιν] "He that planteth and...watereth are one and the same thing": "whether a man planteth or watereth, it is all the same."

1 CORINTHIANS.

CHAPTER IV.

HEBR. 3. εἰς ἐλάχ. 9. Irregularity of article. 15. ἐν Χρ.... ἐγέννησα. 21.

NON-C. 2. ὃ δὲ λ. 6. Latter clause: construction. 9. θέατρον. 11. ἄρτι.

CHAPTER VI.

NON-C. 6. ἀ. μετὰ ἀ. κρίνεται. 11. ταῦτά τινες ἦτε.

---

9. Θ. συνεργοί] "We are *God's* labourers all": ye are *God's* field, *God's* blessing.

12. ξ. χ. κ.] "wood, thatch, reeds."

13. ἐν π. ἀποκ.] "There-is-to-be-a manifestation by fire."

CHAP. IV. 3. εἰς ἐλάχ.] An evident Hebraism: though I find no instance exactly like it in V. A.

4. οὐδὲν ἐμ. σύν.] "I am conscious of no offence": "I know nothing against myself": old use of "by" in E. V., see Cranmer's letter to Henry VIII., Burnet's Hist. of the Reformation, Book 3, near the beginning: "I am exceeding sorry that such things can be proved *by* the Queen":—i.e. "against."

15. ἐν Χριστῷ...ἐγέννησα] "You are my children in Christ..." Or, possibly, ἐν Χρ. = εἰς Χρ., since ב֗ means both *in* and *into;* and in the latter sense is rendered by ἐν occasionally. M. 28. 19. "I have begotten you into Christ," "brought you, as a father, into the family of Christ."

21. ἐν ῥάβδῳ] M. 3. 11, note, Apoc. 2. 27, L. 22. 49. It is one of the most startling instances of the *literal* translation of ב֗ by ἐν: not *Greek*, in any sense, or by any stretch of critical ingenuity, but *Hebraic*: which cannot be too strongly stated, or too often repeated, in this and similar instances of violation of grammar and idiom. It is borrowed, no doubt, from similar uses of ἐν in V. A., e.g. 1 Chr. 12. 11, 14, ἐπαίδευσεν ὑμᾶς ἐν μάστιξι, Ps. 89. 33.

CHAP. V. 5. εἰς ὄλ. τῆς σ.] A violation of the rules of grammar, common in S. Paul: assignable in all probability to a Hebrew source. 2 Cor. 5. 5.

CHAP. VI. 1. κρίνεσθαι ἐπὶ τῶν...] M. 28. 14, Mc. 8. 4, *notes*, and 2 Cor. 13. 1, Acts 25. 9.

5. ἀνὰ μέσον] for בין, V. A. passim. Ex. 22. 26, ἀνὰ μέσον ἁγίου καὶ βεβήλου. Jud. 15. 4, ἀνὰ μ. τῶν δύο κέρκων. The peculiarity here lies in its use with only *one*, τοῦ ἀ. Compare 1 K. 5. 12, ἦν εἰρήνη ἀνὰ μ. Χιρὰμ καὶ ἀνὰ μ. Σαλωμών.

GU. 5

Chapter VII.

Non-C. 31. παράγει. 32. πῶς for ὅπως. 34. μεμέρισται.
Sept. 5. ἐπὶ τὸ αὐτό. 17. εἰ μή, R. 14. 14, note. 37. τοῦ τηρεῖν.

Chapter VIII.

Non-C. 4. ἕτερος εἰ μή. 6. εἰς αὐτόν. 8. περισσεύομεν. 12. τύπτοντες.

Chapter IX.

Non-C. 1. The construction, for interrogation, unusual. 12. στέγομεν. 15. μᾶλλον ἤ...ἵνα.

Chapter X.

Hebr. 5. ἐν τοῖς πλ. 16. τὸ ποτ. τῆς εὐλ. 32. ἀπρόσκοποι.

Non-C. 2. ἐβαπτίσαντο, middle. 7. ἐκάθισε...φαγεῖν. Infinitive after intransitive verb: *universal* almost, in V. A. and N. T. 10. ὀλοθρευτοῦ. 33. μή for οὐ.

Sept. 20. δαιμονίοις, M. 9. 33, note.

---

13. Strong instances of S. Paul's use of the dative (*of the person*, as it used to be called, *inexactly* but *comprehensively*), see Rom. 6. 2, 20, infra 9. 21.

Chap. VII. 15. ἐν εἰρήνῃ] See Gal. 1. 6, 1 Th. 4. 7. In all three the sense of "into" suits best: which בְּ constantly conveys. It is a Hebrew idiom literally rendered by a wrong preposition.

Chap. VIII. 11. ἐπὶ] = עַל "on account of," "leaning upon," "relying upon." Cap. 9. 10.

Chap. X. 3. πνευματικόν] "supernatural." 15. 44, Gal. 4. 29. The manna was not in any sense *spiritual* food, nor the water out of the rock that followed them, *spiritual* drink: but both miraculous and *supernatural*. Πνεῦμα constantly means "the supernatural" as contrasted with σάρξ "the natural."

11. τὰ τέλη τῶν αἰ.] "Upon whom the extremities of the two dispensations, the ante-Christian and Christian æras of the world, have come," in whom have met together the end of the one and the beginning of the other. Heb. 9. 26.

18. The Jews were Ἰσραὴλ κατὰ σάρκα: the Christians Ἰσρ. κατ' ἐπαγγελίαν. S. Paul appeals both to the Jewish and Christian in-

1 CORINTHIANS.

Chapter XI.

Non-C. 4. κατὰ κεφ. ἔχ. 18. μέρος τι. 30. ἱκανοί. 34. ὡς ἂν ἔλθω.

Chapter XII.

Non-C. 2. ὡς ἂν ἤγεσθε. 13. ἐποτίσθημεν. 22. Order of words. 27. ἐκ μέρους. 29. μὴ interrogative.

Chapter XIII.

Non-C. 2. εἰδῶ. 3. ψωμίσω. 8. εἴτε. 12. ἄρτι. 13. μείζων.

---

stinctive belief of what was implied by participation in sacrifices offered to God.

32. See R. 3. 9, John 7. 35.

Chap. XI. 7. δόξα] V. A. for תְּמוּנָה "likeness": Ps. 17. 15, N. 12. 8. Never so found in good Greek.

20. οὐκ ἔστι...φαγεῖν] "There is no eating the *Lord's* supper": Κυρ. contrasted with ἴδιον : they met together to eat *not* the feast of the Lord, in the way instituted by Him, but their own meal.

22. καταισχύνετε] This verb is used by V. A. as = "humilio," "tanquam pudendum rejicio," "coutumeliosè afficio": Ps. 13. 7, Ruth 2. 15. So here "you treat the poor with disrespect," "humiliate them."

27. In V. A. ἔνοχός ἐστι = דָּם לוֹ, "he is guilty," Lev. 20. 9. No instances in V. A. of genitive of *crime* are given in Trommius; only one in Apocrypha. 2 Macc. 13. 6, ἱεροσυλίας ἔνοχος. There seems to have been a generalisation from a particular, from murder to any other crime; "cædis reus" generalised gradually into "reus": "there is blood on his hands," דָּם לוֹ, coming at last to signify "there is guilt on him," ἔνοχός ἐστι. וְהָיָה עָלֶיךָ דָּם, "and so there be blood upon thee," came to mean "...guilt in the midst of thee": V. A. καὶ ἔσται ἐν σοὶ αἵματι ἔνοχος, "some one guilty by reason of bloodshed," originally. M. 5. 22, note, James 2. 10.

Chap. XII. 7. ἡ φανέρωσις] "the illuminating insight," "the power of elucidating divine mysteries and making them clear to others."

10. γένη γλ.] V. A. 2 Chr. 16. 14, γένη μύρων.

Chap. XIII. 6. ἀδικία] Contrasted with ἀληθεία : a very strong instance of ἄδικος = ψευδής, M. 11. 19, note, Luke 16. 9, infra 15. 34.

12. ἐν αἰνίγματι...] Numb. 12. 8, στόμα κατὰ στόμα λαλήσω αὐτῷ ἐν εἴδει καὶ οὐ δι' αἰνιγμάτων. V. A. of which passage Grimm says "observabatur apostolo," and Alford "there is a reference to it."

CHAPTER XIV.

Non-C. 2. λαλῶν γλώσσῃ. 5. ἐκτὸς εἰ μὴ: and subjunctive after εἰ. 7. ὅμως. 10. εἰ τύχοι Past with ἐστι Present.

CHAPTER XV.

Hebr. 15. κατὰ = לְפִי, R. 11. 2, note. 45. ἐγένετο εἰς. 52. ἐν τῇ ἐσχ. σάλπ. 54. κατεπ....εἰς νῖκος.
Non-C. 6. ἐπάνω. 28. ἵνα ᾖ...πᾶσιν. 30. πᾶσαν ὥραν. 31. τὴν ὑμετ. καύχ. my joy in you. 37. τῶν λοιπῶν. 47. χοϊκός. 49. ἐφορέσαμεν. 51. πάντες μὲν οὐ.

CHAPTER XVI.

Hebr. 6. πρὸς ὑ. παραμενῶ, 2 Th. 3. 10. 11. ἐν εἰρήνῃ.
Non-C. 1. λογία. 2. ὅ τι ἂν εὐοδ. 4. ἄξιον τοῦ κἀμὲ π. 12. καὶ πάντως οὐκ ἦν θ. 18. ἀνέπαυσαν.

Chap. XIV. 7. φθόγγοις] = "notes."
16. εὐλογία] = εὐχαριστία. Note M. 26. 26.
37. πνευματικός] = inspired by H. Spirit. 12. 1.

Chap. XV. 8. "To me, the abortion, so to speak."
14. κήρυγμα] not "our preaching": but the subject of it: "the Gospel preached by us."
15. κατὰ τ. Θ.] "with respect to," see Romans 11. 2.
34. δικαίως] For בֶּאֱמֶת, "truly," "in earnest": note M. 11. 19. This rendering of the adverb, justified by the usage of V. A. and N. T., seems in this passage to express the sense better, and is more grammatically correct than those generally suggested.
54. There seems to be a distinction here between φθαρτὸν and θνητὸν: the former comprehending all that were dead before the judgment day and turned already to corruption (vv. 50, 52), the latter those liable to death, but not yet dead.
58. ἐν Κυρίῳ] Confer Col. 3. 18, Ph. 1. 13, notes.

Chap. XVI. 2. μίαν σαββ.] M. 28. 1, Mc. 16. 2, L. 24. 1, μία for πρώτη: Hebraism: Gen. 1. 5, 2. 11, ἡμέρα μία, the first day: τῷ ἑνὶ, the first river: V. A. literal rendering for אֶחָד.
22. μαρὰν ἀθά] Syriac: "the great Lord is coming." ὁ Κύριος ἐγγύς, Phil. 4. 6.

2 CORINTHIANS.

Chapter I.

HEBR. 2. Θεοῦ...Κυρίου, omission of article, Tit. 1. 3. 3. ὁ π. τῶν οἰ. 6. ἐν ὑ. 9. πεπ. ἐφ᾽ ἑαυτ. M. 27. 43, infra 2. 3. 11. ἐκ π. πρ. 12. ἐν ἁπλ.... 18. πιστὸς ὁ Θ.

NON-C. 4. ἧς. 8. ἐβαρήθ. ἐξαπορ. 9. ὦμεν with perf. part. 13. ἀλλ᾽ ἢ ἅ. 14. ἀπὸ μ. 15. δευτέραν. 20. ὅσαι ἐπ.

CHAP. I. 3. ὁ π. τῶν οἰ.] Hebr. use of genitive for adjective. For παρακλ. see J. 14. 16, note.

5. εἰς ἡμᾶς] Vulg. "in nobis." The frequent use of εἰς in V. A. for אֶל apud, or בְּ in and into, may allowably be suggested in explanation of its occurrence in N. T. in such passages as this, where the sense of *apud* or *in*, is required. J. 1. 18.

9. πεποιθ....ἐφ᾽ ἑαυτοῖς] Mc. 1. 15, note. Infra 2. 3, ἐπὶ has acc. εἰς ὃν ἠλπίκ., next verse, is an example of almost parallel usage; see 1 Tim. 5. 5, for our E. V. rendering "trust."

15. ταύτῃ τῇ π.] dative of cause: "because of this persuasion." Infra 24, 2. 12.

18. πιστὸς ὁ Θ. ὅτι] A form of adjuration, purely Hebraic, and corresponding to כִּי יְהוָה חַי, 2 Sam. 2. 27, V. A. ζῇ Κύριος ὅτι, "as surely as God liveth"; "as God is true, *verily* our word...". Is it not possible that here, and in other similar passages, ὅτι answering to כִּי, may have the force of *asseveration* which כִּי has, "*surely, verily*"? See note, M. 7. 23.

20. "How many soever be the promises of God," He will assuredly fulfil them in and through Christ": lit. "in Him is the ναί, and in Him the ἀμήν": the recognition and the fulfilment.

21. ὁ βεβ. ἡμ....εἰς Χρ.] It is hard to translate εἰς adequately here: "for" seems perhaps best.

23. "It was from the wish to spare you, that I never came again."

CHAPTER II.

HEBR. 2. καὶ τίς ἐ. and ἐξ ἐμοῦ, 1 Cor. 1. 30. 3. πεπ. ἐπὶ π. ὑμᾶς. 4. διὰ π. δ. 10. ἐν πρ. Χρ. 12. 14. 17. ἐν Κ. and ἐν Χρ. 14. τὴν ὀσμὴν.

NON-C. 1. ἔκρινα ἐμαυτῷ. 5. ἀπὸ μ. 7. καταποθῇ. 11. πλεονεκτ.

CHAPTER III.

HEBR. 5. ἀφ᾽ ἑαυτῶν. 7. ἡ διακονία τοῦ θ.

CHAP. II. 2. ἐξ ἐμοῦ] ἐξ = ὑπὸ, for מִן, which has both meanings, but is generally rendered by ἐκ or ἀπὸ in V. A., rather than by ὑπὸ. Infra 3. 18, 7. 9, 13. 4, note : 1 Cor. 1. 30.

4. διὰ π. δ.] "out of the midst of": R. 2. 27, note : 2 Tim. 2. 2.

10. ἐν προσώπῳ Χ.] (a), 4. 6 (b), 5. 12 (c), the only instances, apparently, in N. T. of ἐν πρ. And I can only find one (Pr. 8. 30) in V. A. (for לִפְנֵי) amid the innumerable examples of πρὸ, ἀπὸ, κατὰ with πρόσωπον. And in each of the three instances, the meaning is distinctly different (Grimm *sub voce*): (a) *in conspectu Christi*: i.e. approbante Christo. (b) *in facie*, i.e. *in personâ Christi*. (c) *in externâ specie*: compare 1 Sam. 16. 7, ἄνθρωπος ὄψεται εἰς πρόσωπον, ὁ δὲ Θεὸς εἰς καρδίαν.

12. ἐν Κ.] May not the force of ἐν *here*, and in verses 14 and 17, be simply "*by*," "by the help of," derived, of course, from the common use of בְּ ? This meaning seems the most natural and the best, for ἐν Κυρίῳ, in many passages of G. T.: e.g. 1 Cor. 7. 22, 15. 31, 58, Gal. 5. 10, Eph. 6. 10, Ph. 4. 2, τῷ μὴ εὑρεῖν. Supra 1. 15.

17. καπηλ.] "adulterate, dilute, water down."

CHAP. III. In this chapter we have a very remarkable instance of a well-known peculiarity of S. Paul's writings: that is to say, his tendency to be carried away abruptly from the subject he is discussing to another, very slightly, if at all connected with it, by a fresh train of ideas arising out of expressions employed by him in relation to the matter immediately before him. The mention of the ἐπιστολὴ ἐγγεγραμμένη οὐ μέλανι ἀλλὰ πνεύματι Θ. ζῶντος, οὐκ ἐν πλαξὶ λιθίναις ἀλλ᾽ ἐν πλ. καρδίας, seems to have reminded him irresistibly of the parallel distinction between the characteristics of the Law and the Gospel; and he avails himself at once of the opportunity of illustrating the latter contrast by the images suggested by his description of the former. And consequently, the force and meaning of the words and ideas borrowed and transferred, must be modified by the consideration that they are used by way of *illustration*, and *not of dogmatic definition*.

Non-C. 1. συνιστ. and συστατικῶν. 3. διακονηθ. 14. μὴ for οὐ. 18. ἀπὸ δ. εἰς δ.

We must be cautious also not to be misled by our familiarity with the English Version, or by the distinction between *the letter* and *the spirit* of a command, or document, in *our* ordinary phraseology. As S. Paul sums up and concludes his argument by ὁ δὲ Κύριος τὸ πνεῦμά ἐστι (17), it is hard to imagine that the word πνεῦμα, in any part of that argument, means anything but τὸ πνεῦμα Κυρίου (17). The παλαία διαθήκη ἐντετυπωμένη ἐν λίθοις, ἐν πλαξὶ λιθίναις, introductory, transitory, given only for a time,—καταργουμένη, not μένουσα,—was essentially, in Hebraic phrase, γράμματος (6): and Moses the original διάκονος of it, its administrator and expounder, as he was the channel of its communication to Israel. The καινὴ διαθήκη, ἐντετυπωμένη ἐν πλαξὶ καρδίας σαρκίναις,—final, abiding, given once for all, μένουσα,—was, essentially, πνεύματος, the gift and work and dispensation of the Holy Spirit; and Jesus Christ the original διάκονος of it (R. 15. 8), its promulgator and expounder to Jews and Gentiles alike: hence, in this passage, διακονία seems almost to be used as equivalent to διαθήκη. For clearly, in 7 and 8, the contrast lies, not between θανάτου and πνεύματος, but between ἐν γράμμασιν and τοῦ πνεύματος (as in 6): and so ἡ διακ. τοῦ πν. is set against ἡ διακ. ἐν γρ. ἐντετ. ἐν λίθοις, i.e. ἡ παλαιὰ διαθήκη. The *condemnation* and the *death* (9 and 7), as the *justification* (δικαιοσύνη) and the *life through the Spirit*, were the issues, not of the διακονία in its strict sense, but of the διαθήκη. The words τὸ δεδοξασμένον (10) and τὸ καταργούμενον and τὸ μένον (11) seem to refer quite as naturally to the *covenant*, as to the promulgation and administration of it. And if we attach any weight to the tenses employed, ἐγενήθη (7) more accurately describes a single action,—the original enactment of the covenant,—than its continuous and frequently repeated promulgation. Its *first publication* ἐγενήθη ἐν δόξῃ, the traces of which were left on the face of Moses so overpoweringly, ὥστε μὴ δύνασθαι ἀτενίσαι.... It is important also to remember that, in V. A., ἐλπίζω is constantly used for נִבְטַח, confido (1 Tim. 5. 5, note), and ἐλπίς for πεποίθησις, as here in (12) which is but a resumption and restatement of (4). It was not merely *hope*, but *conviction*, that the *hearts* of those to whom he was writing, were soft and open to the influences of God's Holy Spirit, that encouraged S. Paul "to use great plainness of speech," and "to declare to them the whole counsel of God," with no veil drawn between him and them.

13. πρὸς τὸ μὴ ἀτενίσαι] Ought we to translate this,—with E. V.

Chapter IV.

Hebr. 3. ἐν τοῖς ἁ. 16. ὁ ἔξω ἄνθρ.

Non-C. 2. μὴ. πρὸς π. συνείδ. ἀνθρ. 6. εἰπὼν...λάμψαι. 8. ἐν παντὶ. 16. ἡμέρᾳ κ. ἡ. 17. καθ' ὑπερβ. εἰς ὑ.

---

and most commentators,—"that they *could* not," or "that they *should* not," as if describing *the result* or *the object* of Moses putting on the veil? May we not rather take it as referring to the *fact* mentioned in 7, and supply from thence δύνασθαι, and render "out of regard to the fact that they could not?" Surely Moses put on the veil *because* the people were afraid (Ex. 34. 30) to look stedfastly on him, and not *in order that they might not*. And so, doubtless, ἀλλ' ἐπωρώθη ought to be connected with ἀτενίσαι; and in strict grammar we should expect πωρωθῆναι, governed also by πρὸς, "out of regard to the fact that they could not look stedfastly,...but that the thoughts of their hearts were blinded"; "had a film over them." πῶρος = callositas = the film or curtain that drops over the eye from disease, and *blinds* by *hardening* it,—is an apt and forcible emblem of the wilful *hardness of heart* which *blinded* the Jews to the true meaning of the prophecies: the κάλυμμα which they interposed between themselves and the truth, typified by the veil which hid the face of Moses: and which remained even to the time when the Apostle wrote, μὴ ἀνακ., "unless it were rolled back and taken away," as in the case of every one who turned to the Lord (ἡνίκα ἂν ἐπιστρ.); for *then* it was done away with and abolished in and by Christ: ὅτι ἐν Χρ. κατ.

We should observe also in this wonderful passage the strongly marked and pointed antithesis of the contrasted categories.

παλαιὰ διαθήκη	καινὴ διαθήκη
γράμματος	πνεύματος
κατάκρισις	δικαιοσύνη
θάνατος	ζωή
τὸ καταργούμενον	τὸ μένον
πώρωσις	παρρησία
κάλυμμα	ἀνακεκαλυμμένον πρόσωπον
δουλεία (Gal. 5. 1)	ἐλευθερία

Chap. IV. 2. τὰ κρ. τῆς αἰσχ.] "All secret ways of unseemliness," Hebraic for "all unbecoming disguises," "all degrading equivocations and false pretences."

3. "But if, after all, our Gospel *be* (καὶ) veiled": still keeping up the metaphor of the last chapter: verses 14, 15.

2 CORINTHIANS.

Chapter V.

HEBR. 1. οἰκοδ. ἐκ Θ. 7. περιπατοῦμεν, Gal. 5. 25, Mc. 7. 5, notes. 12. ἐν προσώπῳ.

NON-C. 7. εἴδους in sense of *sight*, and not of *the thing seen*.

SEPT. 10. ἔμπροσθεν for "in front of."

Chapter VI.

HEBR. 16. ὅτι, M. 7. 23, note. 18. ἔσομαι εἰς, M. 2. 6, note.

NON-C. 2. καιρῷ δ. without preposition. 3. μηδ. ἐν μ. for οὐδ. ἐν οὐδ.; and 10. 4. ἐν παντί: and 7. 16.

SEPT. 1. εἰς κενὸν, R. 12. 3, note. Gal. 2. 2; Isaiah 29. 8.

---

8. ἐν παντί] This form is only used by S. Paul, of all the Sacred Writers, and is not found in V. A. I doubt whether it has Classical Authority.

10. νέκρωσις] = "mortification": ἡ ν. τοῦ 'I. = "the mortification inculcated by Christ, exemplified in Christ"; ἡ ζωὴ τοῦ 'I. = "the life imparted by Jesus."

CHAP. V. 1. ἡ ἐ. ἡ. οἰκία τοῦ σκ.] Hebraic. "Our tent-house upon earth," metaphorically for "our body," "domus in quâ animus habitat his in terris, velut in tentorio, quod mortis tempore detendetur." Grimm. Sap. 9. 15, βρίθει τὸ γεῶδες σκῆνος νοῦν πολυφρόντιδα. οἰκοδ. ἐκ Θ. "cujus Deus auctor est."

8. εὐδοκέω] constantly used by V. A. for חפץ = gaudeo, volo.

10. "The reward won by and through the body, corresponding to"; πρὸς.

13. Θεῷ...ὑμῖν] dative of person. R. 6. 2, 1 Pet. 2. 24.

CHAP. VI. 3. μωμ.] "מום = labes, macula, corporis vitium (Lev. 21. 23, Deut. 15. 17), in V. A. passim, μῶμος = dedecus, vituperium; unde μωμάομαι: vitupero, culpo." Grimm.

11. πεπλάτυνται] "swells with emotion," "expands and opens": Ps. 119. 32, פִּי תַרְחִיב לִבִּי, ὅταν ἐπλάτυνας τὴν καρδίαν μου. Is. 60. 5 the same words רָחַב לְבָבֵךְ, otherwise rendered in V. A. "Thou shalt see and *be confused*, and thy heart shall fear and *swell with emotion*." E. V. "Thou shalt see and *flow together* and thy heart...*be enlarged*."

12. σπλάγχνοις] = affections, feelings: Hebraic idiom; occurring constantly in O. T. Gen. 43. 30, Jer. 31. 20, Cant. 5. 4. In N. T. found less frequently: L. 1. 78, Acts 1. 18, 1 J. 3. 17, Ph. 1. 8, Col. 3. 12. The bowels were considered by the Jews to be the seat of the affections, as the heart by us.

Chapter VII.

Hebr. 6. 8. 14. ἐν. 9. ἐκ for ὑπὸ, as = מִן. Similarly: infra 13. ἀπὸ. 15. μετὰ φόβου, M. 24. 31, note.

Non-C. 2. χωρήσατε. ἐπλεονεκτ. 5. 11. 16. ἐν παντὶ: and the participle θλ. 11. ἀλλὰ = immo. 11. ἁγνοὺς. 13. ἀνα πέπαυται. 16. θαρρῶ ἐν ὑ.

Chapter VIII.

Hebr. 24. εἰς πρίσωπον = לִפְנֵי.

Non-C. 2. κατὰ βάθους. 12. ἐὰν. 16. διδόντι...ἐν, M. 28. 19, note.

Chapter IX.

Hebr. 5. 6. εὐλογία.

Non-C. 11. ἁπλότητα = liberality: supra 8. 2.

Sept. 9. εἰς τὸν αἰῶνα. Notes Mc. 3. 29 and 1 Th. 4. 15.

Chap. VII. 4. παράκλησις] See note J. 14. 16 for this, and infra vv. 6, 7.

Chap. VIII. 5. διὰ θελήμ. Θ.] A strong instance of the omission of the article, inexplicable by any ordinary rules of Greek construction: and apparently to be referred to the frequent and palpable irregularity as to the use of the definite article in Hebrew.

7. τῇ ἐξ ὑ. ἐν ἡμῖν ἀ.] For the anomalous expression ἡ ἐν ἡμῖν αγ. see 1 J. 4. 16.

19. συνέκδ. ἡμ. σὺν τῇ χ.] A most curious construction: literally and grammatically implying that the χάρις was a companion of S. Pau and his colleague.

Chap. IX. 4. ὑπόστασις] Heb. 3. 14, 11. 1. V. A. for תּוֹחֶלֶת, Ps. 39. 8, and תִּקְוָה, Ruth 1. 12 = "confidence, hope, expectation." Infra 11. 17.

5. εὐλογία] V. A. for בְּרָכָה, one common meaning of which is *donum*, a gift. Prov. 11. 25, נֶפֶשׁ בְּ, a liberal soul. 1 Sam. 25. 27, τὴν εὐλογίαν ταύτην, הַבְּ. In verse 6 ἐπ' εὐλ. = "with liberal intent," "in a liberal spirit," "bountifully."

10. γεννήματα] M. 26. 29, note.

12. "Is not only enough to satisfy to the full the needs of the brethren, but runs over in praise to God."

13. ἡ ὑποταγὴ τῆς ὁμ.] "Your unanimous obedience," Hebraic genitive.

CHAPTER X.

HEBR. 2. κατὰ σάρκα π. 10. ἡ παρ. τοῦ σώμ.

NON-C. 1. π. ύ. διὰ τῆς... 2. τινας τοὺς... 13. 15. τὰ ἄμετρα.

CHAPTER XI.

HEBR. 14. ἄγγ. φωτός.

NON-C. 1. 19. ἀνέχεσθαι, with gen. 6. ἰδιώτης and ἐν. π. 8. ὀψώνιον, and τὴν ύ. διακ. = "service *towards* you," and not "*from* you." 20. εἰς πρόσ. 23. ὑπέρ.

CHAP. X. 4. δυνατὰ τῷ Θ.] A literal rendering of an Hebrew idiom (see note, Acts 7. 20). Jonah 3. 3 is, so far as I know, the only instance of this use of ל after *an adjective*, which Grimm explains as = "Deo judice." It is probably equivalent to לפני, 2 Kings 5. 1, Gen. 10. 9. The idiom ἡ ὑπακοὴ τοῦ Χρ. is found also R. 1. 5, 1 P. 1. 22.

7. τὰ κατὰ πρ. βλ.] "You look at the things before your eyes," "judge only by what you see": as in verse 1, "I, who when amongst you am outwardly," "to the eye" (as my detractors say) "insignificant, but full of boldness towards you in my absence": infra verse 10.

8. For omission of article here and infra 17, 18, see ch. 8. 5, note.

13. The μεμιλτωμένον γράμμα, which marked bounds, was a κανών. Εἰς τὰ ἄμετρα here, and v. 15, *may* possibly be used in the Classical sense of the word, as Grimm takes it, to mean "extravagantly, immoderately": or in a special, non-classical sense, as most Translators and our E. V. have rendered it, "beyond, outside" our measure; as seems to suit the context best. For the adverbial form, εἰς τὰ ἀ., see R. 12. 3, note.

CHAP. XI. 2. ἡρμοσάμην ὑμᾶς] "I have got-you-to-be-betrothed," "have caused you to be..."

10. ἔστιν ἀλ. Χρ. ἐν ἐμοί] A very strange form of expression, irreducible to Greek idiom.

ἡ κ. αὔ. οὐ. φρ.] "Huic gloriationi non præcludetur via": "nemo me impediet quominus hâc re glorier": Grimm. "This boasting shall not be barred against me."

14. ἄγγελον φωτός] The identity of this Hebrew idiom, gen. of noun for adjective, with our own, "an angel of light" = "a bright, glorious, angel," makes the phrase seem quite natural to us; and we forget that it is not a Greek form at all: only a literal rendering of a Hebrew form.

SEPT. 28. ἐπισύστ....."quotidianæ perturbationes": Numb. 26. 9, compare. 31. εἰς τοὺς αἰῶνας.

Chapter XII.

HEBR. 12. ἐν π. ὑπ.... 18. περιεπ.
NON-C. 5. 9. καυχ. ἐν ταῖς... 17. Construction of whole verse. 18. ἐπλεονέκτ.
SEPT. 10. εὐδοκῶ ἐν. Note, M. 3. 17.

---

16. ἄφρων and ἀφροσύνη] in this passage, and infra 12. 6, 11, seem almost equivalent to "*vain*," and "*vanity*": "let no man think me vain" because of my boasting.

25. πεποίηκα] This use of ποιεῖν with nouns of *time* is seldom found in Classical Authors, and not often in V. A., or Apocrypha. Job 10. 7, Ecclesiastes 10. 7, it is the literal rendering of עָשָׂה in same sense. In Vulgate this verse stands "nocte et die...fui," which, if accurately interpreted, has a widely different meaning.

CHAP. XII. 2. ἐν Χρ.] See notes Eph. 6. 21, Ph. 1. 13, Col. 3. 18.

7. τῇ σαρκί] Not *in*, but *for:* "a sharp corrective for my human pride." ἄγγελος in V. A. is used always for מַלְאָךְ, as if it meant only "messenger": whereas in Hag. 1. 13, and Mal. 3. 1, 2. 7, "prophet," or "*minister*," would express its true sense more closely: in accordance with its derivation from the same root, לְאָךְ, as מְלָאכָה, the leading idea of which is "ministerium," "opus alicui delegatum." We lose sight of this, if we always render ἄγγελος in N. T. (when it clearly does not mean *angel*) by *messenger:* as generally in our E. V. Here, for instance, "minister," or "agent," is a more appropriate and correct translation. For bodily sufferings, as connected with the *agency* of Satan, see Job 2. 7, L. 13. 16.

18. This absolute sense of περιπατέω, as = "to live," is distinctly Hebraic: Mc. 7. 5, note, and supra 5. 7. Observe strange use of dative τῷ ἁ. πν., and τοῖς ἁ. ἰχν.: a sort of "dative of the manner," so seldom, in its most natural instances (of which this is certainly not one), found in N. T.

20. εὑρεθῶ ὑμῖν] we translate at once, by intuition as it were, or by recollection of the familiar Eng. Version, "*by you*." Do we consider how rare such a construction is in any Greek Authors? How inexplicable in S. Paul? who omits the preposition here, when absolutely necessary for the Greek idiom: as he inserts it elsewhere, when utterly

Chapter XIII.

Hebr. 1. πᾶν ῥῆμα. 12. ἐν ἁγ. φ.
Non-C. 2. εἰς τὸ πάλιν. 10. ἀποτ. χρῆσ.

---

against the same: with a persistent irregularity, as it were: using it when not wanted, leaving it out when wanted: from old associations, apparently, Hebraic or Alexandrine.

Chap. XIII. 1. ἐπὶ στόματος] Notes M. 28. 14 and Mc. 8. 4.

4. The use of ἐξ in this sense, implying *the cause*, (three times in this verse) ("*through*" and "*by*," E. V., *ex* in Vulg.,) is due most probably to the Septuagint renderings of מִן, when, as so often, it carries this meaning. Supra 2. 2, 7. 9.

GALATIANS.

Chapter I.
Hebr. 6. ἐν χ. X. 16. ἐν ἐμοὶ. 18. πρὸς αὐ.
Non-C. 4. τοῦ ἐν. αἰ. π. 18. ἀν...ἱστ. 22. ἤμην ἀγν. τ. π.

Chapter II.
Hebr. 16. ἐξ ἔ. ν., ἐκ π. and οὐ δικ. π. σ.
Non-C. 2. κατ᾽ ἰδ....ἔδραμον. 5. πρὸς ὥραν.

Chapter III.
Hebr. 6. ἐλογ. αὐ. εἰς δ. 17. εἰς X. 19. δι᾽ ἀγγ. R. 2. 27, and ἐν χ.
Non-C. 19. ἄχρις οὗ ἔ. 23. ὑπὸ with acc.
Sept. 10. τοῦ π. = ל, M.' 2. 6, note.

Chap. I. 6. καλέσαντος ἐν χ.] See notes at 1 Cor. 7. 15, and 1 Th. 4. 7.

9. καὶ ἄρτι] Most probably Hebraic; from similar use of ל.

16. ἐν ἐμοὶ] by me: by my ministry.

Chap. II. 16. ἐξ ἔργων and διὰ πίστεως are clearly not correspondent terms: there must be a special distinct meaning for each preposition. Is it not possibly the same use of διὰ as in 2 Cor. 2. 4, "out of the midst of," "combined with"? πίστις Χρ., can this be "faith *in* Christ"? see R. 3. 22. How can we, by any principles of language, get this meaning out of the phrase? I cannot but think the interpretation, so much reprobated by Grimm, deserves careful consideration: "fides, quæ auctore, approbante, jubente Christo, habetur Deo": the same force of the genitive as in δικαιοσύνη Θεοῦ. "Christ's faith," i.e. "the faith He prescribes and exacts."

Chap. III. 6. ἐλογ. εἰς δ.] There is no ל in Gen. 15. 3, quoted here: but the *form* with εἰς in similar cases was so habitual to the Authors of V. A. that they introduced it here.

GALATIANS.

Chapter IV.

HEBR. 6. ἀββᾶ ὁ π. 18. πρὸς ὑ. 20. ἐν ὑ. 27. ἡ οὐ τ. nom. for voc.

NON-C. 11. μήπως κ. 16. ὥστε. 20. ἄρτι. 24. ἄτινα.

---

9. οἱ ἐκ. π.] M. 5. 37, *note.* "The *faith* people": "all true believers": אַנְשֵׁי אֱמוּנָה.
19. διατ. δι' ἀγγ.] "out of the midst of," "in the presence of."
23. τὴν μ. π. ἀποκ.] Irregular syntax, very common in Hebrew: see 2 Sam. 13. 16, and the V. A. rendering: a specimen of strange mistakes. Eph. 2. 3, M. 25. 34, note.

CHAP. IV. 13. δι' ἀσθένειαν] The accusative here inexplicable, on any principles of grammar. Ellicott translates literally, "because of," "on account of": but this is utterly unsatisfactory. Let us rather admit, at once, that it is an instance of *bad grammar:* acc. for gen., and make it equivalent to מִתוֹךְ, R. 2. 27. "Under the influence of," "out of." 3. 19. What particular ἀσθένεια? Does not the allusion to ὀφθαλμοὺς (15) suggest weakness or disease of the eyes? The result probably of his stroke of blindness at his conversion: which would account for his seldom writing by his own hand: and agrees with many things said about his bodily infirmity. τὸν πειρασμόν μου, "my trial," as he calls it (14).

20. ἄρτι] Apparently never used in V. A.

24. ἀλληγορούμενα] not "an allegory": but "capable of being allegorised": as the Niphal in Hebrew. Make a συστοιχία: and take Agar and Sara, the slave and the free-woman, as allegorical representatives of the bondage of the Mosaic, and the liberty of the Christian, dispensation: under two categories:

1st. κατὰ σάρκα. Agar. Ishmael. Lex in Sina. Jerusalem terrestris. Judæi. Servitus.

2nd. κατ' ἐπαγγελίαν. Sara. Isaac. Evangelium. Jerusalem cælestis. Christiani. Libertas.

27. ἡ οὐ τ....οὐκ ὠ.] Literally quoted from V. A., showing the ungrammatical use of οὐ for μὴ in such expressions, common to V. A. as to N. T.

29. ὁ κατὰ σάρκα...τὸν κ. πνεῦμα] "He whose birth was natural ...him whose birth was supernatural." 1 Cor. 10. 3, 15. 44.

31. ἄρα] Not "so then," as a deduction from the preceding argument; but as expressing antecedent conclusions. "Surely you cannot

Chapter V.

HEBR. 16. πν. περιπ.

NON-C. 6. τι. 9. μικρὰ ζ. 12. ὄφ. κ. ἀποκ. 21. β. Θ., no article.

Chapter VI.

HEBR. 1. ἔν τ. π. 12. ὅσοι θ. εὐπροσ.

---

wish to stand in the first category: to go back to Judaising bondage. Surely we, Christians, Ἰσαὰκ τέκνα κατ' ἐπαγγελίας, are not children of the bondwoman, but of the free: surely we shall not consent to disinherit ourselves."

CHAP. V. 1. τῇ ἐλευθερίᾳ] Infra 13. James 1. 25, νόμον τέλειον, τὸν τῆς ἐλ. "the Gospel, the law" (i.e. dispensation, covenant, enactment) "of freedom : Judaism......of bondage."

17. Our translation in E. V. is undoubtedly wrong, as contradicting S. Paul's previous line of argument, full of encouragement and promise : whereas E. V. suggests helplessness and despair, "*so that ye cannot do* the things that ye would." S. Paul teaches that by the help of God men may master the evil tendencies of their nature (16). And then goes on (17) "For the flesh," i.e. human nature, "is ever struggling against the Spirit : *but* (on the other hand) so is the Spirit against the flesh: and these are set one against the other" (i.e. God has given us the help of His Holy Spirit as a counterpoise against the carnal tendency) "to enable you to avoid doing whatever your lusts desire," "for the very purpose that you need not do whatever you have a mind to." ἵνα μή, "in order that you *may* not," "to the end you should not": much closer to the true meaning than, "so that you *can not*." The Vulgate gives correctly, "Caro enim concupiscit adversus Spiritum: Spiritus autem adversus carnem: hæc enim sibi invicem adversantur: ut non quæcunque vultis ea faciatis."

25. We have πνεύματι in this Chapter, with περιπατέω (16), ζῷ, ἄγομαι (18), and στοιχέω: according to the common Hebrew idiom of "walk" for "life." "If we-are-for living a spiritual life," (as doubtless we are: there is no uncertainty implied by εἰ,) "let us also maintain a spiritual walk." A bold use of dative: representing the Holy Spirit as the regulating cause.

CHAP. VI. 1. ἔν τ. π.] It is remarkable how seldom S. Paul uses, *in this Epistle*, this form (ἐν with dative) to express cause, manner or instrument. οἱ πν., i.e. οἱ Πνεύματι ζῶντες, περιπάτ., supra 5. 16, 25.

Non-C. 3. 9. μηδὲν. 7. ὃ ἐὰν σπ. 12. τῷ στ....διώκωνται. 16. κανένι...στ.

---

2. "Enter into the temptations, try and realise the trials, of others": do not make the weight of their shame heavier.

3. δοκέω = cogito in N. T. Note, M. 3. 9, Phil. 3. 4. Also in V. A. Gen. 38. 15, ἔδοξεν αὐτὴν εἶναι πόρνην יַחְשְׁבֶהָ. Prov. 27. 14.

5. Future, expressing what is *likely* to happen: "every one will, in all probability, have to bear."

10. οἰκείους τῆς π.] "Brethren in the faith," "faith-kindred." V. A. use οἰκεῖτος τοῦ σπέρματος for "consanguineus." Is. 58. 7 מִבְּשָׂרְךָ, ἀπὸ τῶν οἰκ. τοῦ σπ. "blood relations." Numbers 27. 11, שְׁאֵרוֹ הַקָּרֹב לוֹ, "his nearest relation," τῷ οἰκείῳ τῷ ἔγγιστα.

12. τῷ σταυρῷ] Dat. of "cause": a forced expression: like those above, Cap. 5. 16, 18, 25. For striking examples of this dative see 1 Th. 3. 3, Eph. 5. 18.

EPHESIANS.

Chapter I.

Hebr. 3. ἐν π. εὐλ. 7. τὸν πλ. τ. χ. α. 12. εἶναι...εἰς ἐπ. 13. τὸν λ. τῆς ἀλ. and τῷ Πν. τῆς ἐπ. 14. ἀπολ. τῆς π. 15. πίστιν ἐν... 20. ἐν δεξιᾷ α. 22. αὐτὸν ἔδωκε.

Chapter II.

Hebr. 2. περιεπ. κ. τ. αἰῶνα and υἱοῖς τ. ἀ. 3. τῆς σαρκὸς and τέκνα ὀργ. 6. ἐν Χ. 11. ἔθνη ἐν σ. 15. κτίσῃ εἰς ἕνα. 21. 22. Whole verse.

Non-C. 4. πλούσ. ἐν ἐ.

Chapter III.

Hebr. 11. πρόθ. τῶν αἰ. 13. ἐν ταῖς θλ. μου. 16. τὸν πλ. τῆς δ. α. and εἰς τὸν ἔ. ἄ.

Chap. I. 13. τῷ Πν. τῆς ἐπ.] Acts 1. 4.

14. ἀπολ. τῆς περιποιήσεως] "The redemption of the purchasing": i.e. "the redemption which Christ has secured for us at the cost of his own blood"; E. V. translation would require περιποιήματος. But see 1 Pet. 2. 9. ἀπολύτρωσις = "payment in full." "The Holy Spirit, which is the earnest of our inheritance, for (εἰς) the payment in full of every promise" at the great day (ἡμ. ἀπολ. 4. 30) when the Sons of God shall enter into their full inheritance. I doubt if εἰς can mean "until." But see 1 Th. 4. 15, 2 Tim. 1. 12.

Chap. II. 3. τέκνα φ. ὀ.] Gal. 3. 23.

15. κτίσῃ εἰς ἕ. κ. ἄ.] εἰς literal rendering of ל, as Gen. 2. 22, ᾠκοδόμησεν τὴν πλευρὰν εἰς γυναῖκα.

20. ἀκρογωνιαίου] See M. 21. 42, note. "The head stone of the corner," i.e. "key stone or crown of the pointed arch"; γωνη = angle. Infra 4. 16, note.

EPHESIANS.

Chapter IV.

HEBR. 3. 14. 30. ἐν. 13. εἰς μ. ἠλ. τοῦ πλ. 17. ἐν Κ. 22. τὰς ἐ. τῆς ἀπ. 24. ὁσιότ. τῆς ἀλ. 29. πᾶς λ....μὴ. 32. ἐν Χρ.

NON-C. 18. διὰ with acc. ἐσκ. τῇ δ. dat. of part, and infra 23.

Chapter V.

HEBR. 5. πᾶς π....οὐκ. 1 J. 2. 21. 8. τέκνα φ. 14. ὁ καθ. nom. for voc. and 22. 25. 18. ἐν πν. 26. 31. ἔσονται εἰς.

CHAP. IV. 8. Neither an exact quotation from V. A., nor a literal rendering of the Hebrew: in which it is not "*gave*," but "*received*" gifts, בָּאָדָם, "in the form or nature of man," "as man." Our incarnate Lord, ascending in His human body, received gifts for His people.

9. τὰ κατώτερα μ. τῆς γῆς] "the lower region," namely, "that of Earth."

12. πρὸς τ. κ. τῶν ἁ. εἰς] Mark force and relation of the prepositions. The εἰς depends on καταρτισμόν. "With a view to the perfecting" (the full equipment and supply) "of the Saints for...," "ut Christiani indies perfectiones et aptiores reddantur ad opera ministerii, ad ædificationem Ecclesiæ." "Till we all arrive at unity in the faith and knowledge of the Son of God,—at the maturity of our powers,—at the standard of full-age in Christ": "full Christian growth." τοῦ πληρ. Hebr. gen. of qualification. ἵνα μηκ. ὦμεν νήπιοι, ἀλλ' ἄνδρες τέλειοι.

14. ἐν π. πρὸς τὴν μεθ. τῆς πλ.] "by their subtle-practices for waylaying and misleading": μεθοδεία "nomen neque in V. A., neque apud profanos obvium," Grimm.

16. συναρμ. καὶ συμβιβαζ.] These verbs express the exact effect of the key stone of an arch (2. 20). "By Whom the whole body, the Church, symmetrically arranged and firmly compacted and knit together by every joint and articulation of his bountiful supply, maketh continual progress towards its peaceful and harmonious amplification and stability."

17. μαρτύρ. ἐν Κ.] = בְּיַשָּׁבַע: the usual Hebr. form.

29. πρὸς οἰκ. τῆς χρ.] "for necessary and profitable edification"; or "for promotion of the general advantage."

CHAP. V. 6. υἱοὺς τῆς ἀπ.] Suprn 2. 2. = בְּנֵי קְרִי, "contumaces, qui sibi persuaderi nolint." ἀπειθέω in V. A. does not imply *unbelief*, but

Non-C. 15. βλέπετε πῶς. 24. ἐν παντί. 31. ἀντὶ τ.

Chapter VI.

Hebr. 1. 10. 21. ἐν Κ. 2. ἐν ἐπαγγ. 12. τὰ πν. τῆς π. 14. 16. 18. 19. 24.

"resistance to the truth," "refractoriness," "rebellion," "disobedience," and so apparently in N. T. Hebr. 4. 6. Hence as signifying "unpersuadeableness" also it is frequently applied to the Gentiles.

18. οἴνῳ...ἐν πνεύματι] Mark dat. with and without prep., each expressing the instrument. M. 3. 11, 1 Th. 3. 3.

26. ἐν ῥήματι] Comp. James 1. 18, ἀπεκύησεν ἡμᾶς λόγῳ ἀληθείας; "He hath given us a new birth by a word of truth," "by holy words whose virtue never fails," M. 11. 19, i. e. "the prescribed efficacious form of words ordained by our Lord for Baptism": "having cleansed it in the Water-bath by His own solemn word."

27. A metaphor from the Eastern practice of purification before marriage. Esther 2. 12.

32. εἰς Χρ.] "with reference to": Acts 2. 25, Hebr. 1. 7.

Chap. VI. 5. τοῖς κ. κατὰ σάρκα] "your masters in the world," "natural"; as opposed to κατὰ πνεῦμα, "in spiritual affairs."

12. τὰ πν. τῆς πον. ἐν τοῖς ἐπ.] "wicked spirits all above and around us": the Jewish notion of "demons in the air."

15. ἐν ἑτοιμασίᾳ] The usual explanations of this word seem to be without special force or meaning. E. V. "the preparation of the Gospel of peace" is unintelligible, as referring to a piece of defensive armour for the feet. "Alacri et prompto animo quem efficit Evangelium pacis," Grimm's suggestion, is strangely inconsistent with the metaphor, and inappropriate. But there is *one* meaning, derived from V. A., hitherto apparently overlooked or undiscovered, which has a singularly exact coincidence. כֵּן, Dan. 11. 7, 20, 21, מָכוֹן, Ezra 2. 68, 3. 3, Zach. 5. 10, are all ἑτοιμασία in V. A., and all = "basis," "foundation," "something to stand on." Ps. 112. 7, נָכוֹן לִבּוֹ, ἑτοίμη καρδία αὐτοῦ. Ps. 88. 14, δικαιοσύνη...ἑτοιμασία τοῦ θρόνου σου, מָכוֹן, "the firm basis, on which Thy throne stands." Hence metaphorically used here for the strong sole of the *caliga* with which each Roman soldier was shod: the firm support under his feet, on which he stood and stepped, and advanced fearlessly and calmly and securely over dangerous ground. Keble, in his description of the Christian armour, has, for this item of it, "Then heavenly calmness, lest thou fall where dangers line the way": and *this*, "the Gospel of peace" can alone supply. So I suggest,

Non-C. 3. γένηται καὶ ἔσῃ. 8. ὃ ἐάν τι.

"having undergirt your feet," "having your feet shod," "with the sure support and defence and basis," "the solid, firm substratum" "of the Gospel of peace," to carry you safe over the rough ways of the world. "Apparatus" would more nearly express the meaning than "preparation": which is clearly derived, through the Vulgate, "calceati pedes in preparatione ev. pacis," from the primary meaning of ἑτοιμάζω, literally rendered. But this verb is used in V. A. over a hundred times, for כון in its different moods, with all its various shades of meaning, (among which "constituo, stabilio, confirmo," are prominent,) as if equivalent to them all (which of course it is not, "apud Græcos," in the Classical Authors); e.g. 1 Chr. 17. 11 ἑτοιμάσω τὴν βασιλείαν αὐτοῦ, 2 Chr. 12. 1, 2 Kings 2. 12. In each of these the Vulgate has the true meaning: severally, "stabiliam," "cum roboratum fuisset," "firmatum est." In other places it appears to have followed V. A. without discrimination, e.g. Ps. 21. 13, 88. 3, Hab. 2. 12, with the literal *præparare*. Hence we can understand its adopting *præparatio* for ἑτοιμασία here.

17. τοῦ σωτηρίου] A common translation of יְשׁוּעָה in V. A. Is. 59. 17, כּוֹבַע יְשׁ׳, περικεφαλαία σ., 1 Th. 5. 8.

21. πιστὸς δ. ἐν K.] This phrase ἐν K. appears to me very difficult to explain: and I can not feel satisfied with Grimm's elaborate attempts. I believe it to mean "coram Christo." Note at Col. 3. 18 and Phil. 1. 13.

PHILIPPIANS.

Chapter I.
HEBR. 8. ἐν σπλ. 'Ι. X. 26.
NON-C. 13. τοῖς λ. π. 14. λόγον λαλεῖν. 28. ἐν μηδενὶ.

Chapter II.
HEBR. 10. ἐν τῷ ὀ. 13. ὑπὲρ τῆς εὐ. 16. εἰς κενὸν.
NON-C. 2. τὸ ἓν φρ. 16. Whole verse. 23. ὡς ἂν ἀπ. 29. μετὰ π. χ.

CHAP. I. 8. ἐν σπλάγχ.] "with an affection like that of Jesus," "inspired by Jesus."

13. ἐν Χριστῷ] Can this mean "by the help of Christ," "through Christ"? "my imprisonment has, through Christ, become known." Grimm renders: δεσμοὶ ἐν X. "vincula quorum causa posita est in consortio Christi," unsatisfactorily.

CHAP. II. 8. μέχρι θ.] "even as far as death."

9. τὸ ὄνομα] = הַשֵּׁם = *the* name, Jehovah; the same as Κύριος in (11).

10. "That every knee should be bent in the name of Jesus"; i.e. "that all our prayers should be offered in His Name." John 14. 6, 15. 16, 16. 23.

13. ὑπὲρ τῆς εὐδοκίας] = עַל רָצוֹן exactly translated: which V. A. render by δεκτά "acceptably," Is. 60. 7. In 59. 18 עַל, for which ὑπὲρ is the strict and literal equivalent, means "propter," or "secundum": and so ὑπὲρ *here* may possibly have that meaning, as though expressing עַל. Grimm explains quite differently, without any reference to Hebrew. Gesenius says: "עַל substantivis abstractis præmissum adverbiis circumscribendis inservit." עַל שֶׁקֶר, falso. Lev. 5. 22, V. A. ἀδίκως: (compare L. 16. 9). עַל יֶתֶר large, V. A. περισσῶς, Ps. 31. 24; עַל נְקַלָּה leviter, Jerem. 6. 14: and so עַל רָצוֹן, Is. 60. 7 (see above), "in a pleasing manner," which seems to be the meaning of

PHILIPPIANS. 87

CHAPTER III.

HEBR. 3. ἐν σαρκὶ π. 1. 6. 14.
NON-C. 2. βλέπετε. 8. ἀλλὰ μ. οὖν κ. 12. εἰ καταλάβω. 16. στοιχεῖν κανόνι.

CHAPTER IV.

HEBR. 1. 7. 13. 15. εἰς λ. 19. ἐν δ. ἐν Χ.
NON-C. 10. ἤδη......to end. 6. 12.

---

the text; "in a way to please Him," "agreeably to His will." (In V. A. εὐδοκία is almost always put for רָצוֹן.) Gesenius compares the phrase to לְרָצוֹן, Jerem. 6. 20 (V. A. δεκτά) making *that* adverbial, as לַשָּׁוְא, Jerem. 6. 29, 30, in V. A., εἰς κενὸν, εἰς ματαῖον. See Note Rom. 12. 3: and infra verse 16. V. A. use ὑπὲρ very seldom, 2 Kings 18. 5, Ps. 55. 7, Thr. 4. 7. I have found no other instances. It would appear to have been almost unknown to the Translators, which may account for their rendering עַל by a periphrasis as above.

30. τῇ ψυχῇ] = נַפְשׁוֹ, *himself:* "running great risks for himself."

CHAP. III. 2. S. Paul disputes the right of the old Judaising party to call themselves ἡ περιτομή, or οἱ ἐκ περιτομῆς (Acts 10. 45, 11. 2), and asserts his claim to it, and that of all true believers: and coins a new word for the "destructives," κατατομή: the false teachers, who like dogs, *bark down* true doctrine.

3. ἐν σ. πεποιθότες] הֶאֱמִין בְּ, the usual Hebrew form, is translated in V. A. indifferently *with* or *without* ἐν: e.g. Ps. 78. 22, 32. Hence a similar use in N. T. See Notes Mark 1. 15, 2 Thess. 3. 4.

5. Ἑβρ. ἐξ Ἑβρ.] "of Hebrew blood a Hebrew," "a Pharisee to the very letter of the law": κατὰ ν. Φ. 2 Cor. 11. 22, Gal. 1. 14, Acts 6. 1, notes.

16. "But that to which we have attained, is, *to walk...*" may possibly be the correct translation.

CHAP. IV. 5. ὁ Κ. ἐγγύς] = μαρὰν ἀθά. 2 Cor. 16. 22.

6. τῇ πρ. καὶ τῇ δ. μετὰ εὐχαριστίας] Can this have any reference to special prayers at the Eucharist? The use of the article seems to mark a definite and special occasion.

15. εἰς λόγον δόσεως] Hebrew idiom = עַל דְּבַר. M. 5. 32, note.

COLOSSIANS.

Chapter I.
Hebr. 4. 9. 11. 21. 23. 28. 29, all illustrate varying meanings of ἐν, very frequent in this epistle.

Chapter II.
Hebr. 1. ἐν σ. 2. εἰς π. πλ. τῆς πλ. 14. ἐκ τοῦ μ.
Non-C. 8. βλ. μή ἔσται. 14. τὸ χ. τοῖς δ.

Chapter III.
Hebr. 6. υἱ. τῆς ἀπ. 18. nom. for voc. and ἐν Κ.
Non-C. 11. ὅπου = in whom, in which.

Chap. II. 11. τῇ περιτομῇ τοῦ Χρ.] i.e. *Baptism*; which is the Christian *initiation*, as Circumcision was to the Jews.

15. ἐν παρρησίᾳ] "openly," "boldly," "confidently": Mc. 8. 32 note.

Chap. III. 1. εἰ οὖν συνηγέρθητε] = "Seeing then that ye have been raised up," implying a recognised fact. In ordinary Greek, of course, it would mean "if ye had been."

4. φανερ. ἐν δόξῃ] M. 13. 43, James 1. 17: "appear" is far too weak in either case: "manifestation," "showing forth openly," is the idea.

5. τὰ μέλη...] Can this mean "mortify your members *as to* fornication"... : or are we to look upon these and similar offences as *members* making up collectively the whole *body of Sin*: looking on sin as a *body*? Observe the curious introduction of the definite article before only one noun, τὴν πλ.: a strong instance of Hebraic irregularity in its use.

6. ἀπειθείας.] Note Eph. 5. 6, Hebr. 4. 6, R. 11. 30.

7. ἐν αὐτοῖς: i.e. τοῖς υἱοῖς τῆς ἀπ.

10. κατ' εἰκ. τοῦ κτ.] See below 14, συνδ. τῆς ἀλ., and 4. 12 ἐν π. θελ. τοῦ Θ.: all specimens of same class of deviation from strict

COLOSSIANS.

Chapter IV.

Non-C. 3. θ.... λαλῆσαι. 17. βλέπε.

---

grammar (which requires *two* definite articles in such cases,) traceable to Hebraic influence: as also 1 P. 3. 12, οἱ ὀφθ. Κ. and ὦτα αὐτ., and Jude 6, ἀγγ. τοὺς μητ. 1 Th. 2. 13, 4. 3.

12. ἐνδύσασθε...σπλάγχνα] a curiously distorted metaphor. σπλ. οἰκτ. = " pitiful feelings," Hebraic. 2 Cor. 6. 13.

16. ἐν χάριτι] Can this mean "thankfulness, gratitude," as constantly in ordinary Greek? I cannot find any instance of this use in V. A. except the one given by Grimm, 2 Macc. 3. 33: but it is not uncommon in N. T. 1 Tim. 1. 12, Philemon 7, Rom. 6. 17, 7. 25, 2 Cor. 9. 15, Luke 6. 32. Here, "*with gratitude* in your hearts," or "singing, with your hearts, in gratitude": "with grateful heart worship."

18. ἀνῆκε] Eph. 5. 4, Philem. 8, apparently cognate with and used in same sense as προσῆκε. Found in only three passages of N. T. and four times in V. A.: in Apocrypha, 1 Macc. 10. 40, 42, 11. 35, 2 Macc. 14. 8. In Classical Authors, apparently never occurring in this signification.

ἐν Κυρίῳ] This phrase, so frequently employed by S. Paul, but only once, in same sense, by any N. T. writer (Apoc. 14. 13), is most difficult to explain, or account for, or adequately interpret. May I venture some attempt at its elucidation? Can it mean "apud, coram," "in the presence of," "in the sight of," as equivalent to בְּ in V. T. frequently? Gen. 23. 18, בְּאָזְנֵי בְנֵי, V. A. ἐναντίον τῶν εἰσπορευομένων, Ex. 14. 4. Gesenius considers this as an abbreviation of בְּעֵינֵי or בִּפְנֵי; can we imagine S. Paul using ἐν with a similar meaning? I think it will be found that this sense, or one derived from or connected with it, fits and suits most of the passages in his Epistles. Rom. 9. 1, 16. 13, Phil. 1. 1, 3. 1, 6. 1, Eph. 6. 21, 1 Th. 1. 1, 2 Th. 1. 10, and infra Col. 3. 20, 4. 7, σύνδουλος ἐν Χρ. We should understand at once, συνδ. ἐν ἀνθρώποις, "in medio hominum," "apud, coram homines." Can the idea and the phrase possibly have been transferred, from the frequency of its familiar use, in the Hebraistic dialect of the day, when *several* persons were spoken of, to cases where there was *only one*?

22. τοῖς κατὰ σάρκα κ.] as opposed to τοῖς κατὰ τὸ εὐαγγέλιον, or κ. Χριστόν.

Chap. IV. 6. εἰδέναι] The infinitive is often used as if it were a noun, in apposition to another noun going before it, *in any case*: here εἰδέναι seems to be in this relation to ἅλατι; "seasoned with *salt*," i.e. (namely) "the knowing how..."

1 THESSALONIANS.

CHAPTER I.
NON-C. 6. μετὰ χ. πν. ἁ. 9. ἐπεστρ.... δουλ.

CHAPTER II.
HEBR. 2 and 17. 18. καὶ = *but*.
NON-C. 7. ὡς ἂν... θάλπῃ. 10. γίγνομαι, with adverbs.

CHAP. I. 3. Hebraic: "your faith-sprung works, your love-inspired zeal, your hopeful expectation of Christ," "ever making mention" of these "before God."

5. πληροφορίᾳ] metaphor: "either from a ship in full sail and so = βεβαιότης; or from a tree in full bearing, with notion of completeness, satisfaction, full persuasion." Schl.

CHAP II. 6. ἐν βάρει] Schl. sub voce, says, "Paulus respexit sine dubio usum Vocab. Hebr. בָּבוֹד." The original meaning was "gravitas, pondus": and hence "dignity, honour." V. A. renders it by τὸ ἔνδοξον. Is. 22. 24, 59. 19. But in Judges 18. 21,—where it means "res pretiosa," "res gloriosa,"—they have βάρος: which, we may hence infer, with them = "dignity, honor, high repute"; as "gravitas = auctoritas". "When we might justly have claimed high place among you."

13. λόγον Θεοῦ] "The word of God as you heard it from us" = τὸν ἀκοῆς—παρ'—ἥμ. τοῦ Θ. λ.: see notes supra 1. 3, and Col. 4. 12.

17. πρὸς καιρὸν ὥρας] L. 8. 13, John 5. 35, Galatians 2. 5, 1 Cor. 7. 5, 2 Cor. 7. 8, Philem. 15, Hebr. 12. 10, 11, Jac. 4. 14. These are apparently the only instances of this very remarkable use of πρὸς, seldom, if ever, met with in Classical Authors: which seems to be used as if equivalent to εἰς in similar expressions, e. g. εἰς ἐνιαυτόν, which is Homeric; and common also in V. A. and N. T. But I have not found πρὸς in this sense anywhere in V. A. Of course, *we* translate it easily and readily and instinctively, by our own corresponding idiom: but how did it get into N. T. ? I cannot connect it with any Hebrew

1 THESSALONIANS.   91

Chapter III.
HEBR. 4. πρὸς ὑ. 9. ἔμπρ. τ. Θ.
NON-C. 1. μηκ. στέγ. 10. δεόμ. εἰς τὸ ἰδ.

Chapter IV.
HEBR. 8. εἰς ὑ. 15. ἐν λ. Κ. omission of article. 16. ἐν κ... φ... σ. all remarkable. 17. εἰς ἀέρα.
NON-C. 1. ἐρωτ. = request. 10. αὐτὸ. 18. ὥστε π.

Chapter V.
HEBR. 2. ἡ ἡμ. Κ. 23. καὶ... τηρηθ. so that... supra 3. 5.
NON-C. 1. χρ. ἔχ. γραφ. 13. ἡγεῖσθαι... ἐν ἀγ. 18. ἐν παντὶ. 27. ὁρκίζω... ἐπιστ.

---

form. Vulgate renders it by *ad* in all the above, except the three last, where it has *in*. Grimm's citations from Classical Authors do not touch the difficulty, exhibiting an entirely different meaning of πρός.

CHAP. III. 3. τῷ μηδένα σαίνεσθαι] "By the fact that no one is depressed and cowed by these afflictions": i.e. to comfort you about your faith (verse 2), by the example and experience of God's Saints.

5. μήπως] "whether or no," as Gal. 2. 2. How are we to explain the change of mood in μήπως ἐπείρασεν καὶ γένηται? Is it not possibly Hebraic, corresponding to a well-known and frequent use of ן for "so that": "whether or no the Tempter has tempted you, *in order that* our labour might be in vain," infra 5. 22. It is clear that ἐπείρασεν and γένηται cannot be coupled together by a mere *and*. For εἰς κενὸν see R. 12. 3.

CHAP. IV. 1. παράκ. ἐν Κ.] ἐν = בְּ adjurandi, so common in Hebrew and so generally rendered in V. A. by ἐν: 1 Sam. 24. 22, ὄμοσόν μοι ἐν Κ. 2 Sam. 19 7. See M. 5. 34 and 2 Th. 3. 6.

3. "The will of God is your sanctification": three constituent links in which are expressed by the three infinitives, ἀπέχεσθαι, εἰδέναι, μὴ ὑπερβαίνειν.

6. ἐκάλεσεν...ἐν ἀγ.] Most probably ἐν, as equivalent to Hebrew בְּ, stands here for εἰς, which is one of the meanings of that preposition, "has called you unto sanctification." See notes 1 Cor. 7. 15, Gal. 1. 6, M. 28. 19.

15. It is most unusual to have εἰς = until. 2 Tim 1. 12. Perhaps in each case it does not refer to *the time* but *the object*. M. 10. 22, 24. 13, Mc. 13. 13. It would seem to be due to the *literal* rendering of לְ in similar expressions; as constantly found in V. A.

2 THESSALONIANS.

Chapter II.

Non-C. 10. ἀνθ' ὦν. 13. πίστις ἀλ.

Chap. I. 10. ἐν τοῖς ἁγίοις] possibly "coram sanctis Ejus." Col. 3. 18, note: Ex. 14. 4, אִכָּבְדָה בְּפַרְעֹה V. A. ἐνδοξασθήσομαι ἐν Φαραῷ: where the literal ἐν obscures the force of בְּ; which is the same here as in Gen. 23, 18, where V. A. has caught and given the true meaning, ἐναντίον. Or we may translate ἐν here, "*by*," as so very common a sense of בְּ. Matt. 3. 11.

11. πληρώσῃ...ἐν δυνάμει] "complete in you a full delight in all goodness and works that spring of faith, effectually and powerfully."

Chap. II. 1. ὑπὲρ τῆς παρουσίας] "with respect to": ὑπὲρ is the exact literal equivalent of עַל, one of the well-known meanings of which is, "concerning, with respect to," 1 Kings 22. 8, Is. 1. 1, Gen. 26. 21: but in these V. A. have περί. I find ὑπὲρ only three times in V. A.: in two of which it stands for עַל in the above sense: 2 Kings 18. 5, Ps. 55. 7. It is a legitimate inference that such a meaning may have gradually attached to the word, as suiting literally the old familiar mode of expression, when transferred into Greek. Phil. 2. 13. The Thessalonians would seem to have misunderstood his first epistle: cap. 4. 15.

2. δι' ἡμῶν] In V. A. διὰ is frequently used for בְּיַד, "by the hand of," 2 Chr. 29. 25, Jos. 20. 2. So that here it may mean simply "by my hand," "from me."

3. ὁ υἱὸς τῆς ἀπ.] J. 17. 12, note.

10. Here ἀλήθεια and ἀδικία are opposed, as constantly by V. A. See notes at M. 11. 19, L. 16. 9, 1 Tim. 3. 16. Here render "with every lying deceit." Below, verse 12, the opposition is still more pointed and emphatic: ἀδικία clearly means "lying, falsehood," corresponding to τὸ ψεῦδος in verse 11. It is astonishing how all the

Chapter III.

Hebr. 1. 10. πρὸς ὑ.   4. πεπ. ἐν Κ.   6. 15. καὶ = yet.

Versions, following in the wake of the Vulgate, have copied and reproduced this glaring mistake of the V. A., and so have confused and distorted the plain meaning of innumerable passages in O. T.: and our English Version notably so. But what wonder, when the irregular and careless interchange of δίκαιος and ἀληθής, ἄδικος and ψευδής, and the substantives connected with them, in V. A., has affected and coloured so frequently whole sentences in N. T.

Chap. III. 10. ἦμεν πρὸς ὑμᾶς] M. 13. 56. Mc. 9. 19. πρὸς is here not Greek, but Hebraic: in Greek it could not be so used, with an accusative, as expressing an action *in* or *near*, with no sense of *motion to*. It is simply the literal rendering of אֶל, which has *both* meanings. But the translators in V. A., in consequence of their imperfect acquaintance with Greek, unable to discriminate delicate shades of meaning, treated πρὸς as uniformly equivalent to אֶל: and so the occurrence of such utterly ungrammatical phrases as that in the text (which would have defied the comprehension of those who knew only real Classical Greek) becomes intelligible; and can in fact only in this way be accounted for. John 1. 1.

1 TIMOTHY.

CHAP. I. 16. πρὸς ὑποτύπωσιν] not "an example for them to copy," "a pattern for them to imitate"; (as he is speaking of God's wonderful mercy,) but "as a shadowing forth, a sketch, an outline of what should be the experience of all Christians": "for a picture of the case of all, who, like S. Paul, should hereafter believe." ἐν ἐμοὶ πρώτῳ "in" or "by me *first*"; or rather "by me above and before every one else," "by me chiefest of all," verse 15: which sense of πρῶτος is common in N. T., as in V. A. 1 Ch. 27. 43, Ez. 27. 22, πρῶτα ἡδόσματα, 2 Ch. 26. 20; and is found also in Classical Authors.

18. τὴν κ. στρατείαν] = הַצָּבָא, "militia," the service, which every Jewish Priest had to fulfil, לִצְבֹא צָבָא, Numb. 4. 23, "to serve the service": V. A. λειτουργεῖν. In this place it *has nothing whatever to do* with "warfare," as E. V. translates it: but with the functions and service of the priesthood, στρατεύειν στρατείαν being the exact equivalent of the Hebrew idiom given above, which describes the sacred service of the Priests, Levites, &c.

κατὰ τὰς προ. ἐπὶ σὲ προφητείας] "according to supernatural communications from above guiding me to thee":—"in accordance with the intimations of the divine Will previously pointing to thee."

CHAP. III. 13. βαθμὸν, "a step up," advancement, promotion: ἐπαναβαίνειν. But may it not mean "foundation," "standing ground," "a good footing," as θεμέλιον infra, 6. 19?

16. εὐσεβείᾳ] V. A. for יִרְאַת, Prov. 1. 7. In Is. 11. 2 it stands alone for יִרְאַת יְהוָֹה. Is it not possible that this well-known passage may have given the word a fixed and special meaning for the Jews, in which it is used in N. T.? "our Holy Religion."

ἐδικαιώθη] M. 11. 19, L. 16. 2, 2 Thess. 2. 10: here, most probably, in accordance with the views stated in my former notes, "was declared to be true Christ," "*authenticated*" by the Holy Spirit," at His baptism: "declaratus est talis qualis reverâ est," Schl.:—justified, ap-

1 TIMOTHY.   95

CHAPTER V.

HEBR. 4. ἐνωπ. τοῦ Θ. 10. ἐν ἔργ. κ. μ.
NON-C. 12. πίστις. 24. τινῶν before its noun.

---

proved, demonstrated to be the Messiah, by the gifts and credentials of the Holy Spirit, and by His workings in Himself and His Apostles. ἐν πνεύματι "*by* the Spirit," M. 3. 11. ἀνελήφθη is the word used in V. A. of Elijah's Translation, 2 Kings 2. 11; and of our Lord's Ascension in N. T. Acts 1. 11. ἐν δόξῃ, not "*into*," but "*with*" glory.

CHAP. IV. 1. ῥητῶς] i.e. "spoke to S. Paul by inspiration": foreshowing Gnostic and other heresies. δαιμόνια = שֵׁדִים V. A. M. 9. 33, note. Ps. 105. 37, and so in Apocrypha: Baruch 4. 5. Hence its use for *evil* spirits (a notion entirely Jewish) in N. T.

2. ἐν ὑποκρ. ψευδ.] "THROUGH the hypocrisy of lying teachers": ἐν of the *cause*.

5. ἁγιάζεται] See Lev. 11. 44: both for the word (ἁγ.: V. A. for נִקְדַּשׁ) and the idea. "By the word of God." *What* word? the command and explanation given to S. Peter, Acts 10. 15. 1 Cor. 10. 25, Eph. 5. 26.

7. "Harden and train and discipline thyself, with a view to religious improvement," " to the *devout life*"; with *the devout life*, the life of God in the soul, as its end and aim. With this object in view, bodily discipline has its use and advantage: small, comparatively, but still real and important. " Cibis, lautionibus, venere, similibus, ante certamina publica abstinere, γυμνασία appellabatur," Schl. Hence it may mean "religious discipline *of the body*," as distinct from mental and spiritual discipline.

9. πιστὸς ὁ λ.] "The statement is true and to be relied upon."

14. In 2 Tim. 1. 6 S. Paul's agency alone is spoken of: here he speaks of a conjunction of the Body of Presbyters: there it is διὰ ἐπιθέσεως τῶν χειρῶν μου; here μετά, κ.τ.λ. Titus, 1. 5, has it all left to him: in Acts 8. 17, 19. 6, the imposition of hands is used by apostles alone.

διὰ προφητείας] "by directions from Heaven," "by divine intimation and appointment," " by the declaration of God's will": as supra 1. 18.

CHAP. V. 5. Here ἐπί with acc. after ἐλπίζω: supra 4. 10 it has dative. V. A. constantly use this verb followed by ἐπί for בָּטַח, confido, as was no doubt known to the Authors of our E. V., when they translated here "trusteth": as in 4. 10, 6. 17, 1 Pet. 3. 5. In Judg. 18. 7, לָבֶטַח = " securely," is rendered by ἐπ' ἐλπίδι.

CHAP. VI. 2. "Because those who lay claim to the benefit of their services are faithful : i. e. Christian believers."

5. "looking on our Holy Religion as a means of making money": thinking that religion is a source of profit.

12. *not* "fight the good fight," but "run the glorious race," "maintain the noble struggle." 2 Tim. 4. 7 ; τρέχωμεν τὸν ἀγῶνα, Hebr. 12. 1. 1 Cor. 9. 25.   For ὡμολ... see Heb. 4. 14.

19. As βαθμὸς (supra 3. 13) seems possibly = θεμέλιον, may not the latter *here* stand for the former ? or may the meaning be, "laying up," —as men pile up treasures,—"their successive tiers of good works, as a firm basis or foundation, ever rising higher, from which they may stretch upwards to the prize, and spring to lay hold on it at last," ἀφορμή. As though eternal life were hanging up before us, as the prize of our contest, like a ring, to be grasped and held by the winner. θεμέλιον = "a standing ground, a solid basis : something firm beneath the foot." Each advance in holiness is an upward step, on which to rise yet higher : whereas men, whose religion is mainly talk and feeling, are like people walking up sand-hills ; they cannot advance towards the prize : they have nothing to spring from : they slide downwards, and go back.

2 TIMOTHY.

Chap. I. 1. Can κατὰ here = "propter," "with a view to," "for the purpose of," as has been suggested by Winer and others: Tit. 1. 1, κατὰ πίστιν? as עַל often means? If I could cite any instances where V. A. give κατὰ for עַל, I should feel more inclined to support this suggestion.

2. χάρις, ἔλ. εἰρ.] "The triple crown of glory." Keble.

5. ὑπόμν. λαμβ. and 9 πρὸ χρ. αἰ. are Non-C.

Chap. II. 2. διὰ π. μαρτ.] "in the midst of," "coram": notes R. 2. 27, 4. 11, 14. 20, and Gal. 3. 19. Ellicott and others see that this *must* be the meaning, and try to account for it: I have shown *how* it is so, probably.

15. ὀρθοτομεῖν] Found only here in N. T.; and twice in V. A. Prov. 3. 6, 11. 5, and there with ὁδούς: supposed to be a metaphor from cutting a furrow straight, ὀρθὸς = εὐθύς. Not met with in Classical Authors. May we not here (in the absence of ὁδός, or anything like it) keep to the *exact* meaning of the word ὀρθός, "vertical," "upright," and so "true": "dressing it" (as masons say) "by the plumb-line": "setting it up and presenting it to the world, all true, square, uniform: with no deflections or distortions." There does not seem to me to be any idea of *division*: of breaking the truth up into its several portions: but of shaping and arranging the whole truth for exhibition. Grimm, following Schleusner, drops the idea of "cutting": and suggests "rectè tracto," which the Vulgate has: illustrating this by the secondary sense of καινοτομεῖν = "nova facio, muto."—Schl. cites Euseb. H. E. 4. 3, to show that ὀρθοτομία = ὀρθοδοξία, ὀρθοδιδασκαλία: but this, clearly, may be merely derived by them from the use of the word *here:* and may go to prove that they too understood it as suggested above, and did not hold it to imply *division,* as our E. V.

19. "Yet this solid and fundamental doctrine of God's Gospel" (i.e. the Resurrection) "stands firm and sure" (ἕστηκε), "having this seal" and authentication: viz. the same that God gave to the authority

of Moses and Aaron against Korah: Numb. 16. 5, V. A.: ἐπέσκεπται καὶ ἔγνω ὁ Κύριος τοὺς ὄντας αὐτοῦ, the correct translation of the original with its two verbs, בְּקֶר וְיֹדַע יה" אֶת אֲשֶׁר לֹו, from which our E. V. has been diverted by the "tomorrow" in verse 16, and the Vulgate rendering, "mane notum faciet Dominus." "God will discriminate and acknowledge those that are His"; *therefore* "let every one...." As Moses warned the congregation against Korah (Numb. 16. 26), so the Apostle warns the Church against these false teachers and their UNTRUTH (ἀδικία, 1 Cor. 13. 6, M. 11. 19, 2 Th. 2. 10). The *Seal* is Κύριος ἔγνω. καὶ = "therefore," Hebraicè, for וְ, so common in that sense: "therefore let every one...keep clear of all *false doctrine*."

25. μήποτε] M. 13. 15, Mc. 4. 12. "*In case* God, at some future time, may grant them." E. V. "if God peradventure will give them": grasping and exhibiting here the true meaning, which it has obscured in the two other passages, by "*lest*": Vulgate, in them all, has "nequando."

26. εἰς τὸ ἐκ. θέλ.] Hebraic: εἰς = לְ.

TITUS.

CHAP. I. 1. ἀπόστ....κατὰ πίστιν] 2 Tim. 1. 1. εὐσέβεια, 1 Tim. 3. 15 = "The Christian system."

3. ἐν κηρύγματι] "by the promulgation of the Gospel message." The omission of the article is simply Hebraic, and need not surprise any one acquainted with the arbitrary and irregular use of it in Hebrew. I may here again express my opinion of the unsoundness and impracticability of the attempt to account for the anomalies and bewildering perplexities connected with the omission of the definite article in G. T., on any principles of *Classical* Criticism.

10. οἱ ἐκ π.] "The strict *Jewish party* among the Christian converts": not merely, "the Jew-converts": Acts 10. 44, 45, 11. 2, 3.

CHAP. II. 13. ἐπιφ. τῆς δόξης] "The glorious appearing"; as Eph. 4. 13, ἡλικία τοῦ πληρώματος, "the full, complete manhood." "Waiting for our blessed hope, *even* the glorious Epiphany..."

14. περιούσιον] Found only here in N. T., and four times in V. A., Ex. 19. 5, Deut. 7. 6, 14. 2, 26. 8, always with λαός, for עַם סְגֻלָּה, "populus peculiaris": with its derivative περιουσιασμός, twice (Ps. 134. 4, Eccl. 2. 8); the word seems to have been *coined* by the Authors of V. A., to express the same idea, which they have rendered once, Mal. 3. 17, by εἰς περιποίησιν. Quoted 1 Pet. 2. 9. It has no classical authority. They would seem to have concluded that, ὃ περιπεποίηται, περίεστι: and therefore περιπεποιημένον = περιούσιον = peculium.

CHAP. III. 4, 5. Connect last half of 5 with 4, putting οὐκ ἐξ ἔ....ἔλεον in a parenthesis: "he has saved us," i.e. "has provided a way of salvation for us," "by Baptism, and Renewal of the Holy Spirit" (Collect for Christmas Day); "not in consequence of any works of righteousness in us, but according to his mercy."

7. κληρον. γεν.] "that we may, according to our hope, as we hope, come-in-for-the-inheritance-of," "attain to": in which sense κληρονομεῖν

is used constantly by V. A. for יָרַשׁ without any notion of inheritance. For instances see Grimm. And thus both verb and noun are found in N. T., in this wider sense, borrowed doubtless from V. A.; Hebr. 1. 2, 4, 11. 7, 12. 17. This is purely Hebraic, and non-Classical. Polybius has it once. It arose probably from the peculiar light in which the Jews looked on the land of Canaan.

9. περιίστασο] Only found here and 2 Tim. 2. 16: not in V. A.: nor in any Classical Authors in this sense. Josephus, A. J. 4. 6. 12 and Lucian and other later writers use it so. Grimm.

PHILEMON.

6. ἐν ἐπιγνώσει...εἰς Χρ.] "by the recognition *and reference to Christ* of all the good that is in us."

7. τὰ σπλ....ἀναπέπ.] "The hearts of the Saints have been refreshed, re-invigorated, encouraged."

HEBREWS.

Chapter I.

HEBR. 1. ἐν τοῖς π....ἐν υἱῷ. 3. 5. ἔσομαι εἰς π. 8. Nom. for Voc.

NON-C. 3. φέρων. 9. ἔχρισε...ἔλαιον.

The title of this Epistle (as Dr Roberts suggests in his Dissertations on the Gospels) indicates, possibly, *not* the Jews universally, nor even the Jewish converts generally, but the strict Jewish party within or without the Church, οἱ ἐκ περιτομῆς: Acts 6. 1: as opposed to the Ἑλληνισταὶ, the Hellenizers; and the line of argument and the whole tone of the Epistle support this view. That either the difference of style or absence of any personal allusions, or the expression in Chap. 2. 3 ὑπὸ τῶν ἀκ. εἰς ἡμᾶς..., prove S. Paul *not* to be the Author, is untenable. Whoever wrote it, was plainly writing anonymously: and apparently did not wish to be known.

CHAP. I. 1. πολυμερῶς] "The leading thought seems to be that there were many parts or divisions in the Prophetical Harmony; that no *one* utterance embraced the entire mystery: and that each portion had its own style and manner: as S. Paul seems to intimate, 1 Cor. 13. 9 ἐκ μέρους." Maurice.

2. κληρονόμον] = יוֹרֵשׁ = κύριον. Titus 3. 7 and infra 4: κεκληρ. = "adeptus est, proprium accepit," "has by right, as his own."

7, 8. πρὸς τοὺς ἀγγ., πρὸς τὸν υἱὸν] πρὸς = אֶל, "with respect to": Rom. 10. 21, Eph. 5. 32. Hebraic use, though occasionally found in Classical Authors: similarly εἰς, Acts 2. 25. Mark force of μὲν—δὲ, "and whereas he saith of the Angels...of the Son, on the contrary, he saith."

10, 11, 12. The God addressed in Ps. 102 is, all along, *God manifest in the flesh to Sion, the Incarnate Messiah, come down to earth*: hence the applicability of this quotation.

14. "Sent out on errands of help and service for the benefit of those who..."

CHAP. II. 2. δι' ἀγγ.] This *may* mean "in the presence of," "out of the midst of," as 2 Tim. 2. 2, and may refer to Deut. 33. 2, and to the *law* as given from Sinai alone. Or we may understand it of the word and revelation of God conveyed at various times to the Jews by the Prophets, through the intervention of Angels. Chap. 1. 1.

παρακοὴ = "misapprehension."

5. Supply ἀλλ' ἀνθρώπῳ. Schleusner takes τὴν οἰκ. τὴν μ. as = הָעוֹלָם הַבָּא "nova mundi institutio," "œconomia Christiana": the Rabbinic phrase for the post-Messianic æra, ὁ μέλλων αἰών, as הָעֵת הַזֶּה, for the state of things before Messiah: ὁ νῦν or οὗτος αἰών: a distinction most vividly presented to us in N. T., 1 Tim. 6. 17, L. 18. 30, 20. 35, 1 Cor. 1. 20, Heb. 6. 5. But I can find no instance of οἰκουμένη in this sense, though it suits the passage exactly, as expressing "the world of the future": "as it was to be under the coming dispensation." For the government and channels of grace in the Church were to be, not by Angels, but by men: and the Church was to absorb the world and renovate it, and change its character altogether.

10. ἔπρεπε] Can this mean "it SEEMED right"? יִיטַב לוֹ, or טוֹב בְּעֵינָיו, V. A. = καλόν ἐστιν ἐναντίον αὐτοῦ, "becoming, proper, right, before him," "in his eyes": which is the exact meaning of πρέπει, as describing something "*good to the eyes*." We dare not presume to say, —not even an inspired Apostle,—that any particular course of action "*became* God," "*decebat* Deum" (Vulgate). We *may* conclude, from the results, that such a course "*seemed right* to Him."

15. ἔνοχοι] See M. 5. 22, 1 Cor. 11. 27. Here it seems to mean "subject-to-the-penalty-of": Vulg. "obnoxii servituti." But the construction with gen. in this sense, is quite anomalous. It had perhaps come to be used as a substantive.

16. "For assuredly it is not *angels* he comes to help, but the seed of Abraham." ἐπιλαμβ. = "to take by the hand."

CHAP. III. 1. τῆς ὁμολογίας ἡμῶν] = "*our* covenant," "fœderis nostri": as Moses was the ἀπόστολος and Aaron the ἀρχιερεύς of the Jewish.

11. ὡς ὤμοσα] אֲשֶׁר, "how I sware," or "of whom..."

14. ὑπόστασις] parallel to ἐλπὶς in 6: infra 11. 1.

HEBREWS.

CHAPTER IV.
NON-C. 6. ἀπείθ. Eph. 5. 6. 10. κατέπαυσεν. 13. κτίσις.

CHAPTER V.
NON-C. 2. περίκ. ἀσθ. 12. διὰ τὸν χ.

CHAPTER VI.
NON-C. 6. Acc. after γευσαμένους. 17. ἐμεσίτευσε.

CHAP. IV. 2. ὁ λ. τῆς ἀκοῆς] See Rom. 10. 16, M. 4. 24. "The word of the message," i.e. " of the Gospel." Here ἀκοὴ = εὐαγγέλιον.

12. μερισμοῦ] Schleusner "ad intimos animi recessus"; as if parting asunder *implies* the very middle or innermost part: and Grimm, apparently following him, though without acknowledgment, gives "usque ad absconditissimum illum locum, quo animus et anima inter se discernuntur." This appears to be the probable meaning. To take the word in an active sense, as Vulg. "divisio," and our E. V. "dividing asunder," is unjustifiable. Supra 2. 4 it is clearly passive, "gifts." But there is the same ambiguity in many of the Latin and English words signifying "division, distribution, assignment"; active forms used passively.

14. κ. τ. ὁμολογίας] "Let us hold fast to our *vow*," "our *covenant* with God." V. A. use the word for נֶדֶר, votum, Lev. 22. 18, Deut. 12. 6. Comp. 1 Tim. 6. 12 with this passage, and Jerem. 44. 25, τὰς ὁμολογίας ποιήσομεν ὡς ὡμολογήκαμεν. V. A. for נְדָרֵינוּ אֲשֶׁר נָדַרְנוּ. Schl.

CHAP. V. 7. ἀπὸ τῆς εὐλ.] "by reason of," "as the result of..." = מִן, Prov. 13. 11. The *Hebrew* preposition is constantly used in *this* sense among many others (Jude 23, note); whereas ἀπό, its *primary literal* equivalent, is put for it in V. A., without any discrimination of diversity of meaning, almost universally, as though it were its one sole and sufficient exponent. Gen. 9. 11, οὐκ ἀποθανεῖται πᾶσα σάρξ ἔτι ἀπὸ τοῦ ὕδατος τοῦ κατακλυσμοῦ. Ps. 76. 7, τίς ἀντιστήσεταί σοι ἀπὸ τῆς ὀργῆς σου; Hence, probably, it passed into an idiom, and became a vernacular usage. "Having his prayer heard by reason of his piety," "he learnt, from what he suffered himself, Son though he was, the difficulty of obedience."

CHAP. VI. 1. τὸν τῆς ἀρχῆς...λ.] "The initiatory doctrine," "the elementary teaching," of Christ: "the first principles of Christianity."

5. μέλλοντος αἰ.] = οἰκουμένη ἡ μελλ. cf. 2. 5.

7. εὐλογία] "blessing," 2 Cor. 9. 5. V. A. for בְּרָכָה, Lev. 25. 21, Ez. 34. 26, ὑετὸν εὐλογίας.

Chap. VII. 1. Who was Melchisedek? Clearly he must have been, in Abraham's belief, the Patriarch of the Holy Chosen Seed, the family of Shem: Head and Priest of the race: to whom Abraham paid tithe: one of his ancestors; the Representative, by the law of primogeniture, of the rights and dignities of the Sacred Line: whom Abraham, heir of all the promises, acknowledged as his superior, in things human and divine. Which of the descendants of Shem fulfilled these conditions, as first-born in his generation, being alive at the time and within reach of Abraham, on the *same* side of the Euphrates; on the other side of which they were all born, and so far as we know, chiefly lived? *One* there was, who, if we may in any degree trust the Jewish Genealogies, lived to a great age and was alive then: whose very name implies that he *crossed;* who was evidently well known in the country as a Progenitor of Abraham; who has left his name to Abraham and all his seed, as their universal designation: who is especially pointed out in the Bible, as the prominent and most remarkable of the progeny of Shem, signalled out for special distinction above Elam and Asshur and Lud and Aram. For Shem is called emphatically (Gen. 10. 21) "the father of all the children of *Eber*" = עֵבֶר, "qui transivit": (indicating probably his crossing the great River at the time of the dispersion, intimated by the name of his son Peleg = "division"), and Abraham is called, by a patronymic, "the Hebrew," i.e. "the Eberite," or "descendant of Eber": and after *him* and not after Abraham, all the children of Abraham are called. Eber, Priest by birth-right, "a Prince in Religion," מַלְכִּי צֶדֶק = Melchisedek (as he was *temporal* king of Salem), the type and emblem and embodiment of the Priesthood of the First-born,—seems to have been selected by divine appointment, as the impersonation and representative of the Order, of which Christ was a Priest, by his descent from Judah, in whose favour Reuben, Simeon, and Levi were set aside. (Hebr. 7, passim.) If, as seems most probable, Melchisedek is *not a name* but a *title;* no one, in the long list of our Lord's Progenitors, appears so nearly to fulfil the conditions of the tradition, as Eber; a man so wonderfully honoured by what is implied, rather than said, in Holy Writ, —so pre-eminently immortalised as the stem and root of the Hebrew race, by the transmission of his name, through so many ages of the world's history. If *he* was not Melchisedek, *who was?* The words ἀπάτωρ, ἀμ., ἀγενεαλ....in verse 3,—as they cannot, of *course*, be taken *literally*,—may imply no more than the unquestionable fact, that when Melchisedek is introduced into the Sacred Story, no statement is made as to his parentage or descent, or the time of his birth or death. He appears on the scene and disappears mysteriously; but *that* in no way

CHAPTER IX.

HEBR. 3. σκηνὴ...ἁγίων. 5. X. δόξης. 8. τὴν τ. ἁ. ὁ.

---

militates against his being a real personage, subject to all the necessary conditions and laws of human existence.

5, 6. "And whereas those who..." οἱ μὲν, "in contrast to all this, he...," ὁ δέ.

11. "God's people had-been-legislated-for, on it as a basis," "had received the Law on the understanding of the Levitical Priesthood." Compare 8. 6. Grimm.

15. εἰ] Acts 26. 8, 23: "if, *as is the fact*," "seeing that." *What is* περισσ. ἔτι κ.? Clearly, the statement above in 12: "the necessity of a change in *the law*," i.e. the Divine economy and dispensation: "This necessity is more abundantly patent and demonstrable, from the fact that..." As a consequence of the excellency of the new Priesthood, the Religion connected therewith must take a new and higher excellence, i.e. a spiritual.

26. ἔπρεπε] "was proper for us," "befitting, beseeming."

CHAP. VIII. 8. ἡμέραι ἔρχ....καὶ συντ.] Hebraic construction, both in use of ἡμέραι (M. 2. 1, note), and καὶ = ן = when: "a time is coming when..."

11. ἀπὸ μικροῦ αὐτῶν...] לְמִקְטַנָּם וְעַד גְּדוֹלָם, Jerem. 31. 34, literal rendering, except the omission of ן and ן which have great force in the original. εἰδήσουσι, N. C.

CHAP. IX. 1. δικαιώματα] V. A. passim for חֹק, מִשְׁפָּט, ordinationes, generally rendered "statutes" in E. V., Deut. 4. 1, Ps. 119. 5, 8, 12. τό τε ἅγιον κοσμικόν. Pearson on Creed (Art. 6) quotes the Syriac rendering of this passage, בֵּית קוּדְשָׁא עָלְמָנָיא, "*domus sancta mundana*": the part of the Sanctuary which represented this lower world (i.e. the Outer Court and Holy Place), as the Holy of Holies, or Most Holy, represented Heaven: (which Josephus expressly states to have been the belief of the Jews). So, perhaps, the Vulgate "sanctum *sæculare*." Εἶχε μὲν οὖν, a new argument. "Aye, and to take other ground: the first dispensation had its appointed rites of *service*," "common united worship," (λατρεία = cultus Dei *publicus*,) "and its Outer Tabernacle," for general use, of public access, entered day by day, in which men moved constantly to and fro, *as in this lower world*.

5. κατὰ μέρος] "part by part," "in detail"; *particularly*, E. V.

7. ἀγνόημα] like ἁμαρτία, loses its first sense in its adopted one: and includes *all sin* that is not wilful and presumptuous.

Non-C. 17. ἐπεί...ὅτε. 24. ἐμφ. τῷ π.

Chapter X.

Hebr. 19. παρρ. εἰς τ. ε. τῶν ἁ. 38. ἐκ π. and καὶ ἐὰν.
Non-C. 34. ὕπαρξιν.

---

10. Can ἐπὶ βρ. κ.τ.λ. depend upon δικαιώματα σ.? "Authorised and prescribed demands upon the body with respect to meats..." ἐπὶ = עַל. Otherwise the rendering in E. V. seems allowable; "carnal ordinances," i. e. "for the body."

14. διὰ Πν. αἰων.] Compare R. 1. 4, 1 Tim. 3. 16, 1 P. 3. 18.

26. συντελείᾳ] The point in which the τέλη of two things, succeeding one the other, meet. 1 Cor. 10. 11. The confluence, or meeting of the two æras, Ante-Christian and Christian. The Jews had, in their theosophy, three systems, (1) Ante-Mosaic, (2) Mosaic, (3) Messianic. The Sacred Writer is here speaking of the two latter. V. A. have συντέλεια for קֵץ finis, Dan. 12. 4, 13.

Chap. X. 5. σῶμα κατηρτίσω μοι] Exact quotation from V. A. How they ever came so to render the original, אָזְנַיִם כָּרִיתָ לִּי, "mine ears hast thou bored," is inexplicable. We know, Ex. 21. 6, that this means "thou hast claimed me as a servant." Here it would seem as if, in the mind of the Translators of V. A., the providing a human body for Christ, was equivalent to making Him a Servant: as Phil. 2. 8, μορφὴν δούλου λαβών, ἐν ὁμοιώματι ἀνθρ. γενόμενος.

6. V. A. have ᾔτησας here: but Ps. 50. 16, ὁλοκαυτ. οὐκ εὐδοκήσεις, without preposition: as also Ps. 84. 1, Gen. 33. 10. Note, M. 3. 17.

19. ἔχοντες] has three accusatives after it, παρρησίαν, ὁδόν, ἱερέα.

37. ὁ ἐρχ.] One of the common names of Messiah, from Gen. 49. 18, Is. 25. 9. Its use here shows that as yet only part of the purpose of His coming was fulfilled.

38. There is a considerable variation in V. A., as quoted here, from the original Hebrew, to which our E. V. is much closer. For בֶּאֱמוּנָתוֹ, "by *his* faith," V. A. gives ἐκ πίστεώς μου, "by faith in me"; and for נַפְשׁוֹ, "*his* soul," ἡ ψυχή μου. And their substitution of ἐκ for בְּ is curious.

39. V. A. 2 Chr. 14. 13, render by περιποίησις מִחְיָה, "revivification," "restoration," "recovery": which is its exact meaning here.

HEBREWS. 107

Chapter XI.

Non-C. 8. μὴ...ποῦ. 12. τῷ πλ. 37. φόνῳ μ.
Sept. 5. τοῦ μὴ ἰδ. for לֹ.

Chapter XII.

Non-C. 2. ἀντὶ. 10. 11. πρὸς ὀλ. ἡμ. and τὸ παρὸν. 15. ὑστερῶν ἀπό.

Chapter XIII.

Non-C. 5. ἀρκ. τοῖς π. 7. ἔκβασιν.

Chap. XI. 1. ὑπόστασις] Cap. 3. 14, 2 Cor. 9. 4, 11. 17. In all these it means "confidence," "well grounded assurance." *Here* it seems rather to mean, in its stricter and closer sense (both of derivation and construction), "substantiation," "realisation"; the instrument or process, by which we give substance and reality to things: and ἔλεγχος not so much "the test," as "the mode of testing":—"illud, quo subsistunt quæ sperantur; quod demonstrat quæ non cernuntur." Beza. Without faith in a principle or doctrine, acting as if we believed it, we cannot test it, or prove it to be true. "Faith is the process and instrument by which we give substance and reality to things hoped for, and test and ascertain the truth of things unseen."

21. ἐπὶ τὸ ἄ. τῆς ῥάβδου] From V. A. who apparently read מַטֶּה, "a staff," for מִטָּה, "a bed." Vulg. has "lectuli caput." It seems clear there were no vowel points in the Hebrew MSS. used by V. A.

28. πεποίηκε τὸ π.] Special use of ποιέω for θύω. Note, M. 26. 18.

Chap. XII. 15. μή τις ῥίζα π. ἄ. φ.] This is almost an exact quotation from Deut. 29. 18. E. V. "a root that beareth gall and wormwood," and in Margin "a poisonful herb": (πικρία = poison. See Note, Acts 8. 23) i.e. "one who poisons God's people with false teaching or bad example"; as the context shows. And such is the meaning here.

Chap. XIII. 7. ἔκβασις] in Apocrypha = "exitus," "eventus." Sap. 2. 17, 8. 9, 11. 15, "significatione a profanis alienâ," Grimm: —"the issue and outcome of their walk on earth."

15. ὁμολογ. τῷ ὀνόματι] Parallel to R. 15. 9, τῷ ὀν. σου ψαλῶ, which is a direct quotation from V. A. (see note). Here it is a sort of confusion with ἐξομολογεῖσθαι.

S. JAMES.

Chapter I.
HEBR. 6. ἐν π. 11. προσώπου and πορείαις. 13. ὅτι. 1 J. 4. 20. 23. τὸ πρόσ. τῆς γ. 25. ἀκρ. ἐπιλ.

Chapter II.
HEBR. 1. ἐν προσ. 2. 4. Whole verse. 5. 10. 10. ὅστις τηρήσει: fut. 23. ἐλογ. εἰς.

CHAP. I. 3. δοκίμιον] V. A. for מִצְרֵף = the instrument or medium of testing. Prov. 27. 21.

17. πᾶσα δόσις ἀγ....] Hebraic construction. "Every gift, *good*, every bounty, *perfect*, cometh down from above": "Every gift of God is by its very origin altogether and entirely good and perfect"; with no admixture of evil or blemish in it: a reply to the heresy of verse 13, ἀπὸ Θ. πειράζομαι. God permits, but does not send, evil.

τοῦ πατρὸς τῶν φώτων] i. e. "the Creator of the Orbs of Heaven." Jerem. 4. 23, Ps. 135. 7 (apud Aquilam, ἄστρα). The name and attribute which most forcibly suggests *unchangeableness*. Acts 16. 29.

18. ἀπεκύησεν ἡ. λ. ἀλ.] "He gave us a new birth by virtue of a word of truth"; "a word that cannot deceive or fail": i. e. by the holy formula, ordained by our Lord himself, for Baptism. Eph. 5. 26, note.

25. παρακύπτειν] V. A. for הַשְׁקִיף, "to bend down to scrutinise." Gen. 26. 8, Prov. 7. 6. νόμον ἐλευθερίας: note, Gal. 5. 1.

27. θρησκεία = "outward devotion," "*worship*." Deeds of mercy and careful avoidance of the polluting influences of the world, are pure worship: i. e. "elements of it," "essential parts of it": not, of course, the whole of it.

CHAP. II. 4. καὶ for ἄρα, a common meaning of ן. "Have you not, in fact, made partial selections, and acted as judges influenced by wrong considerations?": gen. for adj. "wrong-thinking judges."

Non-C. 14. λέγῃ ἔχ.

Chapter IV.

Non-C. 1. ἡδονῶν. 4. ἔχθρα τοῦ Θ. 13. ἄγε, with plural. 14. πρὸς ὀλίγον.

Chapter V.

Non-C. 4. χώρας. 10. ἐλάλησαν τῷ ὀνόμ. 12. ἤτω.
Sept. 17. προσηύξ. τοῦ μὴ β. M. 2. 6.

---

5. πλ. ἐν π.] "rich in faith": a correct idiom in English, as in Hebrew: but utterly incorrect, and bad in Greek.

8. ν. βασιλικὸς] "The law of our King Jesus."

10. ἔνοχος] See note, 1 Cor. 11. 27.

20. κενός] = μάταιος in V. A.: they are constantly interchanged as renderings of same words, הֶבֶל and שָׁוְא.

Chap. III. 6. Mr W. Randolph suggests a parallelism, in verses 5 and 6:

(5) *a.* ὀλίγον πῦρ, *b.* ἡλίκην ὕ. ἀν.,
(6) *a.* ἡ γλ. πῦρ, *b.* ὁ κόσμ. τῆς ἀδικ. (ἀνάπτεται ὑπ' αὐτῆς),

which he thinks is confirmed by φλογίζ. τ. τρ. τῆς γ. And he quotes in illustration Micah 1. 4:

a. Molten were the mountains, *b.* and the valleys were cleft,
a. as wax before the fire, *b.* as waters poured down a precipice (cleave the face of it).

15, 17. σοφία] = חָכְמָה, and is used in its Hebrew sense, so common in Proverbs, and throughout O. T., of "*religion*," "piety."

Chap. IV. 5. The *quotation* is in verse 6, from Prov. 3. 34. "Do you think that Holy Scripture ever speaks in vain? The spirit within us feels strong desires, that tend to envy: but God giveth grace yet stronger. And therefore the Holy Writer saith...." There is *no quotation* from H. S. in 5: only an introduction to *that* in 6.

1 S. PETER.

CHAPTER I.
HEBR. 4. εἰς ὑμᾶς. 14. τέκνα ὑ.

CHAPTER III.
HEBR. 4. ὁ κρ....ἄνθ. 20. εἰς ἦν for בְּ.
NON-C. 13. μιμηταὶ. 15. μετὰ π.
SEPT. 5. ἐλπ. ἐπὶ. 1 Tim. 5. 5.

CHAP. I. 1. παρεπιδ. διασπ.] "dispersion-sojourners."
11. τὰ εἰς Χρ. παθ.] Some render "the sufferings destined for Christ": but can this meaning be got out of the Greek? May we not possibly regard the words as *the literal* rendering of לְ used, as often, for genitive? 1 K. 15. 31, 1 S. 22. 30.
17. εἰ] with indicative, stating an admitted fact: "seeing that..."
18. μάταιος] = "*heathenish*," as opposed to σοφὸς, which is the Hebrew definition of the true believer. James 3. 17.
22. ὑπακοὴ τῆς ἀλ.] R. 1. 5, 2 Cor. 10. 5. Very remarkable construction.

CHAP. II. 1. λογικὸν] R. 12. 1. "Spiritual": nutriment for the λόγος, the reason or immaterial part of man.
8. λίθος προσκ.] = אֶבֶן מִכְשׁוֹל, צוּר. Is. 8. 14.
9. λαὸς εἰς περιπ.] Tit. 2. 14, note. Compare 1 Chr. 29. 3.

CHAP. III. 9. εἰς τοῦτο......κληρονομ.] "Ye have been called to inherit blessing," i.e. "have been admitted into all the hopes and privileges of the Christian covenant," εἰς τοῦτο, "for this very purpose," "with this object in view," "on this condition," namely, the fulfilment of the rule laid down in 8, 9. St Peter enforces this argument, based

Chapter IV.

Non-C. 2. ἐπιθυμίαις......βιῶσαι. 3. πεπορευμ. 4. ξενίζ. 8. Participle nom. absolute. 12. ξένου. 14. κατά.

Chapter V.

Hebr. 3. κλήρων. 10. ὁ Θ. π. χ. and ἐν Χ. 12. εἰς ἥν.

---

on their intuitive perception of their new religious obligation, by an apt quotation from the writings of a Saint of old. This connexion of the words (ἐκλήθ. ἵνα) agrees with the context and the logical sequence of the passage, which the other combination (εἰς τοῦτο ἵνα) does not.

21. συν. ἀγ. ἐπερώτημα εἰς Θ.] "the earnest prayer for,"—"the searching after,"—a good conscience towards God.

Chap. V. 3. τῶν κλήρων] "the divisions" of God's people: "the portions allotted" to the charge of each Presbyter, i.e. "*Ruler*," in the Church. "Neither as lording it over their allotted fields of labour and administration."

2 S. PETER.

Chapter I.
Hebr. 5. ἐν. 20. πᾶσα...οὐ. 21. Θ. ἄνθ.

Chapter II.
Hebr. 1. αἱρ. ἀπ. 2. ἡ ὁ. τῆς ἀ. 10. ὀπίσω....πορευ. 14. κατ. τέκνα.
Non-C. 7. καταπ. ὑ. 10. κυριότητος. Jude 8. 14. ἀκαταπ. ἁμ. 20. εἰ, with subj.

Chapter III.
Hebr. 3. ἐπ' ἐσχ....ἐμπ. 18. εἰς ἡμ. αἰ.
Non-C. 9. Gen. after βραδ. 11. Plural, ἀναστ.

Chap. I. 3. διὰ δόξης καὶ ἀ.] I cannot translate this, nor can I understand the force of the preposition, by the light of Classical usage or Hebraistic misuse.

17. εἰς ὃν εὐδόκησα] V. A. *generally* has ἐπὶ or ἐν with this verb: not *always*. Gen. 33. 10, Ps. 51. 16, 19, 85. 1, there is no preposition either in Hebr. or Gr.

Chap. III. 12. δι' ἥν] " for *the manifestation* and accomplishment of which day."

1 S. JOHN.

Chapter I.
HEBR. 2. ἦν πρὸς τὸν π. J. 1. 1, note.

Chapter II.
HEBR. 1. παράκ....πρός. 21. πᾶν...οὐκ: infra 3. 15. Rev. 21. 27. 28. ἀπ' αὐτοῦ = מִפָּנָיו, coram illo. Acts 25. 9, note.

NON-C. 6. λέγων μένειν. 18. ἐσχ. ὥ.

Chapter III.
HEBR. 15. 17. κλ. τὰ σπλάγχνα.

NON-C. 5. ἄρῃ = take away. 16. ψυχὴν ἔθηκε = laid down. Note, J. 10. 17.

Chapter V.
NON-C. 15. ἐὰν οἶδ. 16. ἐρωτ. Mc. 4. 10.

CHAP. III. 18. μὴ ἀγ. λόγῳ ἀλλ' ἐν ἔργῳ] Strange diversity of construction after same verb, to express the same meaning, without and with a preposition: the first strictly grammatical, the second, Hebraic. M. 3. 11, note.

CHAP. IV. 2. "That Jesus has come, the Incarnate Messiah": or "that Messiah has come in human nature, the man Jesus."

16. ἐν ἡμῖν] 2 Cor. 8. 7. A most curious use of ἐν: I can give no explanation of it, or of the μεθ' ἡμῶν in 17: and I cannot agree with Grimm's explanation, that ἡ ἀγάπη μεθ' ἡμῶν means "amor mutuus inter nos et Deum": as being against the sense of the passage, and the requirements of fitting reverence: as if ἡμεῖς could comprehend us AND God.

2 S. JOHN.

HEBR. 1. ἐν ἀ. 12. γ. πρὸς ὑ.

---

4. ἐν ἀληθείᾳ] = ἐν δικαιοσύνῃ; just as אֱמֶת = צֶדֶק, Ps. 111. 7, 119. 151, 86. 11, as so frequently found in V. A. and N. T. Notes, M. 11. 19, L. 16. 9, 2 Th. 2. 10. Compare 2 P. 1. 2, 3 John 3, 4, 12.

---

3 S. JOHN.

2. εὔχομαι] followed by inf. pres. ungrammatical.
5. πιστόν] = "an act of Christian principle, of faith."
12. ὑπ' αὐ. τῆς ἀλ.] *Can* this mean "*by his holy life itself?*" 2 J. 4. It seems impossible to get any meaning out of our English Version "by the truth itself."

S. JUDE.

HEBR. 6. εἰς κ. μ. ἡ., no article. 7. ὀπίσω σ. ἑ. 14. ἐν ἁ. μ. 16. θαυμ. πρ. 20. ἐν Πν. 'Α. 23. ἐσπιλ. ἀπὸ.

NON-C. 4. τινες ἀνθ. 4. προγεγρ. 5. τὸ δεύτερον. 8. κυριότητα. 8. δόξας. 11. ἐξεχύθ. 19. μὴ. 22. οὓς μὲν...δὲ.

---

3. ἀν. ἔσχον] Can this be an instance of the Epistolary Imperfect, as in Latin? Compare Gal. 4. 20. Here we clearly, in English, want a *present* tense.

11. τῇ ὁδῷ] Construction without a preposition unusual.

14. τούτοις] The "*de his*" of Vulgate, and "*of these*" of English Version, have no grammatical justification. The word *cannot* be so rendered: the only possible meaning is "prophesied *to* them," "forewarned them," "spoke in the name of God to them." For ἐν ἁγ. μυρ. see note, M. 3. 11. Also L. 14. 31, 22. 49, 1 Cor. 4. 21, Apoc. 13. 10, 19. 15.

23. One of the meanings of the preposition מִן is "*by*," Gen. 9. 11, Job 4. 9, 7. 14, Is. 28. 7: but its literal rendering in V. A. for its almost universal sense "from," is ἀπὸ: they scarcely ever put any other word for it. Hence ἀπὸ being used for ὑπὸ in many instances, as in those passages cited above, came to be regarded as equivalent to it by readers of V. A.; and the usage has crept into N. T. See Apoc. 2. 11 for similar use of ἐκ. I cite a few instances of ἀπὸ put for מִן in V. A., as if at random, without any connexion with the sense. Numb. 32. 22, Deut. 14. 24, Ps. 68. 30, Jer. 26. 9, 32. 43, 34. 22, Is. 52. 14.

REVELATION.

The deviations from grammatical correctness in the Apocalypse are so violent and so astonishing, as to defy explanation. Some few of them may be traceable to Hebraic influences: as I have endeavoured to point out. The others I have simply left untouched. The style of S. John in the Gospel and Epistles is so remarkably pure,—so comparatively free from Hebraisms or non-Classical words and forms,—so much more like the language of the best Greek Authors; that these peculiarities are all the more perplexing. They have given rise to innumerable speculations ancient and modern: but no satisfactory explanation of them has hitherto been found.

CHAP. I. 4. ἀπὸ ὁ ὤν...] Anomalous construction, clearly traceable to the absence of inflexion in Hebrew nouns, which made such a violation of grammar less startling to a Jew writing in Greek.

ὁ ἐρχ.] We say in English, "past, present, and *to come*": and the same idea for "that which is to be, which will exist hereafter," (i.e. the future) is common in Hebrew, expressed by בָּא and אָתָה: V. A. ἔρχομαι. Is. 27. 6, הַבָּאִים, οἱ ἐρχ. "future generations." Jerem. 47. 4, Is. 41. 23, 44. 7, 45. 11. 41. 22 הַבָּאוֹת, 45. 11 אוֹתִיוֹת, τὰ ἐπερχ., "the things that are to come," in Vulgate "ventura." And hence the form is used, with ὁ ἦν, and ὁ ὤν here, as one of the categories of sempiternal existence. It is curious that whereas Hebrew, Latin and English alike use words that imply "coming": the Greek equivalent implies "delay, keeping back," viz. μέλλειν. And it is remarkable that this verb is used *once only* in V. A. to express futurity, Is. 48. 6, ἃ μέλλει γενέσθαι for צְרֻרוֹת, recondita, and not more than six or seven times in Apocrypha.

CHAP. II. 16. πολεμ. μετ᾽ αὐ.] Literal for עִם נִלְחַם, "pugnare contra." 2 K. 14. 5, in V. A. ἐπ. μετά. Infra 11. 7 ποιήσει μετ᾽ αὐτῶν πόλ. So Vulg. "pugnabo cum illis in gladio oris mei." The English idiom coincides with the Hebrew: but μετά in this sense is against all good Greek usage. See Grimm. For ἐν ῥομφαίᾳ see note, L. 22. 49, which Vulgate renders, "Domine, si percutimus in gladio": utterly sacrificing the sense in slavish adherence to a foreign idiom,—which the Translator, apparently, did not understand,—*twice* in one short sentence: as in the verse now before us.

CHAP. III. 4. ὀνόματα] "persons," as Acts 1. 15. Infra 11. 13.

CHAP. IV. 6. κύκλῳ τοῦ θρ.] 7. 11. A form borrowed from V. A. Numb. 11. 24, סְבִיבוֹת הָאֹהֶל, κύκλῳ τῆς σκηνῆς. Ps. 79. 3, κύκλῳ Ἰερουσαλήμ. Ez. 6. 2, Numb. 1. 53 for לְ סָבִיב. Gen. 35. 5 τὰς κύκλῳ αὐτῶν κώμας. Grimm cites Xen. Cyr. 4. 5. 5 as an instance of the phrase in a Classical Author.

10. Future for present: Hebraic irregularity and want of precision as to difference between tenses: with which every student of Hebrew is familiar.

CHAP. VI. 10. ἐκδ. τὸ αἷμα ἡμῶν ἀπό] = דָּרַשׁ דָּם מֵעִם, "sanguinem repetiit ab aliquo," "caedem ultus est." Here we have a blending of the two ideas, in the one verb.

CHAP. XIII. 3. ἐθαύμ. ὀπ.] = "went in wonder after."
12. ἡ πλ. τοῦ θ. αὐτοῦ] "His deadly wound."

CHAP. XIV. 14. The harvest in N. T. parables always represents "the ingathering of the good," M. 13. 30: the vintage, "the judgment of the wicked." See Joel 3. 13.

CHAP. XVI. 3. ψυχὴ ζωῆς] = "living soul." Comp. ξύλον ζ., supra 2. 7.

CHAP. XIX. 8. τὰ δικαιώματα] R. 5. 18, Heb. 9. 1.

INDEX OF GREEK WORDS.

ἀγαπητοὶ Θεοῦ, M. 25. 34, R. 1. 7.
ἄγγελος, "minister," "agent," 2 C. 12. 7.
ἄδικος = ψευδὴς, 1 Cor. 13. 6, L. 16. 9.
αἰσχύνη, "disappointment," R. 5. 4.
αἰτέω = ἐρωτάω, M. 15. 23.
ἀκοή, J. 12. 38.
ἀλλάττειν ἐν, R. 1. 23.
ἀνὰ μέσον, 1 Cor. 6. 5.
ὁ ἄνθρωπος, "mankind," J. 2. 25.
ἀνθ' ὧν, "because," L. 1. 20, R. 5. 12.
ἀπείθεια, Eph. 5. 6.
ἀπὸ for ὑπὸ, 1 Cor. 1. 30, Jude 23.
ἀπὸ for "e numero," L. 24. 42.
ἀπὸ, Acts 25. 9, Heb. 5. 7.
ἀφίημι, "leave," M. 18. 12, L. 18. 16.

βάλλειν = "put," M. 7. 28, 9. 38.
ἐν βάρει, 1 Th. 2. 6.
βαστάζειν τὸν σταυρὸν, L. 14. 27.
βδέλυγμα...ἐρημώσεως, M. 24. 15.
βλέπειν ἀπὸ, Mk. 8. 15.

γὰρ = יִּב = ἀλλὰ, R. 5. 7.
γέεννα, M. 5. 22, 29.
γενεὰ, "history," A. 8. 33.
γράμμα, 2 C. 3. 6.

δαιμόνια, "evil spirits," M. 9. 33.
δέομαί σου, A. 8. 34.
δεῦρο, A. 7. 34.
διὰ τοῦτο, "for all this," J. 19. 11.
διὰ, "out of the midst of," R. 2. 27.
δίκαιος = ἀληθὴς, M. 11. 19, L. 16. 9.
δικαιοσύνη Θεοῦ, R. 1. 17.
δικαίωμα, H. 9. 1.

δόξα, "approval," J. 5. 44.
„   "likeness," 1 C. 11. 7.
δυνάμεις, M. 7. 22, L. 21. 26.

Ἑβραῖος, Ἑλληνιστὴς, A. 6. 1.
εἰ interrogative, M. 12. 10.
εἰ negandi, Mk. 8. 12.
εἰ μὴ = ἀλλὰ, R. 14. 14.
εἶναι εἰς = γίγνεσθαι, M. 2. 6.
σὺ εἶπας, M. 26. 25.
εἰρήνη ὑμῖν, J. 20. 19.
εἰς, "apud," M. 13. 56, 27. 9.
εἰς εἰρήνην, κενὸν... Mk. 5. 34.
εἰς, "with respect to," A. 2. 25.
εἰς, "until," Mk. 3. 29, 1 Th. 4. 15.
ἐκ πίστεως,...περιτομῆς, M. 5. 37.
ἐκ for ὑπὸ, R. 1. 4, 1 Cor. 1. 30.
Ἕλλην, "heathen," Mk. 7. 26.
ἐλπίζειν ἐπὶ, "trust," 1 T. 5. 5.
ἔμπροσθεν for ἐνώπιον, M. 5. 16.
ἐν, literal for בְּ, M. 3. 11, 1 C. 7. 15, A. 1. 15.
ἐν adjurandi, M. 5. 34, R. 9. 1.
ἐν, "coram," ἐν Κυρίῳ, Col. 3. 18.
ἐν for εἰς, 1 C. 7. 15.
ἐν δακτύλῳ Θ. L. 11. 20, A. 1. 15, 27, 28, Vulgate literalisms.
ἔνοχος, M. 5. 22, 1 C. 11. 27.
ἔξελθε τὸ πν., Nom. for Voc. Mk. 5. 8.
ἐξομολογεῖσθαι = "praise," M. 11. 25.
ἐπὶ = "juxta," Mk. 8. 4, 1 Cor. 6. 1.
ἐπὶ, 1 C. 8. 11, R. 5. 12.
ἐπ' ἄρτῳ ζῆν, M. 4. 4, 18. 5.
ἐρχόμενος, Ap. 1. 4.
ἔσεσθε, Fut. for Imp. M. 5. 48.

INDEX OF GREEK WORDS.

ἑτοιμασία = "basis," E. 6. 15.
εὐαγγέλιον Θ. omission of def. article, R. 1. 1, M. 1. 1, J. 1. 1, A. 13. 10.
εὐδοκέω, M. 3. 17.
εὐδοκία, M. 11. 26, 18. 14.
εὐλογέω, M. 26. 26.
εὐλογία, "donum," 2 C. 9. 5.
εὐσέβεια, "our holy religion," 1 T. 3. 16.

ζῶ ἐγώ, R. 14. 11, 2 C. 1. 18.

ἡλικία μικρός, dat. of "part," L. 19. 3.
ἡμέραι, M. 2. 1, Hebr. 8. 8.

Θεῷ ἀστεῖος, A. 7. 20.
θνήσκειν τῇ ἁμαρτίᾳ, dative of "person," R. 6. 2, 20, 1 C. 6. 13, 2 C. 12. 7.
θνητὸν...φθαρτὸν, 1 C. 15. 54.

ἴδια, J. 16. 32, A. 4. 23.
ἵλεώς σοι, "God forbid," M. 16. 22.
ἵνα μή, G. 5. 17.
ἰσχυρὸς, M. 3. 11.

καὶ for ἵνα, 1 Th. 3. 5.
„ οὖν, L. 10. 2.
„ ἄρα, Jac. 2. 4.
καὶ...καὶ, A. 1. 10.
κακολογεῖν = ἀτιμάζειν, M. 15. 4.
κατά, "with respect to," R. 11. 2.
κεφαλὴ γωνίας, M. 21. 42.
κληρονομεῖν, Tit. 3. 7.
κοινὸς, "unclean," M. 15. 11.
κύκλῳ τοῦ..., Ap. 4. 6.

λαμβάνειν πρόσωπον, L. 20. 21.
λόγος πορνείας, M. 5. 32.

μαλακία, M. 4. 23.
μαρὰν ἀθά, 1 C. 16. 22.
μαρτύριον, 1 C. 2. 1.
μάταιος = κενὸς, R. 8. 20.
Μελχισεδὲκ, Heb. 7. 1.
μετά, Hebraic, M. 24. 31, L. 24. 52.
μήποτε, "in case that," M. 13. 14.

ὁδὸς K., A. 9. 2.
οἰκεῖοι τῆς πίστεως, G. 6. 10.
οἰκουμένη μέλλουσα, H. 2. 5.
ὁμολογεῖν ἐν, M. 10. 32.
ὀνόματί σου ψαλῶ, R. 15. 9.
ὀρθοτομεῖν, 2 T. 2. 15.
ὅς for τίς, M. 26. 50.
ὅτι "asseverandi," M. 7. 23, L. 4. 12.
οὗ εἵνεκεν = ἀνθ' ὧν, L. 4. 18.
οὐ φονεύσεις, M. 19. 18. Fut. for Imp.
ὀφείλημα = ἁμαρτία, M. 6. 11.

παθήματα εἰς Χρ., 1 P. 1. 11.
παρά, with acc. "near," Mk. 4. 1.
παράκλησις, "teaching," A. 4. 36, R. 15. 4.
Παράκλητος, J. 14. 16.
παρρησίᾳ, Mk. 8. 32, J. 16. 25.
πεποιθέναι ἐπὶ, M. 27. 43.
περιούσιος, Tit. 2. 14.
περιπατεῖν, Mk. 7. 5, G. 5. 25.
περιποίησις, E. 1. 14, Heb. 10. 39.
περιτομὴ Χρ., "Baptism," Col. 2. 11.
περιτομῆς, οἱ ἐκ, A. 6. 1.
πικρία, "poison," A. 8. 21.
πίστις Ἰ. Χρ., R. 1. 22.
πνευματικὸς, "inspired," 1 C. 14. 37, Mk. 12. 36.
„ "supernatural," 1 C. 10. 3, 14. 1.
ποιεῖν τὸ πάσχα, M. 26. 18.
πολεμεῖν μετά, Ap. 2. 16.
πολιτεύεσθαι, A. 23. 1.
πονηρὸς ὀφθαλμὸς, M. 20. 15.
ποταμοὶ ὕδατος ζῶντος, J. 7. 38.
ποτήριον, παροψὶς, M. 23. 26.
πρέπει, "seems right," Heb. 2. 10.
προθέσεως ἄρτοι, Mk. 2. 26.
πρός, "with respect to," Acts 28. 25.
„ "apud," M. 13. 56, J. 1. 1.
„ ἑαυτούς, J. 20. 10.
„ οὐδὲ ἓν ῥῆμα, M. 27. 14.
„ καιρὸν ὥρας..., 1 Th. 2. 17.
προστεθήσεται, M. 6. 33.
ἐν προσώπῳ, 2 C. 2. 10.
πρὸ προσώπου, Mk. 1. 2.
προφάσει προσεύχονται, dative of "manner, cause, time," L. 18. 33, 20. 47, A. 9. 31, G. 6. 12.

INDEX OF GREEK WORDS.

πτωχὸς for ταπεινὸς, M. 5. 3.
πῶρος, "callositas," 2 C. 3. 14.

ὁ ῥηθεὶς, M. 3. 3.
ῥῆμα = "thing," M. 4. 4, L. 2. 15.
ῥίζα = "surculus," not "radix," R. 15.12.

σημεῖον περιτομῆς, R. 4. 1.
σκάνδαλον, M. 18. 7.
σκῆνος, "corpus," 2 C. 5. 1.
σκιὰ θανάτου, M. 4. 15.
σοφία, "religion," Jac. 3. 15, 1 P. 1. 18.
σπλάγχνα, 2 Cor. 6. 13, Ph. 1. 8.
στρατεύειν στρατείαν, 1 Tim. 1. 18.
στρατία οὐρανοῦ, A. 7. 42.
συγχέω, A. 2. 6.
συντέλεια τῶν αἱ., M. 13. 39.
σώζειν, "sanare," M. 9. 21, A. 14. 9.

τί ἐμοὶ καὶ σοί; J. 2. 4.
τοῦ, with infinitive, M. 2. 6, R. 15. 22.

υἱὸς γεέννης, et similia, M. 8. 12, J. 17. 12.
ὑπακοὴ πίστεως, R. 1. 5.
ὑπὲρ, "with respect to," 2 Th. 2. 1.
ὑπὲρ τῆς εὐδοκίας, Ph. 2. 13.
ὑπόστασις, 2 C. 9. 4.
ὑποτύπωσις, 1 Tim. 1. 16.

φοβεῖσθαι ἀπὸ, M. 10. 28.
φῶς for πῦρ, Mk. 14. 54.
φῶτα = ἄστρα, Jac. 1. 17.

χάρις, "thankfulness," Col. 3. 16.
χώρα = "rus," J. 11. 55.
„ = "ager," L. 21. 21.

ψυχὴ, Ph. 2. 30, πᾶσα, R. 2. 9.

ὠδῖνες θανάτου, A. 2. 24.
ὡσαννὰ ἐν ὑψίστοις, M. 21. 9.

March, 1879.

A CLASSIFIED LIST

OF

EDUCATIONAL WORKS

PUBLISHED BY

GEORGE BELL & SONS.

Full Catalogues will be sent post free on application.

BIBLIOTHECA CLASSICA.

A Series of Greek and Latin Authors, with English Notes, edited by eminent Scholars. 8vo.

Æschylus. By F. A. Paley, M.A. 18*s*.
Cicero's Orations. By G. Long, M.A. 4 vols. 16*s*., 14*s*., 16*s*., 18*s*.
Demosthenes. By R. Whiston, M.A. 2 vols. 16*s*. each.
Euripides. By F. A. Paley, M.A. 3 vols. 16*s*. each.
Homer. By F. A. Paley, M.A. Vol. I. 12*s*.; Vol. II. 14*s*.
Herodotus. By Rev. J. W. Blakesley, B.D. 2 vols. 32*s*.
Hesiod. By F. A. Paley, M.A. 10*s*. 6*d*.
Horace. By Rev. A. J. Macleane, M.A. 18*s*.
Juvenal and Persius. By Rev. A. J. Macleane, M.A. 12*s*.
Plato. By W. H. Thompson, D.D. 2 vols. 7*s*. 6*d*. each.
Sophocles. By Rev. F. H. Blaydes, M.A. Vol. I. 18*s*.
——— Philoctetes. By F. A. Paley, M.A. [*In the Press.*
Tacitus: The Annals. By the Rev. P. Frost. 15*s*.
Terence. By E. St. J. Parry, M.A. 18*s*.
Virgil. By J. Conington, M.A. 3 vols. 12*s*., 14*s*., 14*s*.
An Atlas of Classical Geography; Twenty-four Maps. By W. Hughes and George Long, M.A. New edition, with coloured outlines. Imperial 8vo. 12*s*. 6*d*.

Uniform with above.

A Complete Latin Grammar. By J. W. Donaldson, D.D. 3rd Edition. 14*s*.
A Complete Greek Grammar. By J. W. Donaldson, D.D. 3rd Edition. 16*s*.

GRAMMAR-SCHOOL CLASSICS.

A Series of Greek and Latin Authors, with English Notes. Fcap. 8vo.

Cæsar: De Bello Gallico. By George Long, M.A. 5*s*. 6*d*.
——— Books I.-III. For Junior Classes. By G. Long, M.A. 2*s*. 6*d*.
Catullus, Tibullus, and Propertius. Selected Poems. With Life. By Rev. A. H. Wratislaw. 3*s*. 6*d*

Cicero: De Senectute, De Amicitia, and Select Epistles. By George Long, M.A. 4s. 6d.
Cornelius Nepos. By Rev. J. F. Macmichael. 2s. 6d.
Homer: Iliad. Books I.–XII. By F. A. Paley, M.A. 6s. 6d.
Horace. With Life. By A. J. Macleane, M.A. 6s. 6d. [In 2 parts. 3s. 6d. each.]
Juvenal: Sixteen Satires. By H. Prior, M.A. 4s. 6d.
Martial: Select Epigrams. With Life. By F. A. Paley, M.A. 6s. 6d.
Ovid: the Fasti. By F. A. Paley, M.A. 5s.
Sallust: Catilina and Jugurtha. With Life. By G. Long, M.A. 5s.
Tacitus: Germania and Agricola. By Rev. P. Frost. 3s. 6d.
Virgil: Bucolics, Georgics, and Æneid, Books I.–IV. Abridged from Professor Conington's Edition. 5s. 6d.
(The Bucolics and Georgics in one volume. 3s.)
―――― Æneid, Books V.–XII. Abridged from Professor Conington's Edition. 5s. 6d.
Xenophon: The Anabasis. With Life. By Rev. J. F. Macmichael. 5s.
―――― The Cyropædia. By G. M. Gorham, M.A. 6s.
―――― Memorabilia. By Percival Frost, M.A. 4s. 6d.
A Grammar-School Atlas of Classical Geography, containing Ten selected Maps. Imperial 8vo. 5s.

Uniform with the Series.

The New Testament, in Greek. With English Notes, &c. By Rev. J. F. Macmichael. 7s. 6d.

CAMBRIDGE GREEK AND LATIN TEXTS.

Æschylus. By F. A. Paley, M.A. 3s.
Cæsar: De Bello Gallico. By G. Long, M.A. 2s.
Cicero: De Senectute et de Amicitia, et Epistolæ Selectæ. By G. Long, M.A. 1s. 6d.
Ciceronis Orationes. Vol. I. (in Verrem.) By G. Long, M.A. 3s. 6d.
Euripides. By F. A. Paley, M.A. 3 vols. 3s. 6d. each.
Herodotus. By J. G. Blakesley, B.D. 2 vols. 7s.
Homeri Ilias. I.–XII. By F. A. Paley, M.A. 2s. 6d.
Horatius. By A. J. Macleane, M.A. 2s. 6d.
Juvenal et Persius. By A. J. Macleane, M.A. 1s. 6d.
Lucretius. By H. A. J. Munro, M.A. 2s. 6d.
Sallusti Crispi Catilina et Jugurtha. By G. Long, M.A. 1s. 6d.
Terenti Comœdiæ. By W. Wagner, Ph.D. 3s.
Thucydides. By J. G. Donaldson, D.D. 2 vols. 7s.
Virgilius. By J. Conington, M.A. 3s. 6d.
Xenophontis Expeditio Cyri. By J. F. Macmichael, B.A. 2s. 6d.
Novum Testamentum Græcum. By F. H. Scrivener, M.A. 4s. 6d An edition with wide margin for notes, half bound, 12s.

CAMBRIDGE TEXTS WITH NOTES.

A Selection of the most usually read of the Greek and Latin Authors, Annotated for Schools. Fcap. 8vo. 1s. 6d. each.

Euripides. Alcestis. By F. A. Paley, M.A.
——— Medea. By F. A. Paley, M.A.
——— Hippolytus. By F. A. Paley, M.A.
——— Hecuba. By F. A. Paley, M.A.
——— Bacchæ. By F. A. Paley, M.A.
——— Ion. By F. A. Paley, M.A. [Price 2s.]
Æschylus. Prometheus Vinctus. By F. A. Paley, M.A.
——— Septem contra Thebas. By F. A. Paley, M.A.
Ovid. Selections. By A. J. Macleane, M.A.

PUBLIC SCHOOL SERIES.

A Series of Classical Texts, annotated by well-known Scholars. Crown 8vo.

Aristophanes. The Peace. By F. A. Paley, M.A. 4s. 6d.
——— The Acharnians. By F. A. Paley, M.A. 4s. 6d.
——— The Frogs. By F. A. Paley, M.A. 4s. 6d.
Cicero. The Letters to Atticus. Bk. I. By A. Pretor. M.A. 4s. 6d.
Demosthenes de Falsa Legatione. By R. Shilleto, M.A. 6s.
——— The Law of Leptines. By B. W. Beatson, M.A.
Plato. The Apology of Socrates and Crito. By W. Wagner, Ph.D. 4th Edition. 4s. 6d.
——— The Phædo. By W. Wagner, Ph.D. 5s. 6d.
——— The Protagoras. By W. Wayte, M.A. 4s. 6d.
Plautus. The Aulularia. By W. Wagner, Ph.D. 2nd edition. 4s. 6d.
——— Trinummus. By W. Wagner, Ph.D. 2nd edition. 4s. 6d.
——— The Menaechmei. By W. Wagner, Ph.D. 4s. 6d.
Sophoclis Trachiniæ. By A. Pretor, M.A. 4s. 6d.
Terence. By W. Wagner, Ph.D. 10s. 6d.
Theocritus. By F. A. Paley, M.A. 4s. 6d.

Others in preparation.

CRITICAL AND ANNOTATED EDITIONS.

Ætna. By H. A. J. Munro, M.A. 3s. 6d.
Aristophanis Comœdiæ. By H. A. Holden, LL.D. 8vo. 2 vols. 23s. 6d. Plays sold separately.
——— Pax. By F. A. Paley, M.A. Fcap. 8vo. 4s. 6d.
Catullus. By H. A. J. Munro, M.A. 7s. 6d.
Horace. Quinti Horatii Flacci Opera. By H. A. J. Munro, M.A. Large 8vo. 1l. 1s.
Livy. The first five Books. By J. Prendeville. 12mo. roan, 5s. Or Books I.-III. 3s. 6d. IV. and V. 3s. 6d.

Lucretius. Titi Lucretii Cari de Rerum Natura Libri Sex. With a Translation and Notes. By H. A. J. Munro, M.A. 2 vols. 8vo. Vol. I. Text, 16s. Vol. II. Translation, 6s. (Sold separately.)

Ovid. P. Ovidii Nasonis Heroides XIV. By A. Palmer, M.A. 8vo. 6s.

Propertius. Sex Aurelii Propertii Carmina. By F. A. Paley, M.A. 8vo. Cloth, 9s.

Sophocles. The Ajax. By C. E. Palmer, M.A. 4s. 6d.

Thucydides. The History of the Peloponnesian War. By Richard Shilleto, M.A. Book I. 8vo. 6s. 6d. (Book II. *in the press.*)

Greek Testament. By Henry Alford, D.D. 4 vols. 8vo. (Sold separately.) Vol. I. 1l. 8s. Vol. II. 1l. 4s. Vol. III. 18s. Vol. IV. Part I. 18s.; Part II. 14s.; or in one Vol. 32s.

LATIN AND GREEK CLASS-BOOKS.

Auxilia Latina. A Series of Progressive Latin Exercises. By Rev. J. B. Baddeley, M.A. Fcap. 8vo. 2s.

An Introductory Part to the above on Accidence. [*In the Press.*]

Latin Prose Lessons. By A. J. Church, M.A. 2nd Edit. Fcap. 8vo. 2s. 6d.

Latin Exercises and Grammar Papers. By T. Collins, M.A. 2nd Edition. Fcap. 8vo. 2s. 6d.

Analytical Latin Exercises. By C. P. Mason, B.A. 2nd Edit. 3s. 6d.

Scala Græca: a Series of Elementary Greek Exercises. By Rev. J. W. Davis, M.A., and R. W. Baddeley, M.A. 3rd Edition. Fcap. 8vo. 2s. 6d.

Greek Verse Composition. By G. Preston, M.A. Crown 8vo. 4s. 6d.

BY THE REV. P. FROST, M.A., ST. JOHN'S COLLEGE, CAMBRIDGE.

Eclogæ Latinæ; or, First Latin Reading-Book, with English Notes and a Dictionary. New Edition. Fcap. 8vo. 2s. 6d.

Materials for Latin Prose Composition. New Edition. Fcap. 8vo. 2s. 6d. Key, 4s.

A Latin Verse-Book. An Introductory Work on Hexameters and Pentameters. New Edition. Fcap. 8vo. 3s. Key, 5s.

Analecta Græca Minora, with Introductory Sentences, English Notes, and a Dictionary. New Edition. Fcap. 8vo. 3s. 6d.

Materials for Greek Prose Composition. New Edit. Fcap. 8vo. 3s. 6d. Key, 5s.

Florilegium Poeticum. Elegiac Extracts from Ovid and Tibullus. New Edition. With Notes. Fcap. 8vo. 3s.

BY THE REV. F. E. GRETTON.

A First Cheque-book for Latin Verse-makers. 1s. 6d.

A Latin Version for Masters. 2s. 6d.

Reddenda; or Passages with Parallel Hints for Translation into Latin Prose and Verse. Crown 8vo. 4s. 6d.

Reddenda Reddita (*see next page*).

BY H. A. HOLDEN, LL.D.

Foliorum Silvula. Part I. Passages for Translation into Latin Elegiac and Heroic Verse. 8th Edition. Post 8vo. 7s. 6d.

—— Part II. Select Passages for Translation into Latin Lyric and Comic Iambic Verse. 3rd Edition. Post 8vo. 5s.

—— Part III. Select Passages for Translation into Greek Verse. 2rd Edition. Post 8vo. 8s.

Folia Silvulæ, sive Eclogæ Poetarum Anglicorum in Latinum et Græcum conversæ. 8vo. Vol. I. 10s. 6d. Vol. II. 12s.

Foliorum Centuriæ. Select Passages for Translation into Latin and Greek Prose. 6th Edition. Post 8vo. 8s.

TRANSLATIONS, SELECTIONS, &c.

*** Many of the following books are well adapted for School Prizes.

Æschylus. Translated into English Prose by F. A. Paley, M.A. 2nd Edition. 8vo. 7s. 6d.

—— Translated into English Verse by Anna Swanwick. Crown 8vo. 2 vols. 12s.

—— Folio Edition, with 33 Illustrations after Flaxman. 2l. 2s.

Anthologia Græca. A Selection of Choice Greek Poetry, with Notes. By F. St. John Thackeray. 4th and Cheaper Edition. 16mo. 4s. 6d.

Anthologia Latina. A Selection of Choice Latin Poetry, from Nævius to Boëthius, with Notes. By Rev. F. St. John Thackeray. Fcap. 8vo. 6s. 6d.

Aristophanes: The Peace. Text and Metrical Translation. By B. B. Rogers, M.A. Fcap. 4to. 7s. 6d.

—— The Wasps. Text and Metrical Translation. By B. B. Rogers, M.A. Fcap. 4to. 7s. 6d.

Corpus Poetarum Latinorum. Edited by Walker. 1 vol. 8vo. 18s.

Horace. The Odes and Carmen Sæculare. In English Verse by J. Conington, M.A. 7th edition. Fcap. 8vo. 5s. 6d.

—— The Satires and Epistles. In English Verse by J. Conington, M.A. 4th edition. 6s. 6d.

—— Illustrated from Antique Gems by C. W. King, M.A. The text revised with Introduction by H. A. J. Munro, M.A. Large 8vo. 1l. 1s.

Mvsæ Etonenses, sive Carminvm Etonæ Conditorvm Delectvs. By Richard Okes. 2 vols. 8vo. 15s.

Propertius. Verse translations from Book V., with revised Latin Text. By F. A. Paley, M.A. Fcap. 8vo. 3s.

Plato. Gorgias. Translated by E. M. Cope, M.A. 8vo. 7s.

—— Philebus. Translated by F. A. Paley, M.A. Small 8vo. 4s.

—— Theætetus. Translated by F. A. Paley, M.A. Small 8vo, 4s.

—— Analysis and Index of the Dialogues. By Dr. Day. Post 8vo. 5s.

Reddenda Reddita: Passages from English Poetry, with a Latin Verse Translation. By F. E. Gretton. Crown 8vo. 6s.

Sabrinæ Corolla in hortulis Regiæ Scholæ Salopiensis contexuerunt tres viri floribus legendis. Editio tertia. 8vo. 8s. 6d.

Sertum Carthusianum Floribus trium Seculorum Contextum. By W. H. Brown. 8vo. 14s.

Theocritus. In English Verse, by C. S. Calverley, M.A. Crown 8vo. 7s. 6d.

Translations into English and Latin. By C. S. Calverley, M.A. Post 8vo. 7s. 6d.

—— By R. C. Jebb, M.A.; H. Jackson, M.A., and W. E. Currey, M.A. Crown 8vo. 8s.

—— into Greek and Latin Verse. By R. C. Jebb. 4to. cloth gilt. 10s. 6d.

REFERENCE VOLUMES.

A Latin Grammar. By T. H. Key, M.A. 6th Thousand. Post 8vo. 8s.
A Short Latin Grammar for Schools. By T. H. Key, M.A., F.R.S. 11th Edition. Post 8vo. 3s. 6d.
A Guide to the Choice of Classical Books. By J. B. Mayor, M.A. Crown 8vo. 2s.
The Theatre of the Greeks. By J. W. Donaldson, D.D. 8th Edition. Post 8vo. 5s.
A Dictionary of Latin and Greek Quotations. By H. T. Riley. Post 8vo. 5s. With Index Verborum, 6s.
A History of Roman Literature. By W. S. Teuffel, Professor at the University of Tübingen. By W. Wagner, Ph.D. 2 vols. Demy 8vo. 21s.
Student's Guide to the University of Cambridge. Revised and corrected. 3rd Edition. Fcap. 8vo. 6s. 6d.

CLASSICAL TABLES.

Greek Verbs. A Catalogue of Verbs, Irregular and Defective; their leading formations, tenses, and inflexions, with Paradigms for conjugation, Rules for formation of tenses, &c. &c. By J. S. Baird, T.C.D. 2s. 6d.
Greek Accents (Notes on). By A. Barry, D.D. New Edition. 1s.
Homeric Dialect. Its Leading Forms and Peculiarities. By J. S. Baird, T.C.D. New edition, revised by W. Gunion Rutherford. 1s.
Greek Accidence. By the Rev. P. Frost, M.A. New Edition. 1s.
Latin Accidence. By the Rev. P. Frost, M.A. 1s.
Latin Versification. 1s.
Notabilia Quædam; or the Principal Tenses of most of the Irregular Greek Verbs and Elementary Greek, Latin, and French Construction. New edition. 1s.
Richmond Rules for the Ovidian Distich, &c. By J. Tate, M.A. 1s.
The Principles of Latin Syntax. 1s.

CAMBRIDGE SCHOOL AND COLLEGE TEXT-BOOKS.

A Series of Elementary Treatises for the use of Students in the Universities, Schools, and Candidates for the Public Examinations. Fcap. 8vo.

Arithmetic. By Rev. C. Elsee, M.A. Fcap. 8vo. 7th Edit. 3s. 6d.
Algebra. By the Rev. C. Elsee, M.A. 4th Edit. 4s.
Arithmetic. By A. Wrigley, M.A. 3s. 6d.
——— A Progressive Course of Examples. With Answers. By J. Watson, M.A. 3rd Edition. 2s. 6d.
Algebra. Progressive Course of Examples. By Rev. W. F. M'Michael, M.A., and R. Prowde Smith, M.A. 3s. 6d.

Plane Astronomy, An Introduction to. By P. T. Main, M.A. 3rd Edition. [*In the Press.*
Conic Sections treated Geometrically. By W. H. Besant, M.A. 2nd Edition. 4s. 6d.
Elementary Conic Sections treated Geometrically. By W. H. Besant, M.A. [*In the Press.*
Statics, Elementary. By Rev. H. Goodwin, D.D. 2nd Edit. 3s.
Hydrostatics, Elementary. By W. H. Besant, M.A. 7th Edit. 4s.
Mensuration, An Elementary Treatise on. By B. T. Moore, M.A. 5s.
Newton's Principia, The First Three Sections of, with an Appendix; and the Ninth and Eleventh Sections. By J. H. Evans, M.A. 5th Edition, by P. T. Main, M.A. 4s.
Trigonometry, Elementary. By T. P. Hudson, M.A. 3s. 6d.
Optics, Geometrical. With Answers. By W. S. Aldis, M.A. 3s. 6d.
Analytical Geometry for Schools. By T. G. Vyvyan. 3rd Edit. 4s. 6d.
Greek Testament, Companion to the. By A. C. Barrett, A.M. 3rd Edition. Fcap. 8vo. 5s.
Book of Common Prayer, An Historical and Explanatory Treatise on the. By W. G. Humphry, B.D. 5th Edition. Fcap. 8vo. 4s. 6d.
Music, Text-book of. By H. C. Banister 7th Edit. revised. 5s.
―――― Concise History of. By H. G. Bonavia Hunt, B. Mus. Oxon. 3rd Edition revised. 3s. 6d.

ARITHMETIC AND ALGEBRA.

Principles and Practice of Arithmetic. By J. Hind, M.A. 9th Edit. 4s. 6d.
Elements of Algebra. By J. Hind, M.A. 6th Edit. 8vo. 10s. 6d.
Choice and Chance. A Treatise on Permutations and Combinations. By W. A Whitworth. 2nd Edition. Crown 8vo. 6s.
See also foregoing Series.

GEOMETRY AND EUCLID.

Text-Book of Geometry. By T. S. Aldis, M.A. Small 8vo. 4s. 6d. Part I. 2s. 6d. Part II. 2s.
The Elements of Euclid. By H. J. Hose. Fcap. 8vo. 4s. 6d. Exercises separately, 1s.
―――― The First Six Books, with Commentary by Dr. Lardner. 10th Edition. 8vo. 6s.
―――― The First Two Books explained to Beginners. By C. P. Mason, B.A. 2nd Edition. Fcap. 8vo. 2s. 6d.
The Enunciations and Figures to Euclid's Elements. By Rev. J. Brasse, D.D. 3rd Edition. Fcap. 8vo. 1s. On Cards, in case, 5s. 6d. Without the Figures, 6d.
Exercises on Euclid and in Modern Geometry. By J. McDowell, B.A. Crown 8vo. 2nd Edition revised. 6s.

Geometrical Conic Sections. By W. H. Besant, M.A. 3rd Edit. 4s. 6d.
Elementary Geometrical Conic Sections. By W. H. Besant, M.A. [*In the Press.*
The Geometry of Conics. By C. Taylor, M.A. 2nd Edit. 8vo. 4s. 6d.
Solutions of Geometrical Problems, proposed at St. John's College from 1830 to 1846. By T. Gaskin, M.A. 8vo. 12s.

TRIGONOMETRY.

The Shrewsbury Trigonometry. By J. C. P. Aldous. Crown 8vo. 2s.
Elementary Trigonometry. By T. P. Hudson, M.A. 3s. 6d.
Elements of Plane and Spherical Trigonometry. By J. Hind, M.A. 5th Edition. 12mo. 6s.
An Elementary Treatise on Mensuration. By B. T. Moore, M.A. 5s.

ANALYTICAL GEOMETRY AND DIFFERENTIAL CALCULUS.

An Introduction to Analytical Plane Geometry. By W. P. Turnbull, M.A. 8vo. 12s.
Treatise on Plane Co-ordinate Geometry. By M. O'Brien, M.A. 8vo. 9s.
Problems on the Principles of Plane Co-ordinate Geometry. By W. Walton, M.A. 8vo. 16s.
Trilinear Co-ordinates, and Modern Analytical Geometry of Two Dimensions. By W. A. Whitworth, M.A. 8vo. 16s.
An Elementary Treatise on Solid Geometry. By W. S. Aldis, M.A. 2nd Edition revised. 8vo. 8s.
Geometrical Illustrations of the Differential Calculus. By M. B. Pell. 8vo. 2s. 6d.
Elementary Treatise on the Differential Calculus. By M. O'Brien, M.A. 8vo. 10s. 6d.
Notes on Roulettes and Glissettes. By W. H. Besant, M.A. 8vo. 3s. 6d.
Elliptic Functions, Elementary Treatise on. By A. Cayley, M.A. Demy 8vo. 15s.

MECHANICS & NATURAL PHILOSOPHY.

Statics, Elementary. By H. Goodwin, D.D. Fcap. 8vo. 2nd Edition. 3s.
Statics, Treatise on. By S. Earnshaw, M.A. 4th Edition. 8vo. 10s. 6d.
Dynamics, A Treatise on Elementary. By W. Garnett, B.A. 2nd Edition. Crown 8vo. 6s.
Statics and Dynamics, Problems in. By W. Walton, M.A. 8vo. 10s. 6d.

Theoretical Mechanics, Problems in. By W. Walton. 2nd Edit. revised and enlarged. Demy 8vo. 16s.
Mechanics, An Elementary Treatise on. By Prof. Potter. 4th Edition revised. 8s. 6d.
Hydrostatics, Elementary. By Prof. Potter. 7s. 6d.
Hydrostatics. By W. H. Besant, M.A. Fcap. 8vo. 7th Edition. 4s.
Hydromechanics, A Treatise on. By W. H. Besant, M.A. 8vo. New Edition revised. 10s. 6d.
Dynamics of a Particle, A Treatise on the. By W. H. Besant, M.A. [*Preparing.*
Dynamics of a Rigid Body, Solutions of Examples on the. By W. N. Griffin, M.A. 8vo. 6s. 6d.
Motion, An Elementary Treatise on. By J. R. Lunn, M.A. 7s. 6d.
Optics, Geometrical. By W. S. Aldis, M.A. Fcap. 8vo. 3s. 6d.
Double Refraction, A Chapter on Fresnel's Theory of. By W. S. Aldis, M.A. 8vo. 2s.
Optics, An Elementary Treatise on. By Prof. Potter. Part I. 3rd Edition. 9s. 6d. Part II. 12s. 6d.
Optics, Physical; or the Nature and Properties of Light. By Prof. Potter, A.M. 6s. 6d. Part II. 7s. 6d.
Heat, An Elementary Treatise on. By W. Garnett, B.A. Crown 8vo. 2nd Edition revised. 3s. 6d.
Geometrical Optics, Figures Illustrative of. From Schelbach. By W. B. Hopkins. Folio. Plates. 10s. 6d.
Newton's Principia, The First Three Sections of, with an Appendix; and the Ninth and Eleventh Sections. By J. H. Evans, M.A. 5th Edition. Edited by P. T. Main, M.A. 4s.
Astronomy, An Introduction to Plane. By P. T. Main, M.A. Fcap. 8vo. cloth. 4s.
Astronomy, Practical and Spherical. By R. Main, M.A. 8vo. 14s.
Astronomy, Elementary Chapters on, from the 'Astronomie Physique' of Biot. By H. Goodwin, D.D. 8vo. 3s. 6d.
Pure Mathematics and Natural Philosophy, A Compendium of Facts and Formulæ in. By G. R. Smalley. Fcap. 8vo. 3s. 6d.
Elementary Course of Mathematics. By H. Goodwin, D.D. 6th Edition. 8vo. 16s.
Problems and Examples, adapted to the 'Elementary Course of Mathematics.' 3rd Edition. 8vo. 5s.
Solutions of Goodwin's Collection of Problems and Examples. By W. W. Hutt, M.A. 3rd Edition, revised and enlarged. 8vo. 9s.
Pure Mathematics, Elementary Examples in. By J. Taylor. 8vo. 7s. 6d.
Euclid, Mechanical. By the late W. Whewell, D.D. 5th Edition. 5s.
Mechanics of Construction. With numerous Examples. By S. Fenwick, F.R.A.S. 8vo. 12s.
Anti-Logarithms, Table of. By H. E. Filipowski. 3rd Edition. 8vo. 15s.
Mathematical and other Writings of R. L. Ellis, M.A. 8vo. 16s.
Pure and Applied Calculation, Notes on the Principles of. By Rev. J. Challis, M.A. Demy 8vo. 15s.
Physics, The Mathematical Principle of. By Rev. J. Challis, M.A. Demy 8vo. 5s.

HISTORY, TOPOGRAPHY, &c.

Rome and the Campagna. By R. Burn, M.A. With 85 Engravings and 26 Maps and Plans. With Appendix. 4to. 3*l*. 3*s*.

Modern Europe. By Dr. T. H. Dyer. 2nd Edition revised and continued. 5 vols. Demy 8vo. 2*l*. 12*s*. 6*d*.

The History of the Kings of Rome. By Dr. T. H. Dyer. 8vo. 16*s*.

A Plea for Livy. By Dr. T. H. Dyer. 8vo. 1*s*.

Roma Regalis. By Dr. T. H. Dyer. 8vo. 2*s*. 6*d*.

The History of Pompeii: its Buildings and Antiquities. By T. H. Dyer. 3rd Edition, brought down to 1874. Post 8vo. 7*s*. 6*d*.

Ancient Athens: its History, Topography, and Remains. By T. H. Dyer. Super-royal 8vo. Cloth. 1*l*. 5*s*.

The Decline of the Roman Republic. By G. Long. 5 vols. 8vo. 14*s*. each.

A History of England during the Early and Middle Ages. By C. H. Pearson, M.A. 2nd Edition revised and enlarged. 8vo. Vol. I. 16*s*. Vol. II. 14*s*.

Historical Maps of England. By C. H. Pearson. Folio. 2nd Edition revised. 31*s*. 6*d*.

History of England, 1800–15. By Harriet Martineau, with new and copious Index. 1 vol. 3*s*. 6*d*.

History of the Thirty Years' Peace, 1815–46. By Harriet Martineau. 4 vols. 3*s*. 6*d*. each.

A Practical Synopsis of English History. By A. Bowes. 4th Edition. 8vo. 2*s*.

Student's Text-Book of English and General History. By D. Beale. Crown 8vo. 2*s*. 6*d*.

Lives of the Queens of England. By A. Strickland. Library Edition, 8 vols. 7*s*. 6*d*. each. Cheaper Edition, 6 vols. 5*s*. each. Abridged Edition, 1 vol. 6*s*. 6*d*.

Eginhard's Life of Karl the Great (Charlemagne). Translated with Notes, by W. Glaister, M.A., B.C.L. Crown 8vo. 4*s*. 6*d*.

Outlines of Indian History. By A. W. Hughes. Small post 8vo. 3*s*. 6*d*.

The Elements of General History. By Prof. Tytler. New Edition, brought down to 1874. Small post 8vo. *s*. 6*d*.

ATLASES.

An Atlas of Classical Geography. 24 Maps. By W. Hughes and G. Long, M.A. New Edition. Imperial 8vo. 12*s*. 6*d*.

A Grammar-School Atlas of Classical Geography. Ten Maps selected from the above. New Edition. Imperial 8vo. 5*s*.

First Classical Maps. By the Rev. J. Tate, M.A. 3rd Edition. Imperial 8vo. 7*s*. 6*d*.

Standard Library Atlas of Classical Geography. Imp. 8vo. 7*s*. 6*d*.

PHILOLOGY.

WEBSTER'S DICTIONARY OF THE ENGLISH LAN-
GUAGE. Re-edited by N. Porter and C. A. Goodrich. With Dr. Mahn's Etymology. 1 vol. 21s. With Appendices and 70 additional pages of Illustrations, 31s. 6d.
'THE BEST PRACTICAL ENGLISH DICTIONARY EXTANT.'—*Quarterly Review.*
Prospectuses, with specimen pages, post free on application.

New Dictionary of the English Language. Combining Explanation with Etymology, and copiously illustrated by Quotations from the best Authorities. By Dr. Richardson. New Edition, with a Supplement. 2 vols. 4to. 4l. 14s. 6d.; half russia, 5l. 15s. 6d.; russia, 6l. 12s. Supplement separately. 4to. 12s.
An 8vo. Edit. without the Quotations, 15s.; half russia, 20s.; russia, 24s.

The Elements of the English Language. By E. Adams, Ph.D. 15th Edition. Post 8vo. 4s. 6d.

Philological Essays. By T. H. Key, M.A., F.R.S. 8vo. 10s. 6d.

Language, its Origin and Development. By T. H. Key, M.A., F.R.S. 8vo. 14s.

Synonyms and Antonyms of the English Language. By Archdeacon Smith. 2nd Edition. Post 8vo. 5s.

Synonyms Discriminated. By Archdeacon Smith. Demy 8vo. 16s.

Etymological Glossary of nearly 2500 English Words in Common Use derived from the Greek. By the Rev. E. J. Boyce. Fcap. 8vo. 3s. 6d.

A Syriac Grammar. By G. Phillips, D.D. 3rd Edition, enlarged. 8vo. 7s. 6d.

A Grammar of the Arabic Language. By Rev. W. J. Beaumont, M.A. 12mo. 7s.

Who Wrote It? A Dictionary of Common Poetical Quotations. Fcap. 8vo. 2s. 6d.

DIVINITY, MORAL PHILOSOPHY, &c.

Novum Testamentum Græcum, Textus Stephanici, 1550. By F. H. Scrivener, A.M., LL.D. New Edition. 16mo. 4s. 6d. Also on Writing Paper, with Wide Margin. Half-bound. 12s.

By the same Author.

Codex Bezæ Cantabrigiensis. 4to. 26s.

A Full Collation of the Codex Sinaiticus with the Received Text of the New Testament, with Critical Introduction. 2nd Edition, revised. Fcap. 8vo. 5s.

A Plain Introduction to the Criticism of the New Testament. With Forty Facsimiles from Ancient Manuscripts. 2nd Edition. 8vo. 16s.

Six Lectures on the Text of the New Testament. For English Readers. Crown 8vo. 6s.

The New Testament for English Readers. By the late H. Alford, D.D. Vol. I. Part I. 3rd Edit. 12s. Vol. I. Part II. 2nd Edit. 10s. 6d. Vol. II. Part I. 2nd Edit. 16s. Vol. II. Part II. 2nd Edit. 16s.

The Greek Testament. By the late H. Alford, D.D. Vol. I. 6th Edit. 1l. 8s. Vol. II. 6th Edit. 1l. 4s. Vol. III. 5th Edit. 18s. Vol. IV. Part I. 4th Edit. 18s. Vol. IV. Part II. 4th Edit. 14s. Vol. IV. 1l. 12s.

Companion to the Greek Testament. By A. C. Barrett, M.A. 3rd Edition. Fcap. 8vo. 5s.

Liber Apologeticus. The Apology of Tertullian, with English Notes, by H. A. Woodham, LL.D. 2nd Edition. 8vo. 8s. 6d.

The Book of Psalms. A New Translation, with Introductions, &c. By Very Rev. J. J. Stewart Perowne, D.D. 8vo. Vol. I. 4th Edition, 18s. Vol. II. 4th Edit. 16s.

—— Abridged for Schools. 2nd Edition. Crown 8vo. 10s. 6d.

History of the Articles of Religion. By C. H. Hardwick. 3rd Edition. Post 8vo. 5s.

Pearson on the Creed. Carefully printed from an early edition. With Analysis and Index by E. Walford, M.A. Post 8vo. 5s.

Doctrinal System of St. John as Evidence of the Date of his Gospel. By Rev. J. J. Lias, M.A. Crown 8vo. 6s.

An Historical and Explanatory Treatise on the Book of Common Prayer. By Rev. W. G. Humphry, B.D. 5th Edition, enlarged. Small post 8vo. 4s. 6d.

The New Table of Lessons Explained. By Rev. W. G. Humphry, B.D. Fcap. 1s. 6d.

A Commentary on the Gospels for the Sundays and other Holy Days of the Christian Year. By Rev. W. Denton, A.M. New Edition. 3 vols. 8vo. 54s. Sold separately.

Commentary on the Epistles for the Sundays and other Holy Days of the Christian Year. By Rev. W. Denton, A.M. 2 vols. 36s. Sold separately.

Commentary on the Acts. By Rev. W. Denton, A.M. Vol. I. 8vo. 18s. Vol. II. 14s.

Notes on the Catechism. By Rev. A. Barry, D.D. 5th Edit. Fcap. 2s.

Catechetical Hints and Helps. By Rev. E. J. Boyce, M.A. 3rd Edition, revised. Fcap. 2s. 6d.

Examination Papers on Religious Instruction. By Rev. E. J. Boyce. Sewed. 1s. 6d.

Church Teaching for the Church's Children. An Exposition of the Catechism. By the Rev. F. W. Harper. Sq. fcap. 2s.

The Winton Church Catechist. Questions and Answers on the Teaching of the Church Catechism. By the late Rev. J. S. B. Monsell, LL.D. 3rd Edition. Cloth, 3s.; or in Four Parts, sewed.

The Church Teacher's Manual of Christian Instruction. By Rev. M. F. Sadler. 16th Thousand. 2s. 6d.

Short Explanation of the Epistles and Gospels of the Christian Year, with Questions. Royal 32mo. 2s. 6d.; calf, 4s. 6d.

Butler's Analogy of Religion; with Introduction and Index by Rev. Dr. Steere. New Edition. Fcap. 3s. 6d.

—— Three Sermons on Human Nature, and Dissertation on Virtue. By W. Whewell, D.D. 4th Edition. Fcap. 8vo. 2s. 6d.

Lectures on the History of Moral Philosophy in England. By W. Whewell, D.D. Crown 8vo. 8s.

Elements of Morality, including Polity. By W. Whewell, D.D. New Edition, in 8vo. 15s.

Astronomy and General Physics (Bridgewater Treatise). New Edition. 5s.

Kent's Commentary on International Law. By J. T. Abdy, LL.D. New and Cheap Edition. Crown 8vo. 10s. 6d.

A Manual of the Roman Civil Law. By G. Leapingwell, LL.D. 8vo. 12s.

FOREIGN CLASSICS.

A series for use in Schools, with English Notes, grammatical and explanatory, and renderings of difficult idiomatic expressions.
Fcap. 8vo.

Schiller's Wallenstein. By Dr. A. Buchheim. New Edit. 6s. 6d. Or the Lager and Piccolomini, 3s. 6d. Wallenstein's Tod, 3s. 6d.
—— Maid of Orleans. By Dr. W. Wagner. 3s. 6d.
—— Maria Stuart. By V. Kastner. 3s.
Goethe's Hermann and Dorothea. By E. Bell, M.A., and E. Wölfel. 2s. 6d.
German Ballads, from Uhland, Goethe, and Schiller. By C. L. Bielefeld. 3s. 6d.
Charles XII., par Voltaire. By L. Direy. 3rd Edition. 3s. 6d.
Aventures de Télémaque, par Fénélon. By C. J. Delille. 2nd Edition. 4s. 6d.
Select Fables of La Fontaine. By F. E. A. Gasc. New Edition. 3s.
Picciola, by X. B. Saintine. By Dr. Dubuc. 4th Edition. 3s. 6d.

FRENCH CLASS-BOOKS.

Twenty Lessons in French. With Vocabulary, giving the Pronunciation. By W. Brebner. Post 8vo. 4s.
French Grammar for Public Schools. By Rev. A. C. Clapin, M.A. Fcap. 8vo. 6th Edit. 2s. 6d. Separately, Part I. 2s.; Part II. 1s. 6d.
French Primer. By Rev. A. C. Clapin, M.A. 3rd Edition. Fcap. 8vo. 1s.
Primer of French Philology. By Rev. A. C. Clapin. Fcap. 8vo. 1s.
Le Nouveau Tresor; or, French Student's Companion. By M. E. S. 16th Edition. Fcap. 8vo. 3s. 6d.

F. E. A. GASC'S FRENCH COURSE.

First French Book. Fcap 8vo. New Edition. 1s. 6d.
Second French Book. New Edition. Fcap. 8vo. 2s. 6d.
Key to First and Second French Books. Fcap. 8vo. 3s. 6d.
French Fables for Beginners, in Prose, with Index. New Edition. 12mo. 2s.
Select Fables of La Fontaine. New Edition. Fcap. 8vo. 3s.
Histoires Amusantes et Instructives. With Notes. New Edition. Fcap. 8vo. 2s. 6d.

Practical Guide to Modern French Conversation. Fcap. 8vo. 2s. 6d.

French Poetry for the Young. With Notes. Fcap. 8vo. 2s.

Materials for French Prose Composition; or, Selections from the best English Prose Writers. New Edition. Fcap. 8vo. 4s. 6d. Key, 6s.

Prosateurs Contemporains. With Notes. 8vo. New Edition, revised. 5s.

Le Petit Compagnon; a French Talk-Book for Little Children. 16mo. 2s. 6d.

An Improved Modern Pocket Dictionary of the French and English Languages. 25th Thousand, with additions. 16mo. Cloth. 4s. Also in 2 vols., in neat leatherette, 5s.

Modern French-English and English-French Dictionary. 2nd Edition, revised. In 1 vol. 12s. 6d. (formerly 2 vols. 25s.)

GOMBERT'S FRENCH DRAMA.

Being a Selection of the best Tragedies and Comedies of Molière, Racine, Corneille, and Voltaire. With Arguments and Notes by A. Gombert. New Edition, revised by F. E. A. Gasc. Fcap. 8vo. 1s. each; sewed, 6d.

CONTENTS.

MOLIERE:—Le Misanthrope. L'Avare. Le Bourgeois Gentilhomme. Le Tartuffe. Le Malade Imaginaire. Les Femmes Savantes. Les Fourberies de Scapin. Les Précieuses Ridicules. L'Ecole des Femmes. L'Ecole des Maris. Le Médecin malgré Lui.

RACINE:—Phédre. Esther. Athalie. Iphigénie. Les Plaideurs. Thébaïde; or, Les Frères Ennemis. Andromaque. Britannicus.

P. CORNEILLE:—Le Cid. Horace. Cinna. Polyeucto.

VOLTAIRE:—Zaïre.

GERMAN CLASS-BOOKS.

Materials for German Prose Composition. By Dr Buchheim. 5th Edition, revised, with an Index. Fcap. 4s. 6d.

A German Grammar for Public Schools. By the Rev. A. C. Clapin and F. Holl Müller. Fcap. 2s. 6d.

Kotzebue's Der Gefangene. With Notes by Dr. W. Stromberg. 1s.

ENGLISH CLASS-BOOKS.

The Elements of the English Language. By E. Adams, Ph.D. 15th Edition. Post 8vo. 4s. 6d.

The Rudiments of English Grammar and Analysis. By E. Adams, Ph.D. New Edition. Fcap. 8vo. 2s.

BY C. P. MASON, B.A. LONDON UNIVERSITY.

First Notions of Grammar for Young Learners. Fcap. 8vo. Cloth. 8d.

First Steps in English Grammar for Junior Classes. Demy 18mo. New Edition. 1s.

Outlines of English Grammar for the use of Junior Classes. Cloth. 5th Edition. 1s. 6d.

English Grammar, including the Principles of Grammatical Analysis. 22nd Edition. Post 8vo. 3s. 6d.

Shorter English Grammar, with copious carefully graduated Exercises. Crown 8vo. 3s. 6d. [*Just published.*]

English Grammar Practice, being the Exercises from the above, in a separate volume. 1s. [*Just published.*]

The Analysis of Sentences applied to Latin. Post 8vo. 1s. 6d.

Analytical Latin Exercises: Accidence and Simple Sentences, &c. Post 8vo. 3s. 6d.

Edited for Middle-Class Examinations.

With Notes on the Analysis and Parsing, and Explanatory Remarks.

Milton's Paradise Lost, Book I. With Life. 3rd Edit. Post 8vo. 2s.

———— Book II. With Life. 2nd Edit. Post 8vo. 2s.

———— Book III. With Life. Post 8vo. 2s.

Goldsmith's Deserted Village. With Life. Post 8vo. 1s. 6d.

Cowper's Task, Book II. With Life. Post 8vo. 2s.

Thomson's Spring. With Life. Post 8vo. 2s.

———— Winter. With Life. Post 8vo. 2s.

Practical Hints on Teaching. By Rev. J. Menet, M.A. 4th Edit. Crown 8vo. cloth, 2s. 6d. ; paper, 2s.

Test Lessons in Dictation. Paper cover, 1s. 6d.

Questions for Examinations in English Literature. By Rev. W. W. Skeat. 2s. 6d.

Drawing Copies. By P. H. Delamotte. Oblong 8vo. 12s. Sold also in parts at 1s. each.

Poetry for the School-room. New Edition. Fcap. 8vo. 1s. 6d.

Select Parables from Nature, for Use in Schools. By Mrs. A. Gatty. Fcap. 8vo. Cloth. 1s.

School Record for Young Ladies' Schools. 6d.

Geographical Text-Book; a Practical Geography. By M. E. S. 12mo. 2s.

The Blank Maps done up separately, 4to. 2s. coloured.

A First Book of Geography. By Rev. C. A. Johns, B.A., F.L.S. &c. Illustrated. 12mo. 2s. 6d.

Loudon's (Mrs.) Entertaining Naturalist. New Edition. Revised by W. S. Dallas, F.L.S. 5s.

———— **Handbook of Botany.** New Edition, greatly enlarged by D. Wooster. Fcap. 2s. 6d.

The Botanist's Pocket-Book. With a copious Index. By W. R. Hayward. 2nd Edit. revised. Crown 8vo. Cloth limp. 4s. 6d.

Experimental Chemistry, founded on the Work of Dr. Stöckhardt. By C. W. Heaton. Post 8vo. 5s.

Double Entry Elucidated. By B. W. Foster. 7th Edit. 4to. 8s 6d.

A New Manual of Book-keeping. By P. Crellin, Accountant. Crown 8vo. 3s. 6d.

Picture School-Books. In Simple Language, with numerous Illustrations. Royal 16mo.

School Primer. 6d.—School Reader. By J. Tilleard. 1s.—Poetry Book for Schools. 1s.—The Life of Joseph. 1s.—The Scripture Parables. By the Rev. J. E. Clarke. 1s.—The Scripture Miracles. By the Rev. J. E. Clarke. 1s.—The New Testament History. By the Rev. J. G. Wood, M.A. 1s.—The Old Testament History. By the Rev. J. G. Wood, M.A. 1s.—The Story of Bunyan's Pilgrim's Progress. 1s.—The Life of Christopher Columbus. By Sarah Crompton. 1s.—The Life of Martin Luther. By Sarah Crompton. 1s.

BOOKS FOR YOUNG READERS.

In 8 vols. Limp cloth, 6d. each.

The New-born Lamb; Rosewood Box; Poor Fan; Wise Dog——The Cat and the Hen; Sam and his Dog Red-leg; Bob and Tom Lee; A Wreck——The Three Monkeys——Story of a Cat, told by Herself——The Blind Boy; The Mute Girl; A New Tale of Babes in a Wood——The Dey and the Knight; The New Bank-note; The Royal Visit; A King's Walk on a Winter's Day——Queen Bee and Busy Bee——Gull's Crag, a Story of the Sea.

BELL'S READING-BOOKS.

FOR SCHOOLS AND PAROCHIAL LIBRARIES.

The popularity which the 'Books for Young Readers' have attained is a sufficient proof that teachers and pupils alike approve of the use of interesting stories, with a simple plot in place of the dry combination of letters and syllables, making no impression on the mind, of which elementary reading-books generally consist.

The Publishers have therefore thought it advisable to extend the application of this principle to books adapted for more advanced readers.

Now Ready. Post 8vo. Strongly bound.

Masterman Ready. By Captain Marryat, R.N. 1s. 6d.
The Settlers in Canada. By Captain Marryat, R.N. 1s. 6d.
Parables from Nature. (Selected.) By Mrs. Gatty. 1s.
Friends in Fur and Feathers. By Gwynfryn. 1s.
Robinson Crusoe. 1s. 6d.
Andersen's Danish Tales. (Selected.) By E. Bell, M.A. 1s.
Southey's Life of Nelson. (Abridged.) 1s.
Grimm's German Tales. (Selected.) By E. Bell, M.A. 1s.
Life of the Duke of Wellington, with Maps and Plans. 1s.

Others in Preparation.

London: Printed by JOHN STRANGEWAYS, Castle St. Leicester Sq.

www.ingramcontent.com/pod-product-compliance
Lightning Source LLC
Chambersburg PA
CBHW031828230426
43669CB00009B/1271